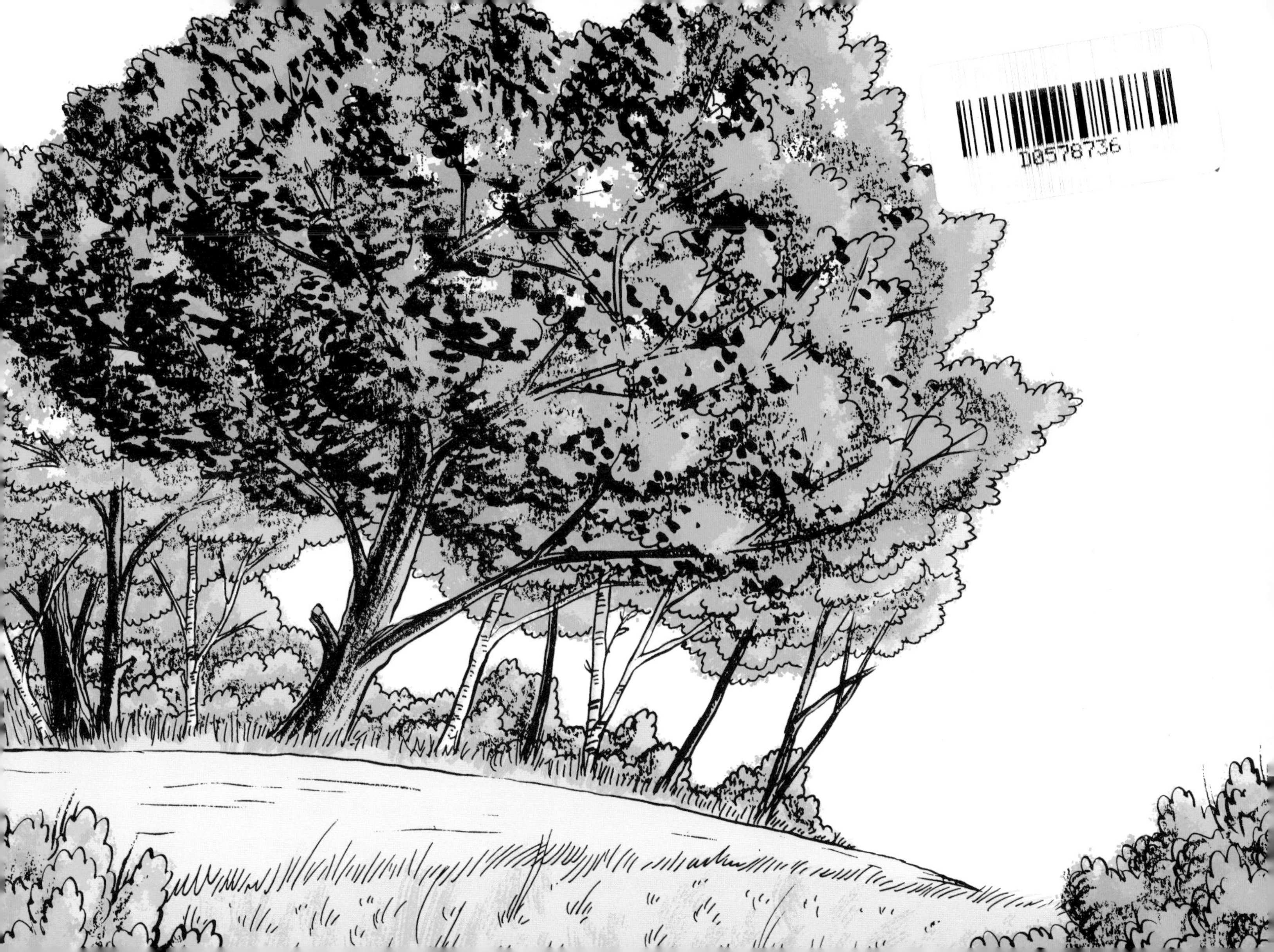

Motel Art
Improvement
Service

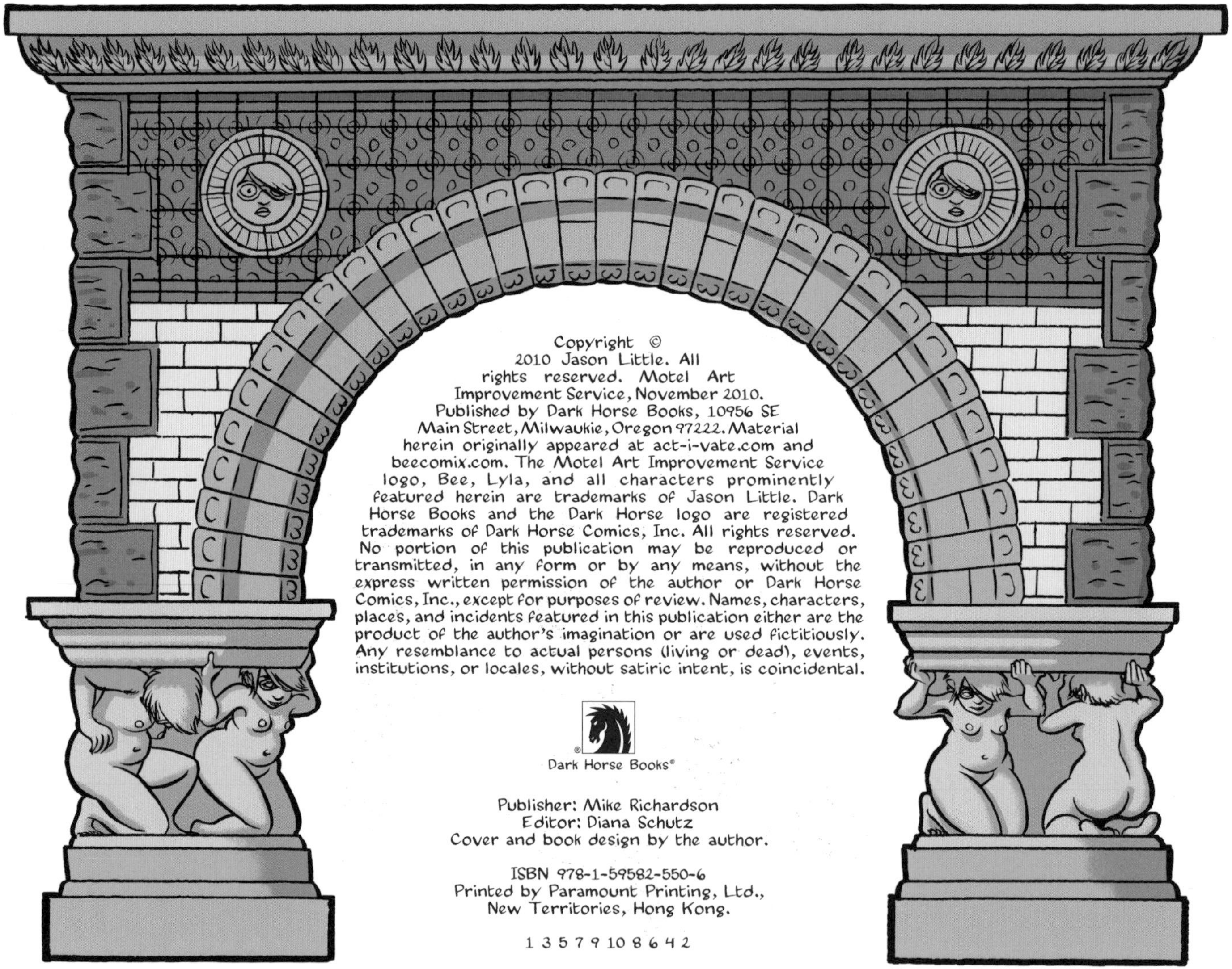

 Motel Art Improvement Service, November 2010. Published by Dark Horse Books, 10956 SE Main Street, Milwaukie, Oregon 97222. Material herein originally appeared at act-i-vate.com and beecomix.com.

Dark Horse Books®

Publisher: Mike Richardson
Editor: Diana Schutz
Cover and book design by the author.

ISBN 978-1-59582-550-6
Printed by Paramount Printing, Ltd., New Territories, Hong Kong.

1 3 5 7 9 10 8 6 4 2

Thanks, Mom.

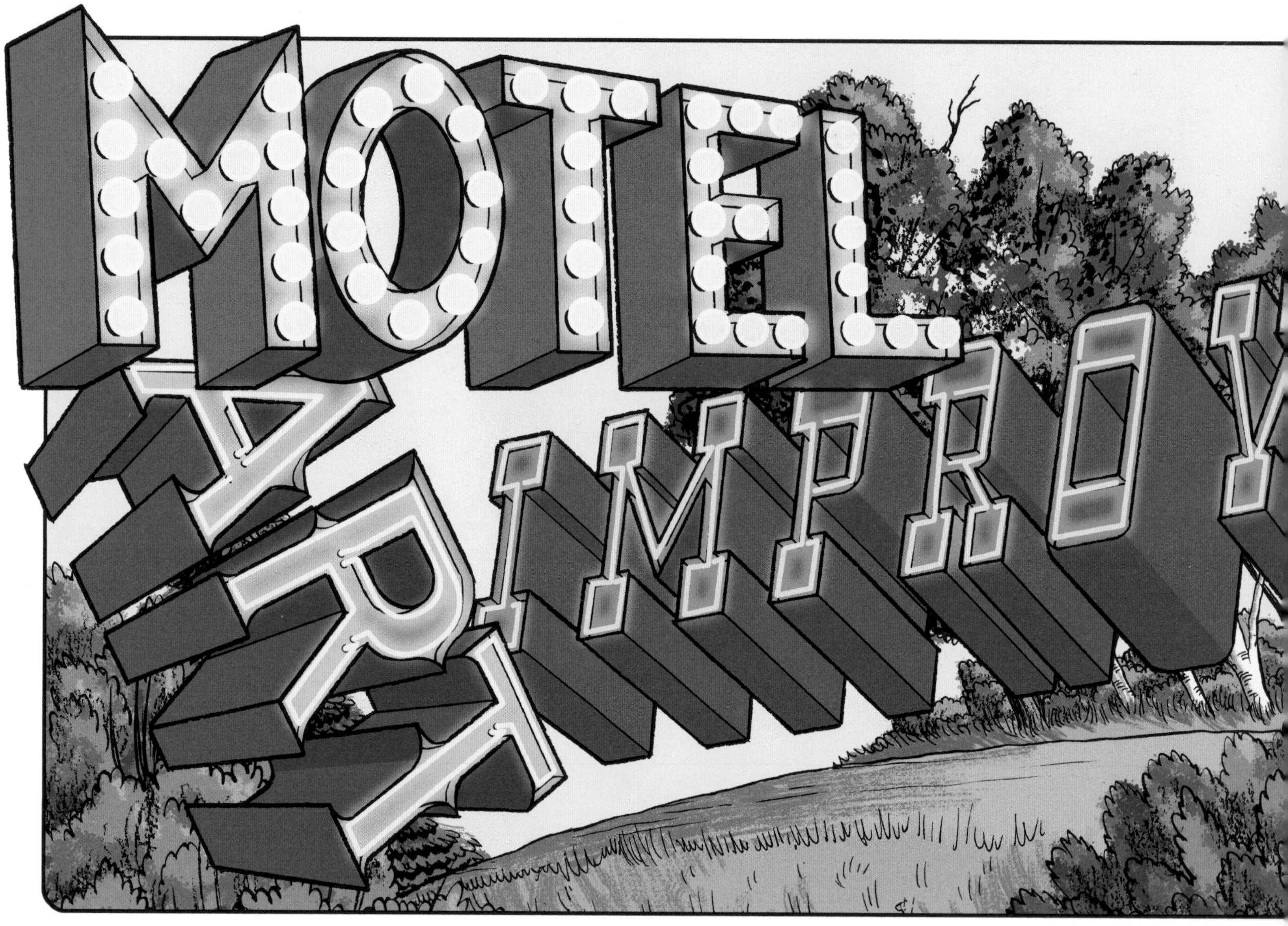
MOTEL
ART
IMPROV

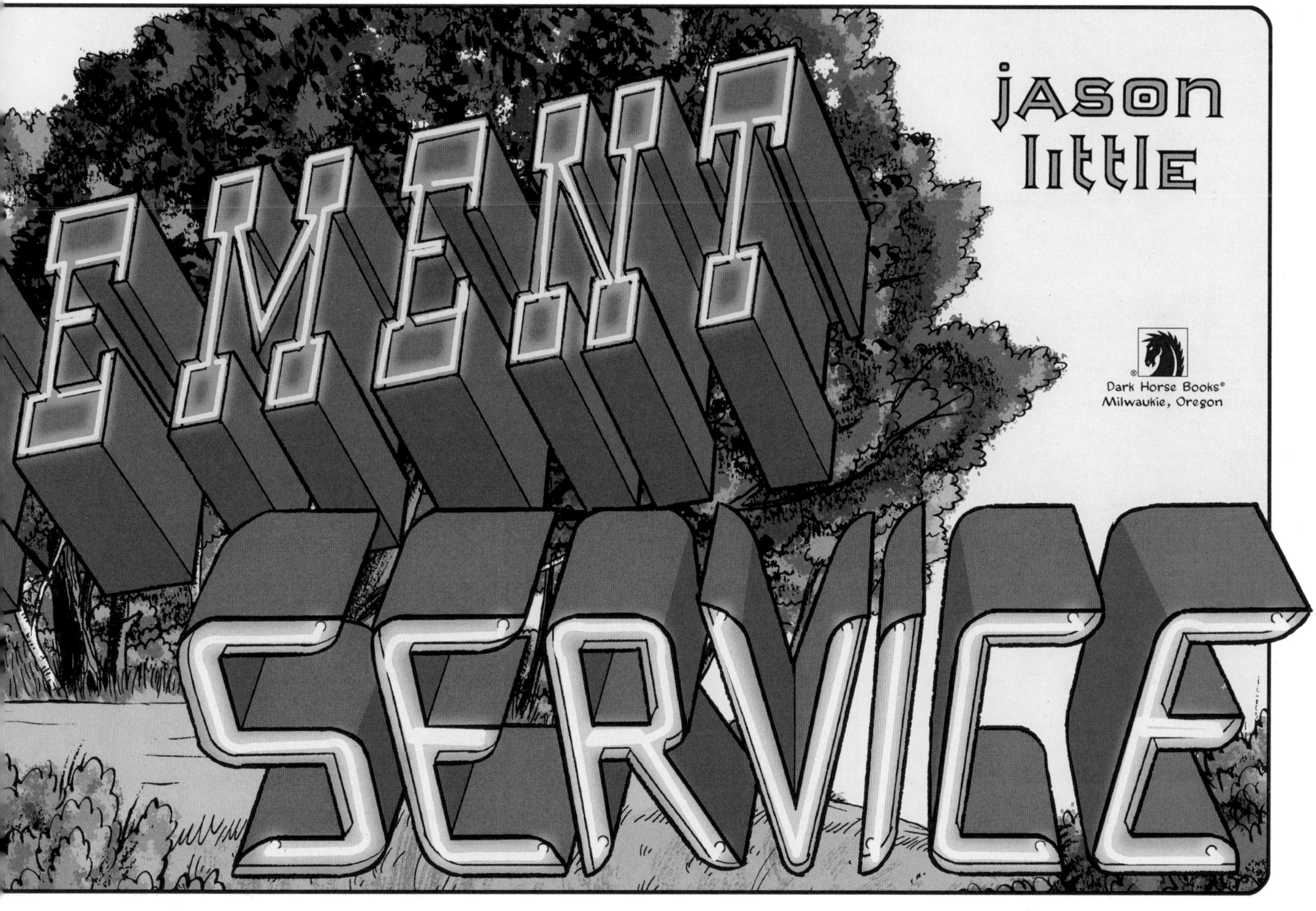
EMENT
SERVICE
jason little
Dark Horse Books®
Milwaukie, Oregon

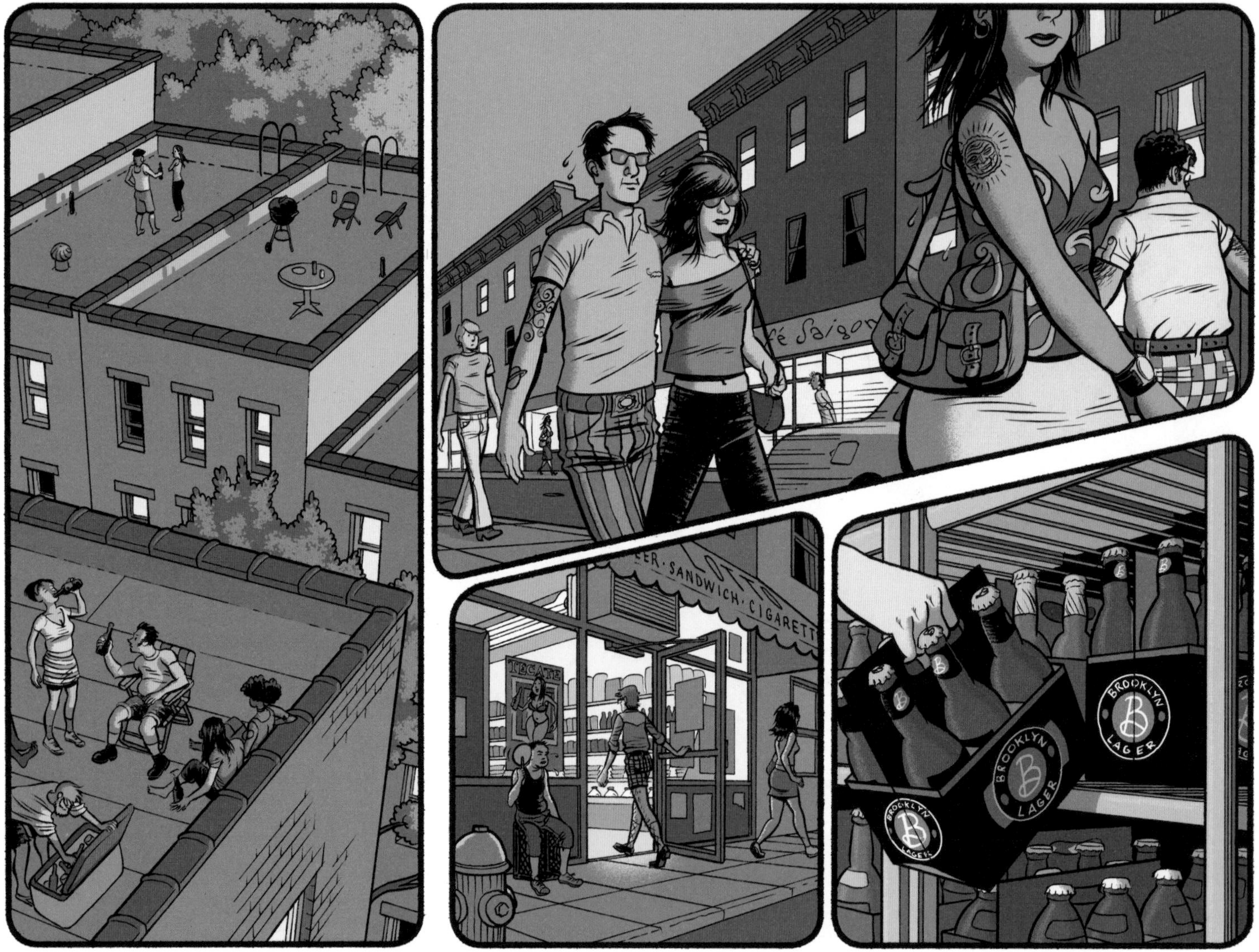
SANDWICH · CIGARETT
TECATE
BROOKLYN LAGER
BROOKLYN LAGER
BROOKLYN LAGER

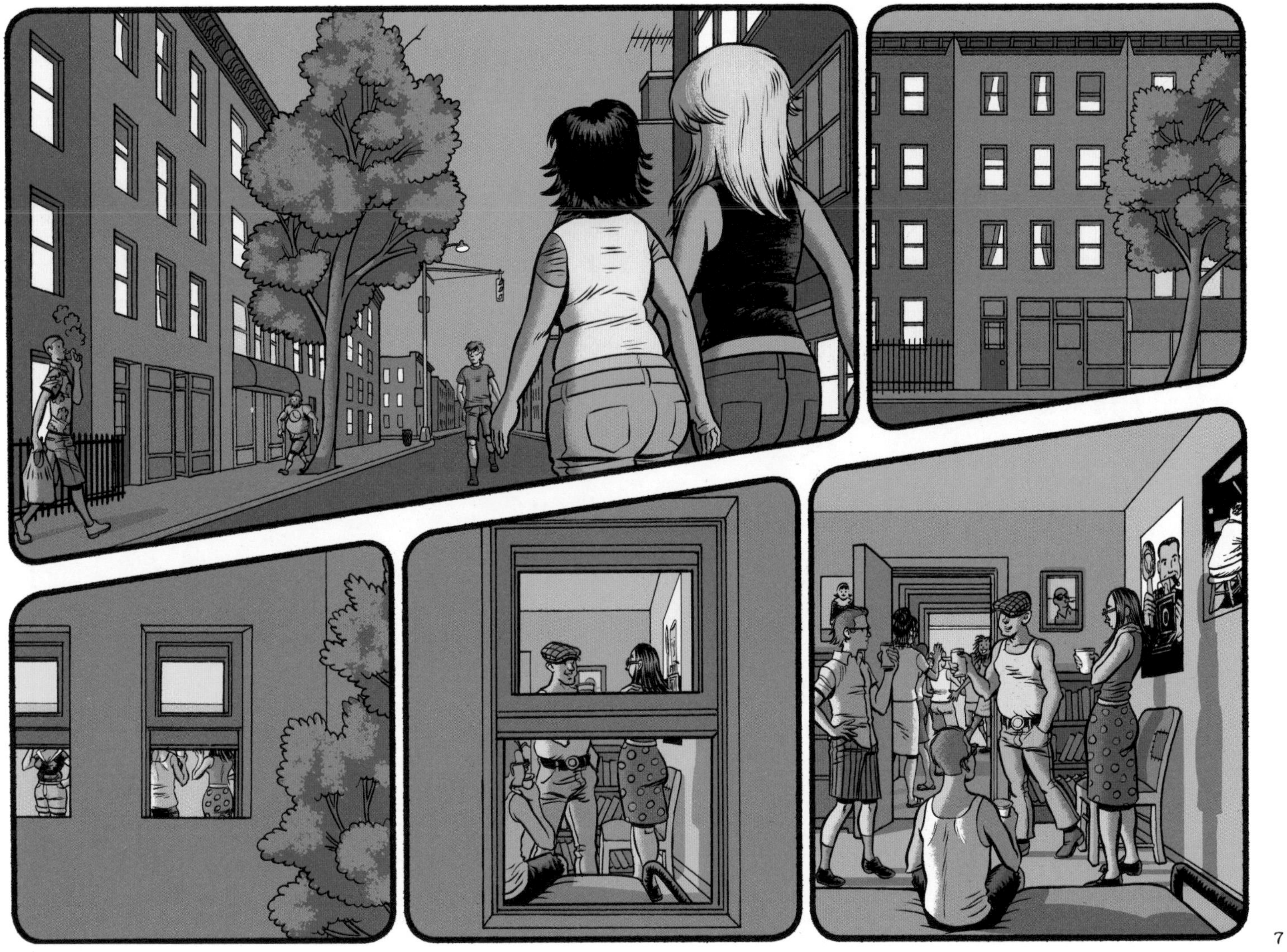

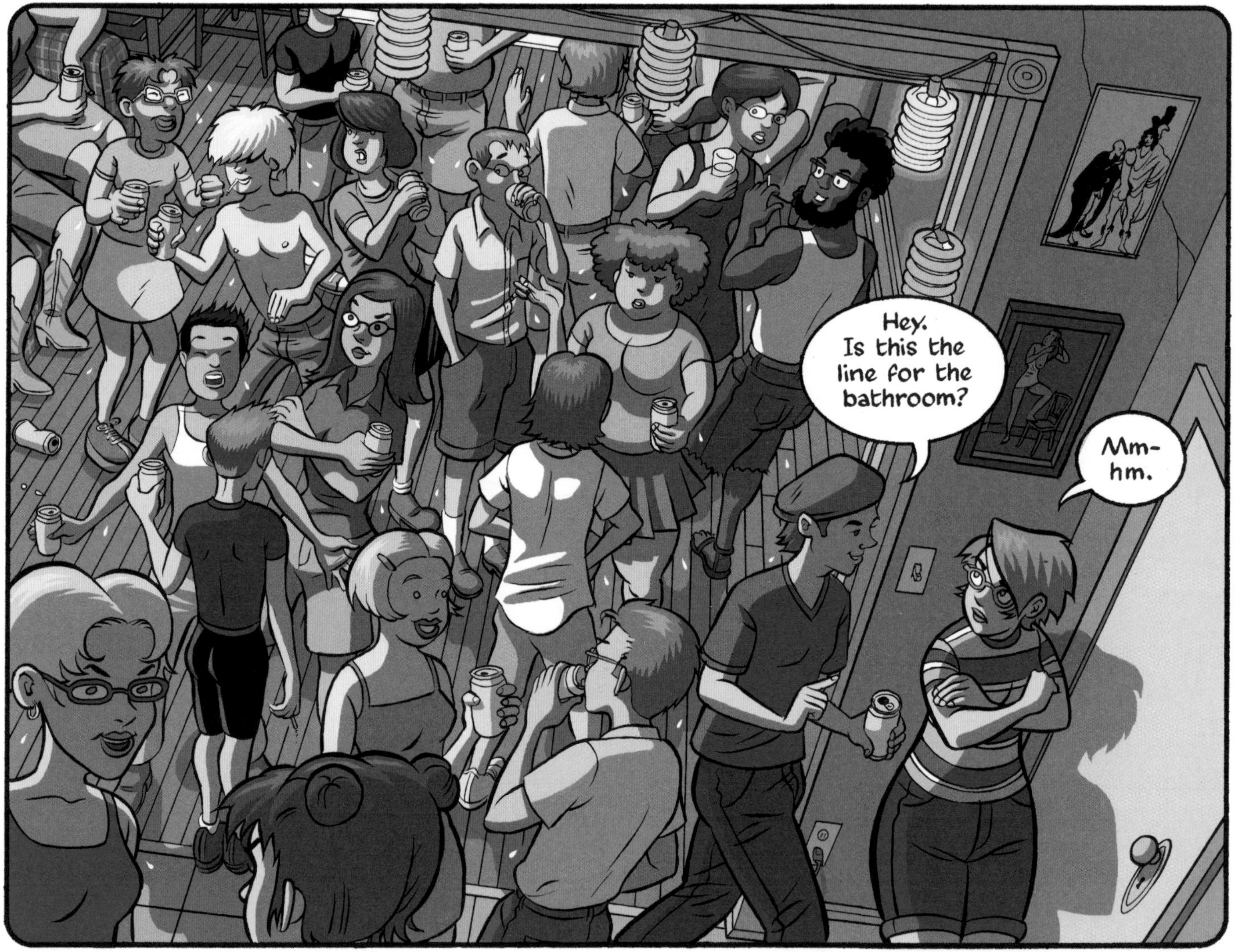
Hey. Is this the line for the bathroom?
Mm-hm.

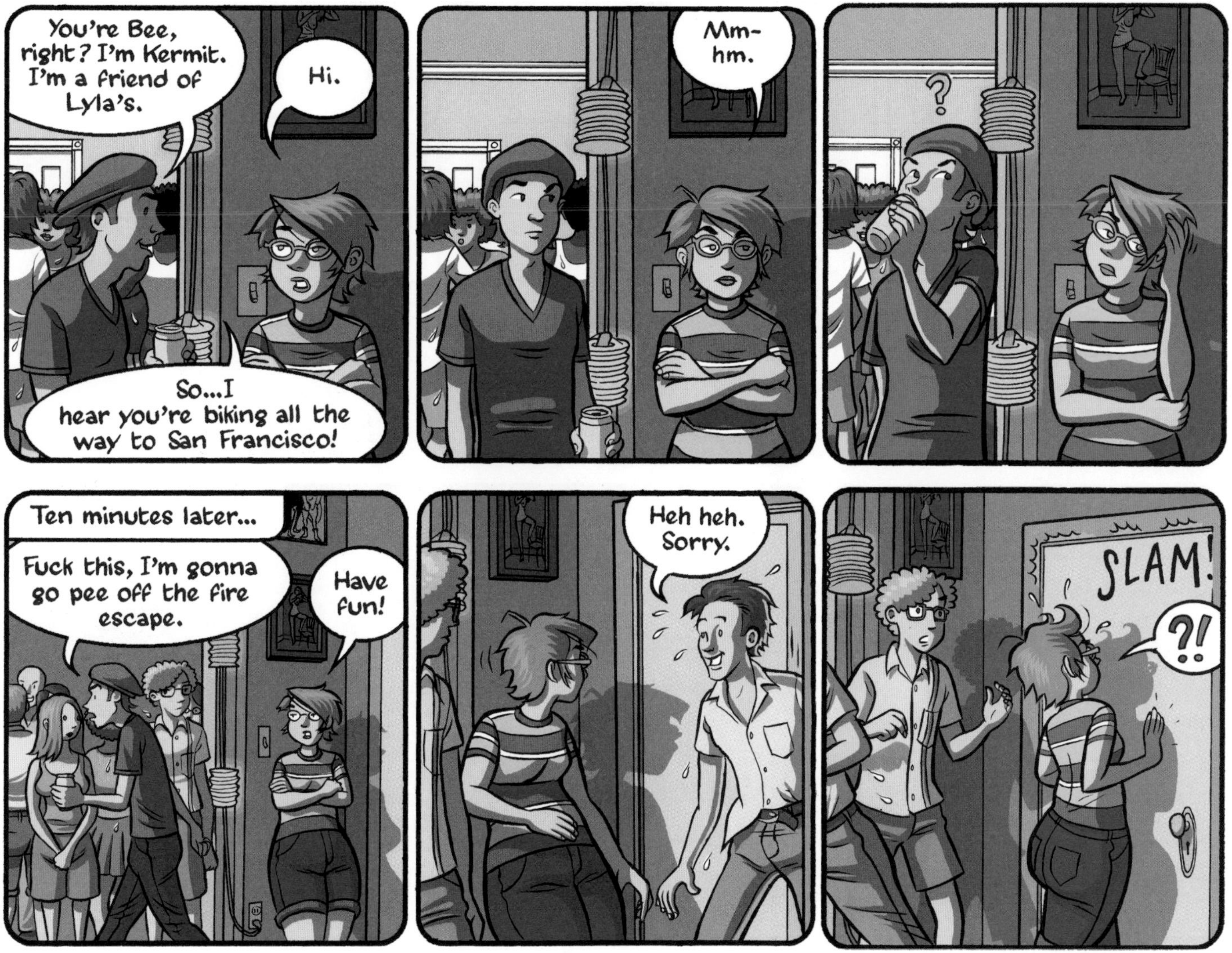
You're Bee, right? I'm Kermit. I'm a friend of Lyla's.
Hi.
So...I hear you're biking all the way to San Francisco!
Mm-hm.
?
Ten minutes later...
Fuck this, I'm gonna go pee off the fire escape.
Have fun!
Heh heh. Sorry.
SLAM!
?!

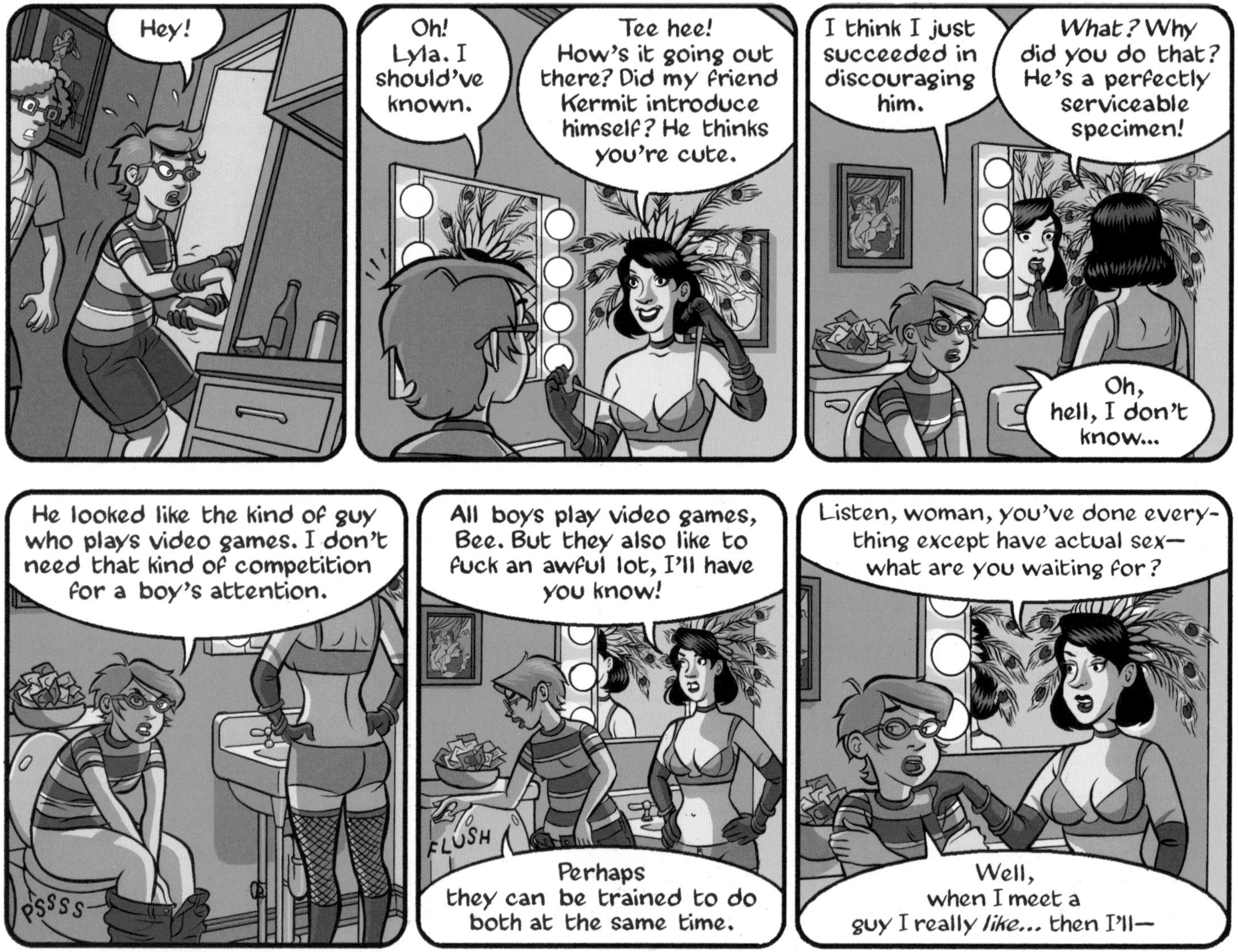
Hey!
Oh! Lyla. I should've known.
Tee hee! How's it going out there? Did my friend Kermit introduce himself? He thinks you're cute.
I think I just succeeded in discouraging him.
What? Why did you do that? He's a perfectly serviceable specimen!
Oh, hell, I don't know...
He looked like the kind of guy who plays video games. I don't need that kind of competition for a boy's attention.
PSSSS-
All boys play video games, Bee. But they also like to fuck an awful lot, I'll have you know!
FLUSH
Perhaps they can be trained to do both at the same time.
Listen, woman, you've done every-thing except have actual sex— what are you waiting for?
Well, when I meet a guy I really *like...* then I'll—

Well, don't be caught unprepared. Here! Take these with you on your bike trip.

But— all these—I don't—

Please! I insist. It's the least I can do.

Now, let's get you a drink.

I can't drink tonight. I've got cramps and took a couple of my heavy-duty pain pills. My period came early this month.

You poor thing! And on the eve of your voyage, too.

Anyway... maybe you'll meet some hot guys on your bike trip.

The next morning...

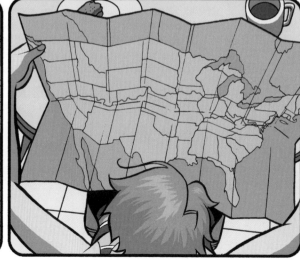

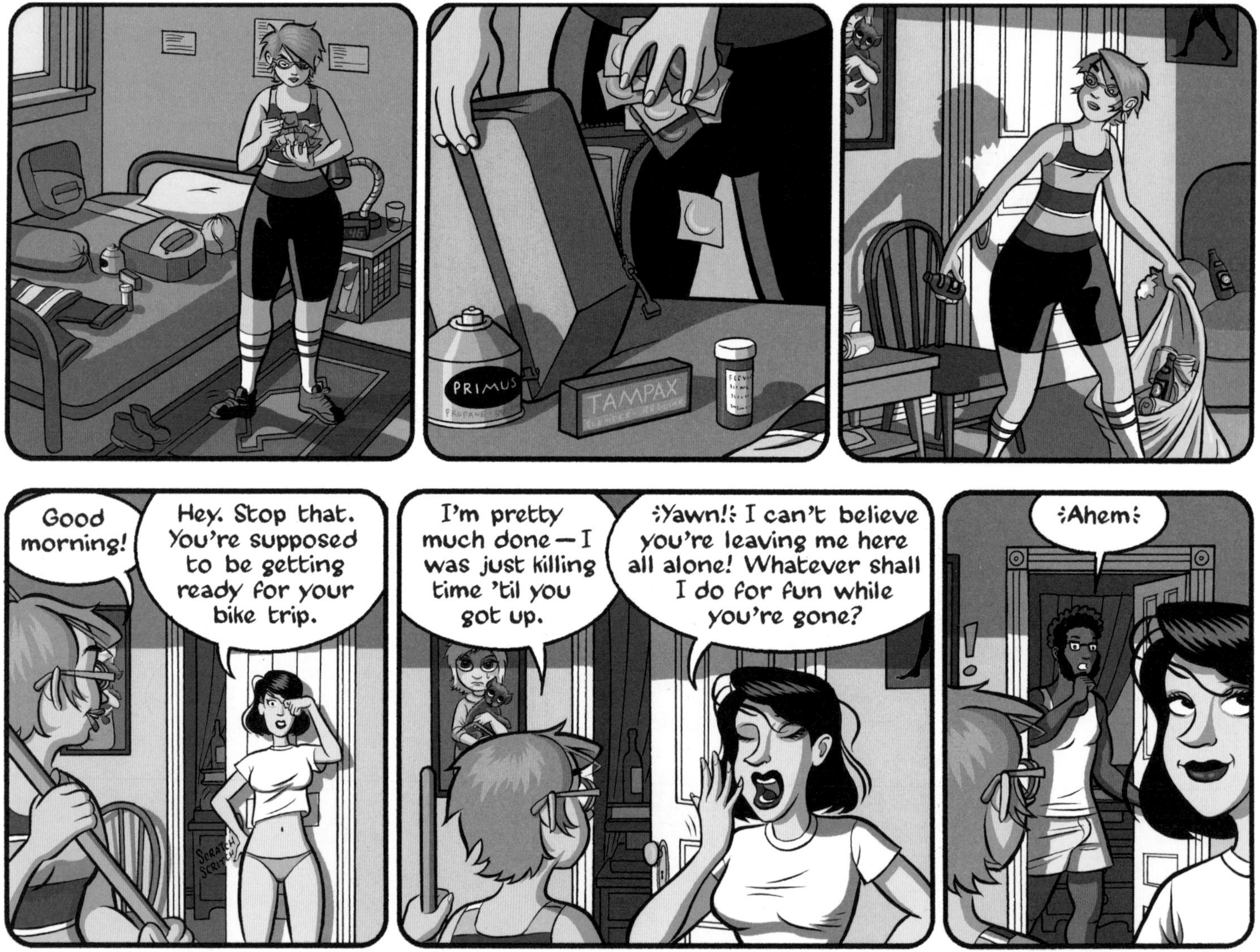
PRIMUS
TAMPAX
Good morning!
Hey. Stop that. You're supposed to be getting ready for your bike trip.
SCRATCH SCRATCH
I'm pretty much done—I was just killing time 'til you got up.
⁖Yawn!⁖ I can't believe you're leaving me here all alone! Whatever shall I do for fun while you're gone?
⁖Ahem⁖
!

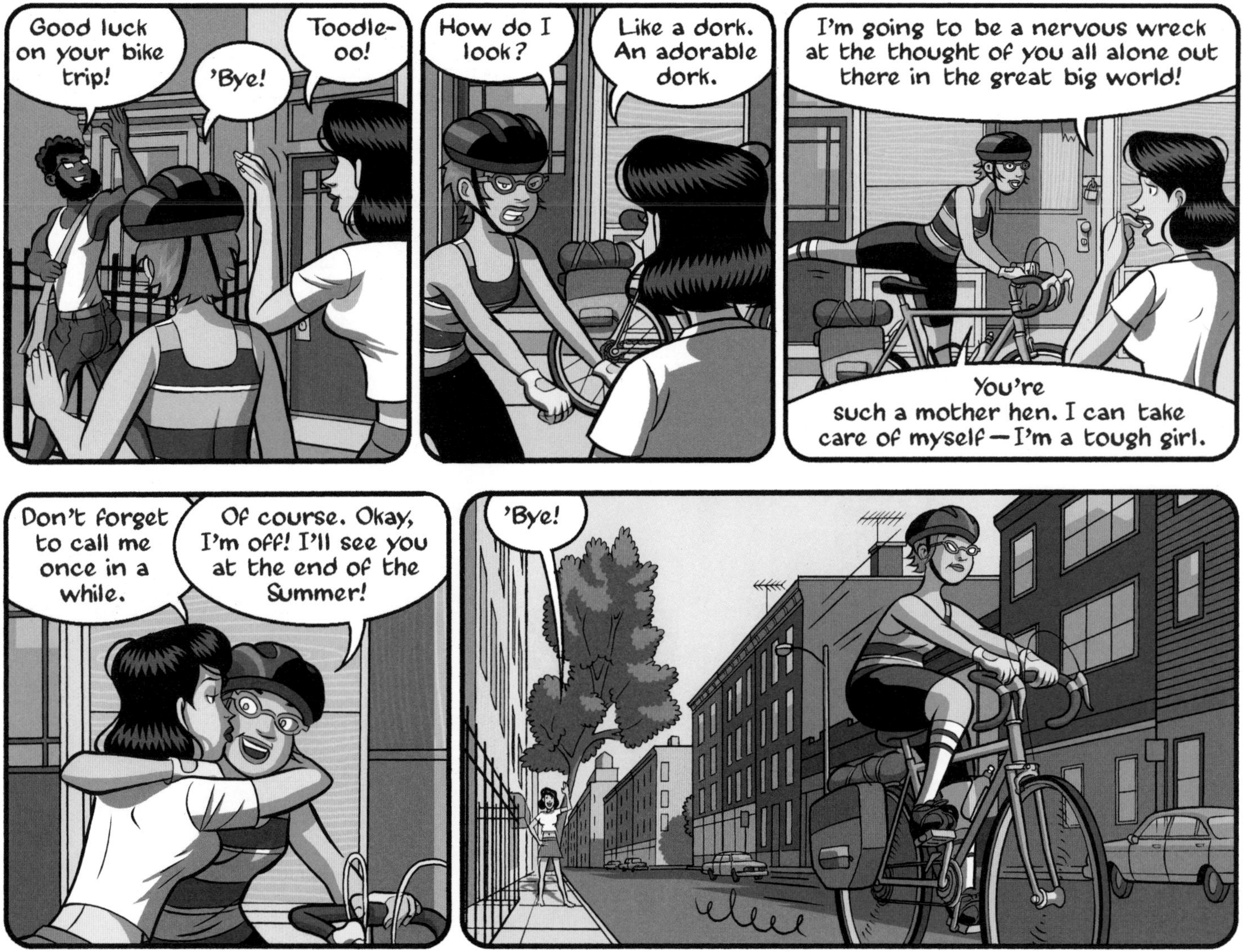
Good luck on your bike trip!
'Bye!
Toodle-oo!
How do I look?
Like a dork. An adorable dork.
I'm going to be a nervous wreck at the thought of you all alone out there in the great big world!
You're such a mother hen. I can take care of myself—I'm a tough girl.
Don't forget to call me once in a while.
Of course. Okay, I'm off! I'll see you at the end of the Summer!
'Bye!

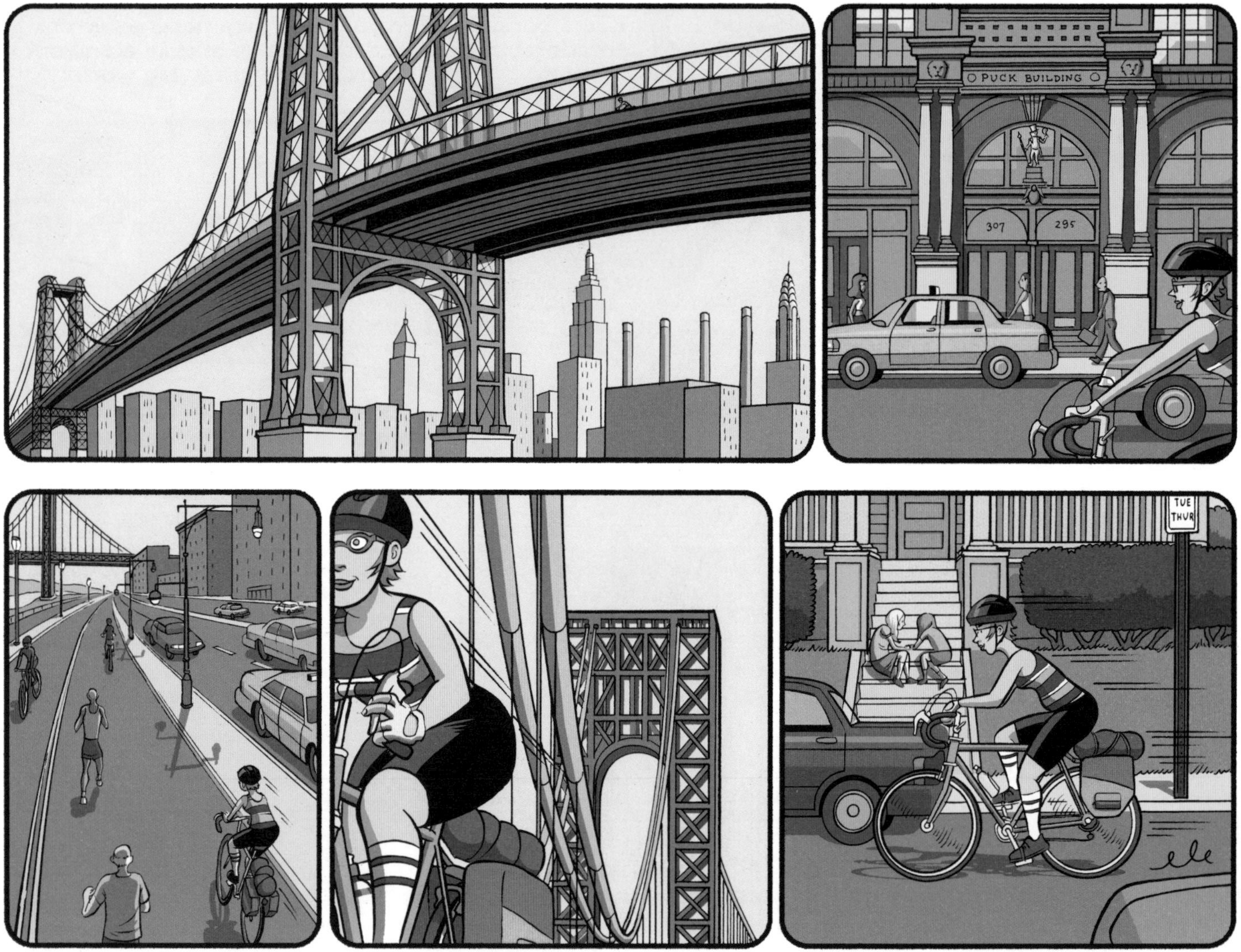
PUCK BUILDING
307
295
TUE
THUR

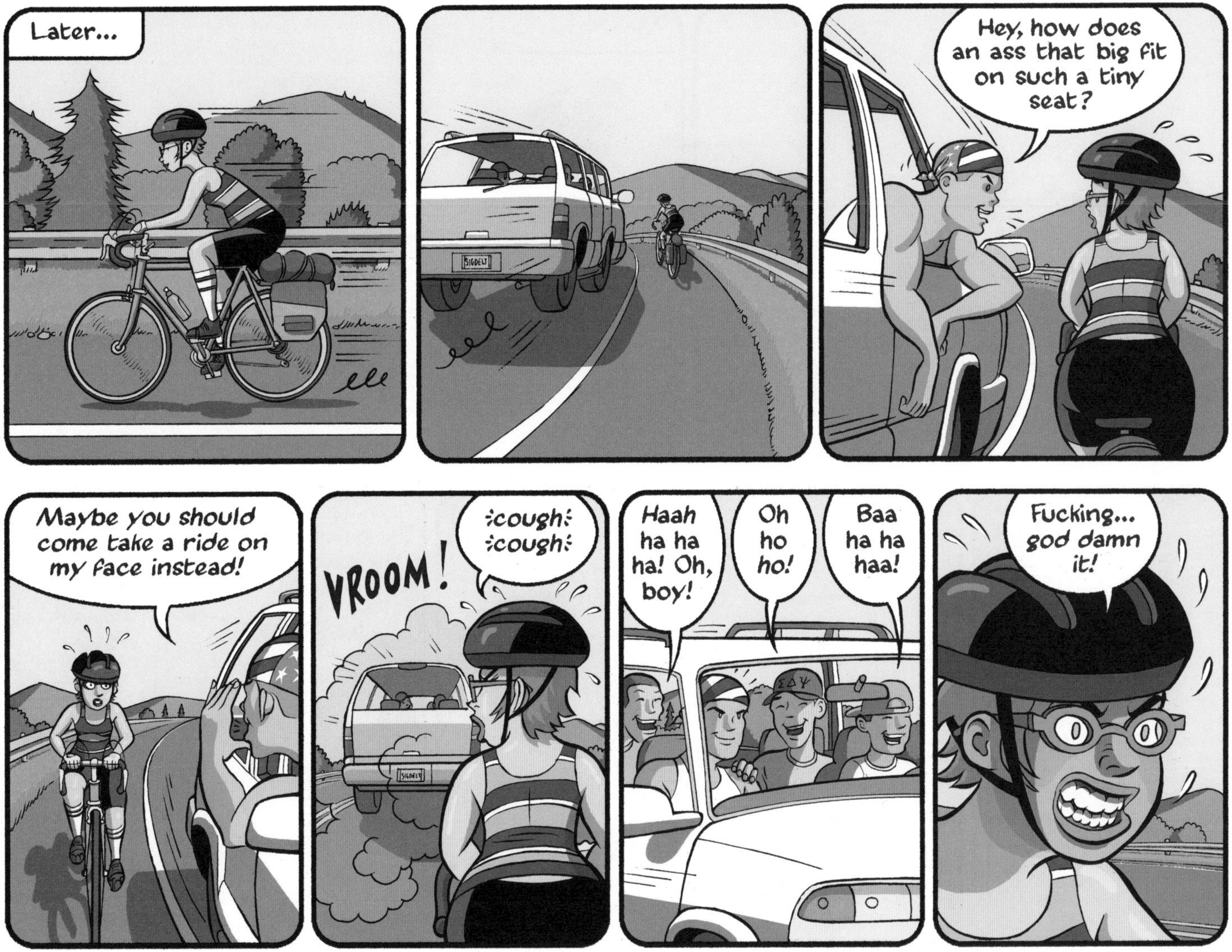
Later...
SIGDELT
Hey, how does an ass that big fit on such a tiny seat?
Maybe you should come take a ride on my face instead!
VROOM!
:cough: :cough:
SIGDELT
Haah ha ha ha! Oh, boy!
Oh ho ho!
Baa ha ha haa!
ΣΔΨ
Fucking... god damn it!

Meanwhile...

The GREEN PINE Inn
NO VACANCY

‡Zzzz...‡

‡Zzzzaw...‡

‡Ahem‡... Mister Campbell...

‡Zzzsnort!‡ Huh?

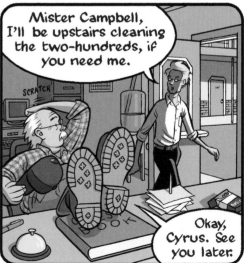
Mister Campbell, I'll be upstairs cleaning the two-hundreds, if you need me.

SCRATCH

Okay, Cyrus. See you later.

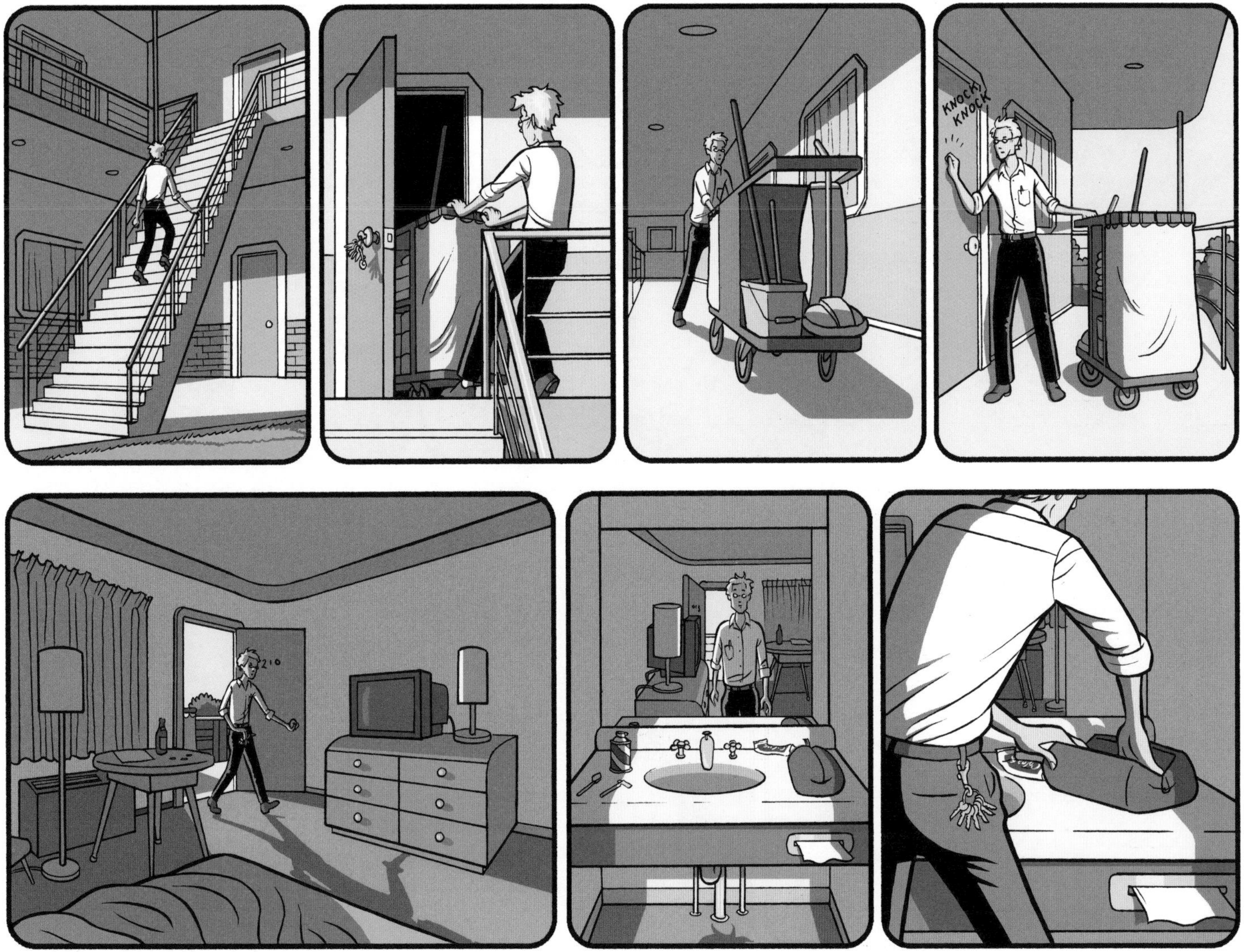
KNOCK KNOCK

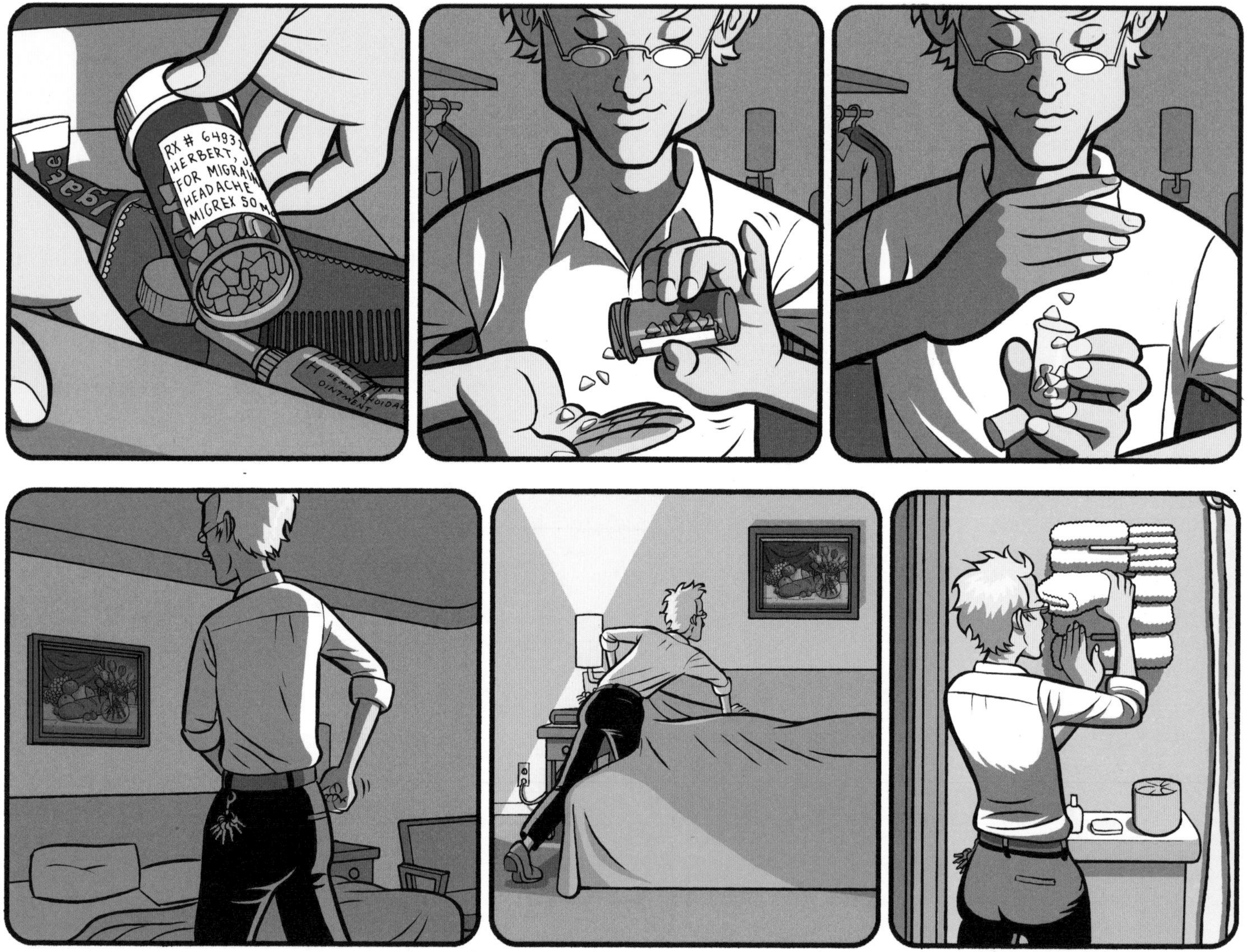
RX # 64932
HERBERT, J.
FOR MIGRAINE
HEADACHE
MIGREX 50 MG
HEMMORHOIDAL
OINTMENT

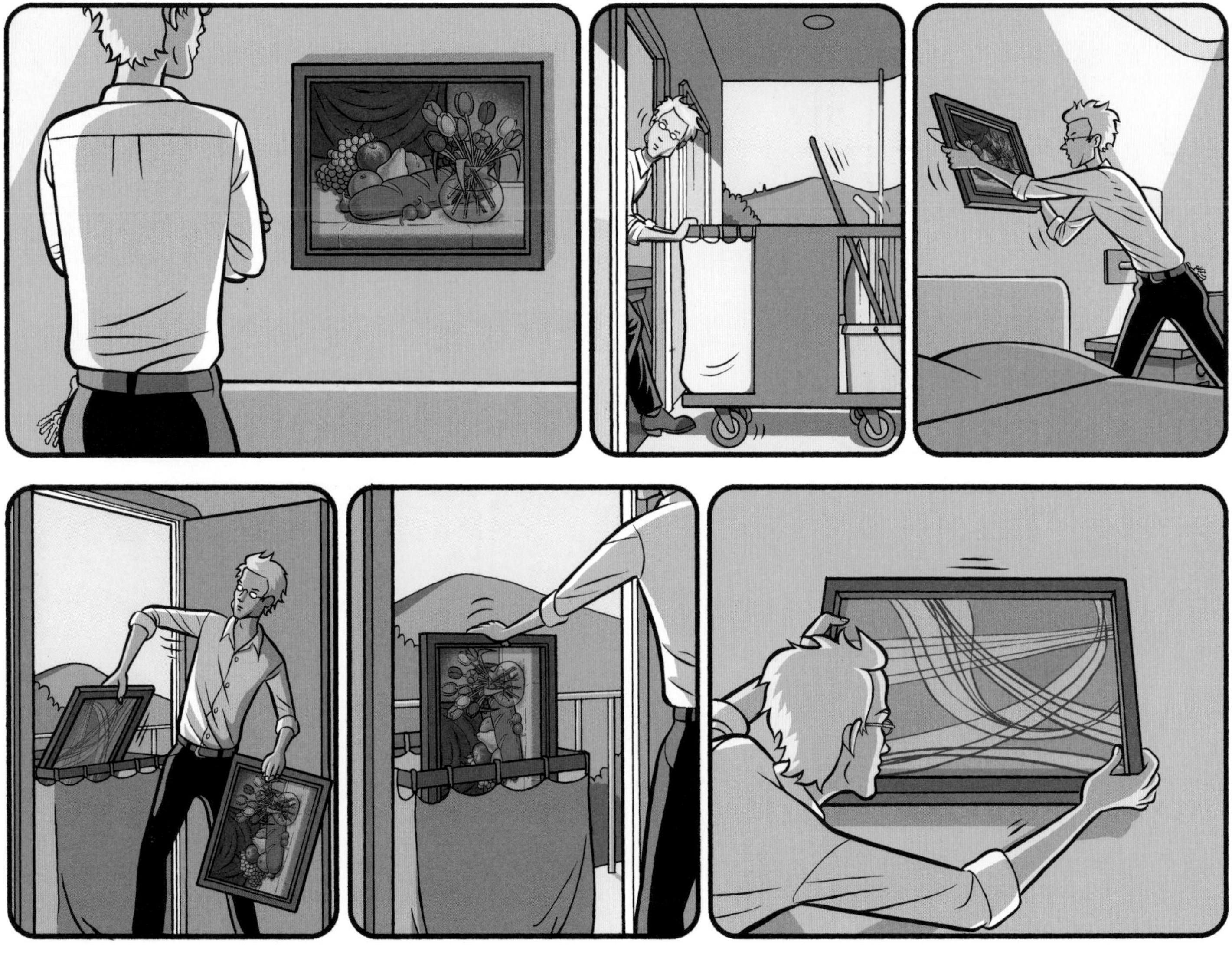

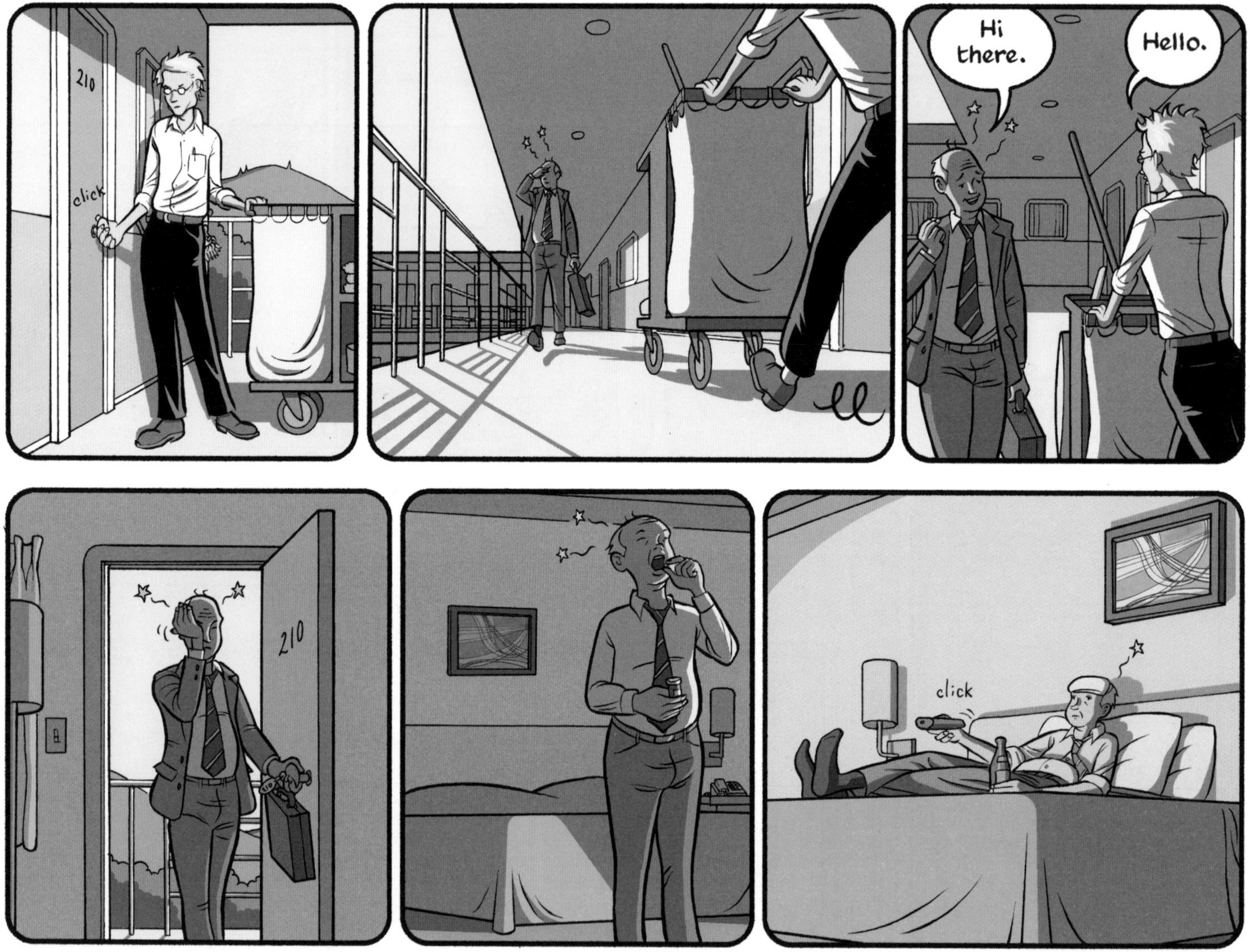
210
click
Hi there.
Hello.
210
click

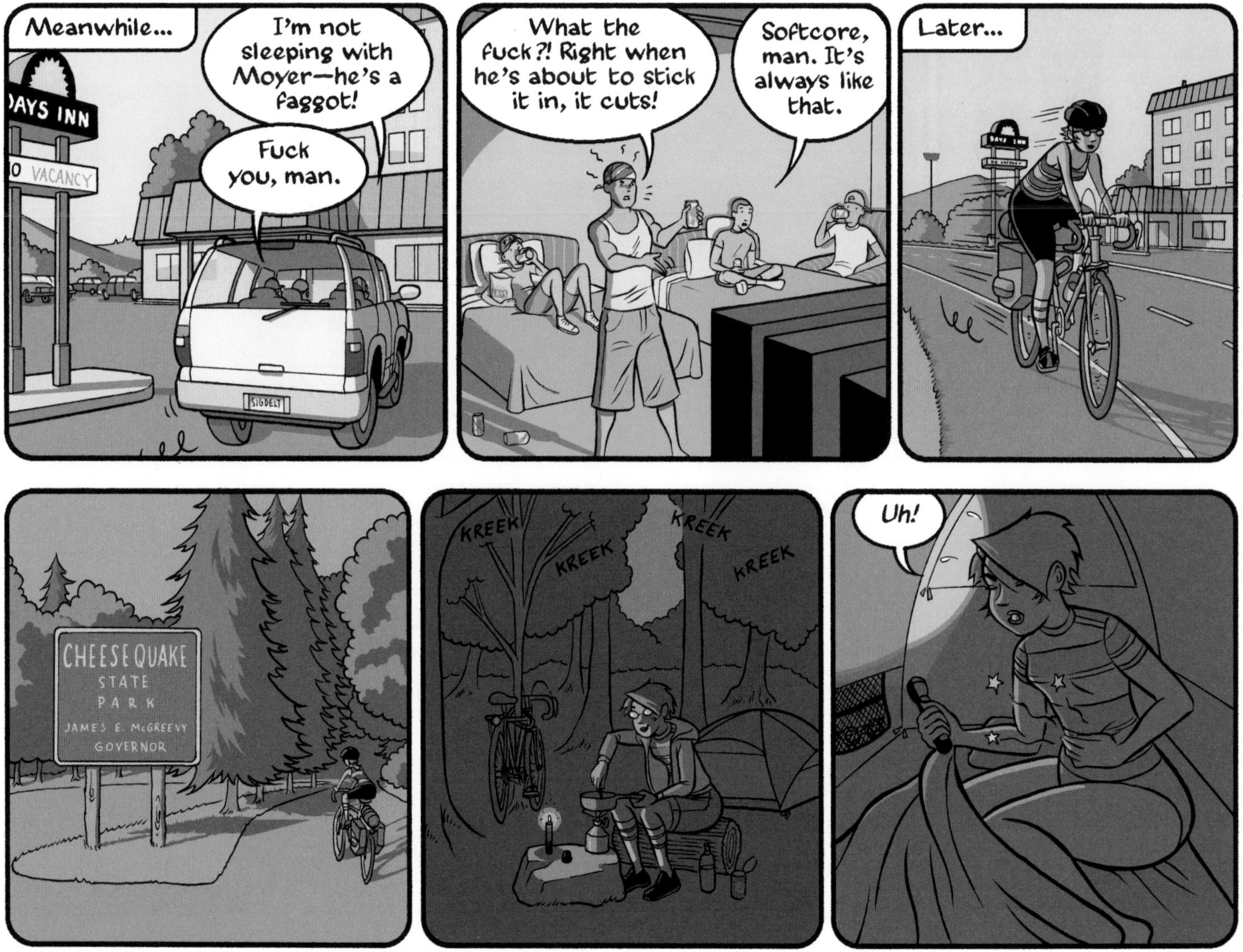
Meanwhile...
I'm not sleeping with Moyer—he's a faggot!
Fuck you, man.
VACANCY
SIGDELT
What the fuck?! Right when he's about to stick it in, it cuts!
Softcore, man. It's always like that.
Later...
CHEESE QUAKE
STATE
PARK
JAMES E. McGREEVY
GOVERNOR
KREEK
KREEK
KREEK
KREEK
Uh!

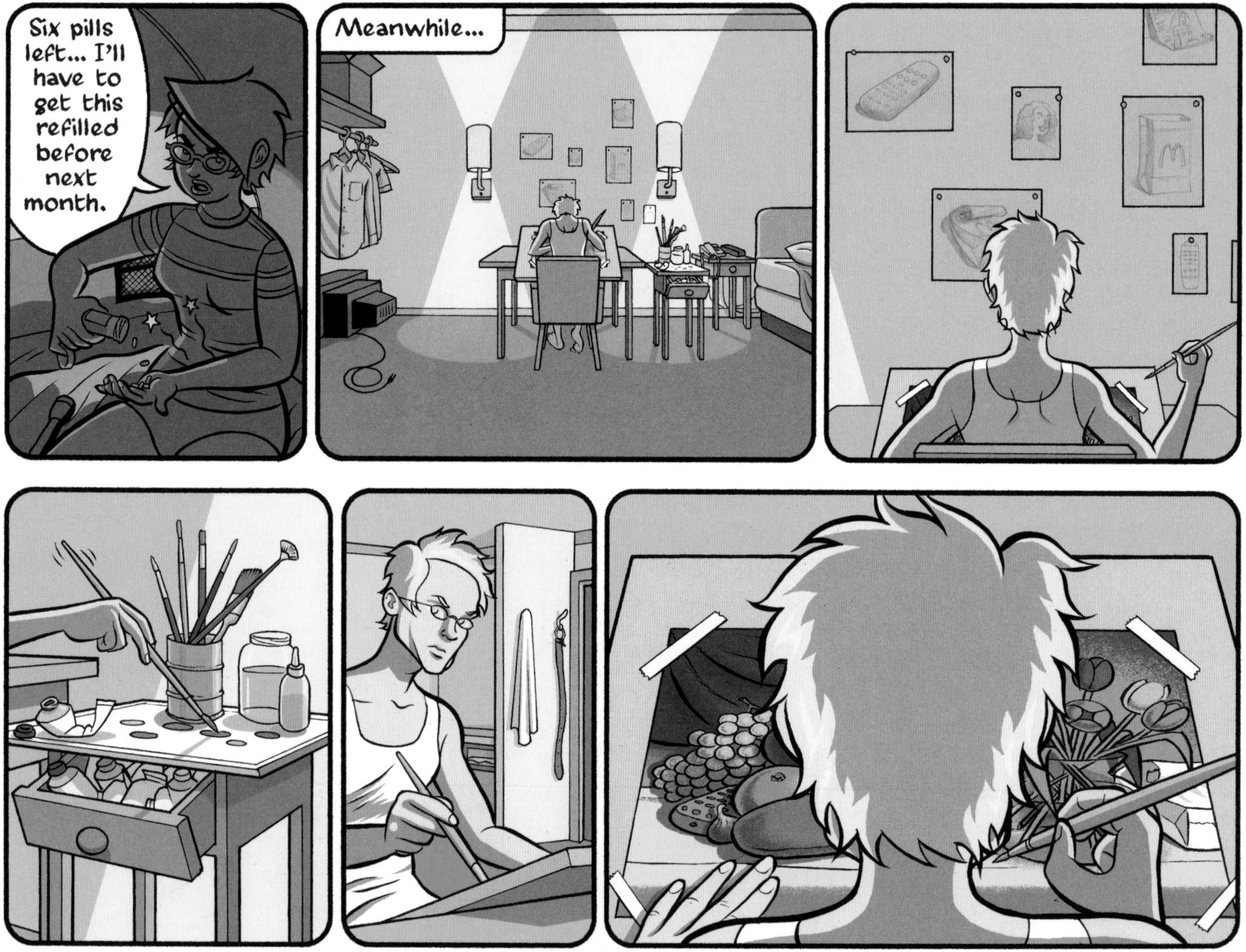
Six pills left... I'll have to get this refilled before next month.
Meanwhile...

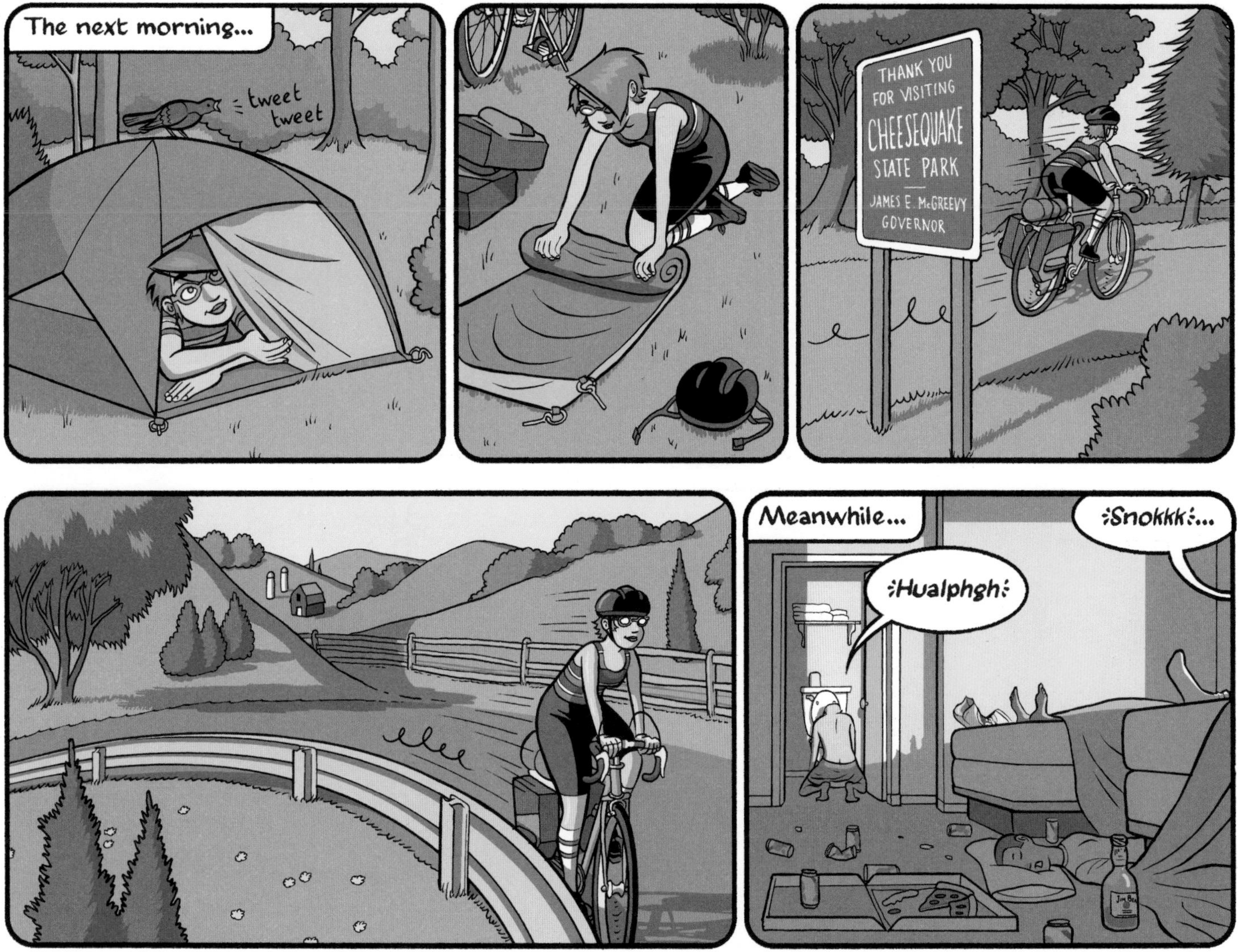
The next morning...
tweet
tweet
THANK YOU
FOR VISITING
CHEESEQUAKE
STATE PARK
JAMES E. McGREEVY
GOVERNOR
Meanwhile...
Snokkk...
Hualphgh

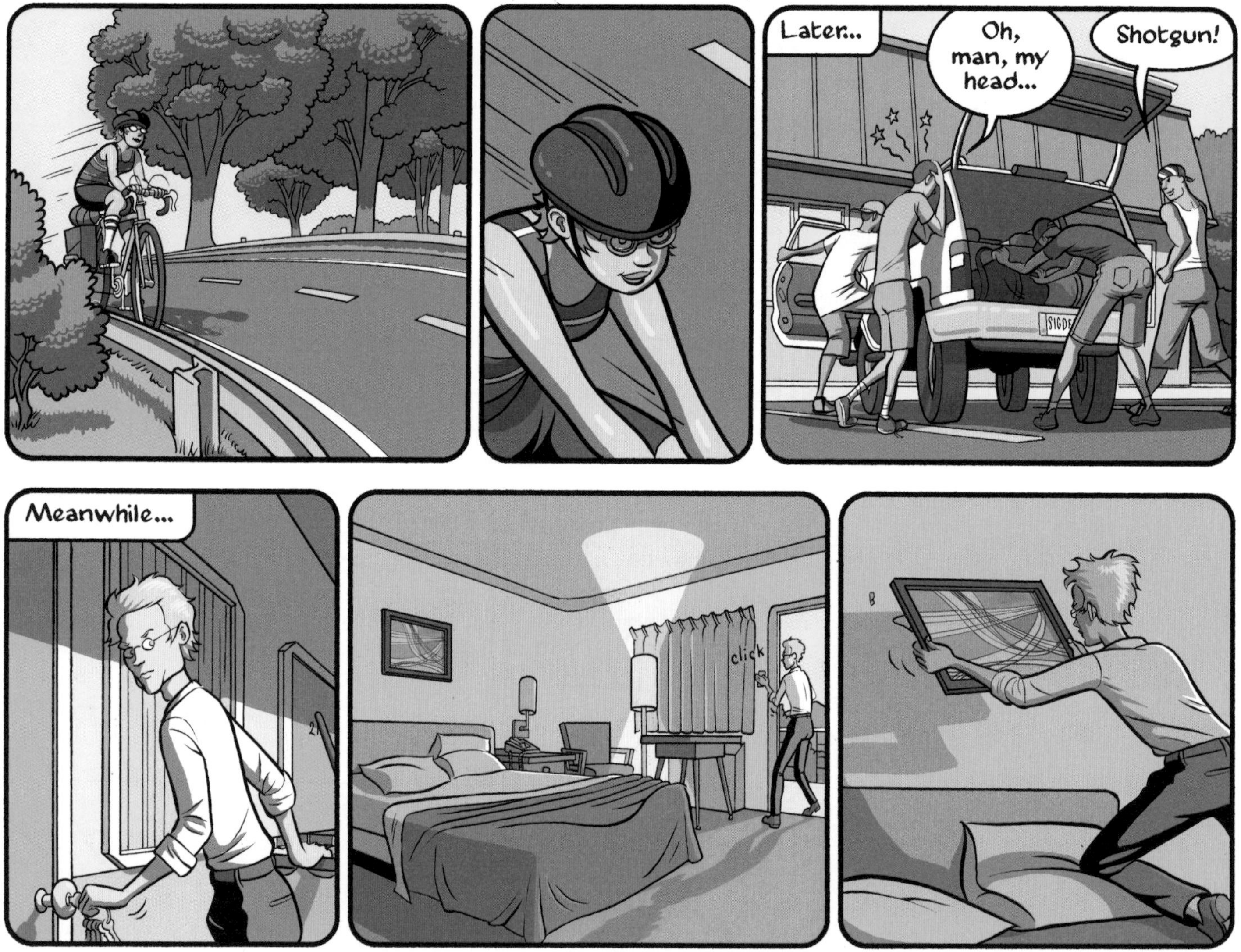
Later...
Oh, man, my head...
Shotgun!
Meanwhile...
click

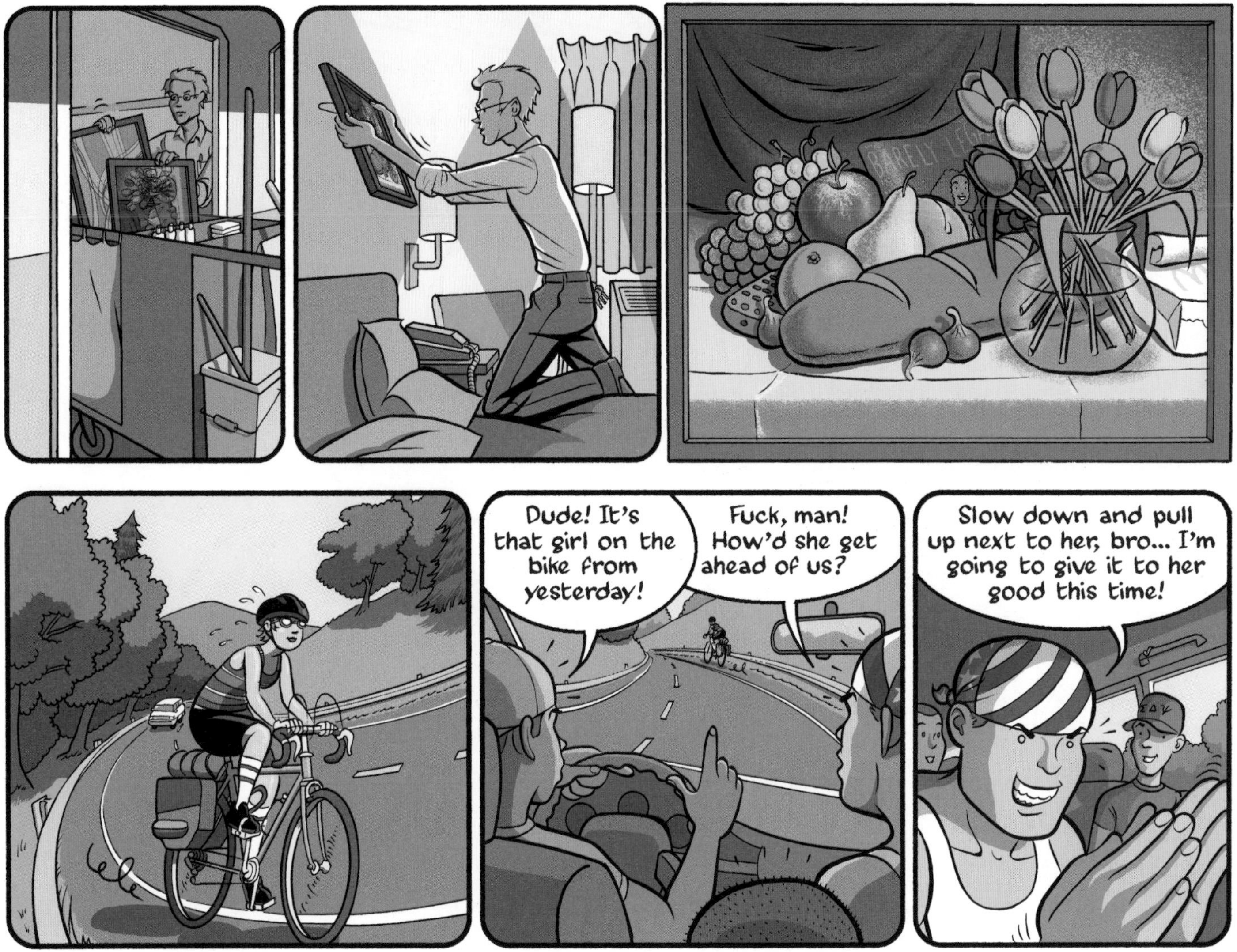
Dude! It's that girl on the bike from yesterday!
Fuck, man! How'd she get ahead of us?
Slow down and pull up next to her, bro... I'm going to give it to her good this time!

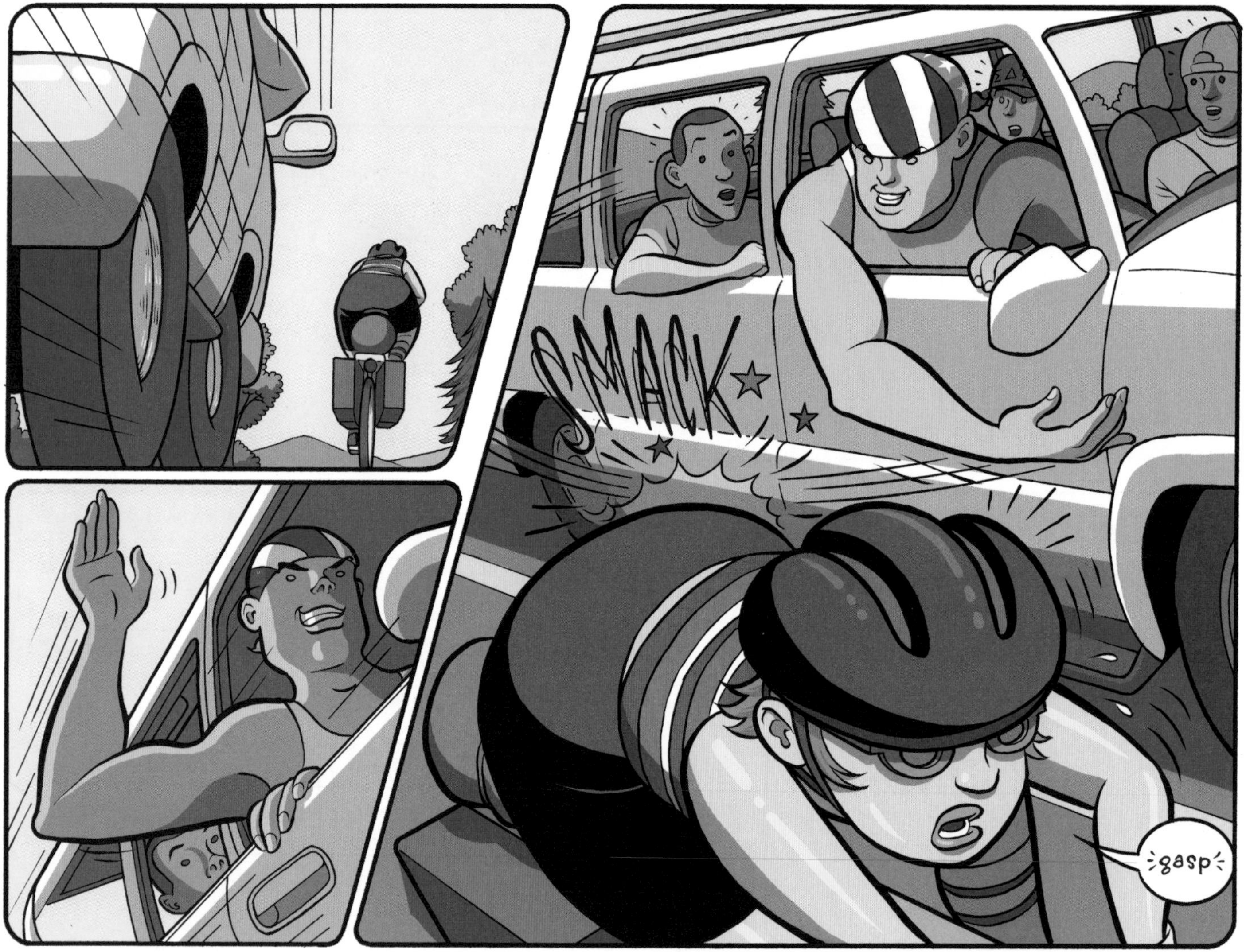
SMACK
gasp

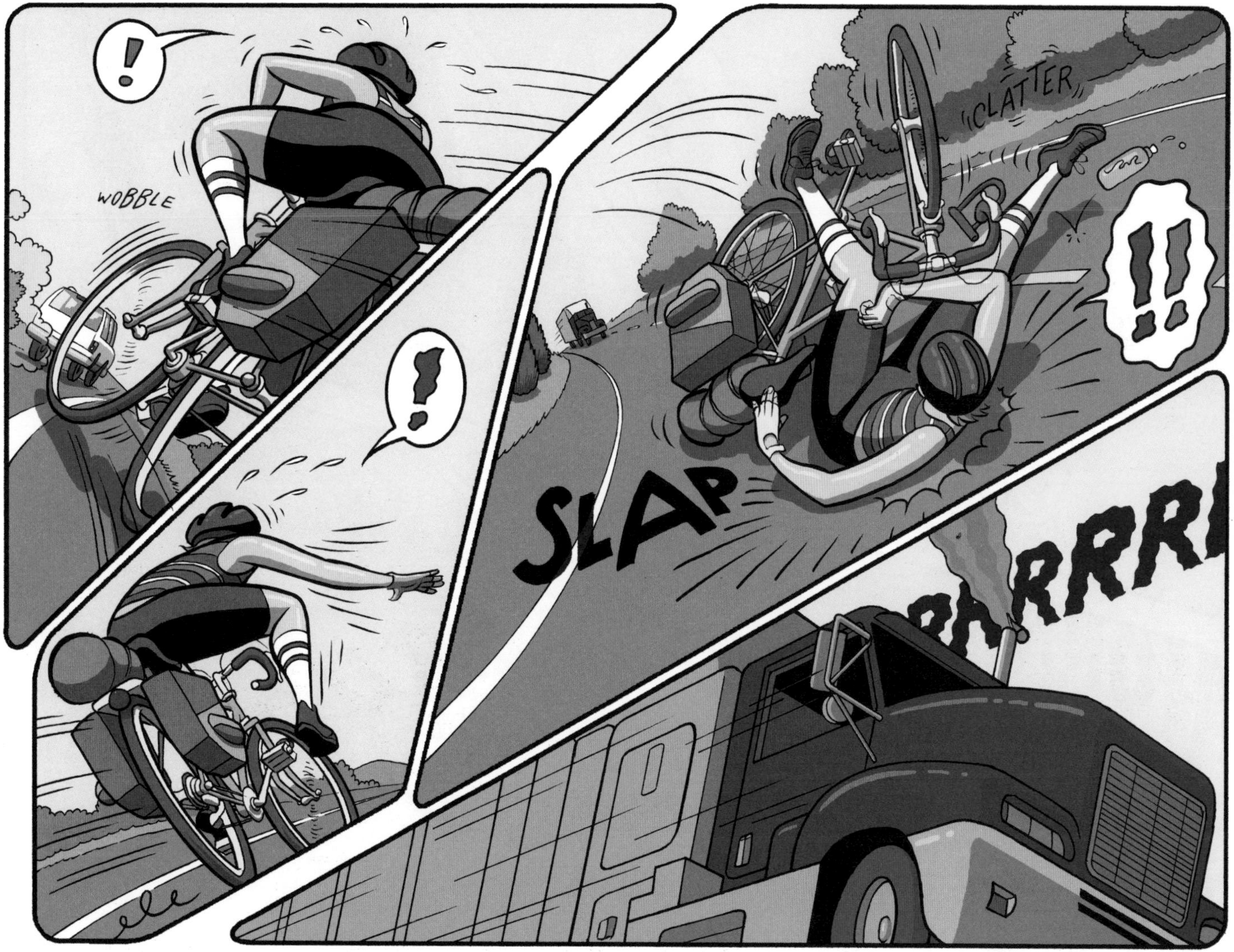
!
WOBBLE
!
CLATTER
!!
SLAP
RRRRRRR

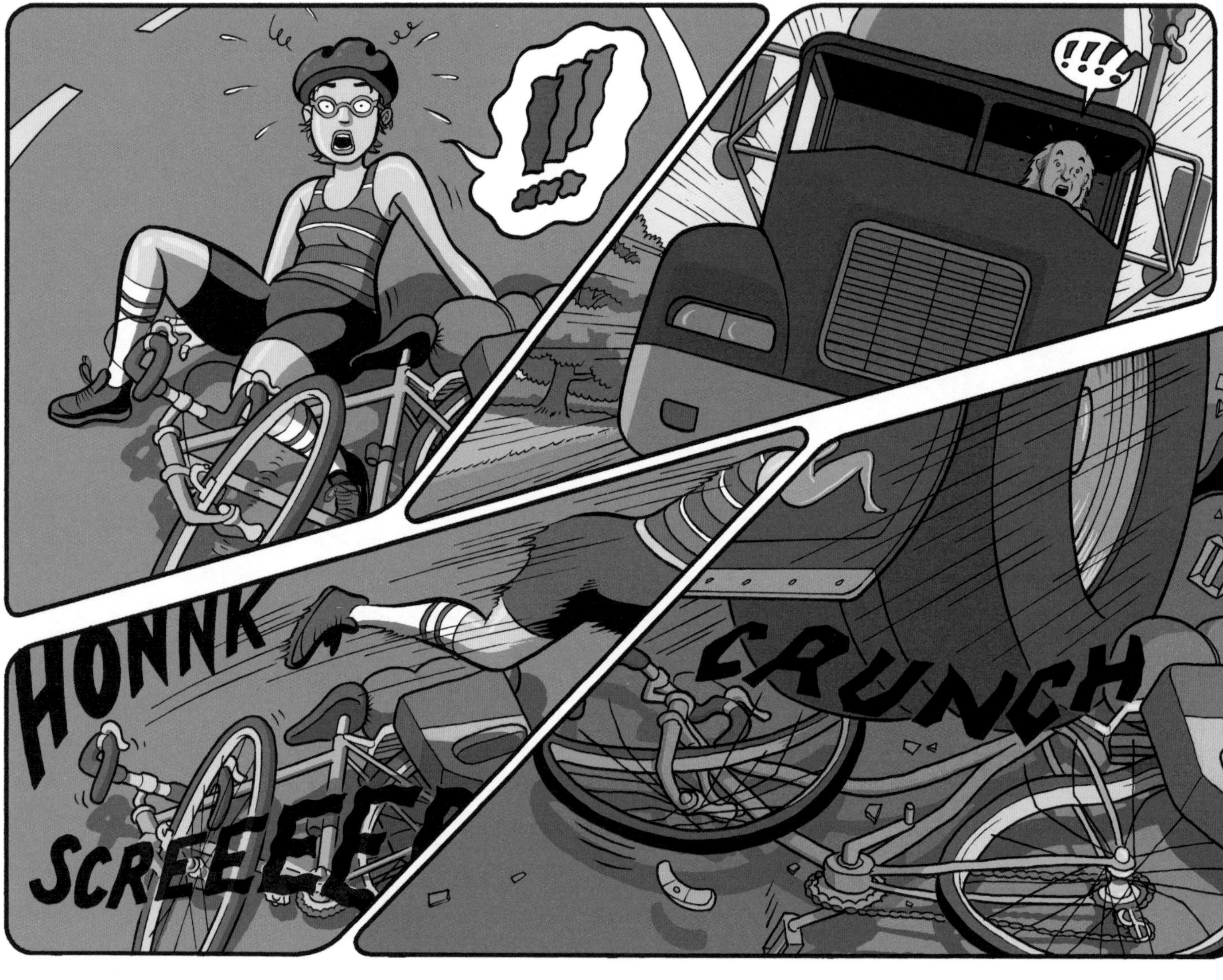
!!!
!!!!
HONNK
SCREEEEE
CRUNCH

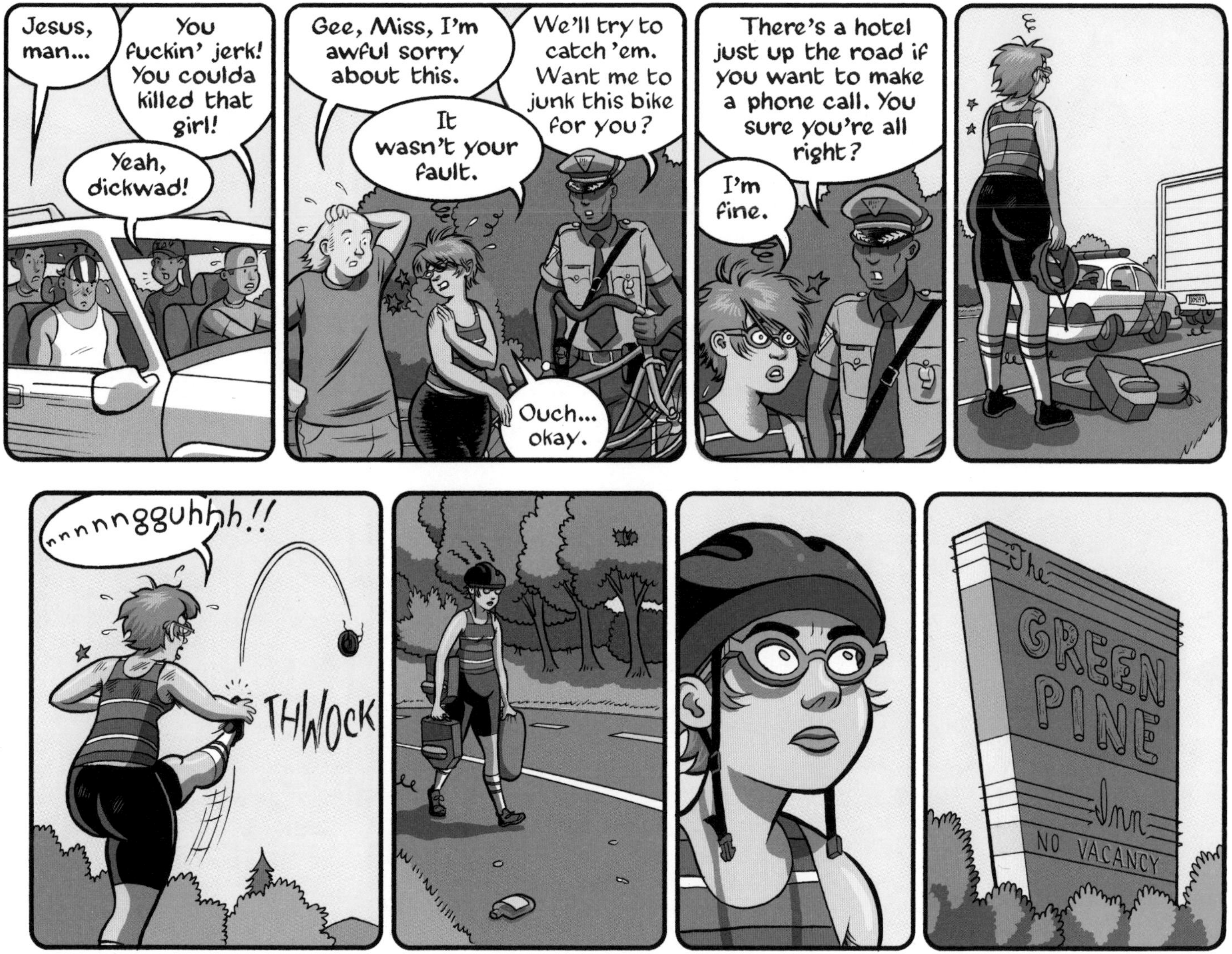

Jesus, man...
You fuckin' jerk! You coulda killed that girl!
Yeah, dickwad!
Gee, Miss, I'm awful sorry about this.
It wasn't your fault.
We'll try to catch 'em. Want me to junk this bike for you?
Ouch... okay.
There's a hotel just up the road if you want to make a phone call. You sure you're all right?
I'm fine.
nnnnngguhhh!!
THWOCK
The GREEN PINE Inn
NO VACANCY

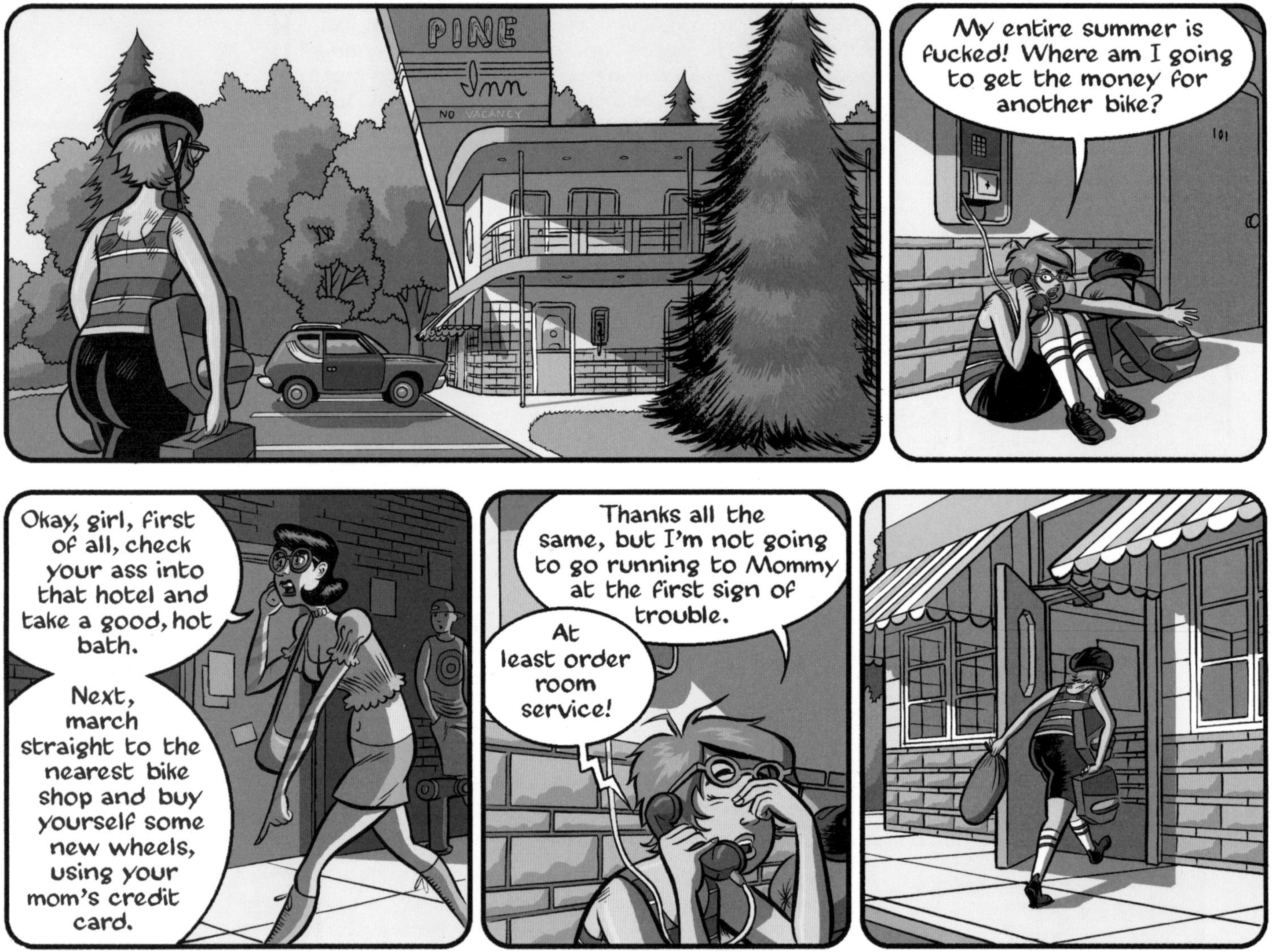

PINE Inn
NO VACANCY
My entire summer is fucked! Where am I going to get the money for another bike?
101
Okay, girl, first of all, check your ass into that hotel and take a good, hot bath.
Next, march straight to the nearest bike shop and buy yourself some new wheels, using your mom's credit card.
Thanks all the same, but I'm not going to go running to Mommy at the first sign of trouble.
At least order room service!

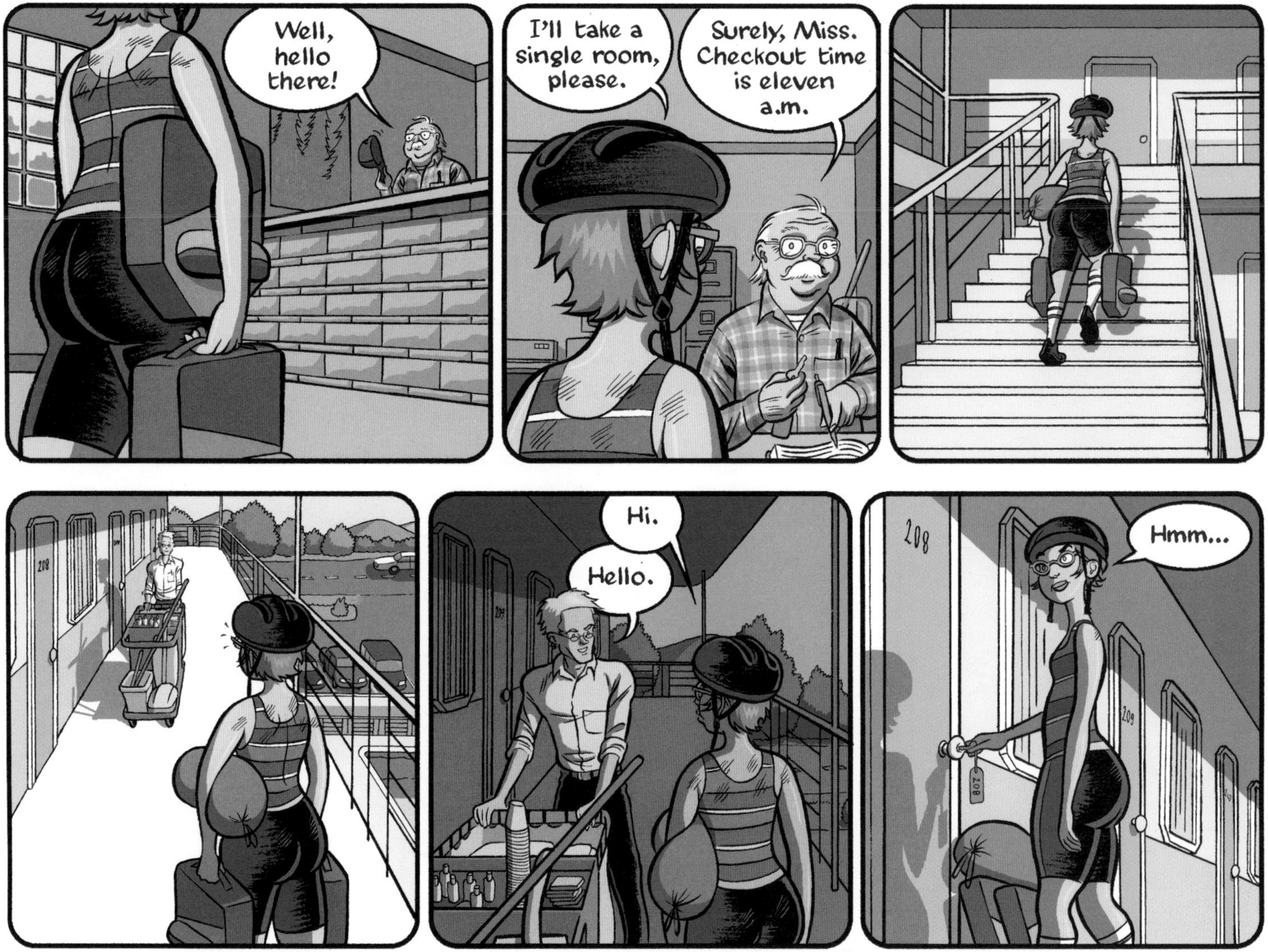
Well, hello there!
I'll take a single room, please.
Surely, Miss. Checkout time is eleven a.m.
Hi.
Hello.
Hmm...

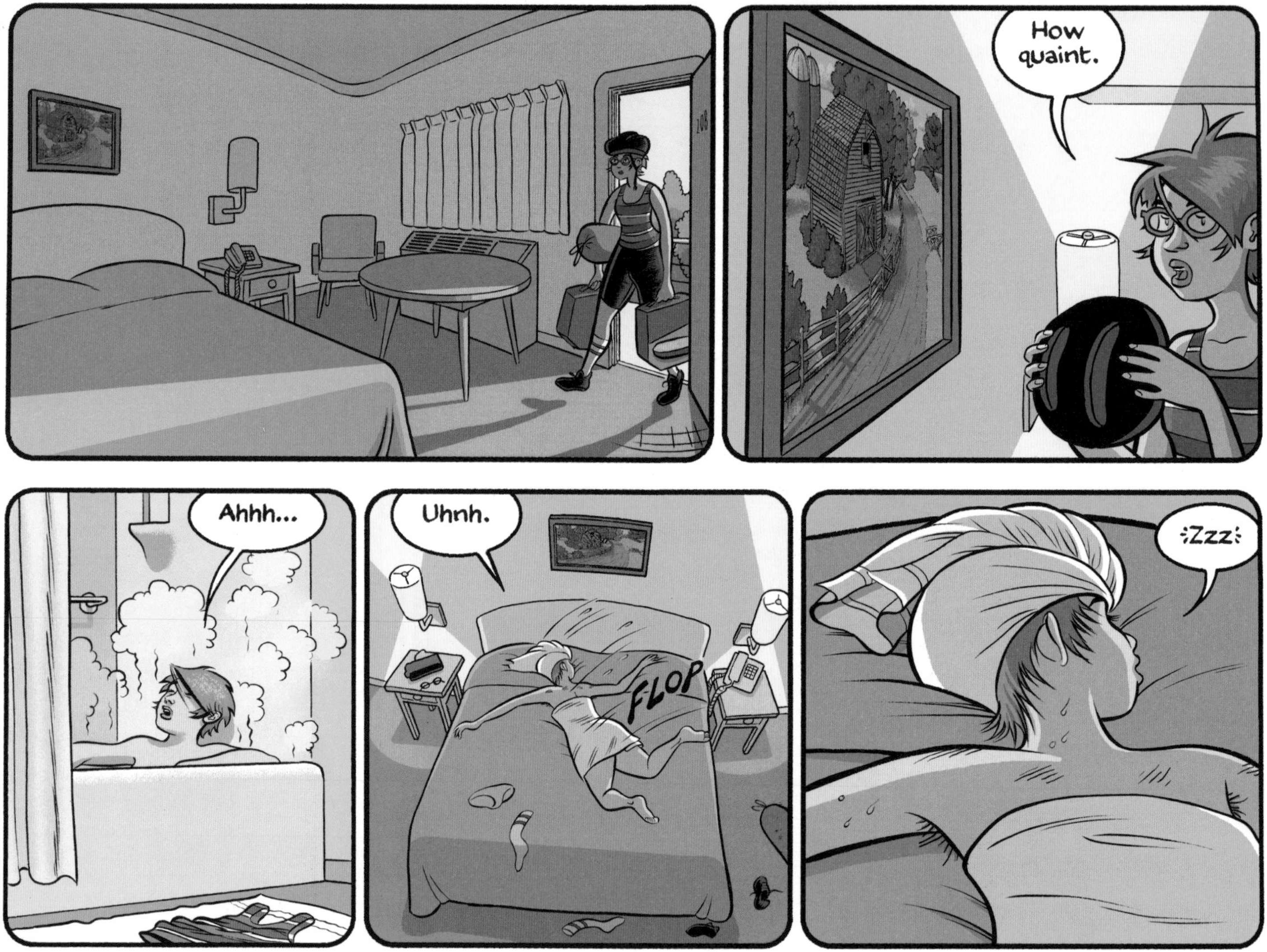
How quaint.
Ahhh...
Uhnh.
FLOP
Zzz

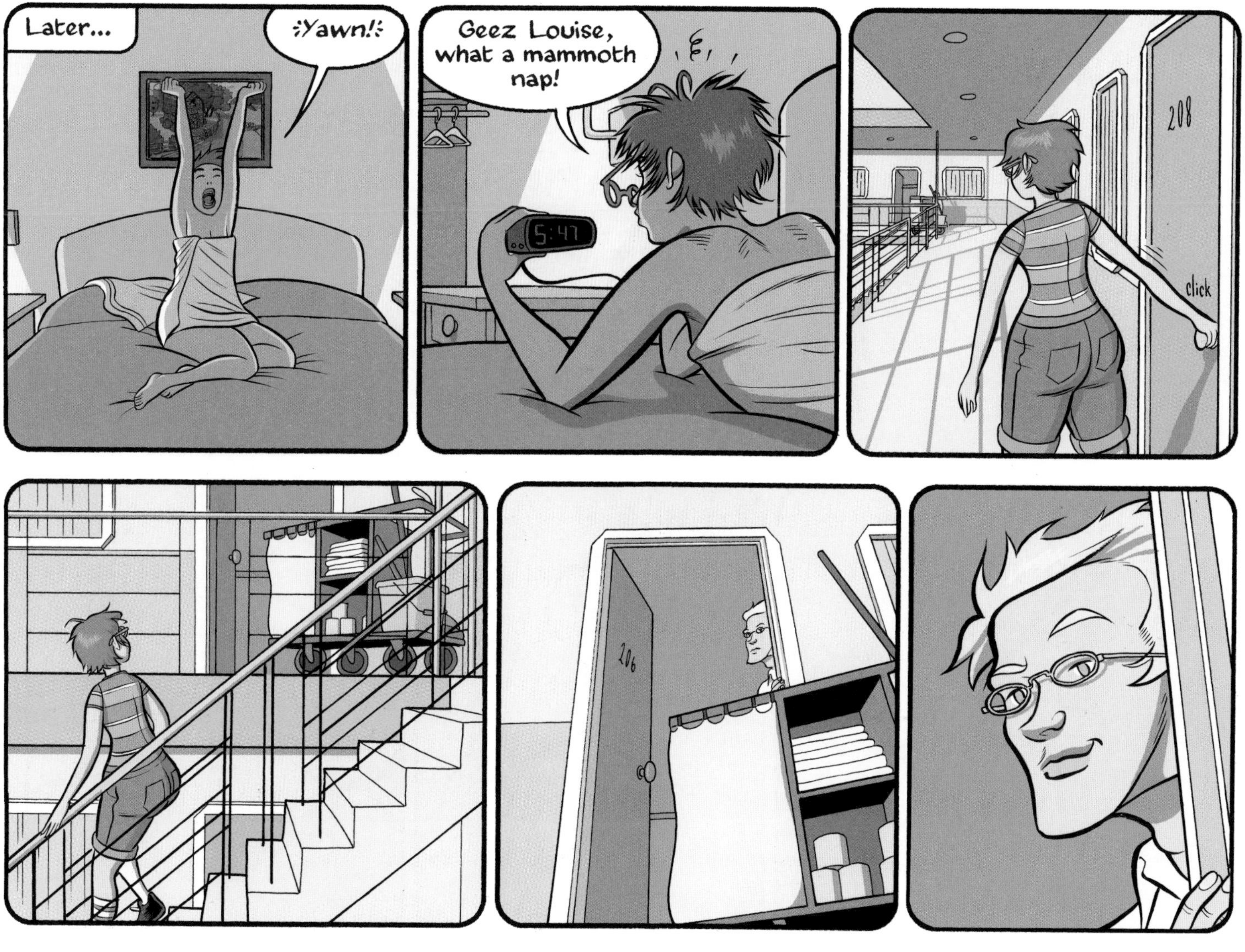
Later...
:Yawn!:
Geez Louise, what a mammoth nap!
5:47
208
click
206

DINER
The GREEN PINE Inn
Meanwhile...
208
FLOVIL

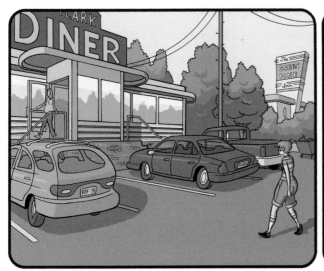

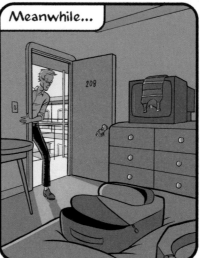

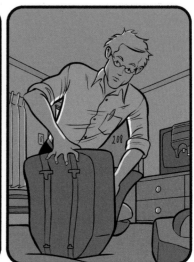

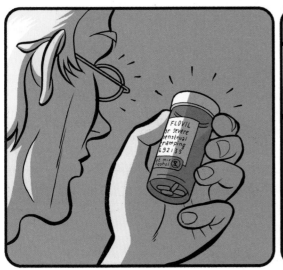

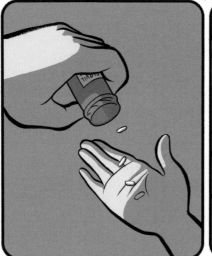

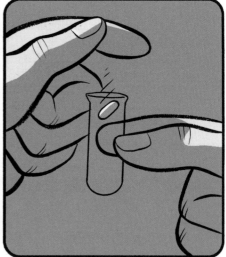

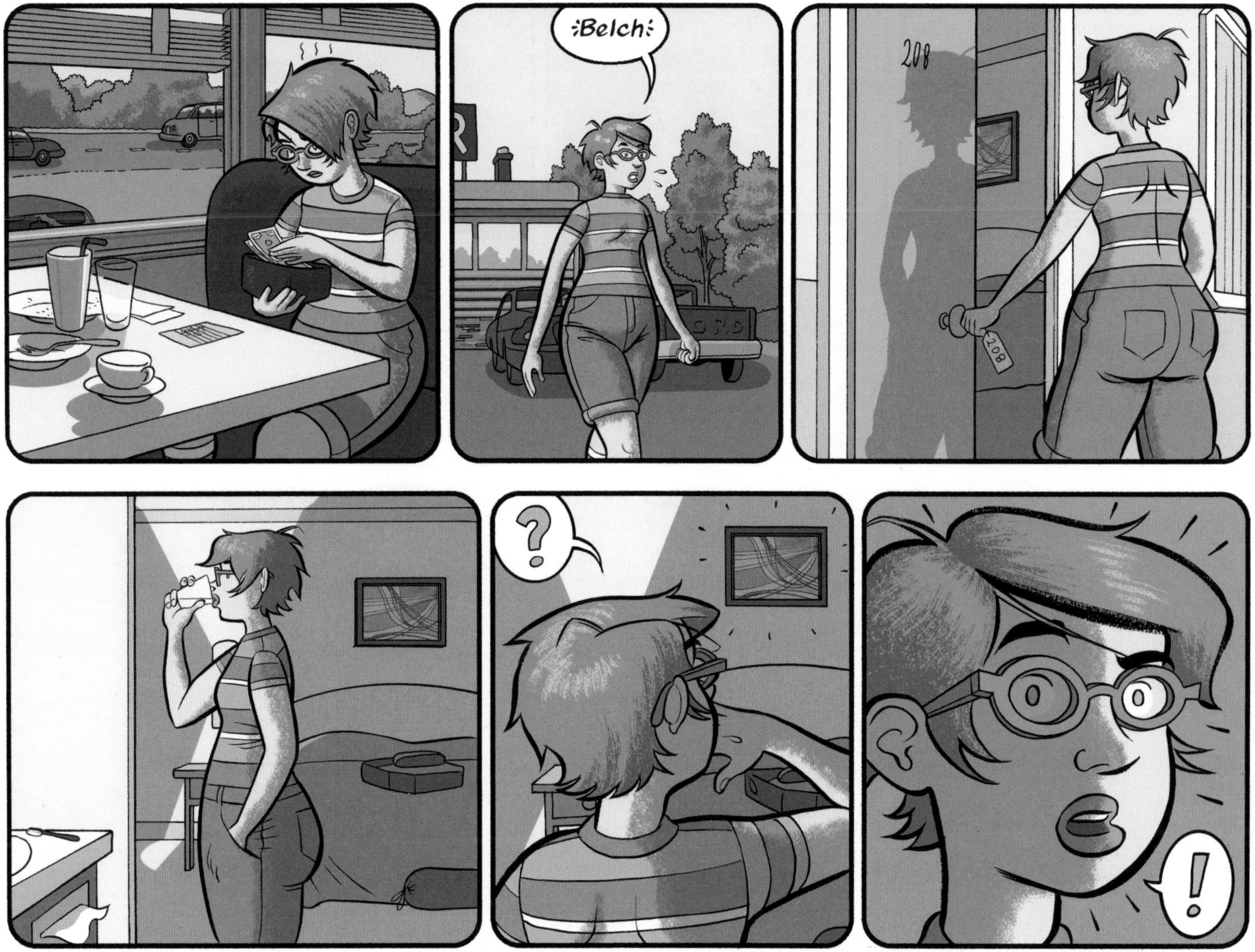
:Belch:
208
208
?
!

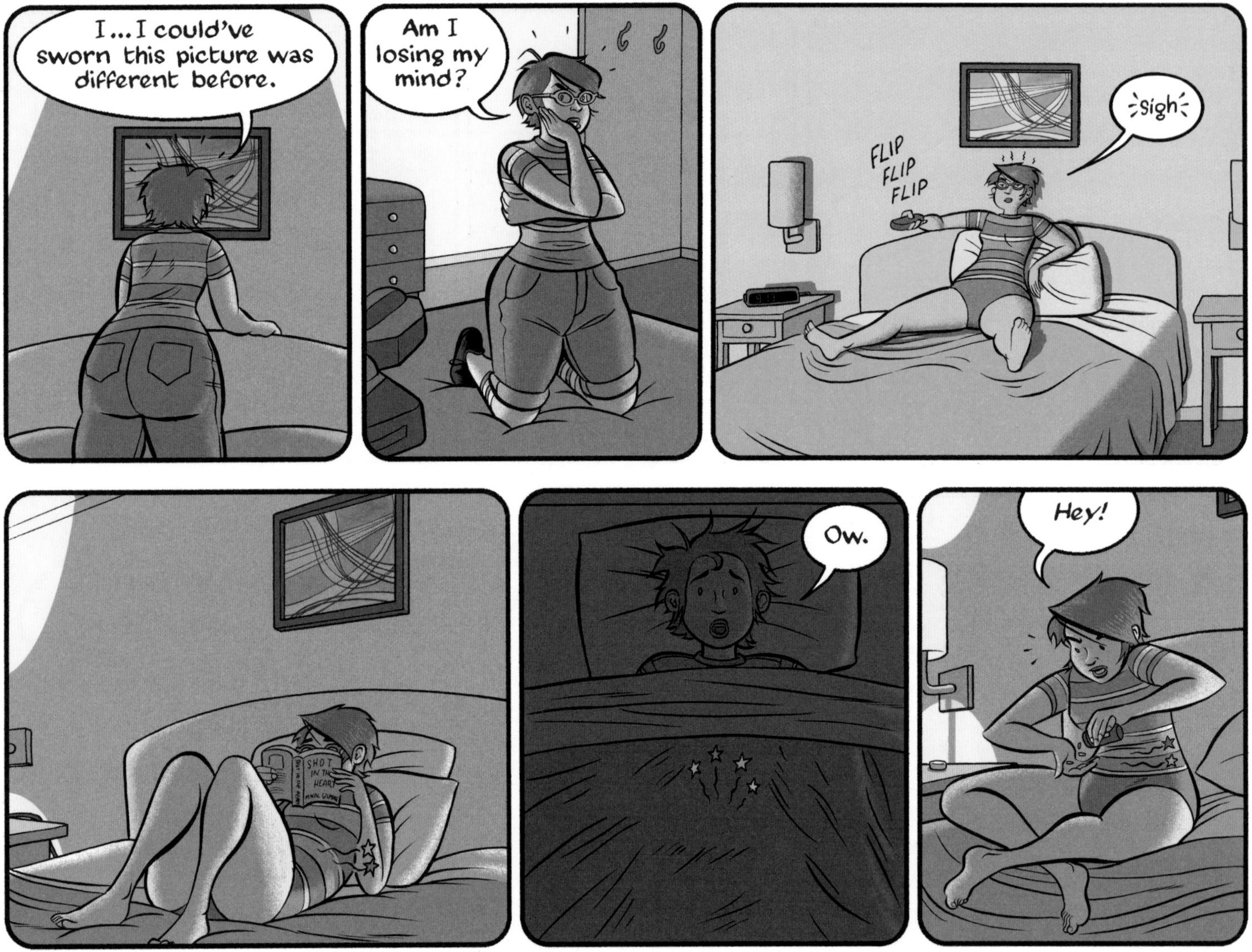
I...I could've sworn this picture was different before.
Am I losing my mind?
FLIP FLIP FLIP
sigh
SHOT IN THE HEART
Ow.
Hey!

I thought I had four of these left.

SCRAPE

207

?

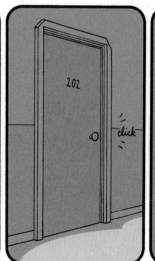

202

click

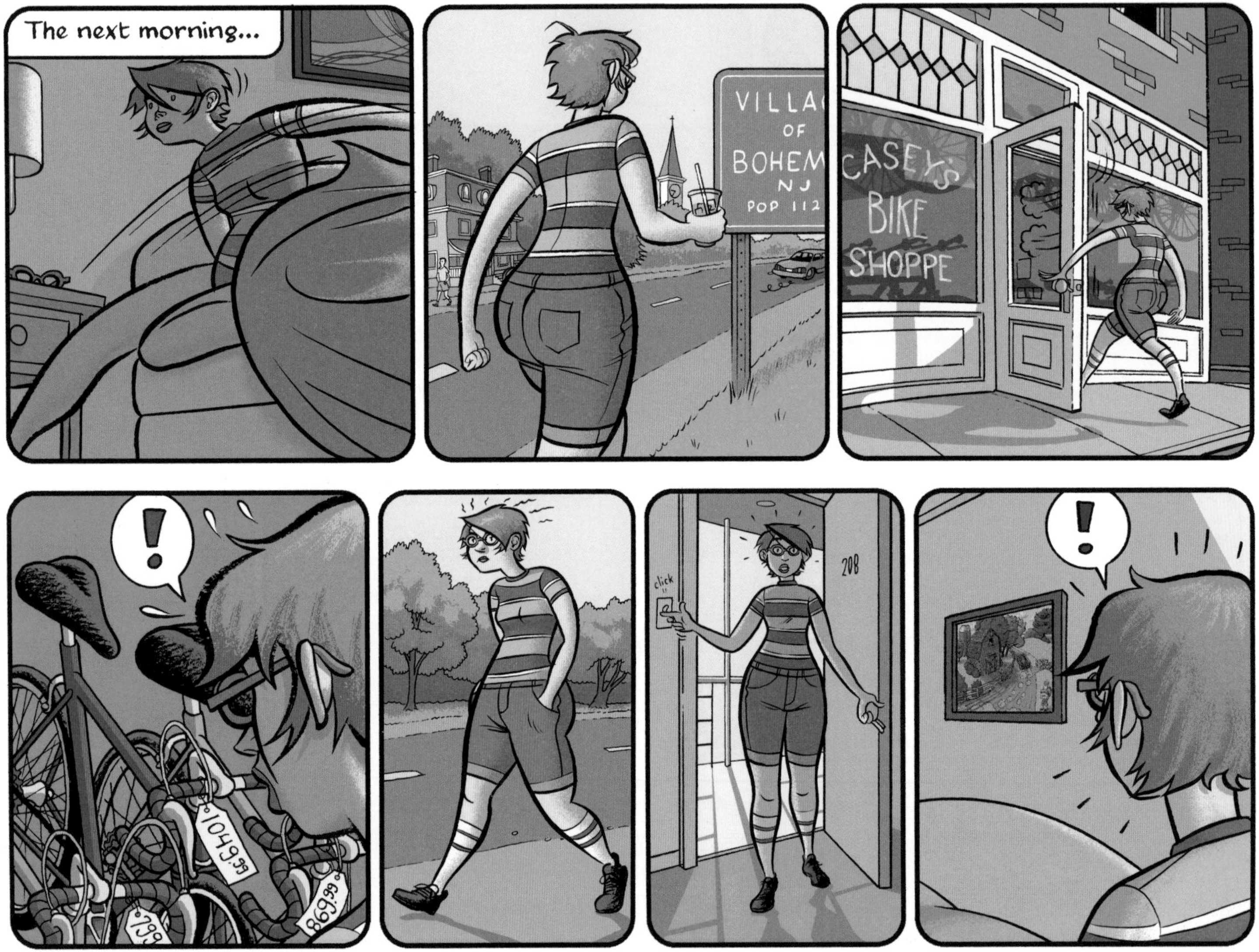

The next morning...
VILLA
OF
BOHEM
NJ
POP 112
CASEY'S
BIKE
SHOPPE
!
1049.99
869.99
click
208
!

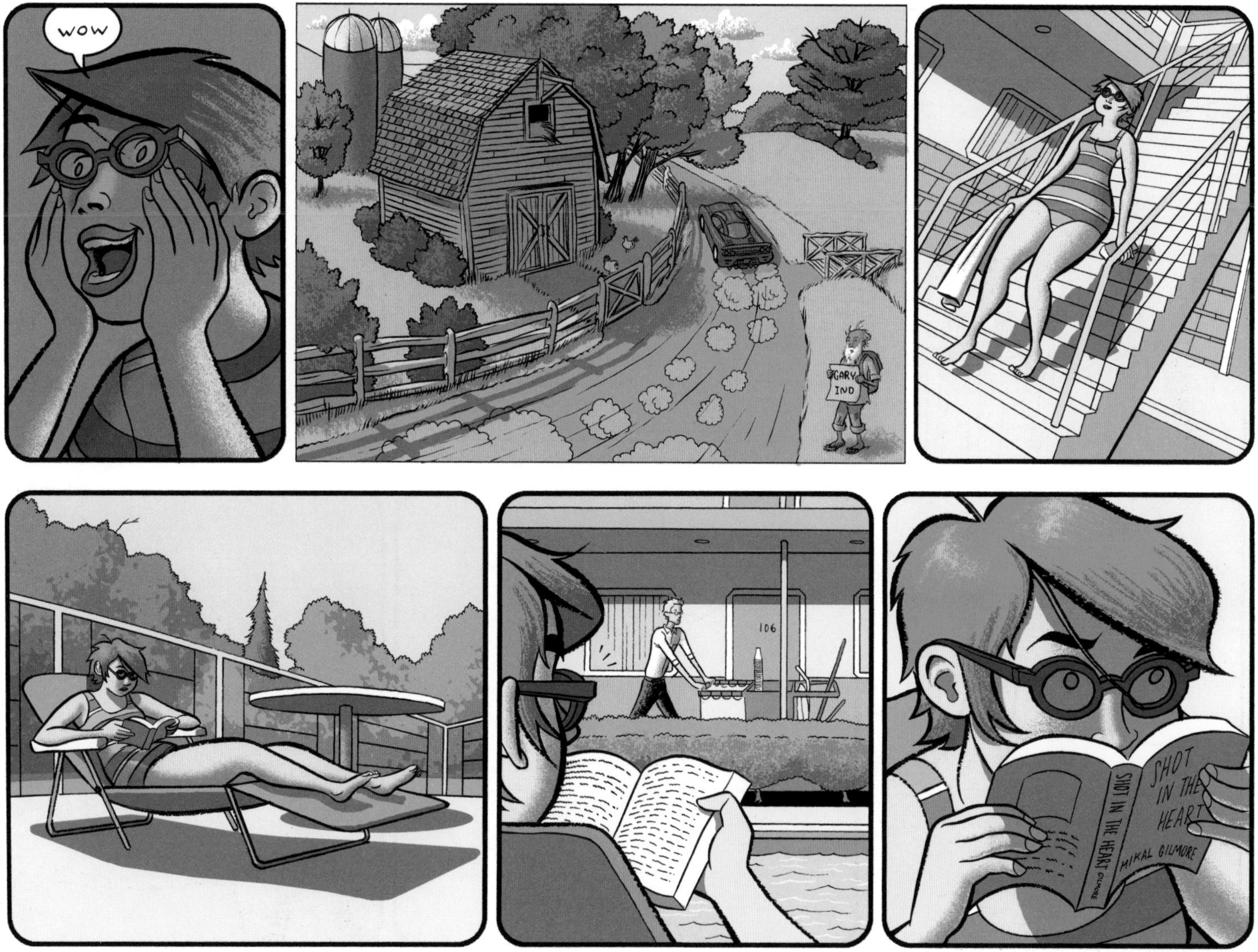
WOW
GARY
IND
106
SHOT IN THE HEART
MIKAL GILMORE

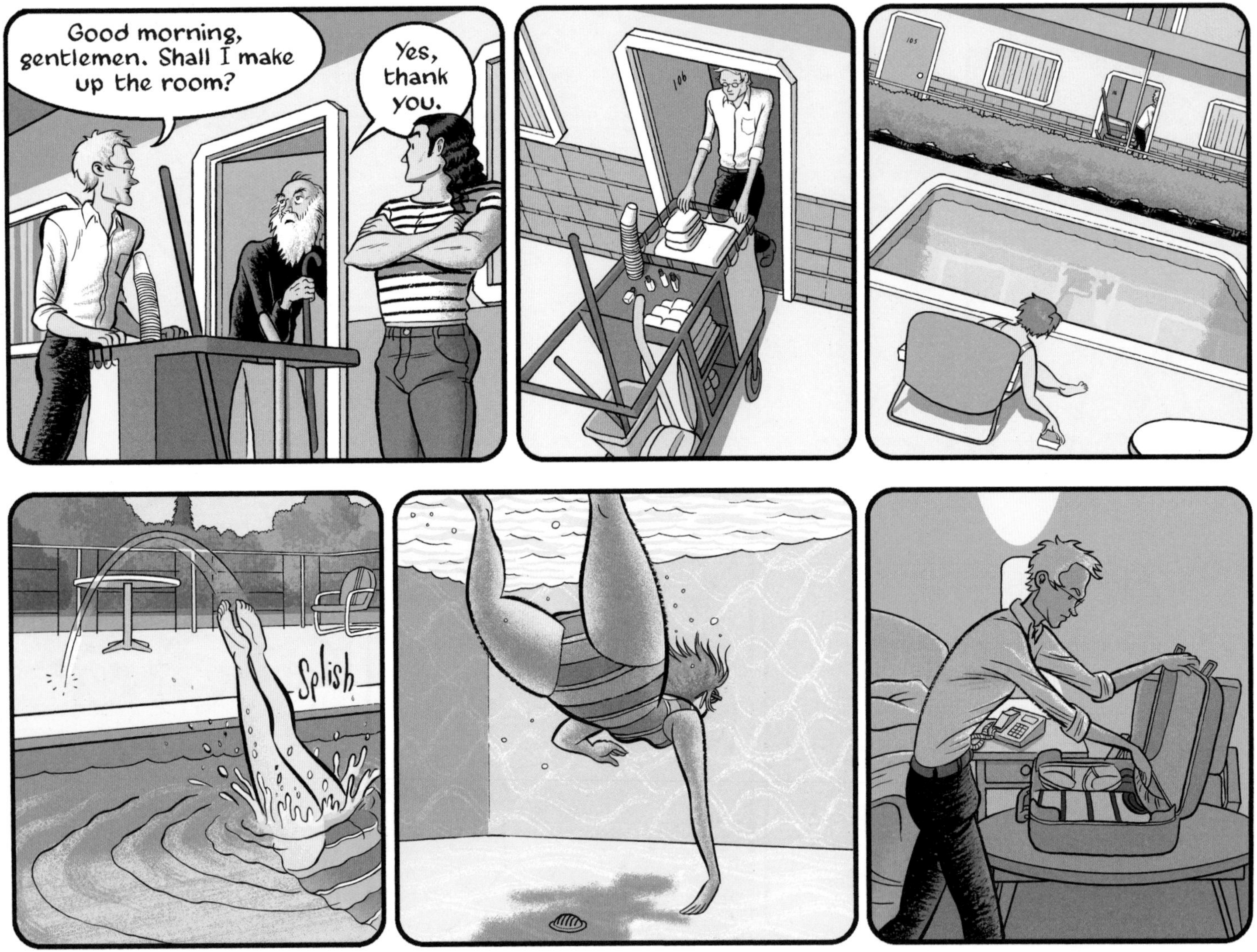
Good morning, gentlemen. Shall I make up the room?
Yes, thank you.
106
Splish

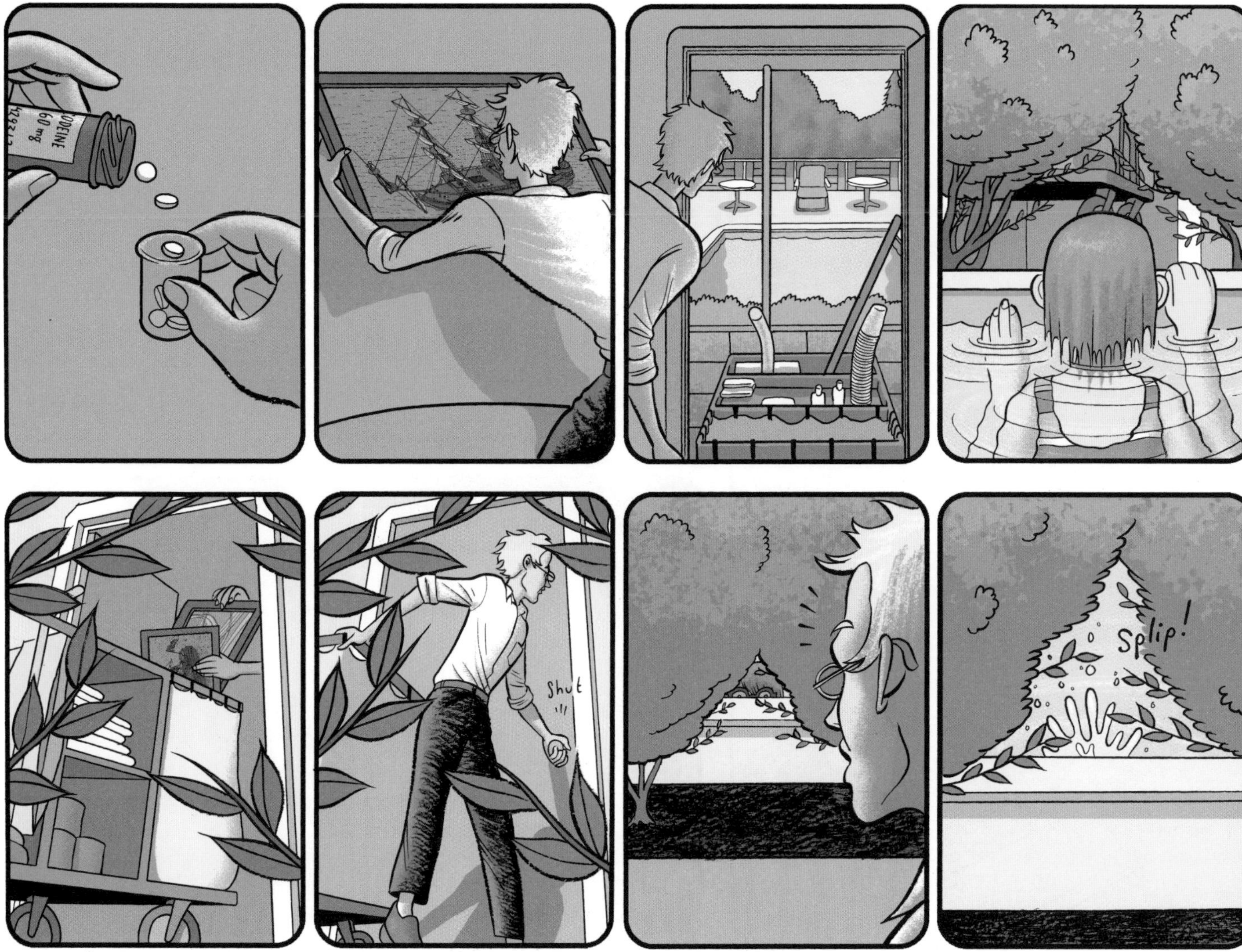
ODEINE
60 mg
Shut
Splip!

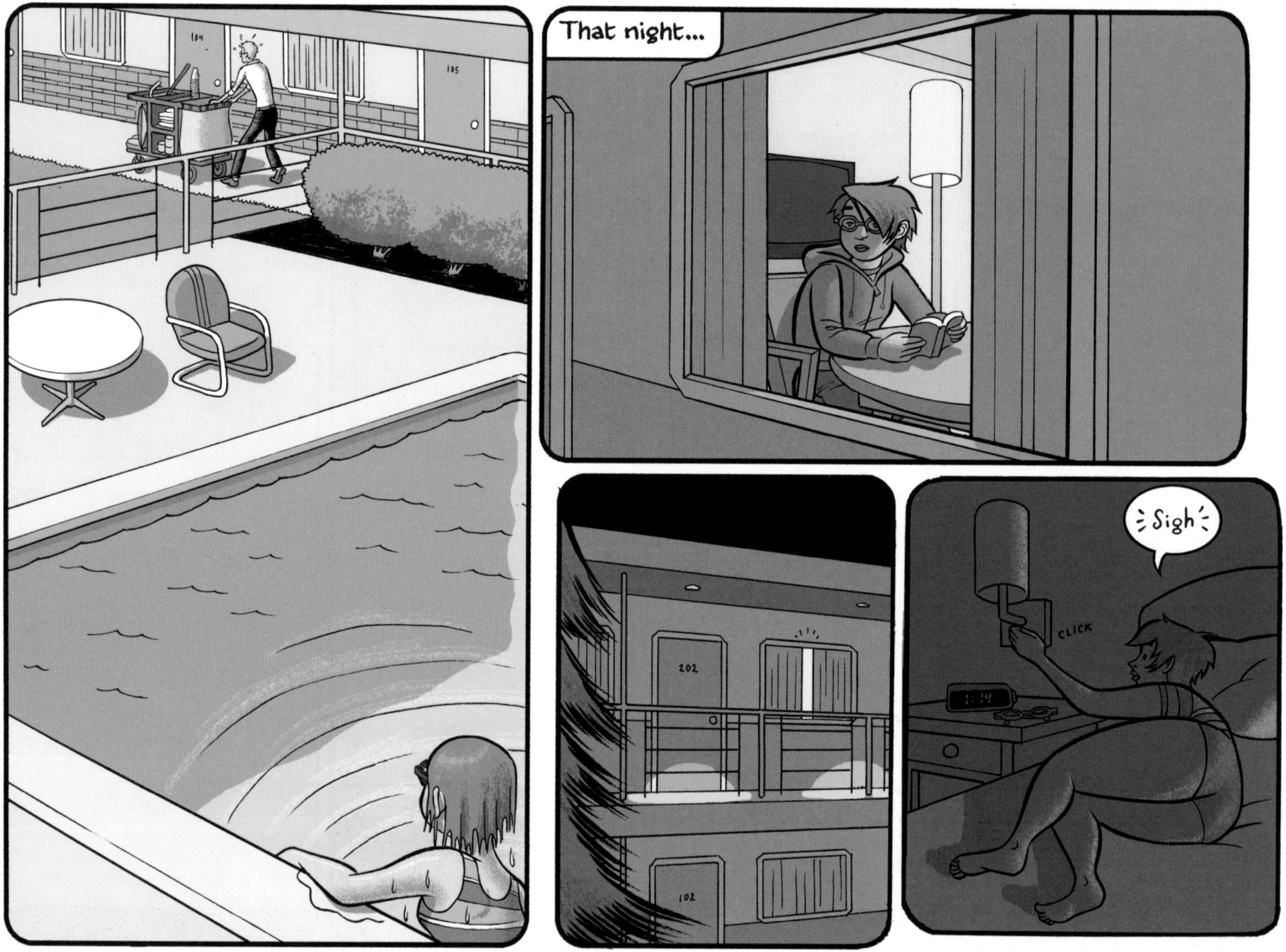

That night...
Sigh
CLICK

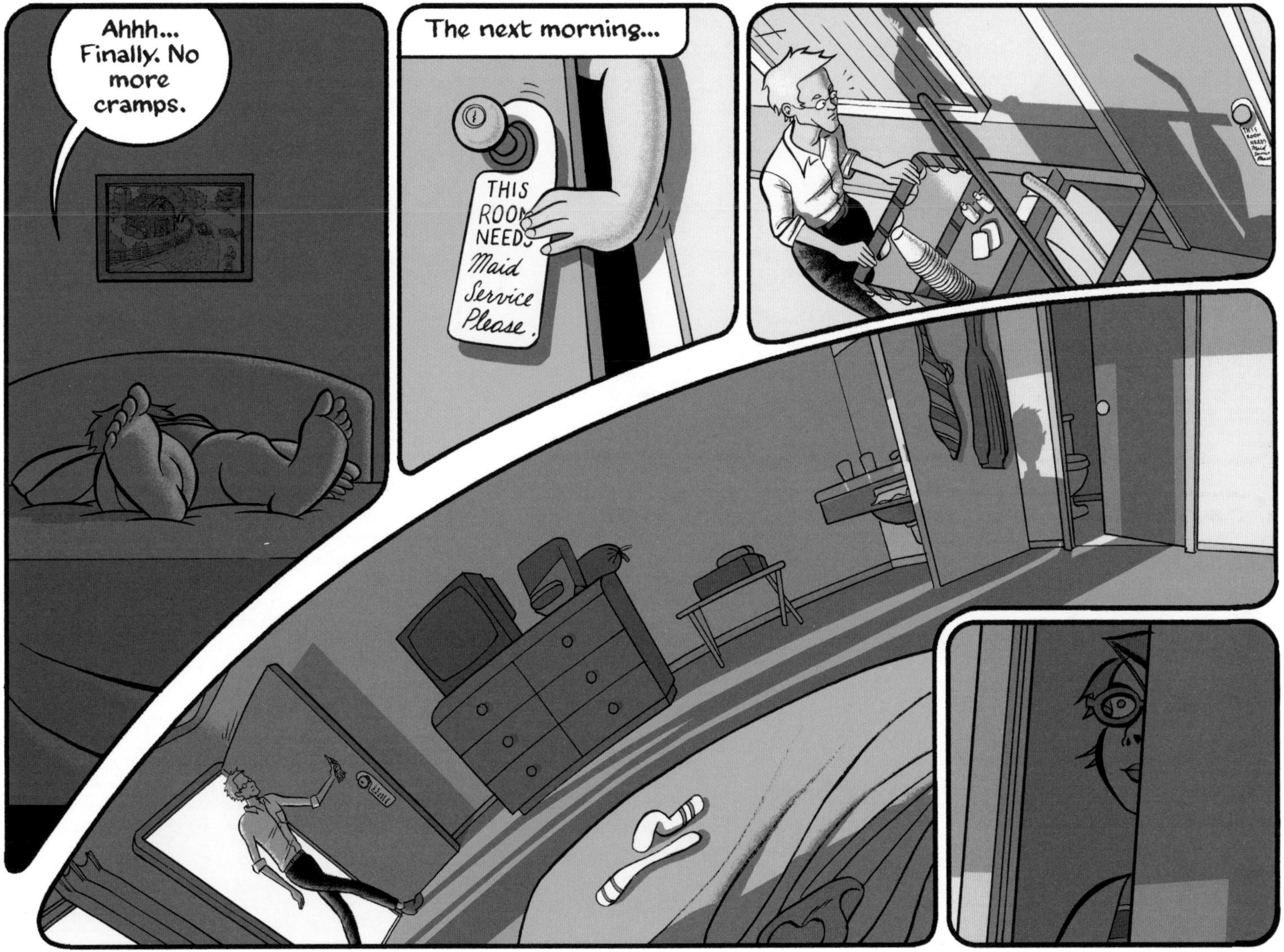
Ahhh... Finally. No more cramps.
The next morning...
THIS ROOM NEEDS Maid Service Please.

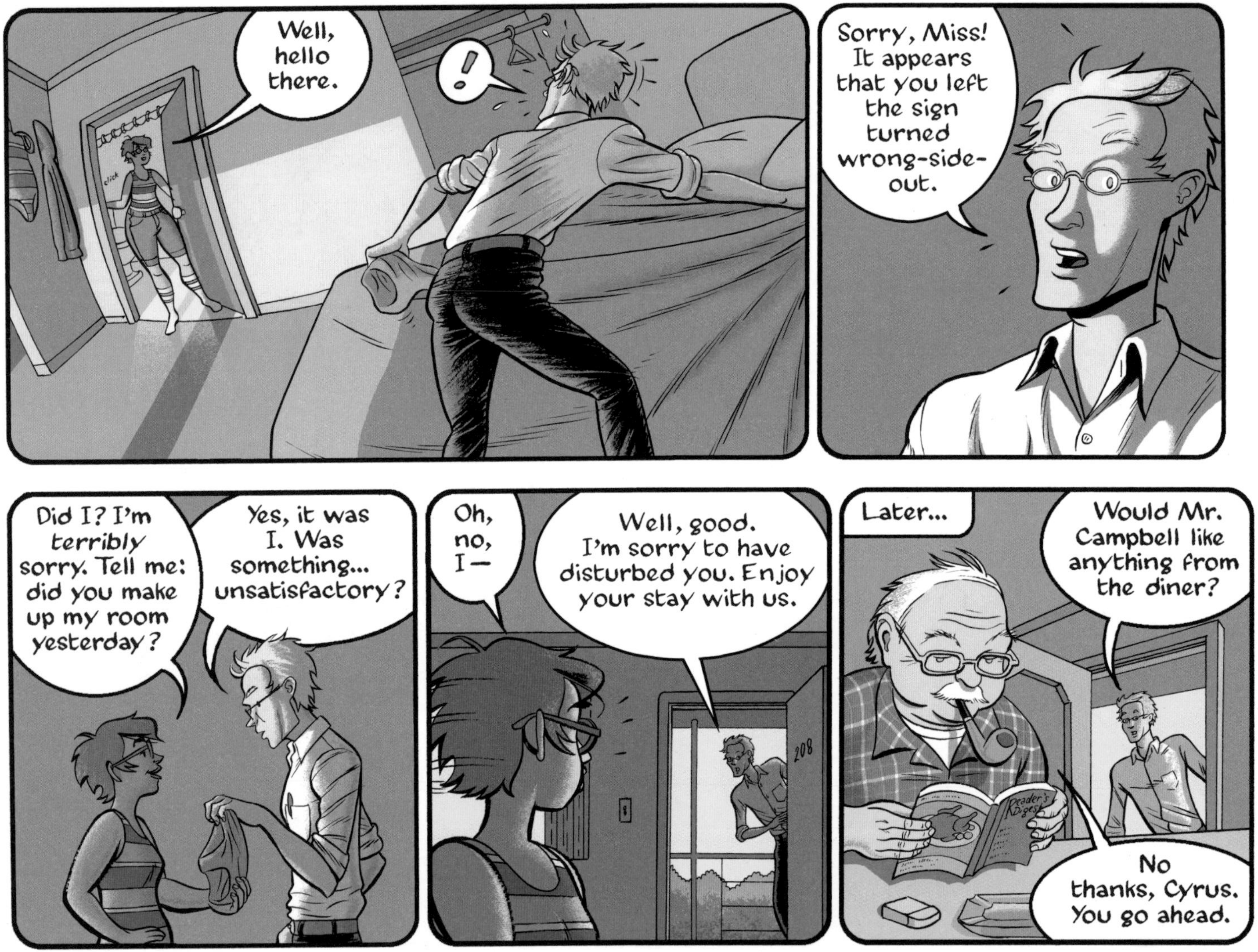
Well, hello there.
click
!
Sorry, Miss! It appears that you left the sign turned wrong-side-out.
Did I? I'm terribly sorry. Tell me: did you make up my room yesterday?
Yes, it was I. Was something... unsatisfactory?
Oh, no, I—
Well, good. I'm sorry to have disturbed you. Enjoy your stay with us.
208
Later...
Would Mr. Campbell like anything from the diner?
Reader's Digest
No thanks, Cyrus. You go ahead.

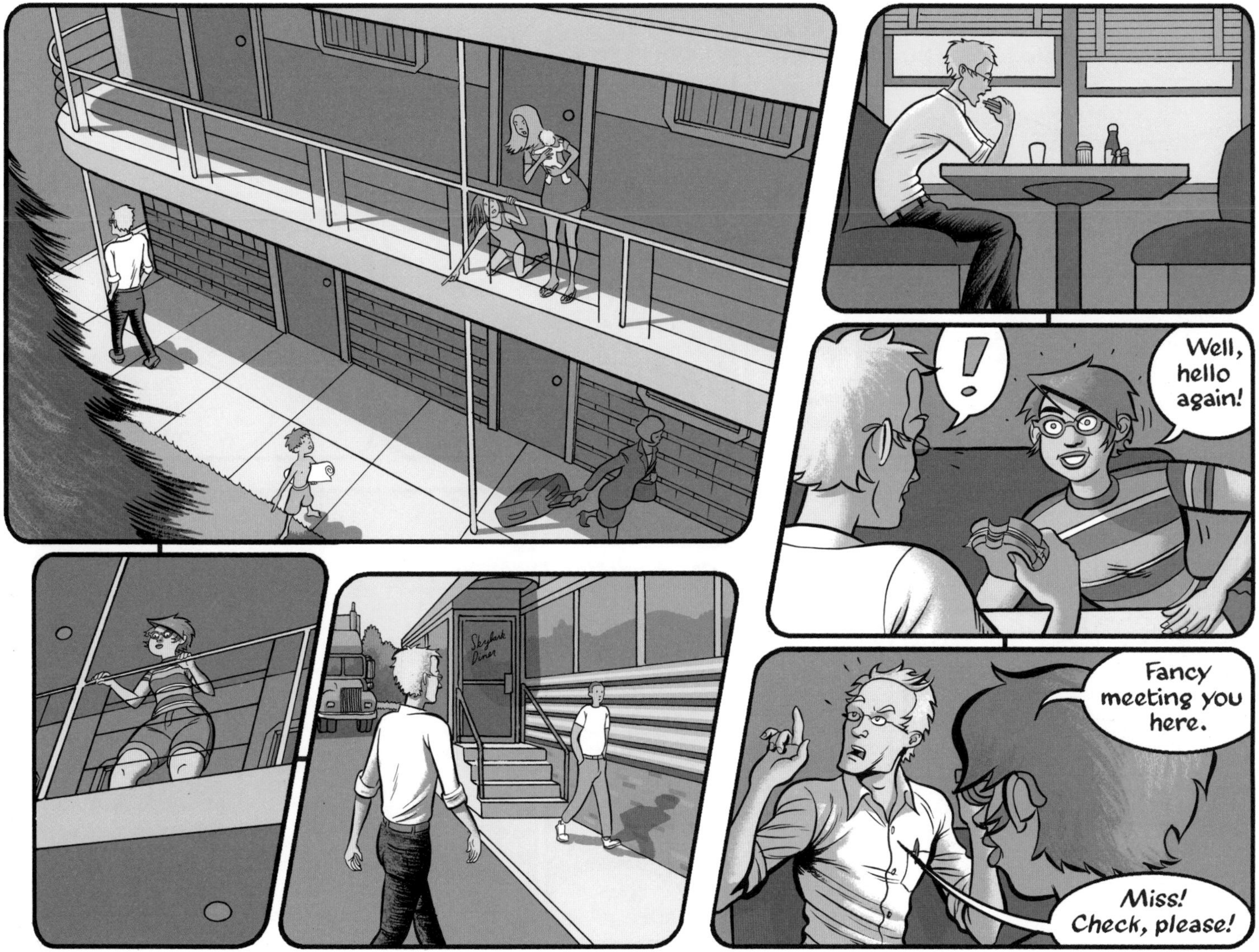
!
Well, hello again!
Fancy meeting you here.
Miss! Check, please!

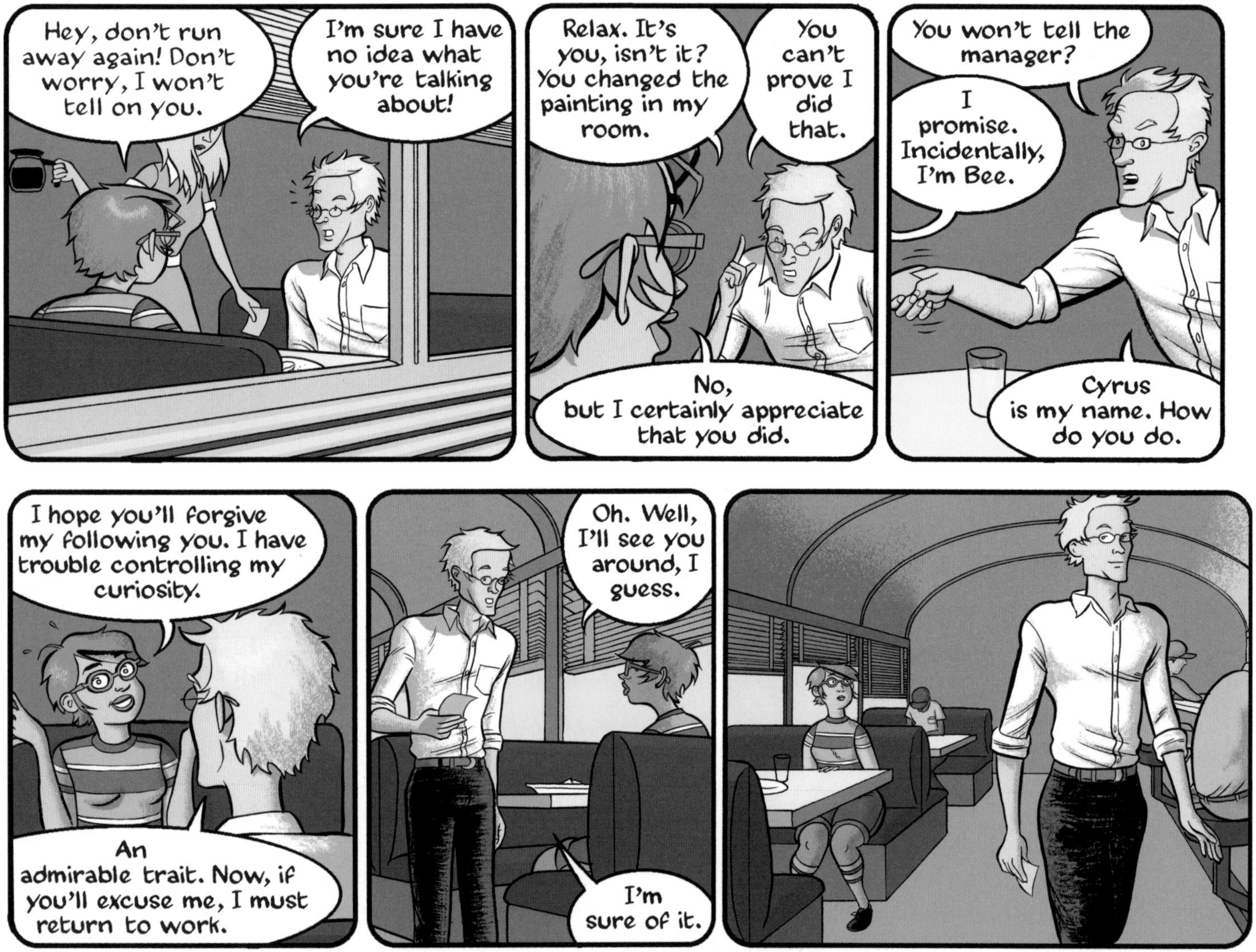
Hey, don't run away again! Don't worry, I won't tell on you.
I'm sure I have no idea what you're talking about!
Relax. It's you, isn't it? You changed the painting in my room.
You can't prove I did that.
No, but I certainly appreciate that you did.
You won't tell the manager?
I promise. Incidentally, I'm Bee.
Cyrus is my name. How do you do.
I hope you'll forgive my following you. I have trouble controlling my curiosity.
An admirable trait. Now, if you'll excuse me, I must return to work.
Oh. Well, I'll see you around, I guess.
I'm sure of it.

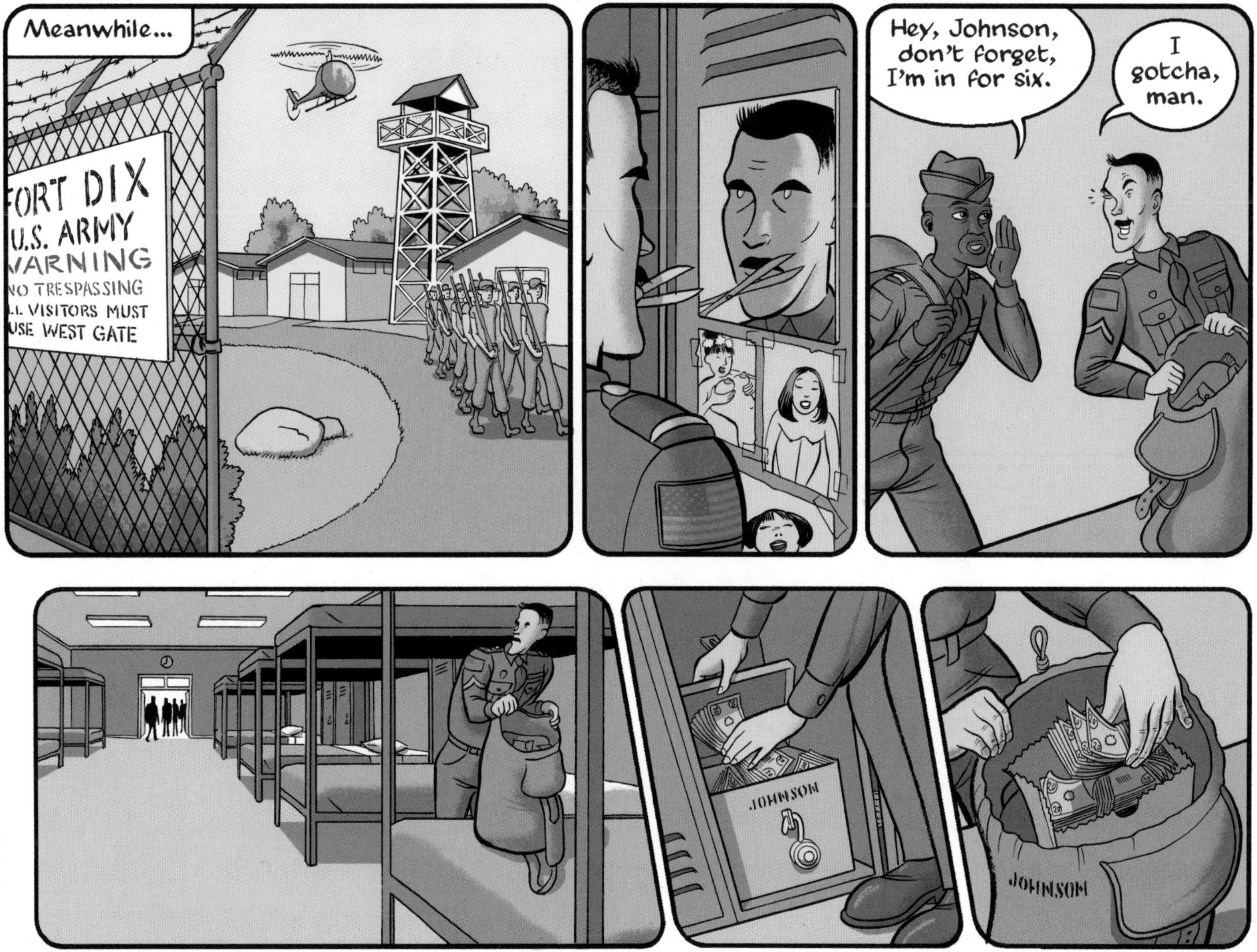
Meanwhile...
FORT DIX
U.S. ARMY
WARNING
NO TRESPASSING
ALL VISITORS MUST
USE WEST GATE
Hey, Johnson, don't forget, I'm in for six.
I gotcha, man.
JOHNSON
JOHNSON

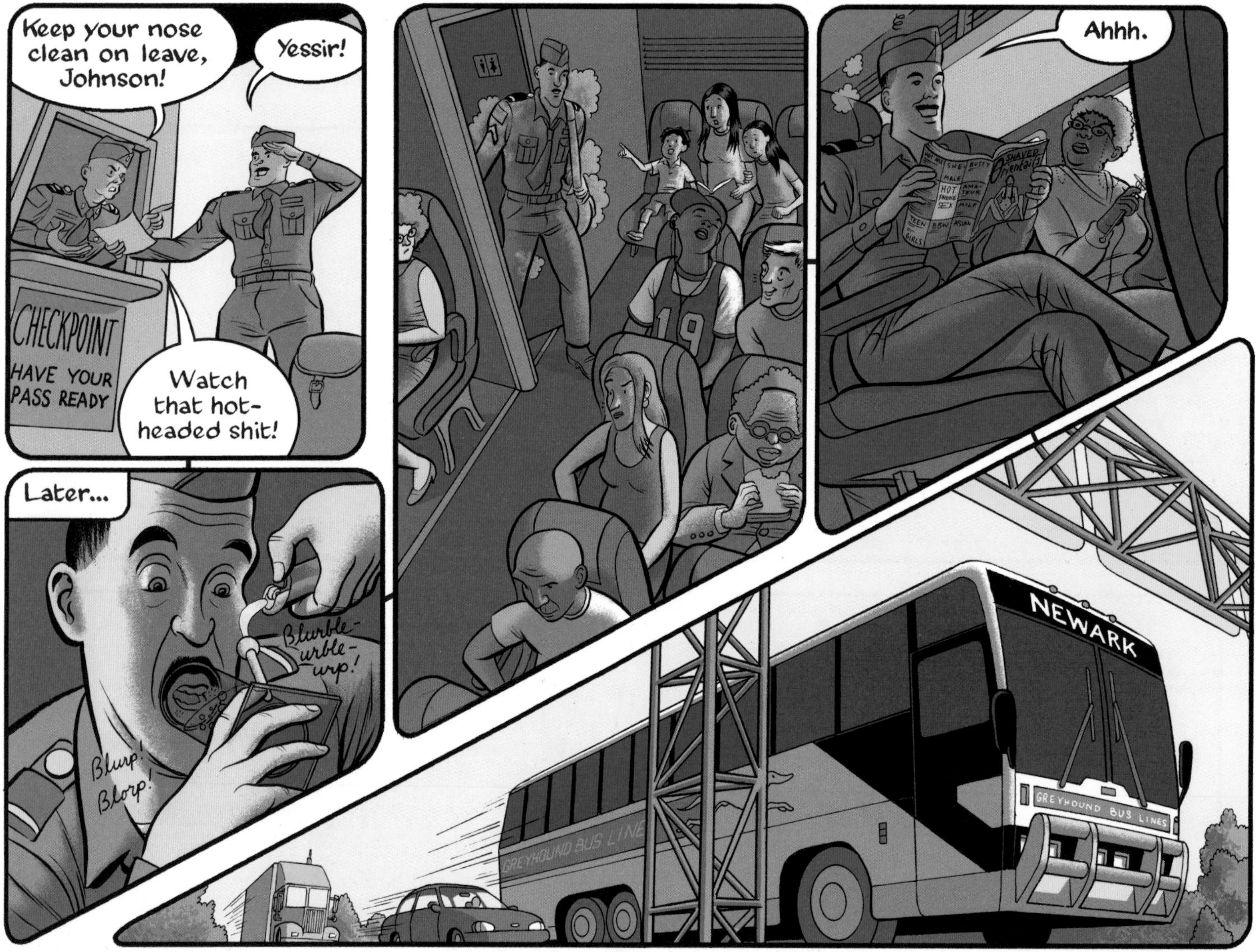
Keep your nose clean on leave, Johnson!
Yessir!
CHECKPOINT
HAVE YOUR PASS READY
Watch that hot-headed shit!
Later...
Blurble-urble-urp!
Blurp! Blorp!
19
HOT ASS
SHE-MALE
BUSTY
HOT PHONE SEX
AMA-TEUR
MILF
TEEN GIRLS
BBW
ASIAN
SHAVED Orientals
Ahhh.
NEWARK
GREYHOUND BUS LINES
GREYHOUND BUS LINES

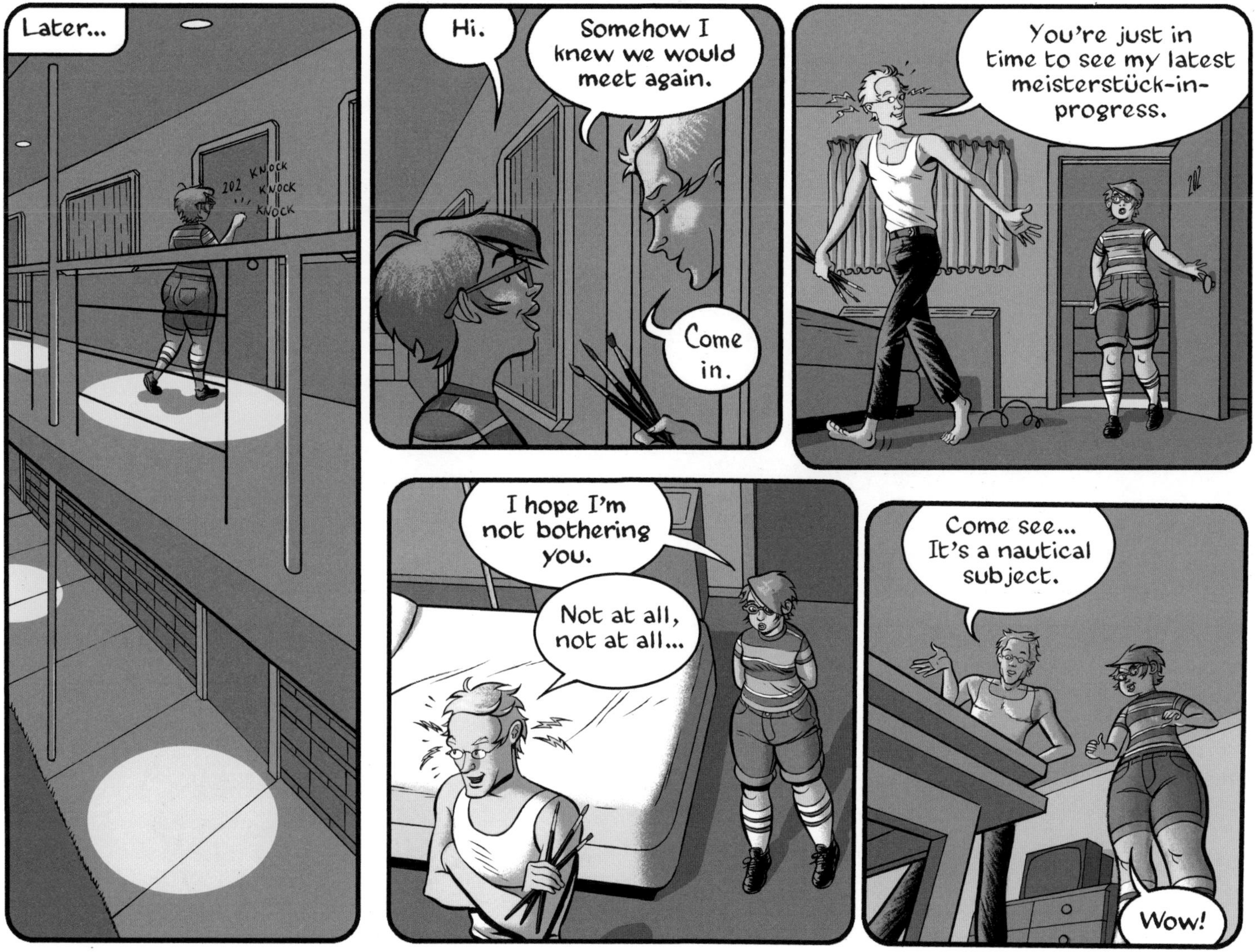
Later...
202
KNOCK KNOCK KNOCK
Hi.
Somehow I knew we would meet again.
Come in.
You're just in time to see my latest meisterstück-in-progress.
202
I hope I'm not bothering you.
Not at all, not at all...
Come see... It's a nautical subject.
Wow!

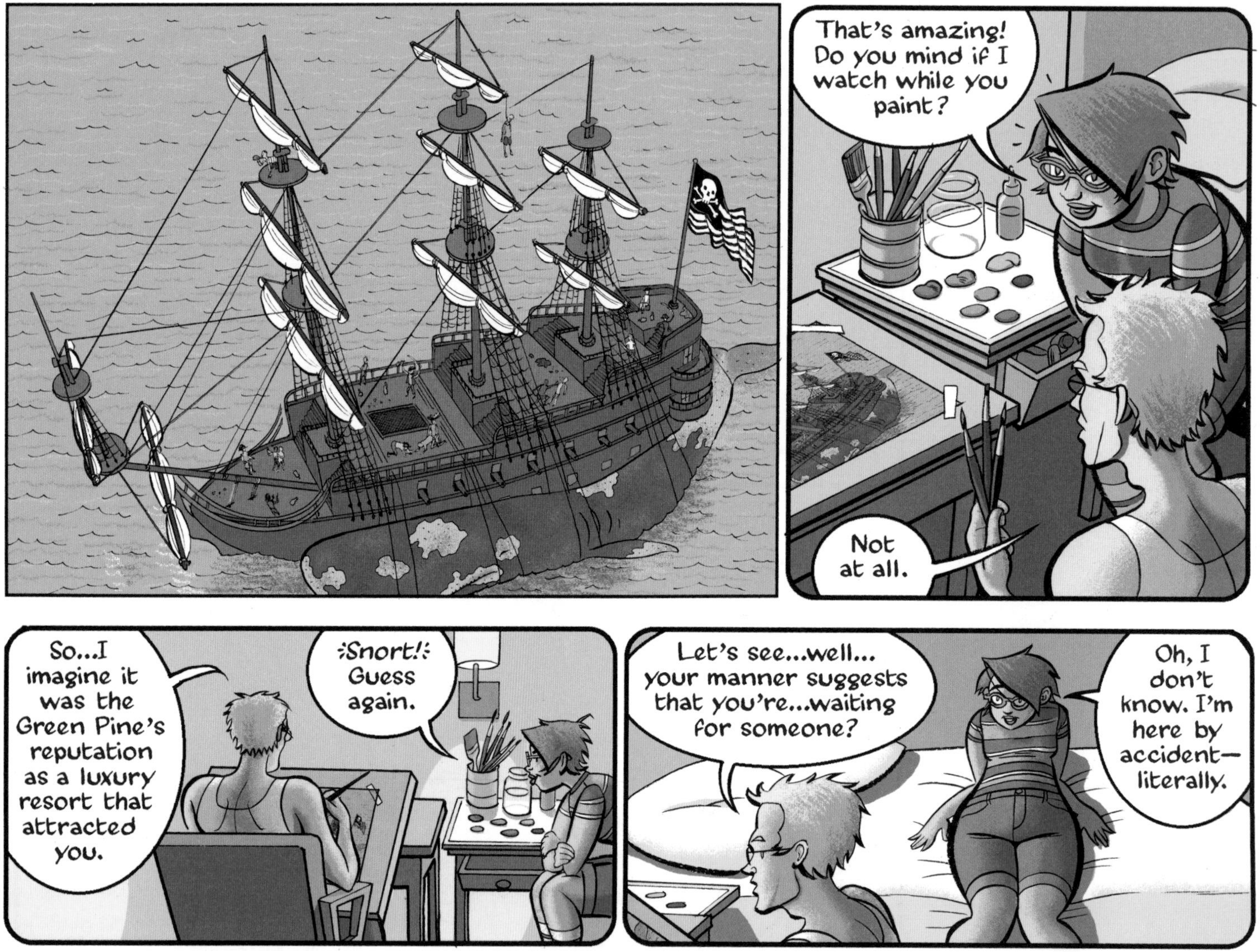
That's amazing! Do you mind if I watch while you paint?
Not at all.
So...I imagine it was the Green Pine's reputation as a luxury resort that attracted you.
⁘Snort!⁘ Guess again.
Let's see...well... your manner suggests that you're...waiting for someone?
Oh, I don't know. I'm here by accident—literally.

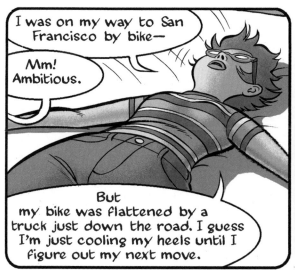

I was on my way to San Francisco by bike—

Mm! Ambitious.

But my bike was flattened by a truck just down the road. I guess I'm just cooling my heels until I figure out my next move.

Perhaps a new bicycle would be in order?

Sure... as long as the price is right.

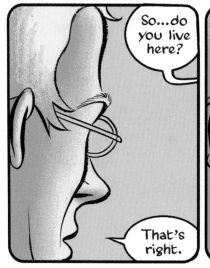

So... do you live here?

That's right.

Must get lonely.

Oh, well, you know. I keep myself occupied with my painting. I—

51

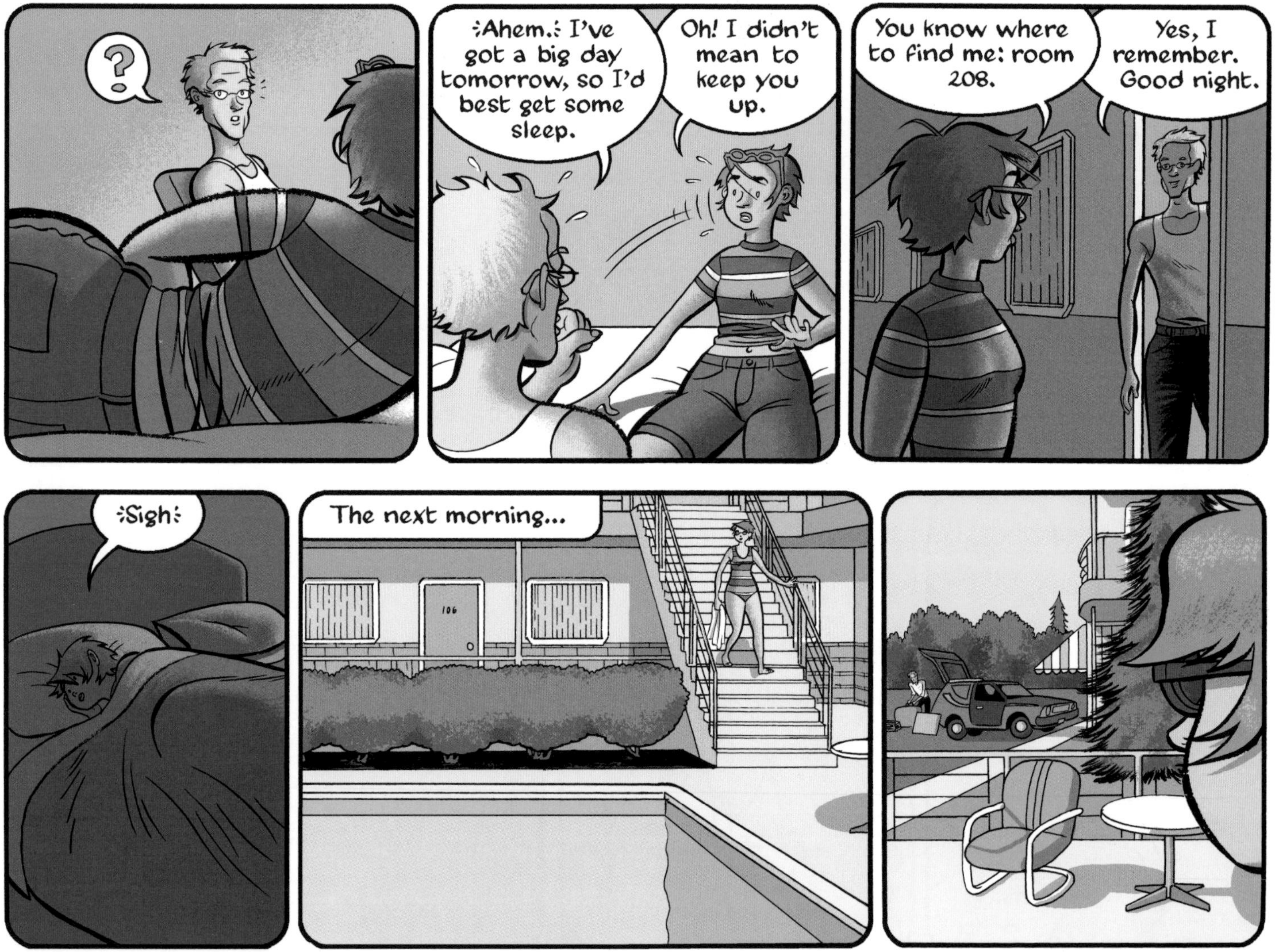
?
:Ahem.: I've got a big day tomorrow, so I'd best get some sleep.
Oh! I didn't mean to keep you up.
You know where to find me: room 208.
Yes, I remember. Good night.
:Sigh:
The next morning...
106

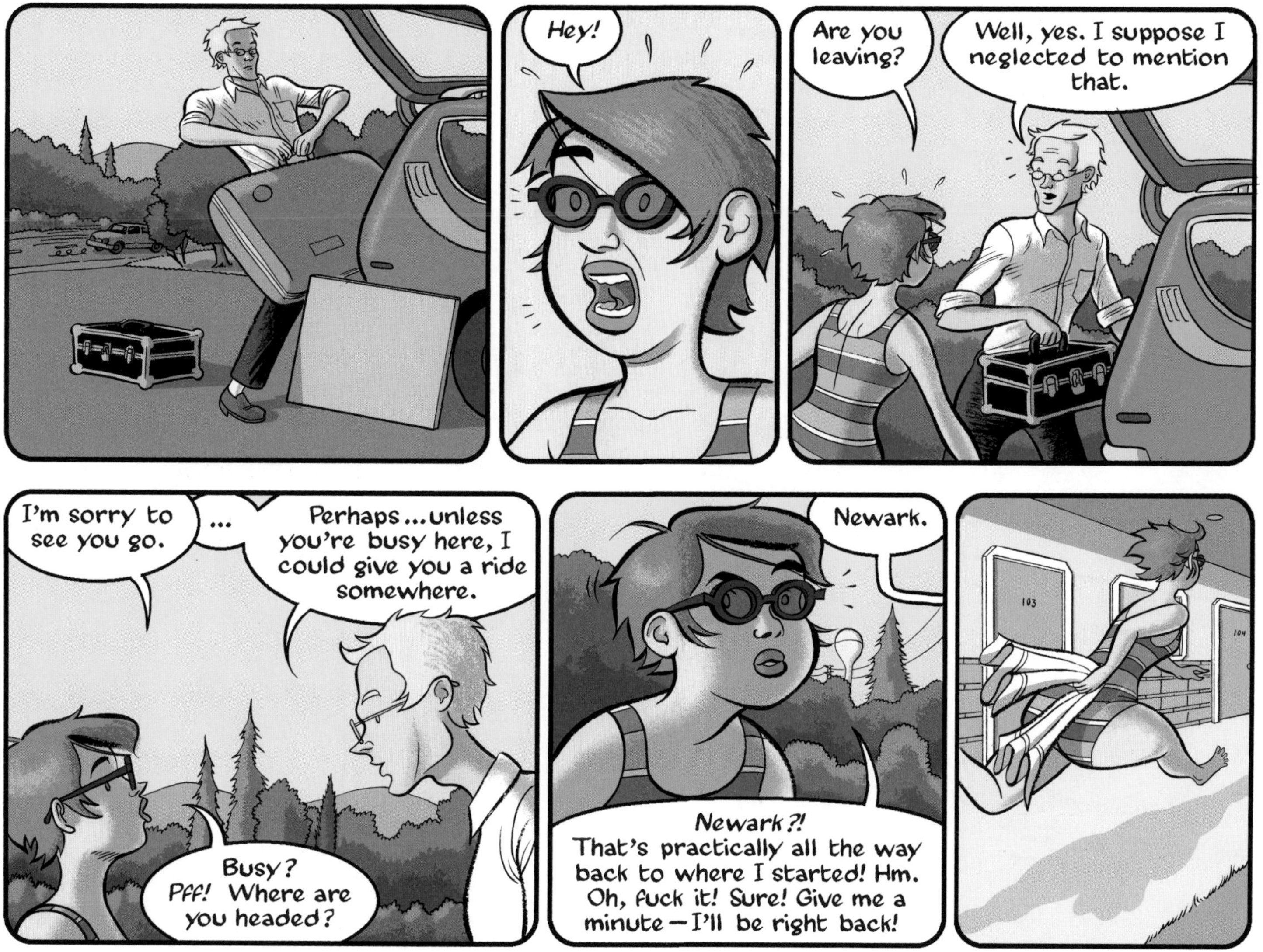
Hey!
Are you leaving?
Well, yes. I suppose I neglected to mention that.
I'm sorry to see you go.
...
Perhaps...unless you're busy here, I could give you a ride somewhere.
Busy? Pff! Where are you headed?
Newark.
Newark?! That's practically all the way back to where I started! Hm. Oh, fuck it! Sure! Give me a minute—I'll be right back!
103
104

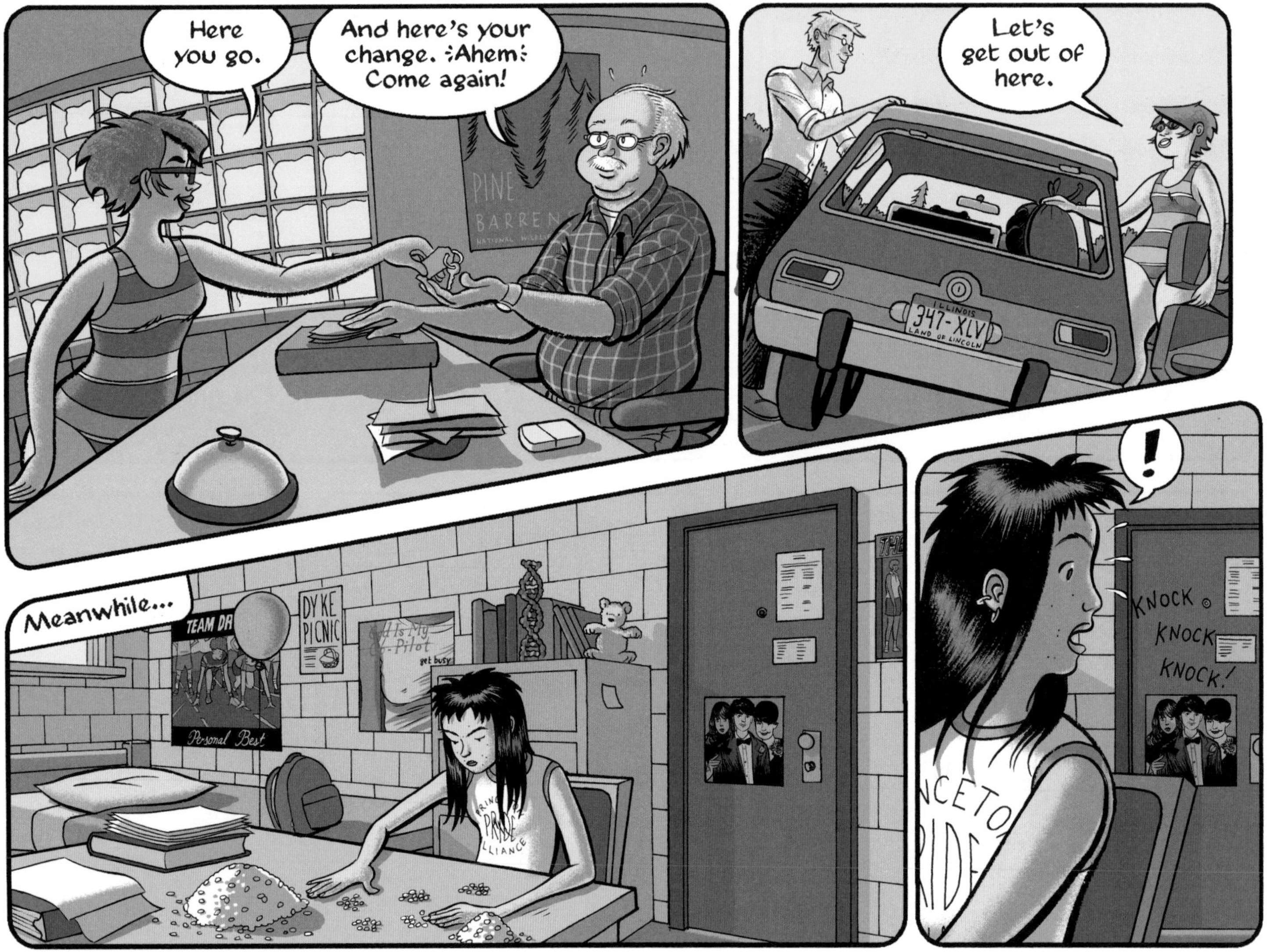
Here you go.
And here's your change. ¡Ahem¡ Come again!
PINE BARRENS
Let's get out of here.
ILLINOIS 347-XLV LAND OF LINCOLN
Meanwhile...
TEAM DR
Personal Best
DYKE PICNIC
God Is My Co-Pilot
get busy
PRINCETON PRIDE ALLIANCE
!
KNOCK KNOCK KNOCK!

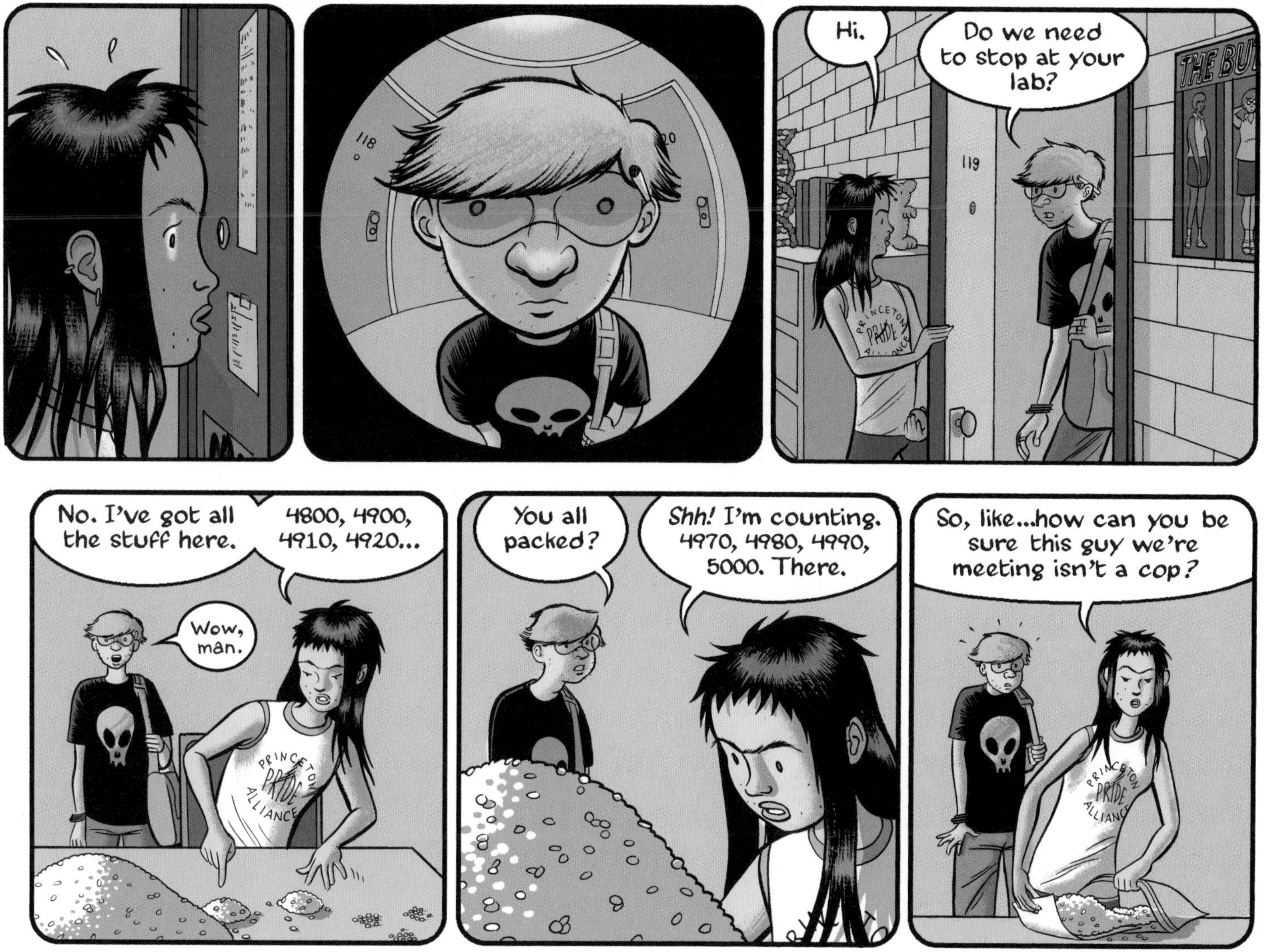
118
120
Hi.
Do we need to stop at your lab?
119
No. I've got all the stuff here.
4800, 4900, 4910, 4920...
Wow, man.
You all packed?
Shh! I'm counting. 4970, 4980, 4990, 5000. There.
So, like...how can you be sure this guy we're meeting isn't a cop?

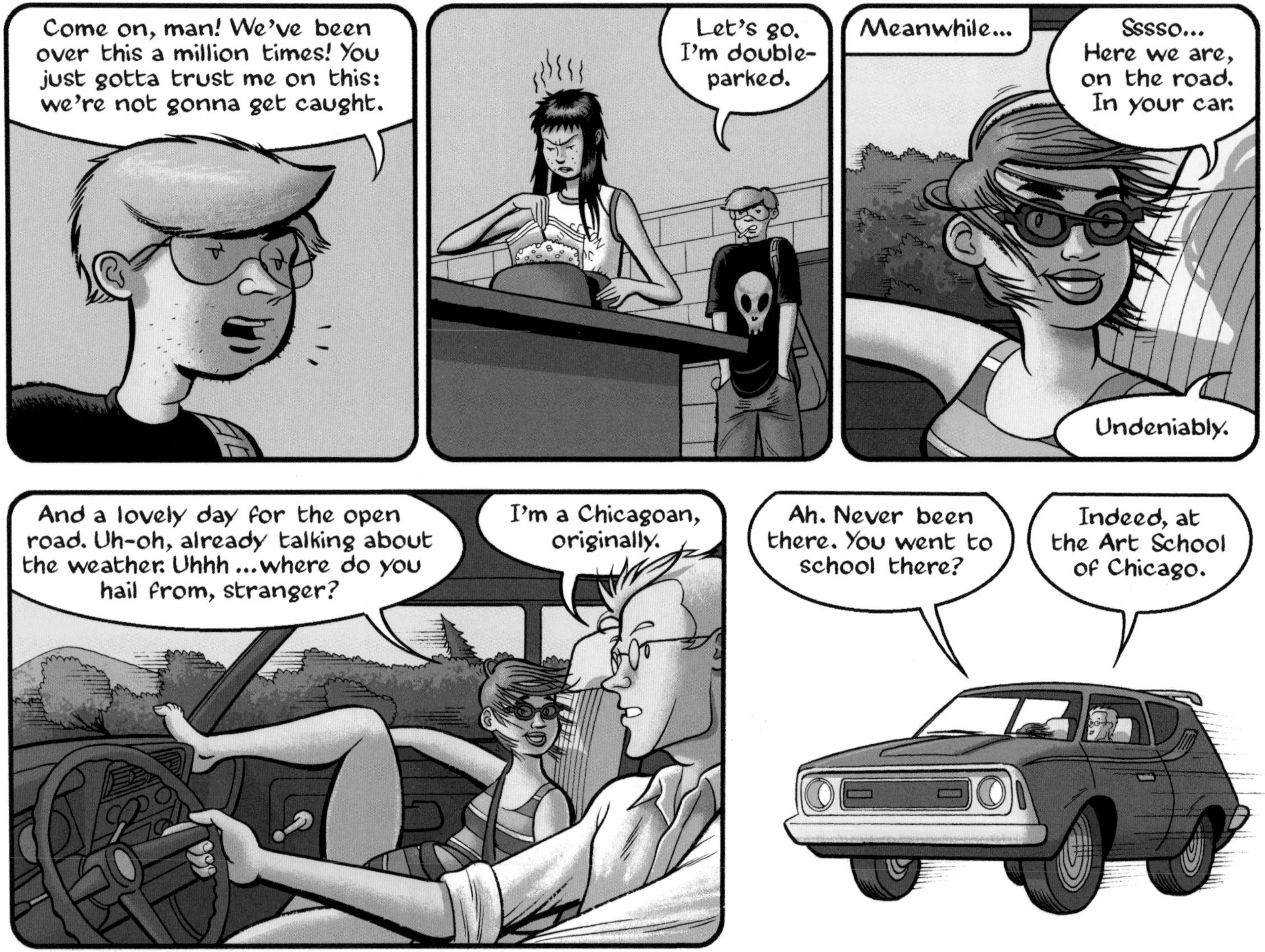

Come on, man! We've been over this a million times! You just gotta trust me on this: we're not gonna get caught.
Let's go. I'm double-parked.
Meanwhile...
Sssso... Here we are, on the road. In your car.
Undeniably.
And a lovely day for the open road. Uh-oh, already talking about the weather. Uhhh ...where do you hail from, stranger?
I'm a Chicagoan, originally.
Ah. Never been there. You went to school there?
Indeed, at the Art School of Chicago.

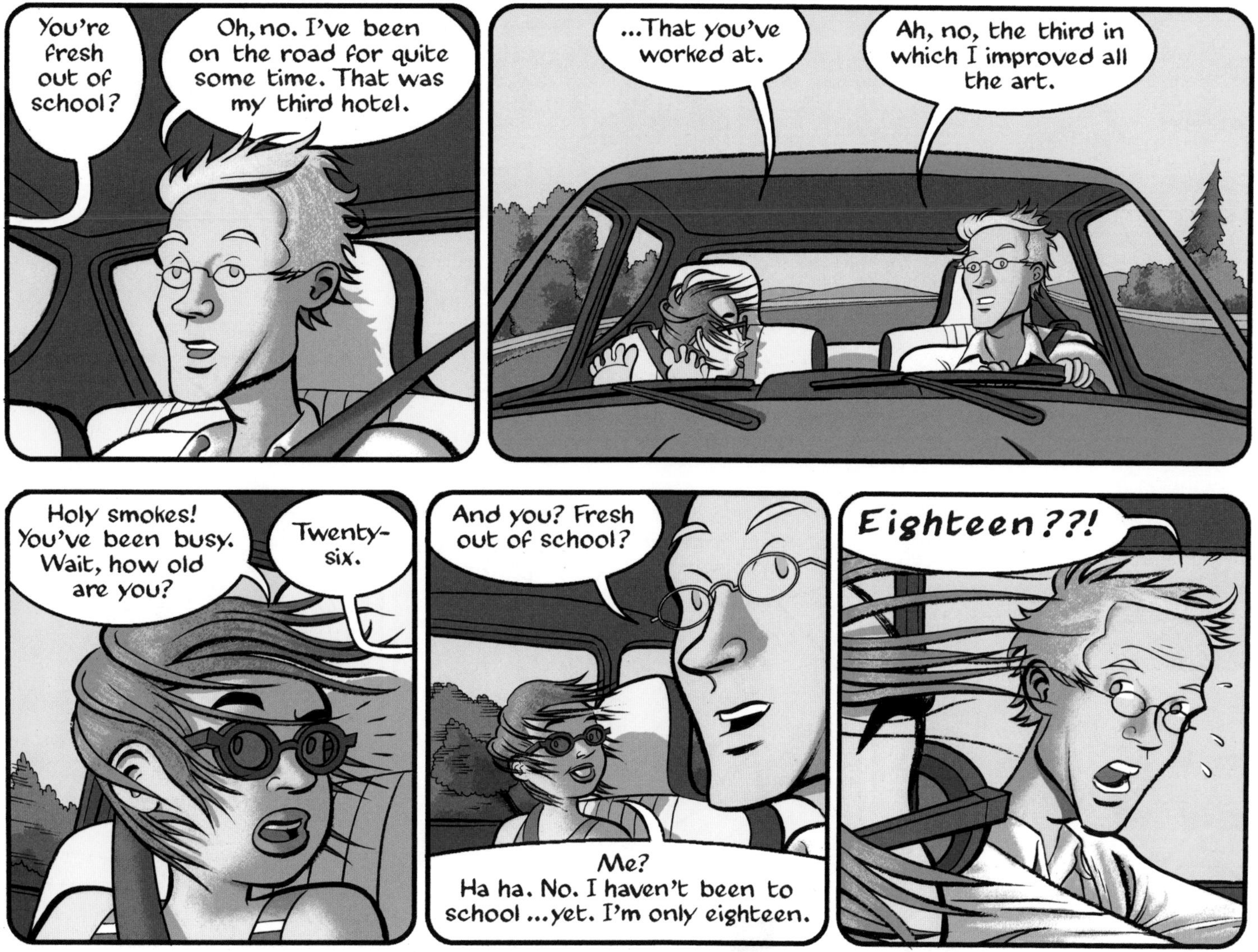
You're fresh out of school?
Oh, no. I've been on the road for quite some time. That was my third hotel.
...That you've worked at.
Ah, no, the third in which I improved all the art.
Holy smokes! You've been busy. Wait, how old are you?
Twenty-six.
And you? Fresh out of school?
Me? Ha ha. No. I haven't been to school ...yet. I'm only eighteen.
Eighteen??!

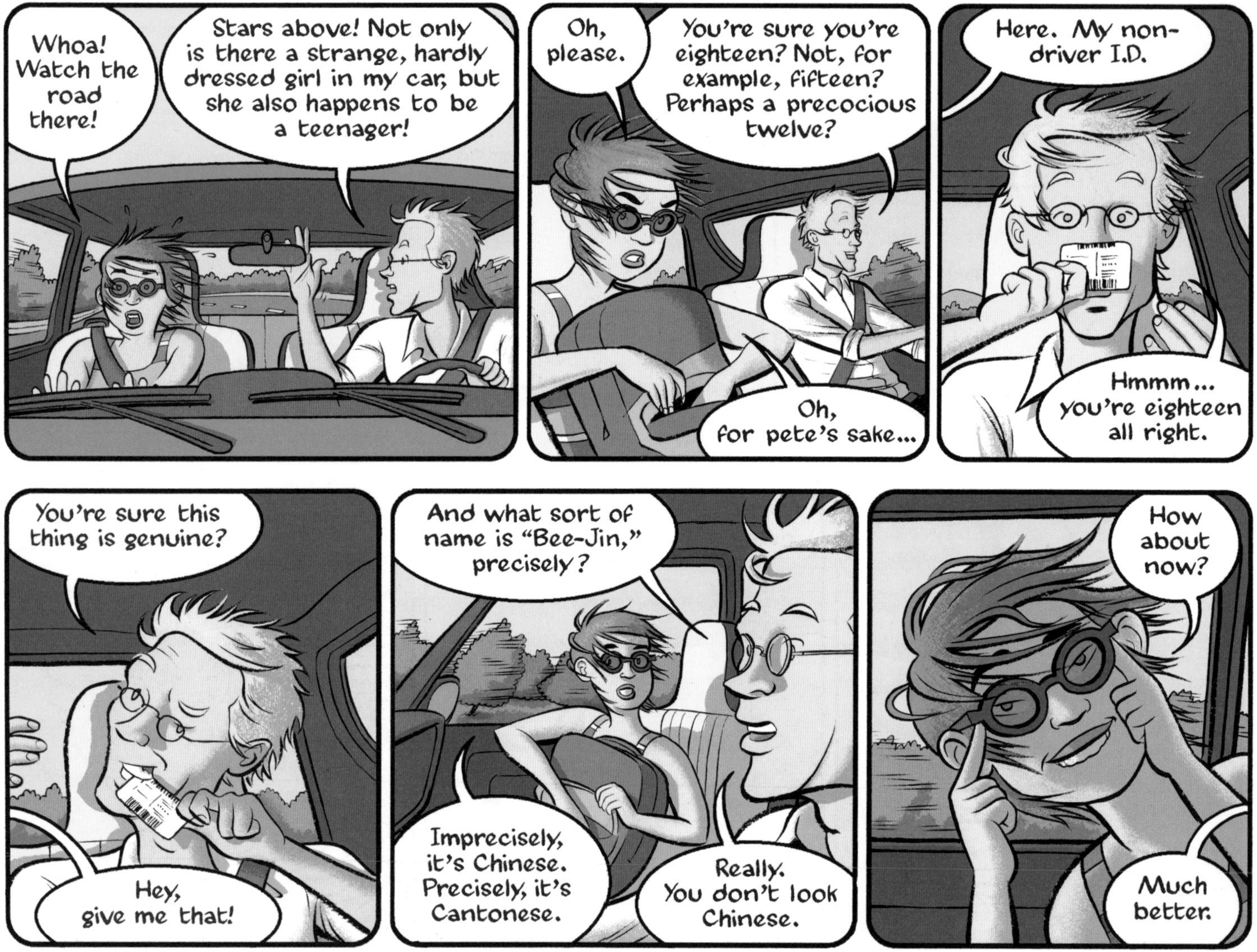
Whoa! Watch the road there!
Stars above! Not only is there a strange, hardly dressed girl in my car, but she also happens to be a teenager!
Oh, please.
You're sure you're eighteen? Not, for example, fifteen? Perhaps a precocious twelve?
Oh, for pete's sake...
Here. My non-driver I.D.
Hmmm... you're eighteen all right.
You're sure this thing is genuine?
Hey, give me that!
And what sort of name is "Bee-Jin," precisely?
Imprecisely, it's Chinese. Precisely, it's Cantonese.
Really. You don't look Chinese.
How about now?
Much better.

Is there an explanation for the red hair?

I get that from my dad, a red-haired Jew.

Bee-Jin, the red-headed Chinese Jew.

Yes. I'm a living, breathing, ethnic joke.

Meanwhile...

You still haven't gotten your car fixed.

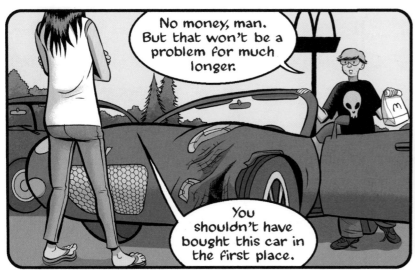

No money, man. But that won't be a problem for much longer.

You shouldn't have bought this car in the first place.

Hey, man, I needed wheels! And you should be, like, *thankful* I bought this car. If I wasn't so hard up, I wouldn'a thought up the deal that's gonna save your sorry ass.

...

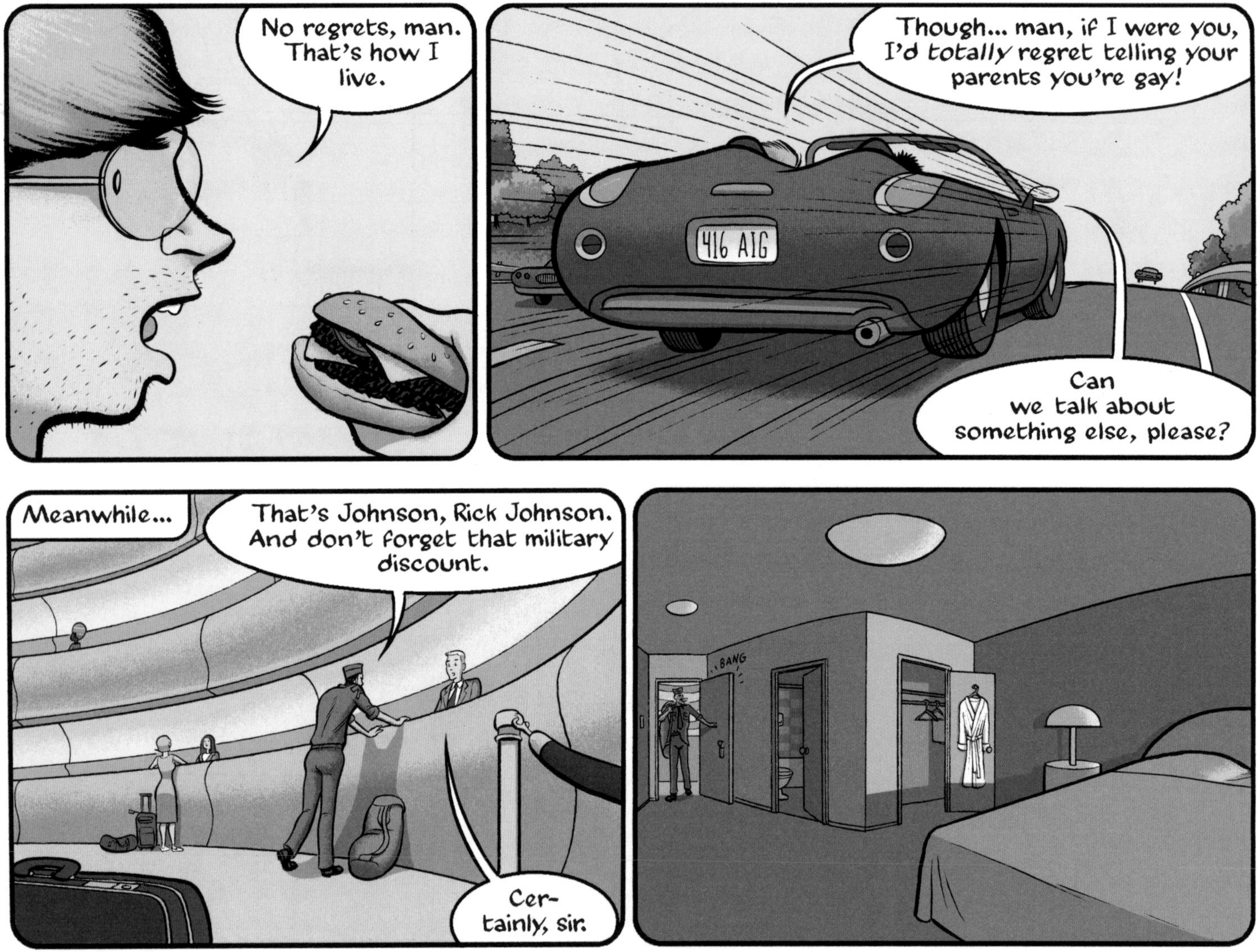
No regrets, man. That's how I live.
Though... man, if I were you, I'd *totally* regret telling your parents you're gay!
416 AIG
Can we talk about something else, please?
Meanwhile...
That's Johnson, Rick Johnson. And don't forget that military discount.
Cer-tainly, sir.
BANG

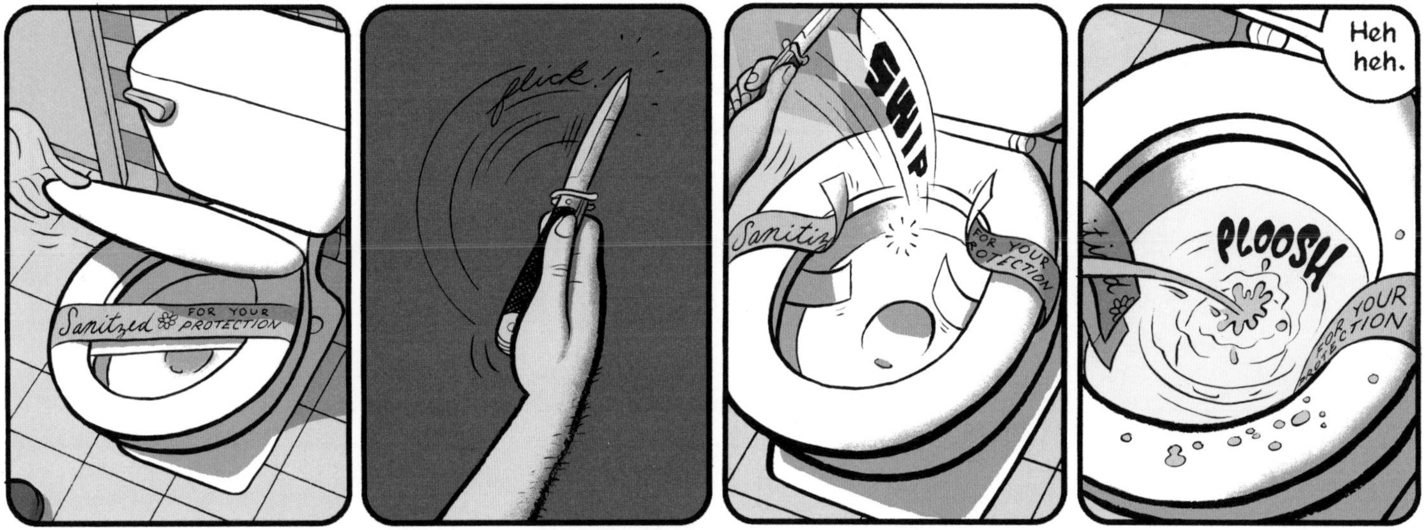
Sanitized FOR YOUR PROTECTION
flick!
SWIP
Sanitiz
FOR YOUR PROTECTION
PLOOSH
FOR YOUR PROTECTION
Heh heh.

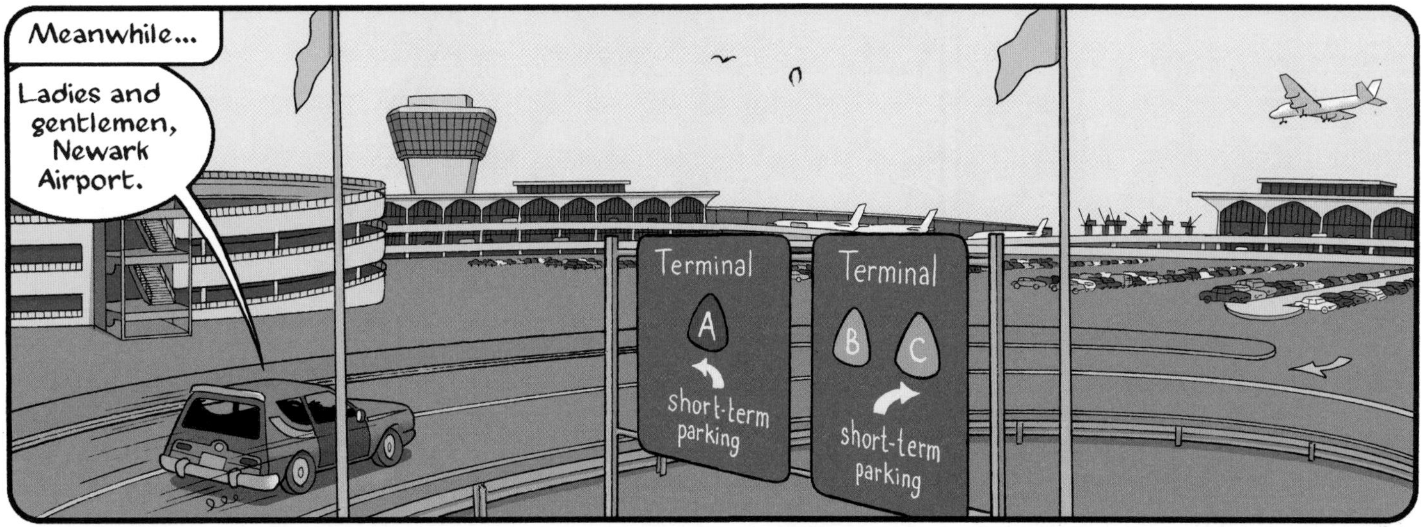
Meanwhile...
Ladies and gentlemen, Newark Airport.
Terminal A short-term parking
Terminal B C short-term parking

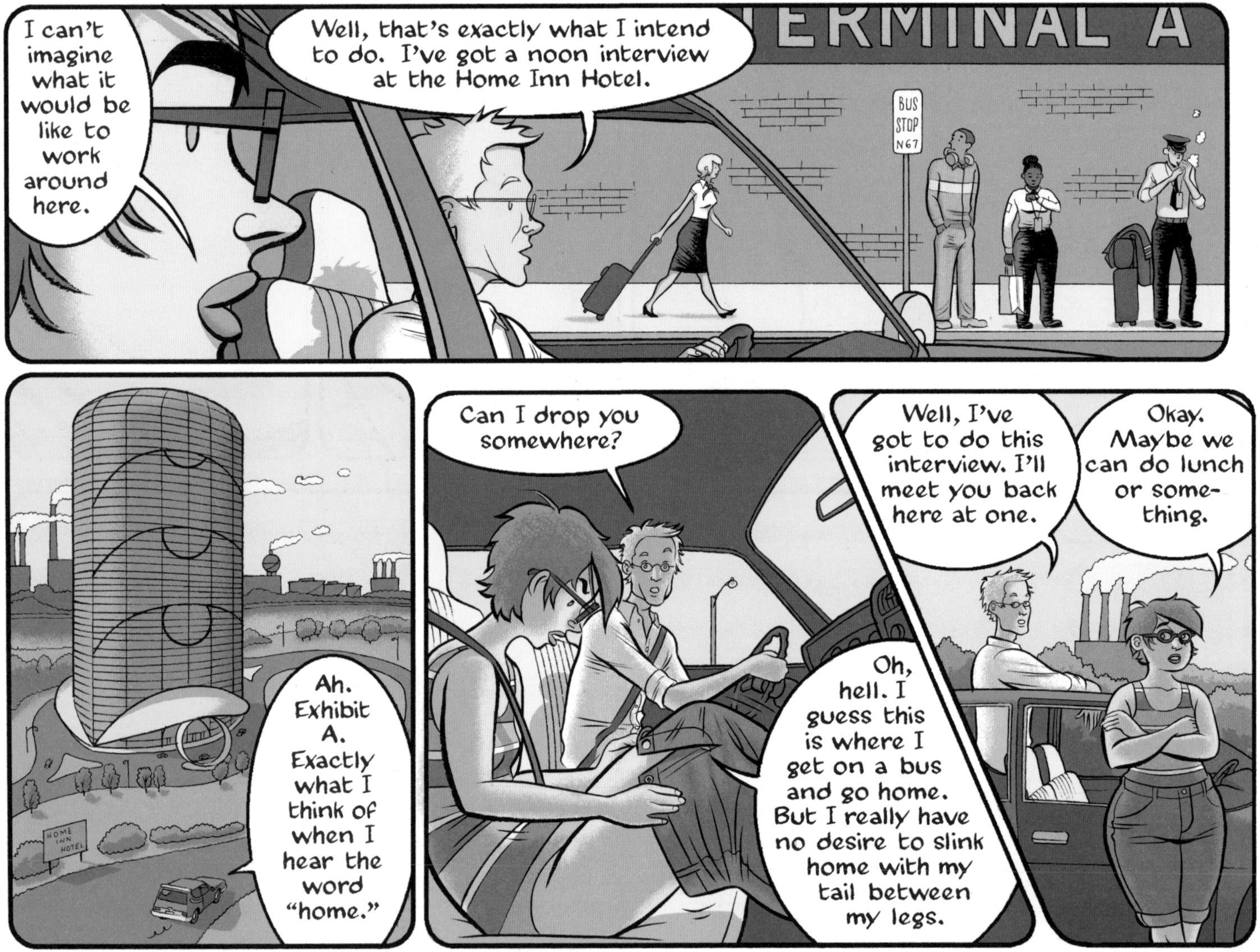
TERMINAL A
I can't imagine what it would be like to work around here.
Well, that's exactly what I intend to do. I've got a noon interview at the Home Inn Hotel.
BUS STOP N67
Ah. Exhibit A. Exactly what I think of when I hear the word "home."
HOME INN HOTEL
Can I drop you somewhere?
Oh, hell. I guess this is where I get on a bus and go home. But I really have no desire to slink home with my tail between my legs.
Well, I've got to do this interview. I'll meet you back here at one.
Okay. Maybe we can do lunch or some-thing.

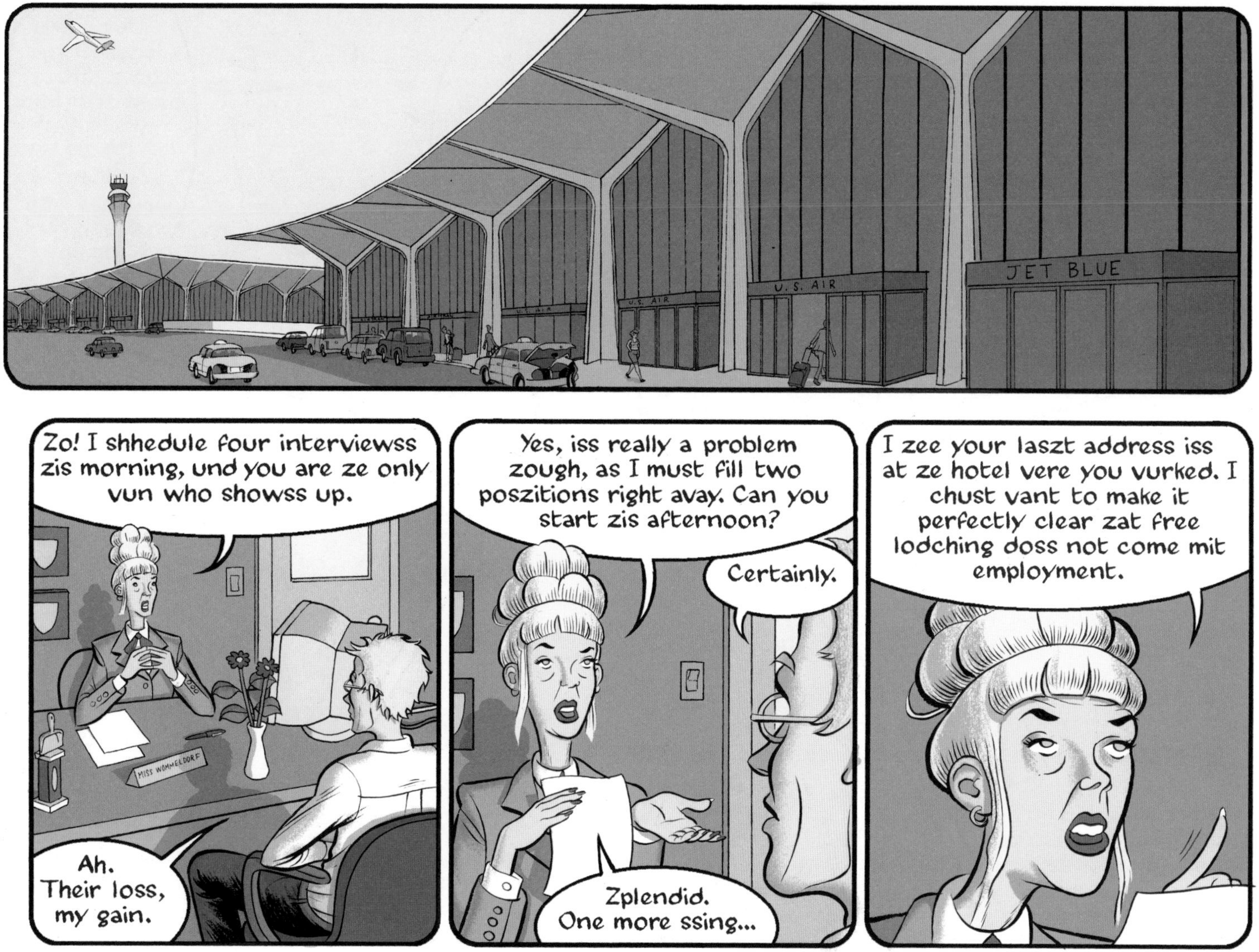
JET BLUE
U.S. AIR
Zo! I shhedule four interviewss zis morning, und you are ze only vun who showss up.
MISS WOMMELDORF
Ah. Their loss, my gain.
Yes, iss really a problem zough, as I must fill two poszitions right avay. Can you start zis afternoon?
Certainly.
Zplendid. One more ssing...
I zee your laszt address iss at ze hotel vere you vurked. I chust vant to make it perfectly clear zat free lodching doss not come mit employment.

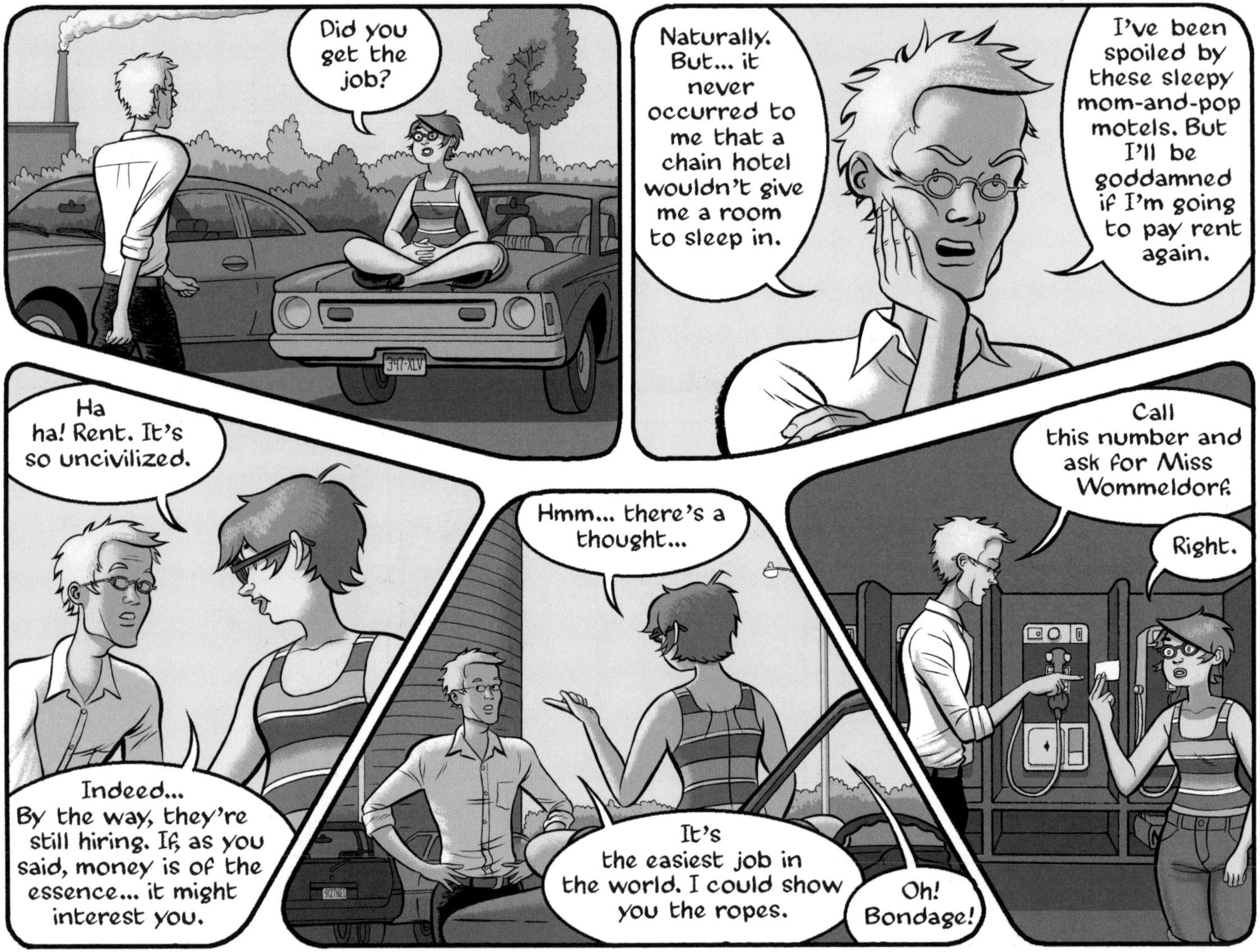
Did you get the job?
Naturally. But... it never occurred to me that a chain hotel wouldn't give me a room to sleep in.
I've been spoiled by these sleepy mom-and-pop motels. But I'll be goddamned if I'm going to pay rent again.
Ha ha! Rent. It's so uncivilized.
Indeed... By the way, they're still hiring. If, as you said, money is of the essence... it might interest you.
Hmm... there's a thought...
It's the easiest job in the world. I could show you the ropes.
Oh! Bondage!
Call this number and ask for Miss Wommeldorf.
Right.

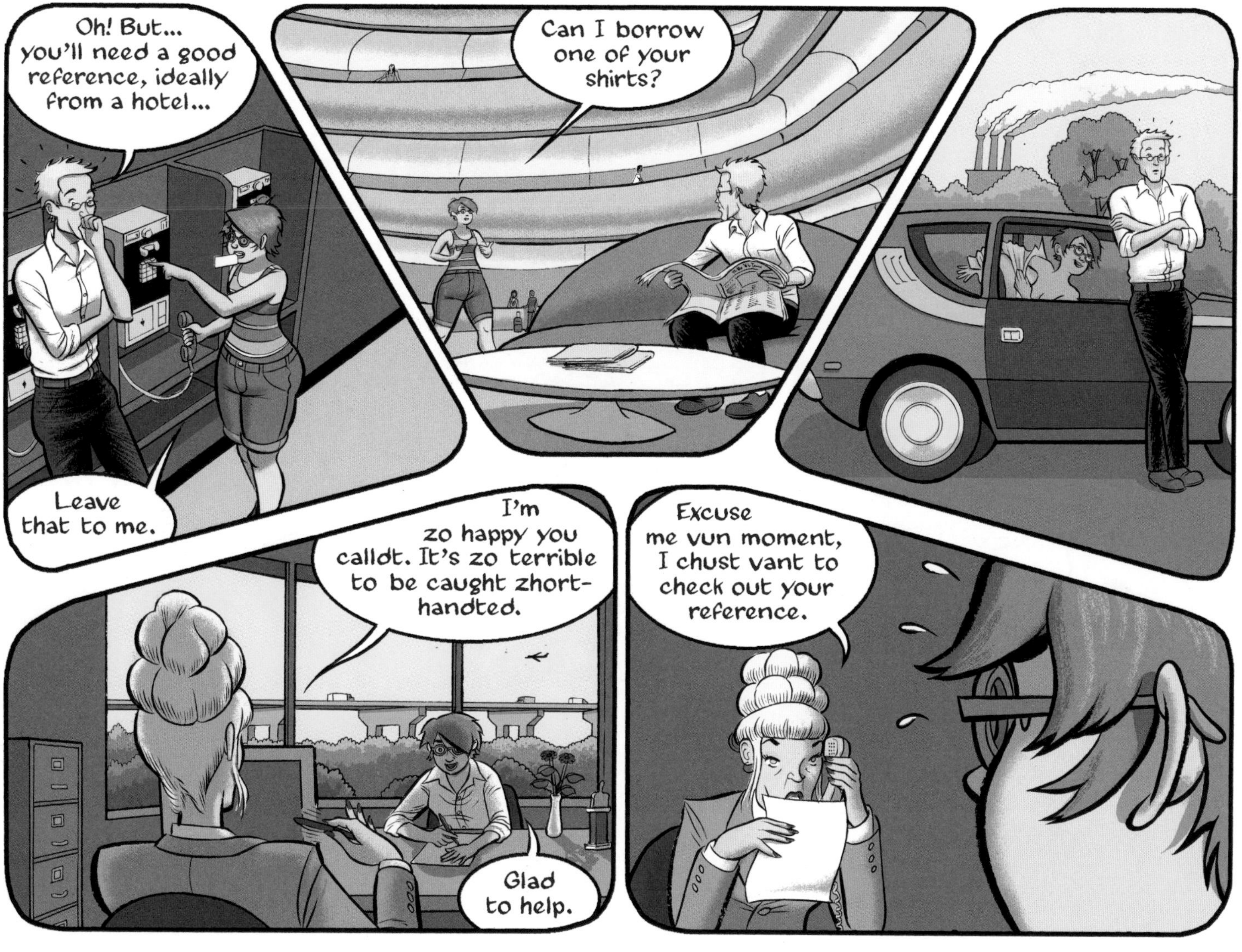
Oh! But... you'll need a good reference, ideally from a hotel...
Leave that to me.
Can I borrow one of your shirts?
I'm zo happy you calldt. It's zo terrible to be caught zhort-handted.
Glad to help.
Excuse me vun moment, I chust vant to check out your reference.

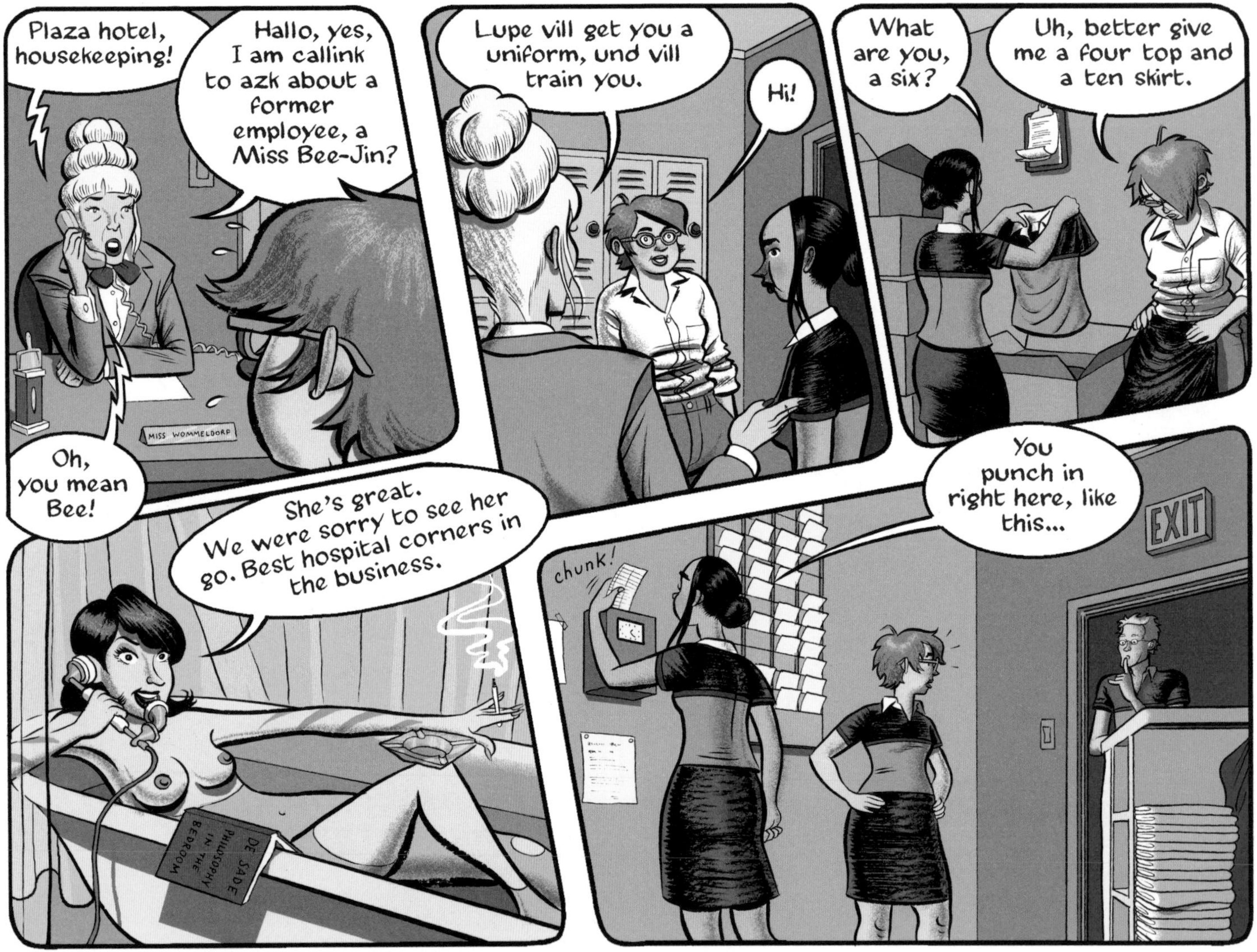
Plaza hotel, housekeeping!
Hallo, yes, I am callink to azk about a former employee, a Miss Bee-Jin?
MISS WOMMELDORF
Lupe vill get you a uniform, und vill train you.
Hi!
What are you, a six?
Uh, better give me a four top and a ten skirt.
Oh, you mean Bee!
She's great. We were sorry to see her go. Best hospital corners in the business.
DE SADE PHILOSOPHY IN THE BEDROOM
You punch in right here, like this...
chunk!
EXIT

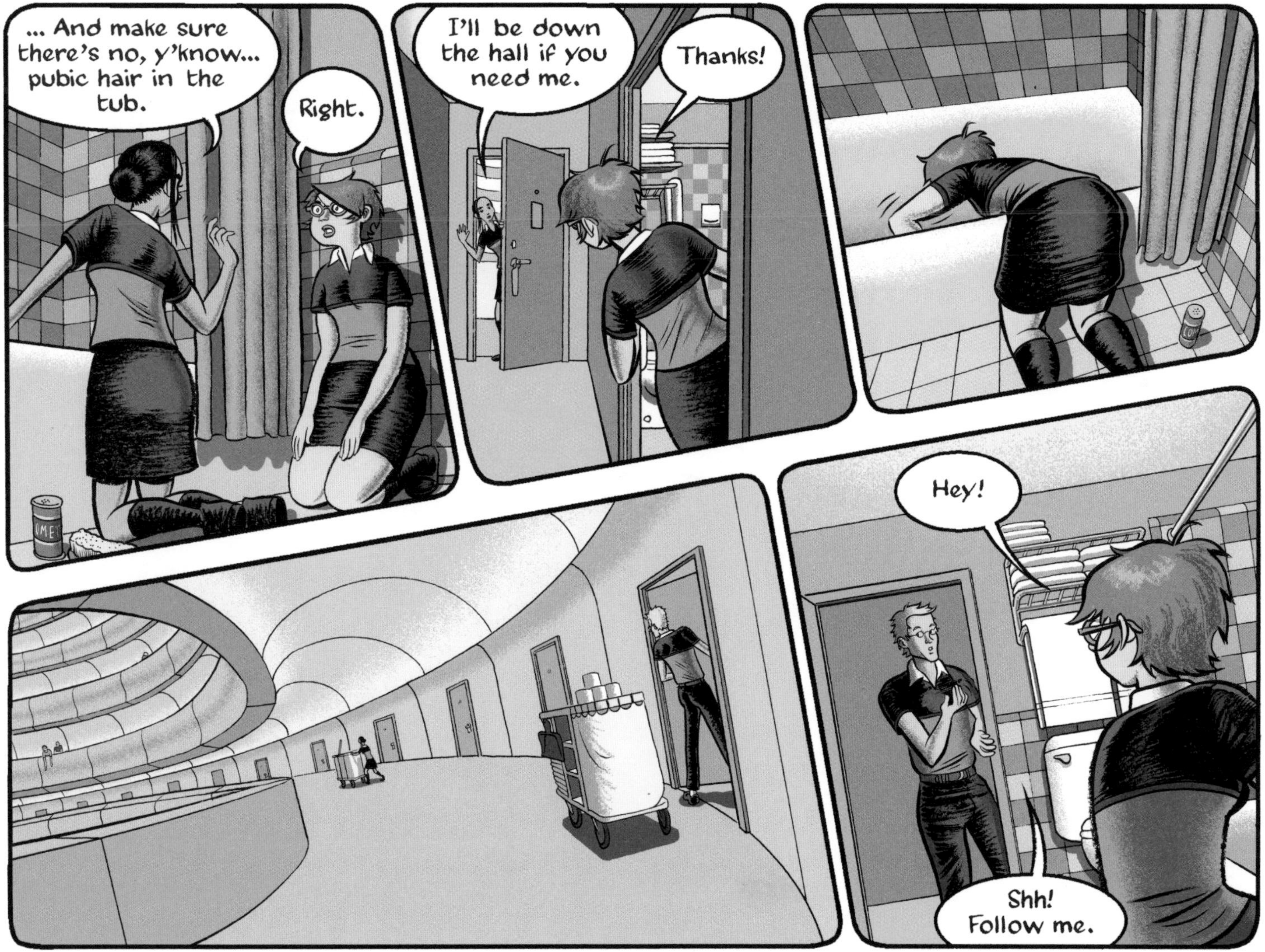
... And make sure there's no, y'know... pubic hair in the tub.
Right.
I'll be down the hall if you need me.
Thanks!
Hey!
Shh! Follow me.

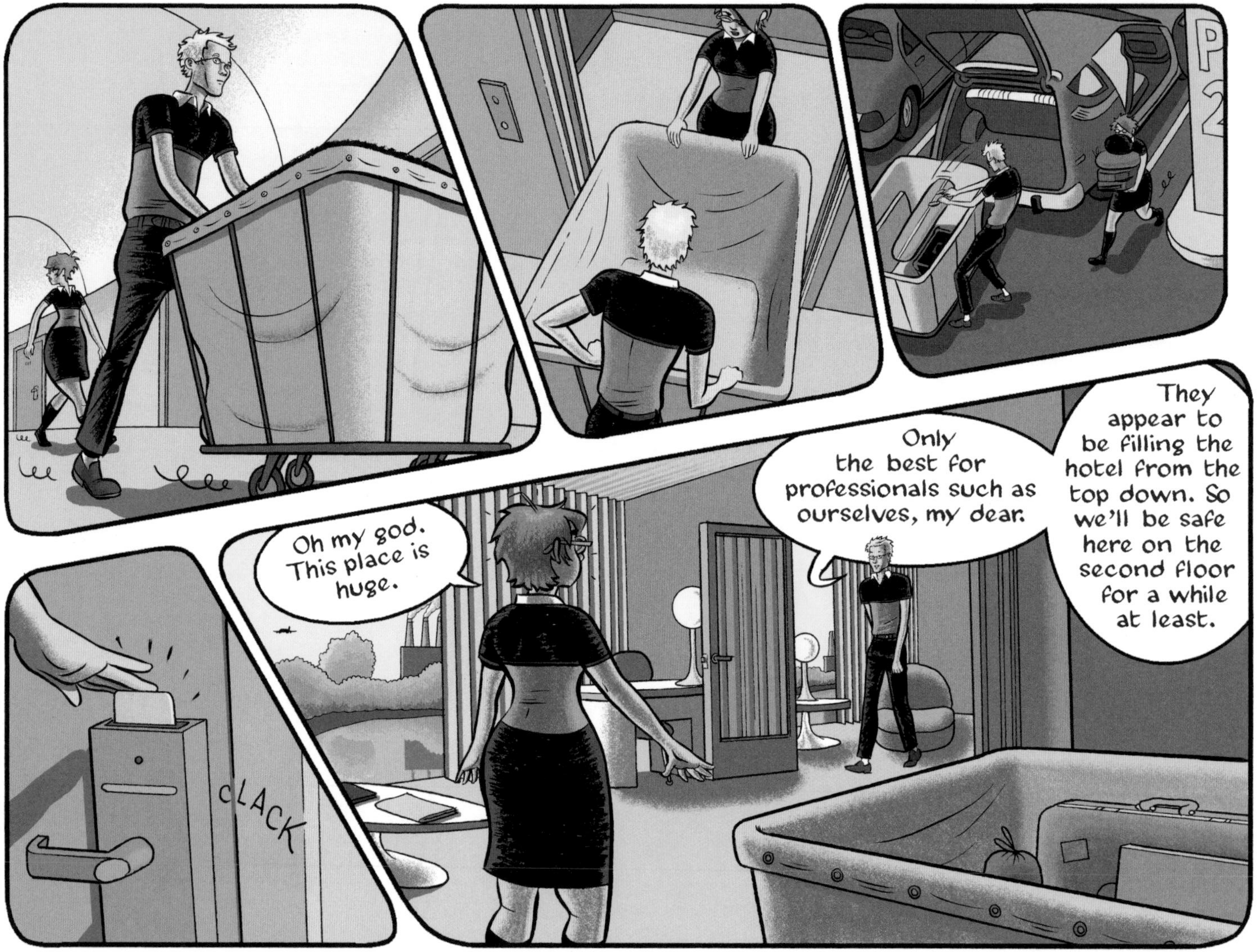
Oh my god. This place is huge.
Only the best for professionals such as ourselves, my dear.
They appear to be filling the hotel from the top down. So we'll be safe here on the second floor for a while at least.
CLACK
P2

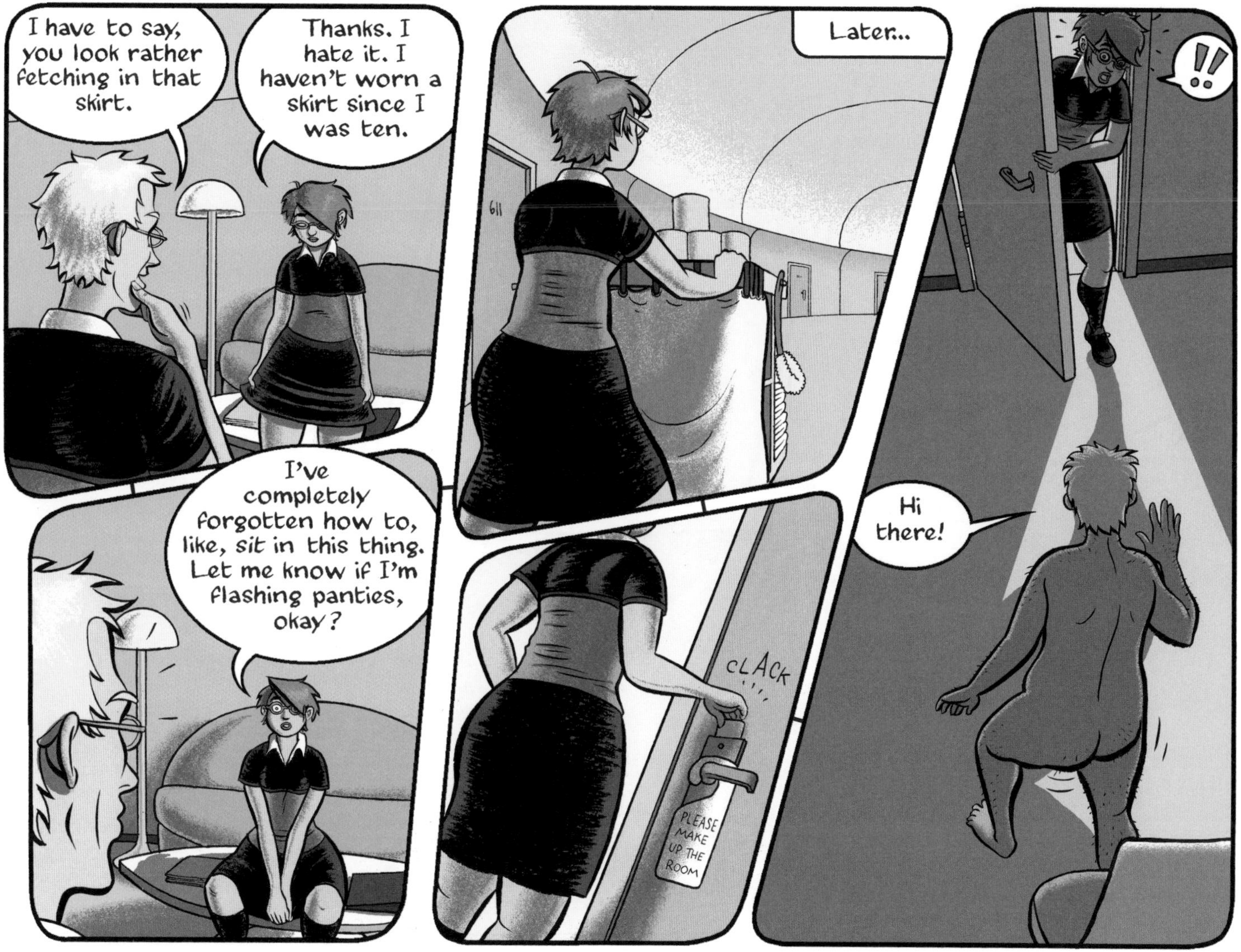
I have to say, you look rather fetching in that skirt.
Thanks. I hate it. I haven't worn a skirt since I was ten.
I've completely forgotten how to, like, *sit* in this thing. Let me know if I'm flashing panties, okay?
Later...
611
CLACK
PLEASE MAKE UP THE ROOM
!!
Hi there!

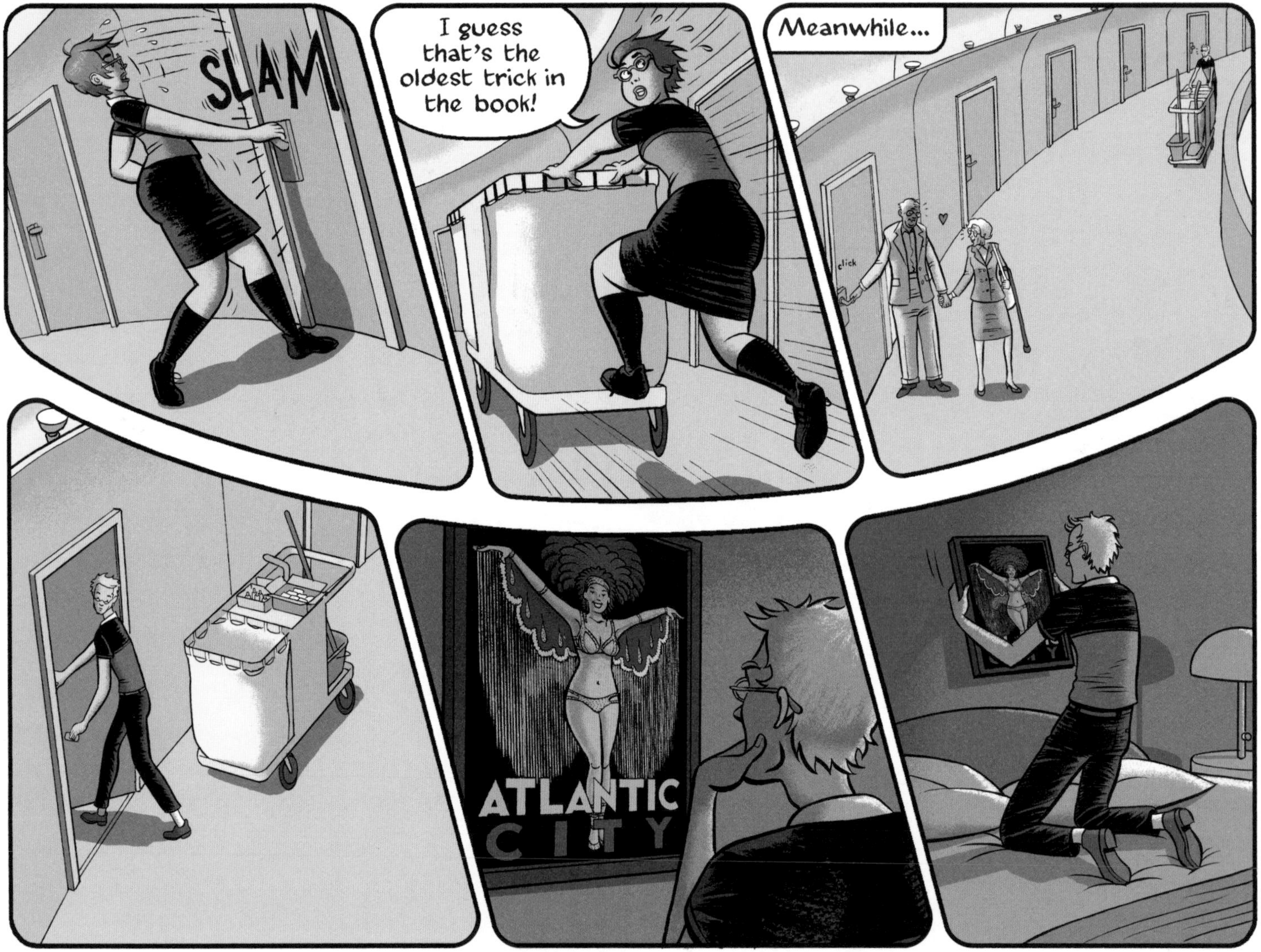
SLAM
I guess that's the oldest trick in the book!
Meanwhile...
click
ATLANTIC CITY

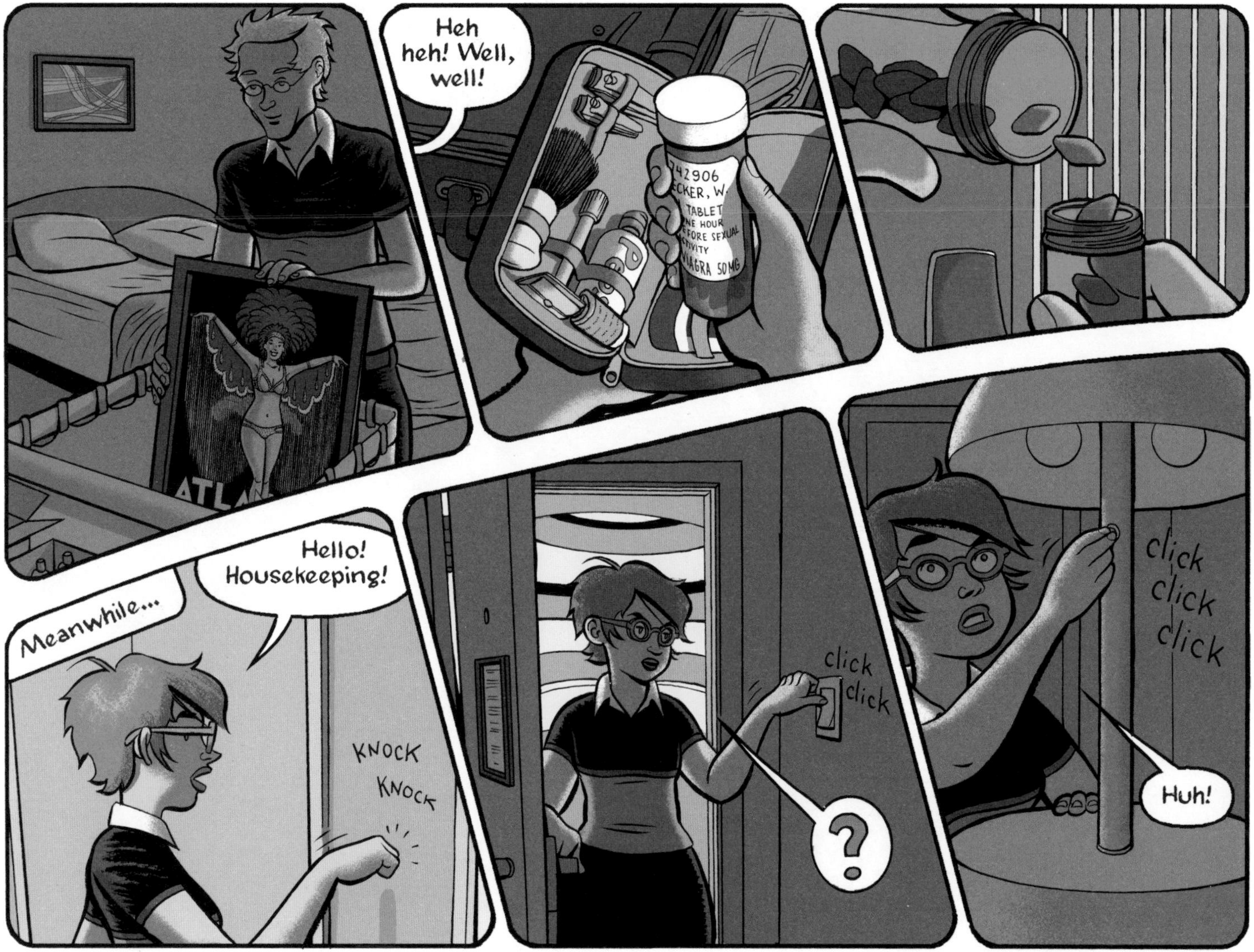
Heh heh! Well, well!
VIAGRA 50MG
Meanwhile...
Hello! Housekeeping!
KNOCK KNOCK
click click
?
click click click
Huh!

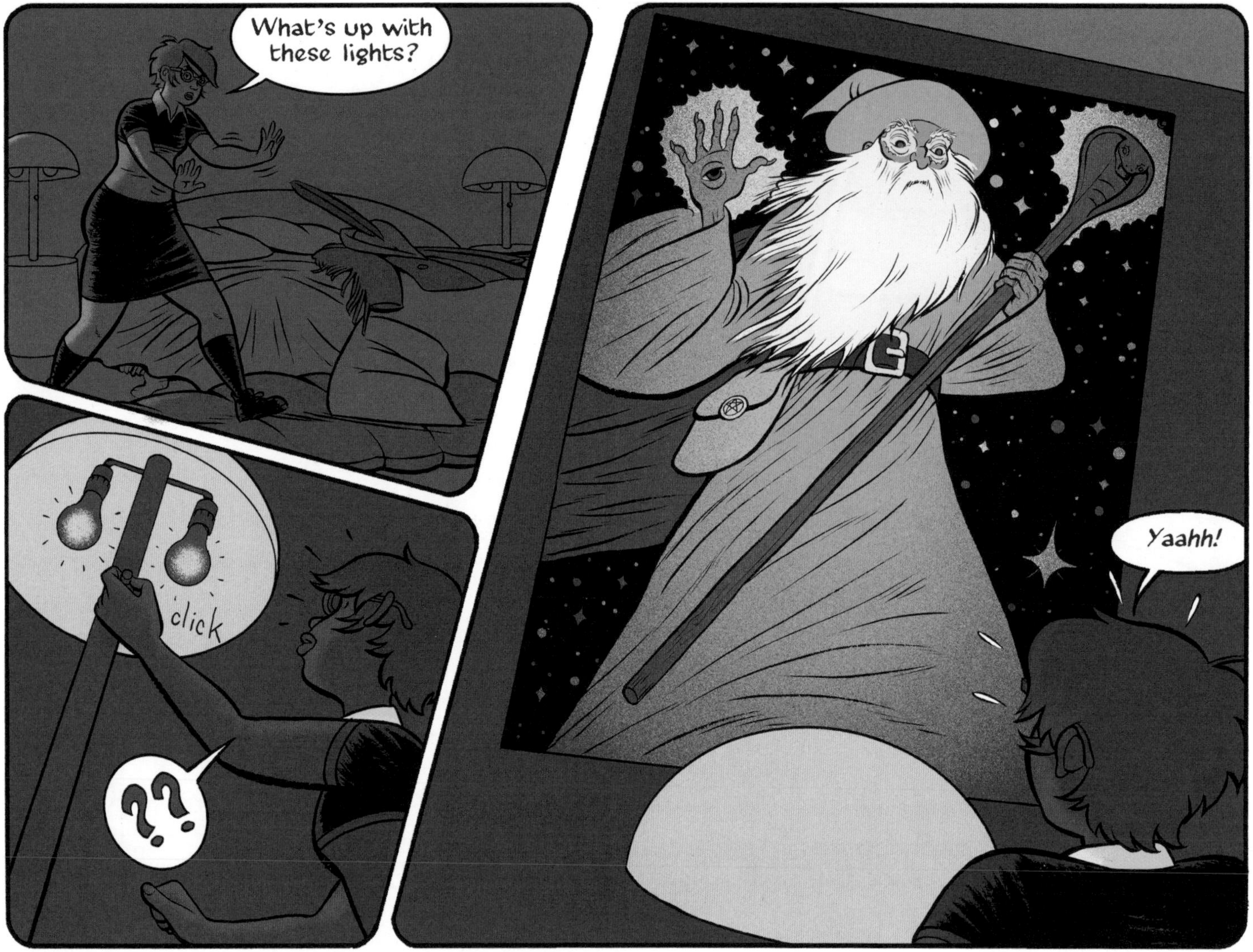
What's up with these lights?
click
??
Yaahh!

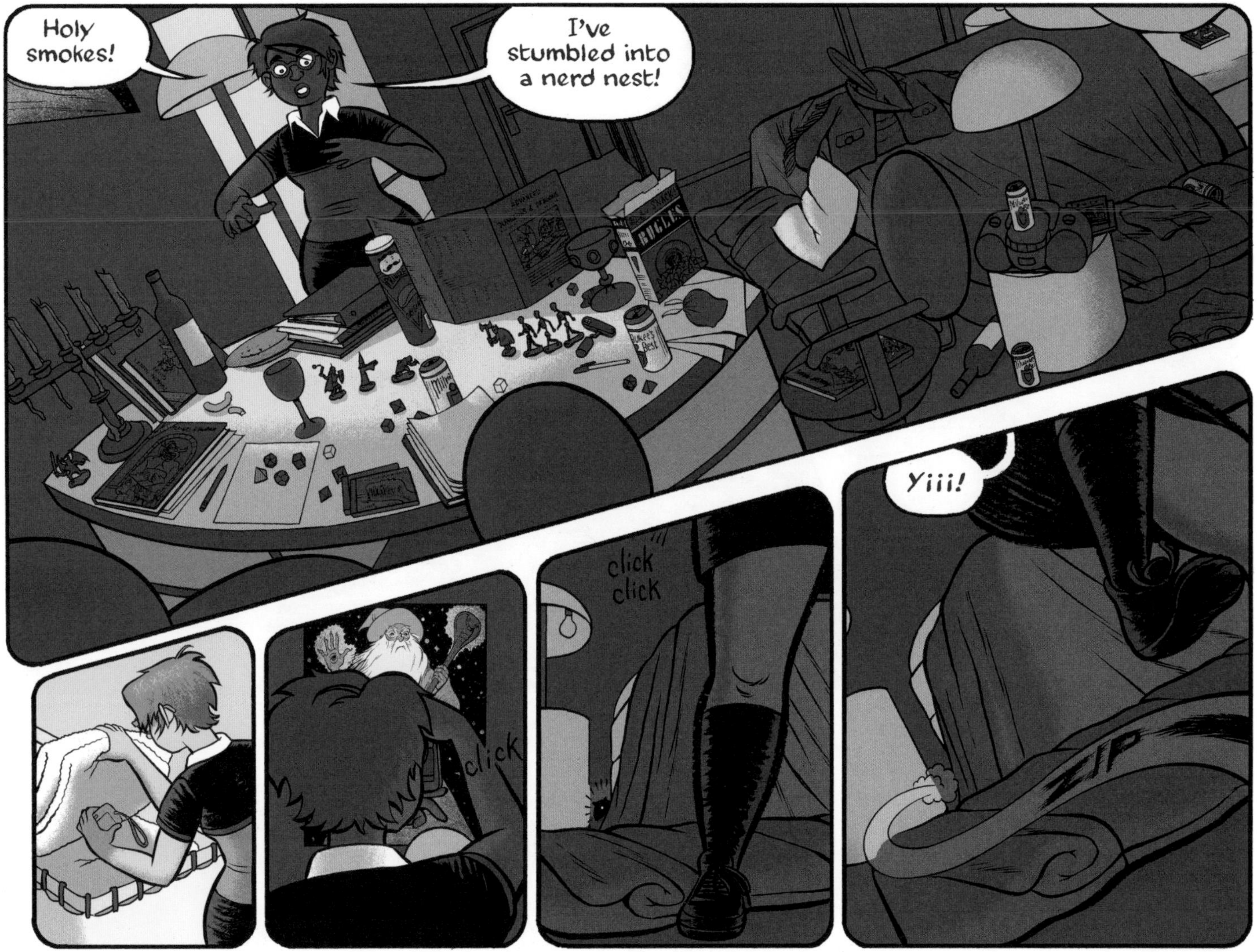
Holy smokes!
I've stumbled into a nerd nest!
click
click click
Yiii!
ZIP

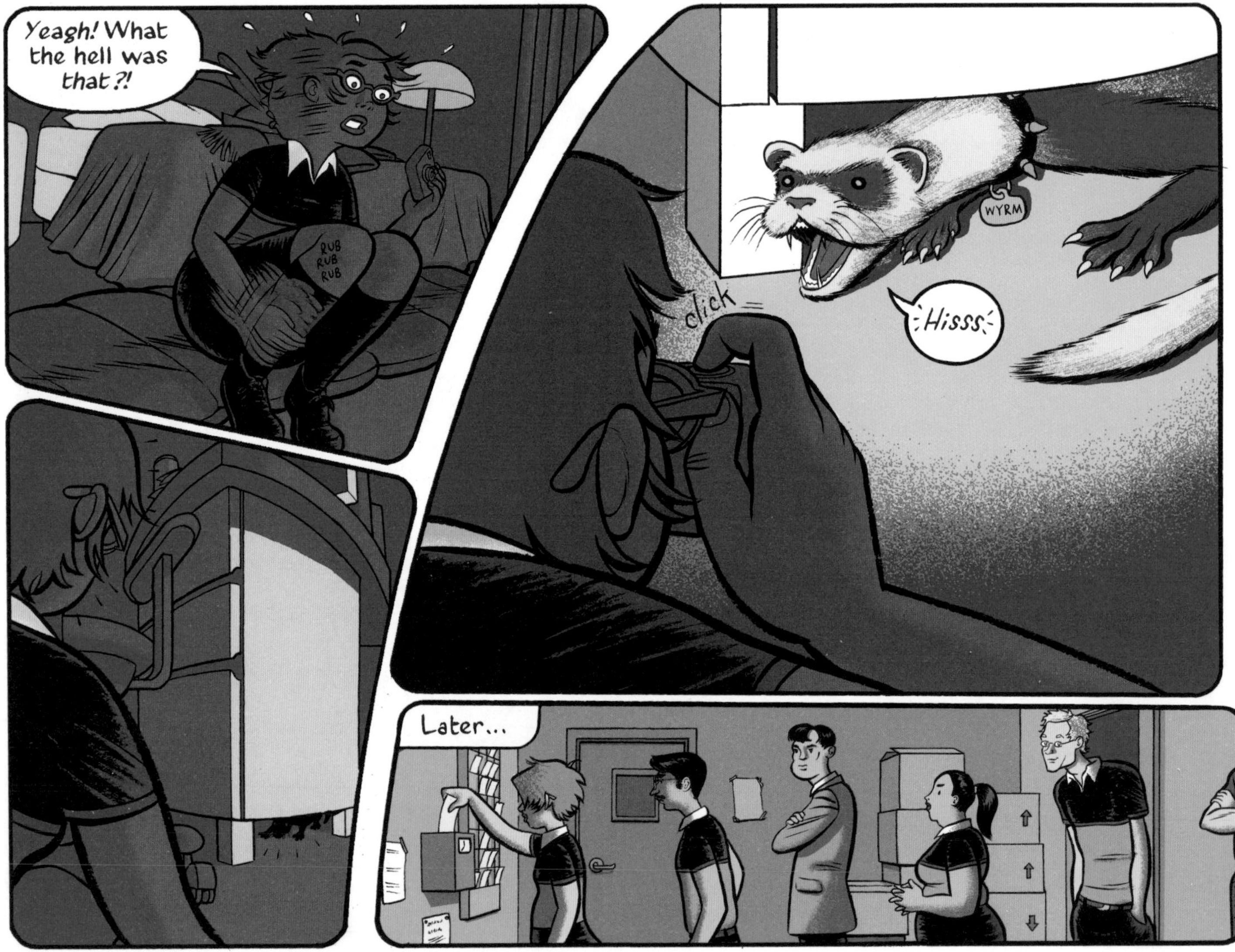
Yeagh! What the hell was that?!
RUB RUB RUB
click
WYRM
Hisss
Later...

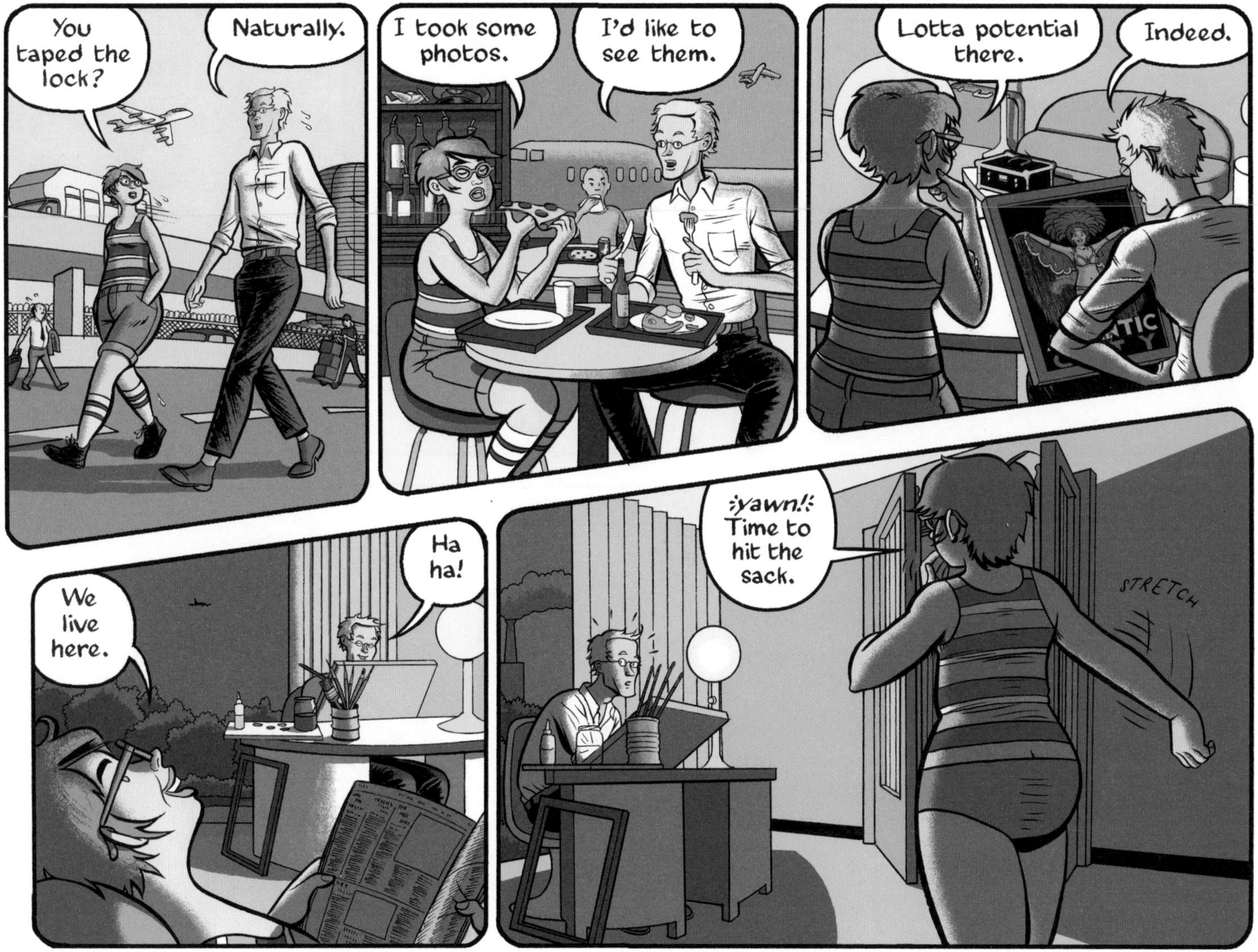
You taped the lock?
Naturally.
I took some photos.
I'd like to see them.
Lotta potential there.
Indeed.
We live here.
Ha ha!
:yawn!: Time to hit the sack.
STRETCH

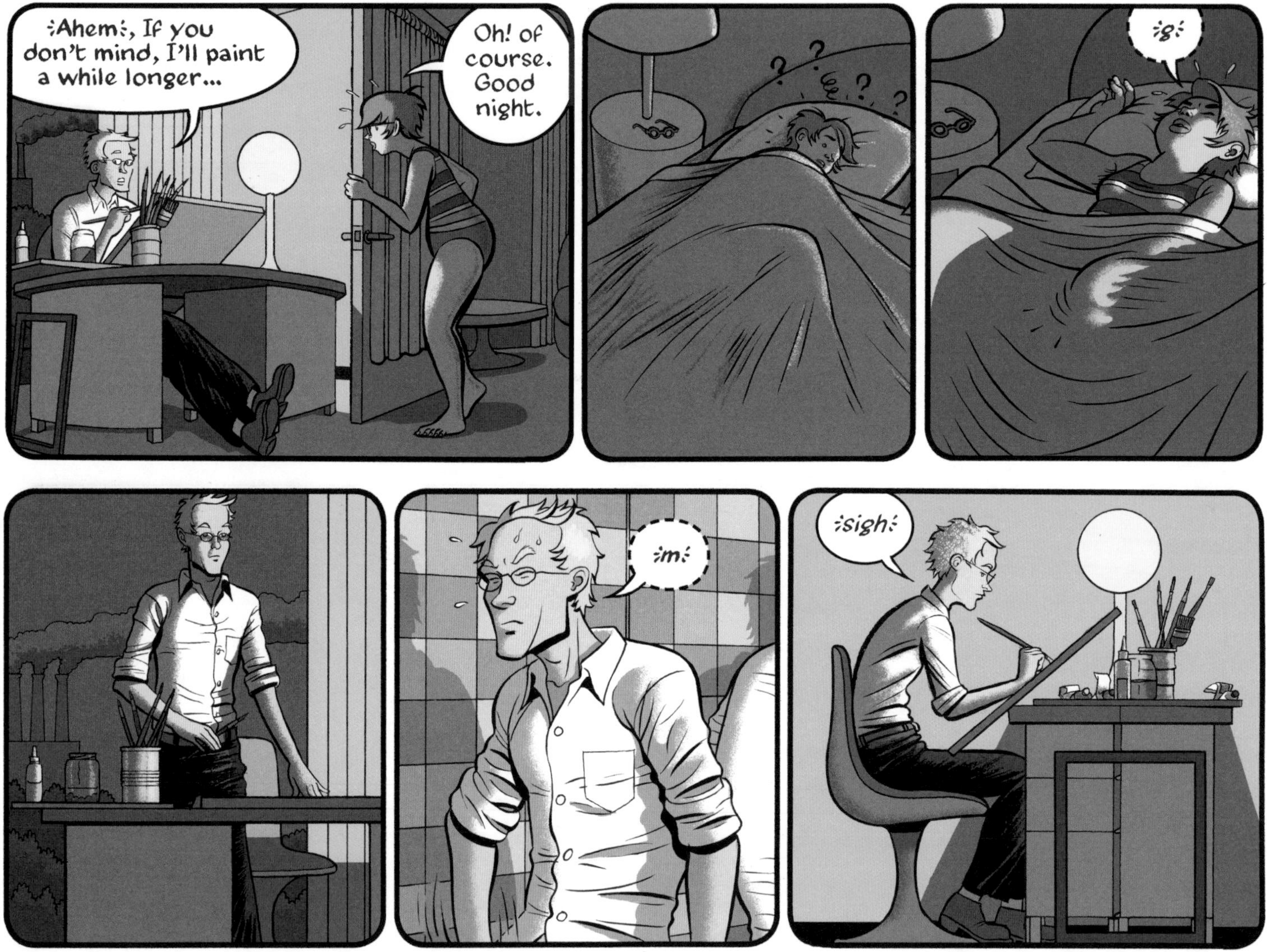

:Ahem:, If you don't mind, I'll paint a while longer...
Oh! of course. Good night.
? ? ? ?
:g:
:m:
:sigh:

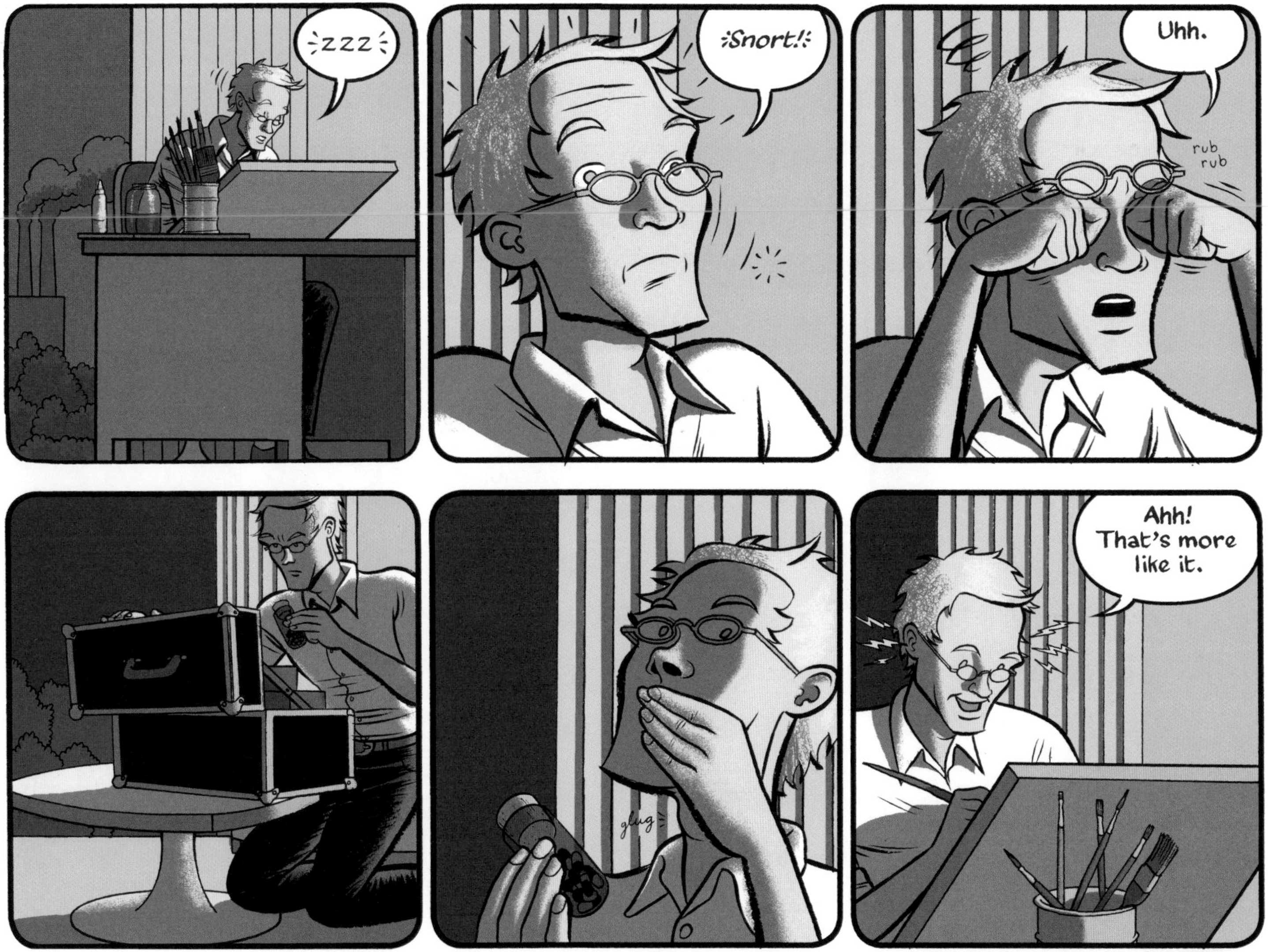
zzz
Snort!
Uhh.
rub rub
glug
Ahh! That's more like it.

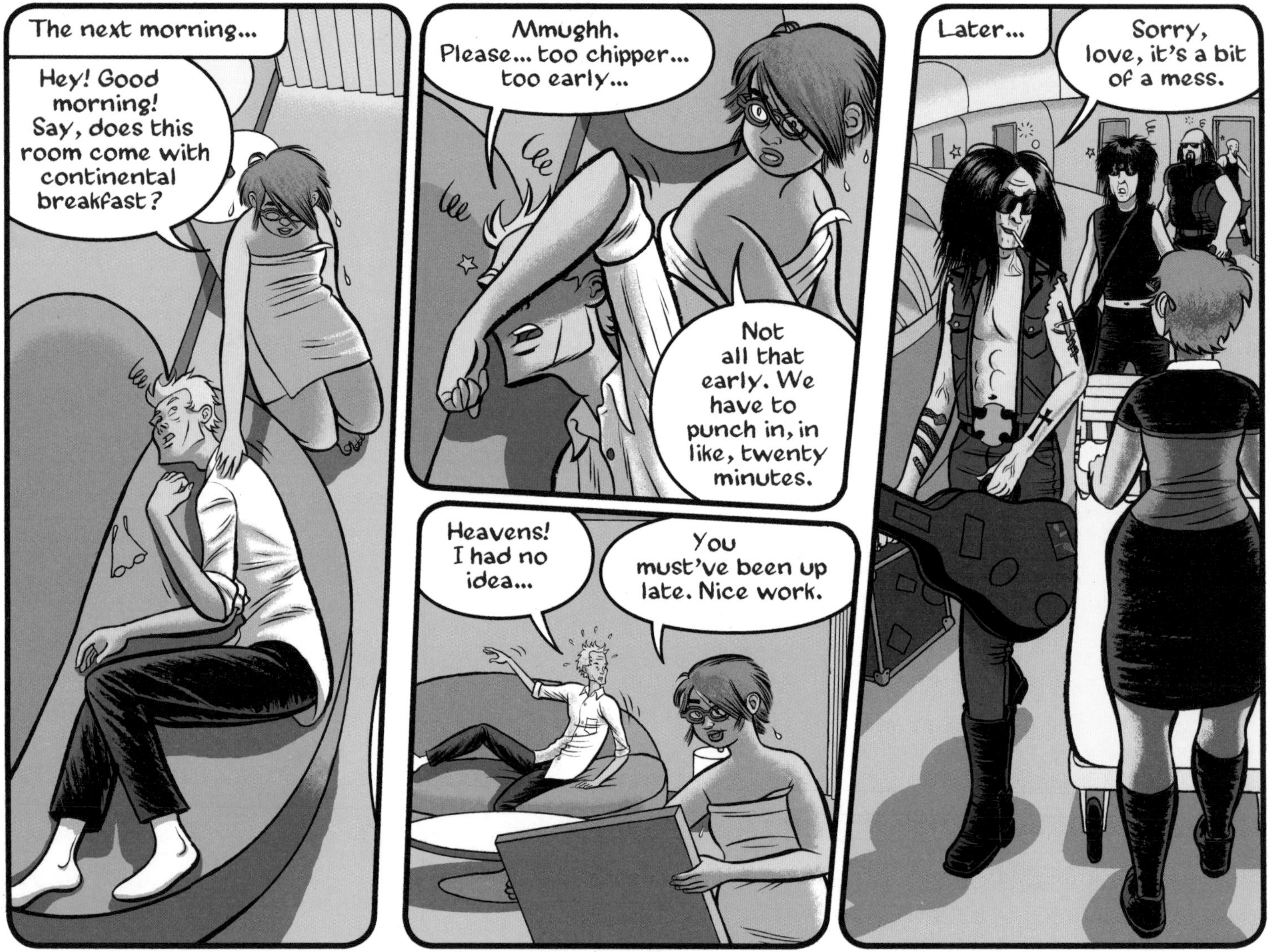
The next morning...
Hey! Good morning! Say, does this room come with continental breakfast?
Mmughh. Please... too chipper... too early...
Not all that early. We have to punch in, in like, twenty minutes.
Heavens! I had no idea...
You must've been up late. Nice work.
Later...
Sorry, love, it's a bit of a mess.

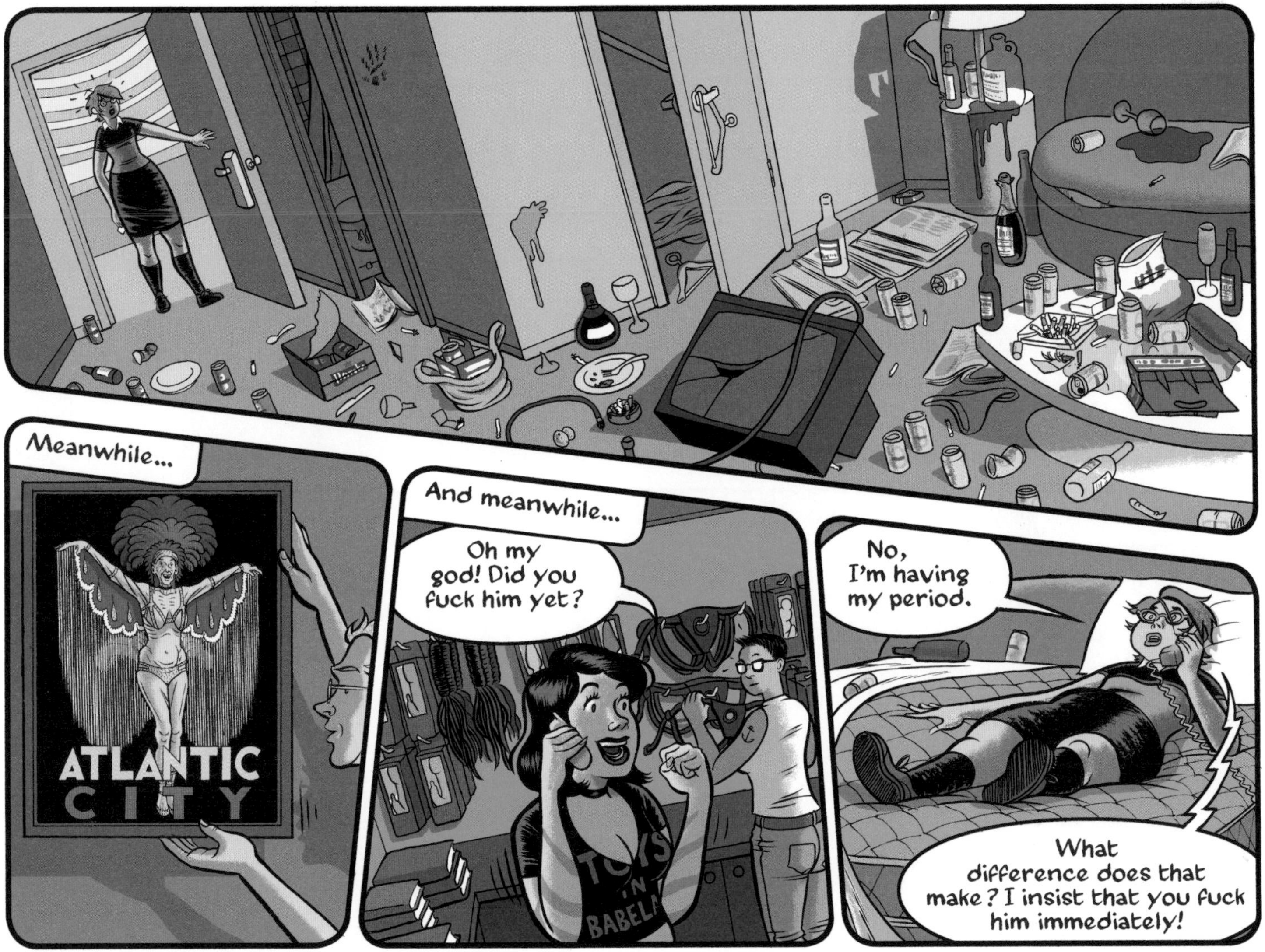
Meanwhile...
ATLANTIC CITY
And meanwhile...
Oh my god! Did you fuck him yet?
TOYS IN BABELA
No, I'm having my period.
What difference does that make? I insist that you fuck him immediately!

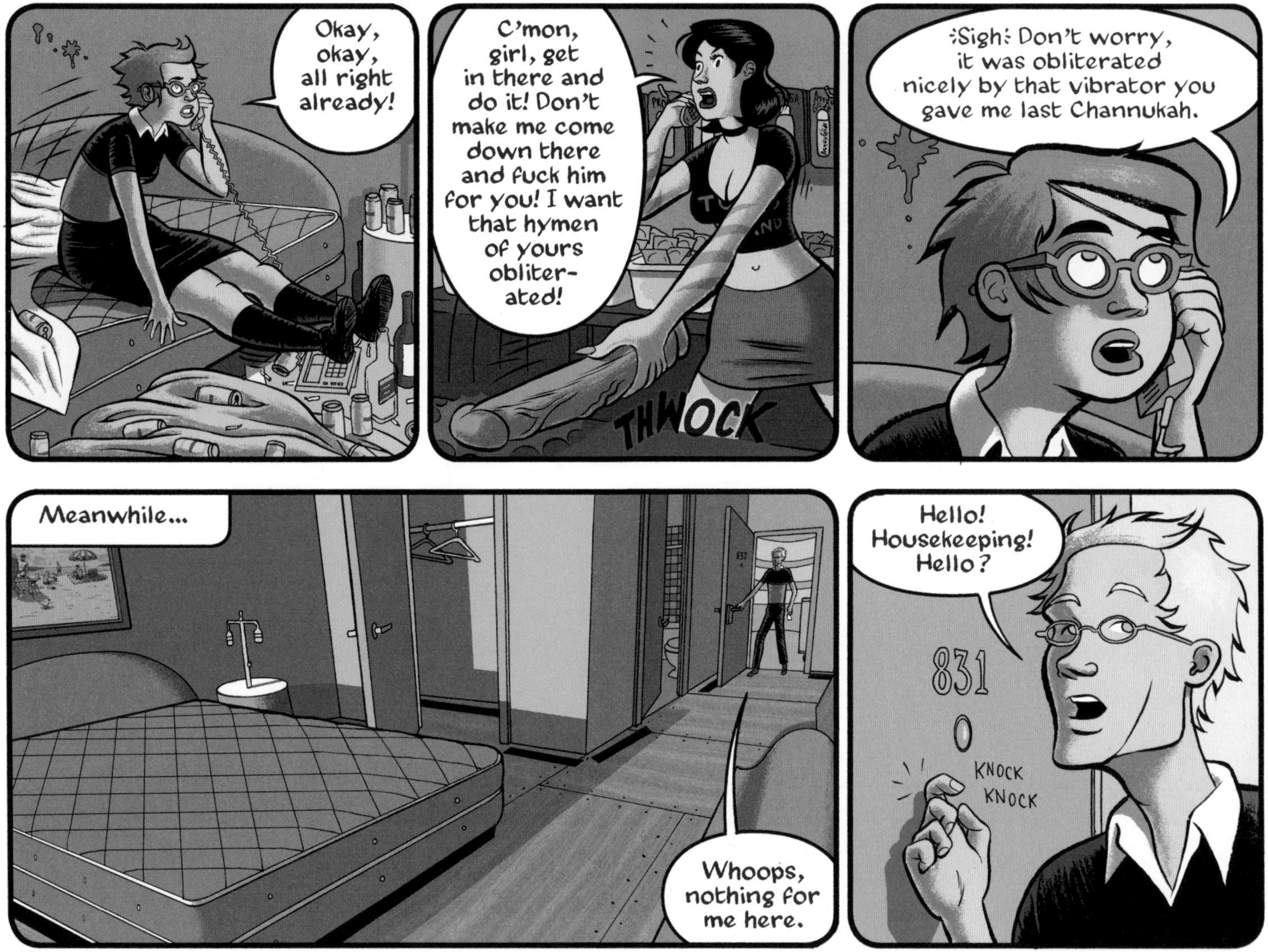

Okay, okay, all right already!
C'mon, girl, get in there and do it! Don't make me come down there and fuck him for you! I want that hymen of yours obliter-ated!
THWOCK
:Sigh: Don't worry, it was obliterated nicely by that vibrator you gave me last Channukah.
Meanwhile...
837
Whoops, nothing for me here.
Hello! Housekeeping! Hello?
831
KNOCK KNOCK

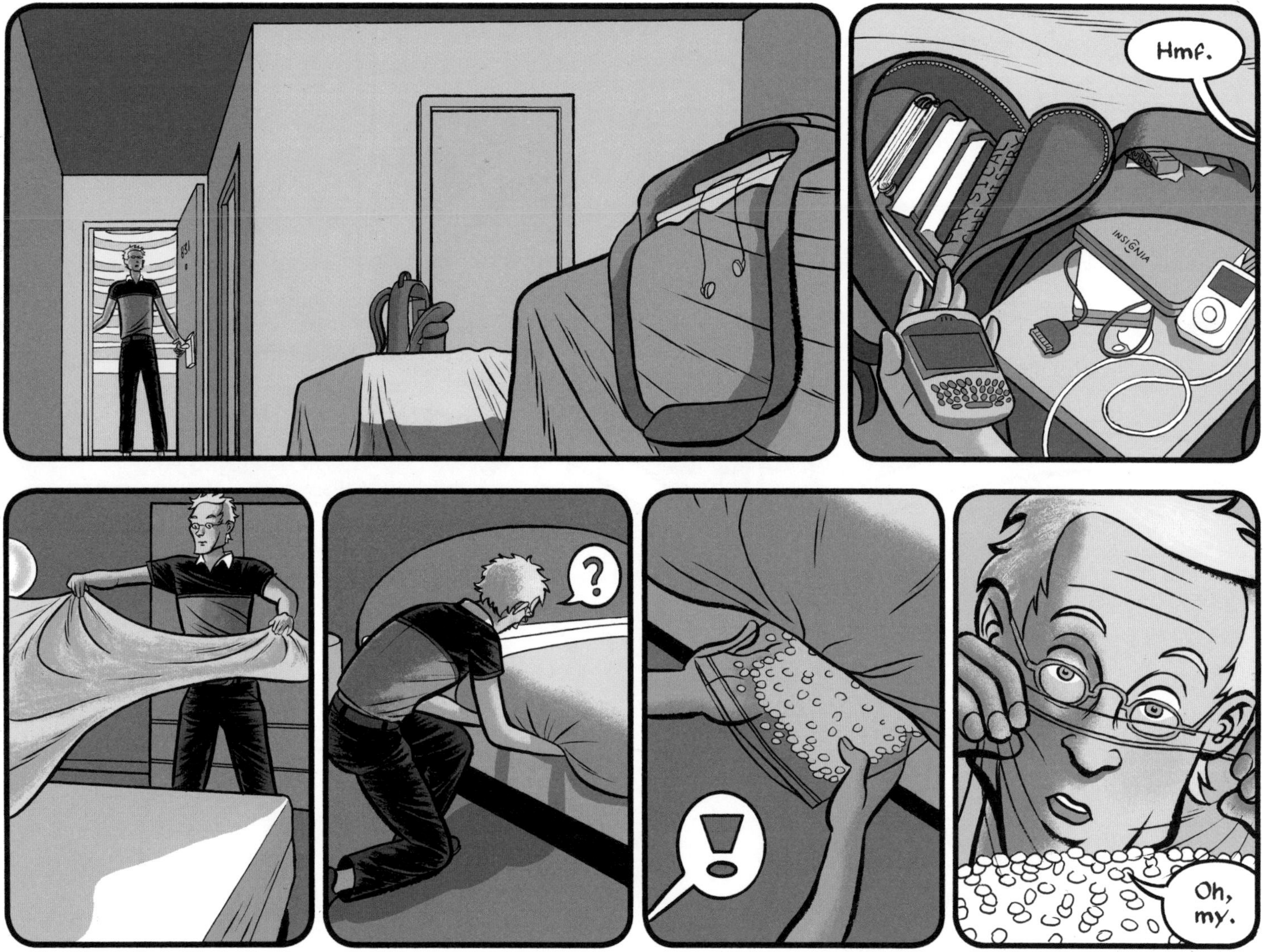
Hmf.
?
!
Oh, my.

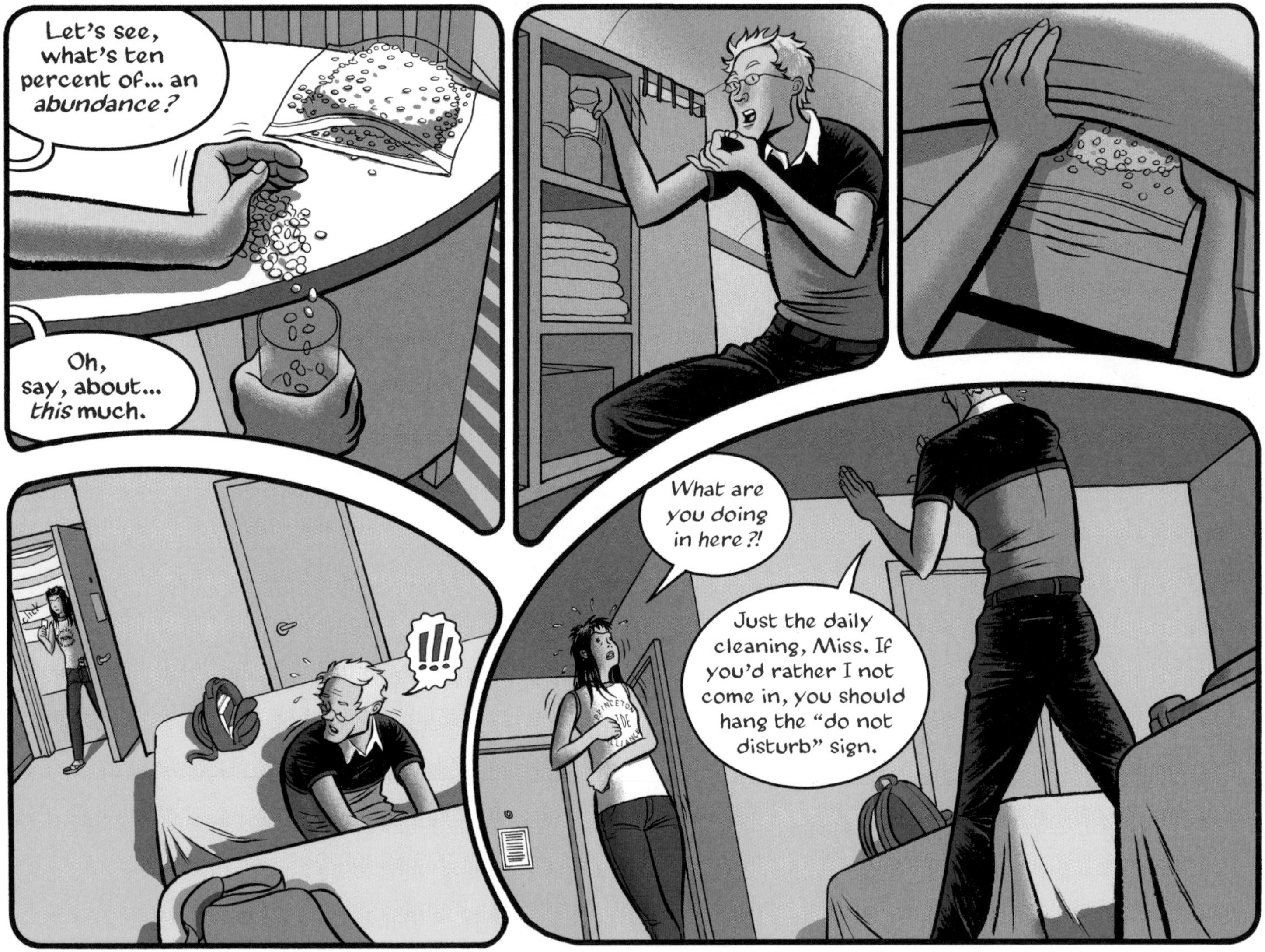

Let's see, what's ten percent of... an *abundance?*
Oh, say, about... *this* much.
click
!!!
What are you doing in here?!
Just the daily cleaning, Miss. If you'd rather I not come in, you should hang the "do not disturb" sign.

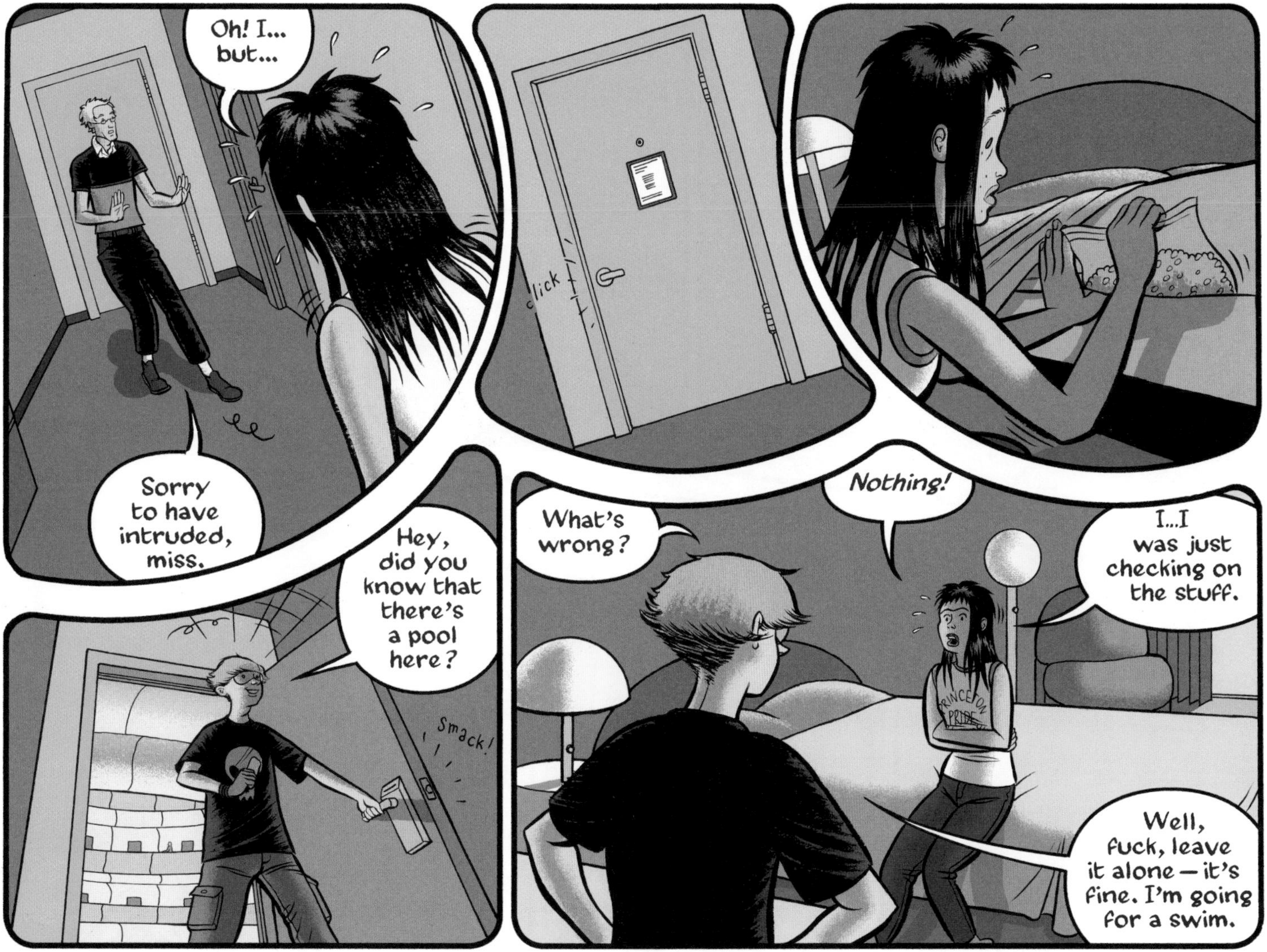
Oh! I... but...
Sorry to have intruded, miss.
click
Hey, did you know that there's a pool here?
Smack!
What's wrong?
Nothing!
I...I was just checking on the stuff.
PRINCETON PRIDE
Well, fuck, leave it alone — it's fine. I'm going for a swim.

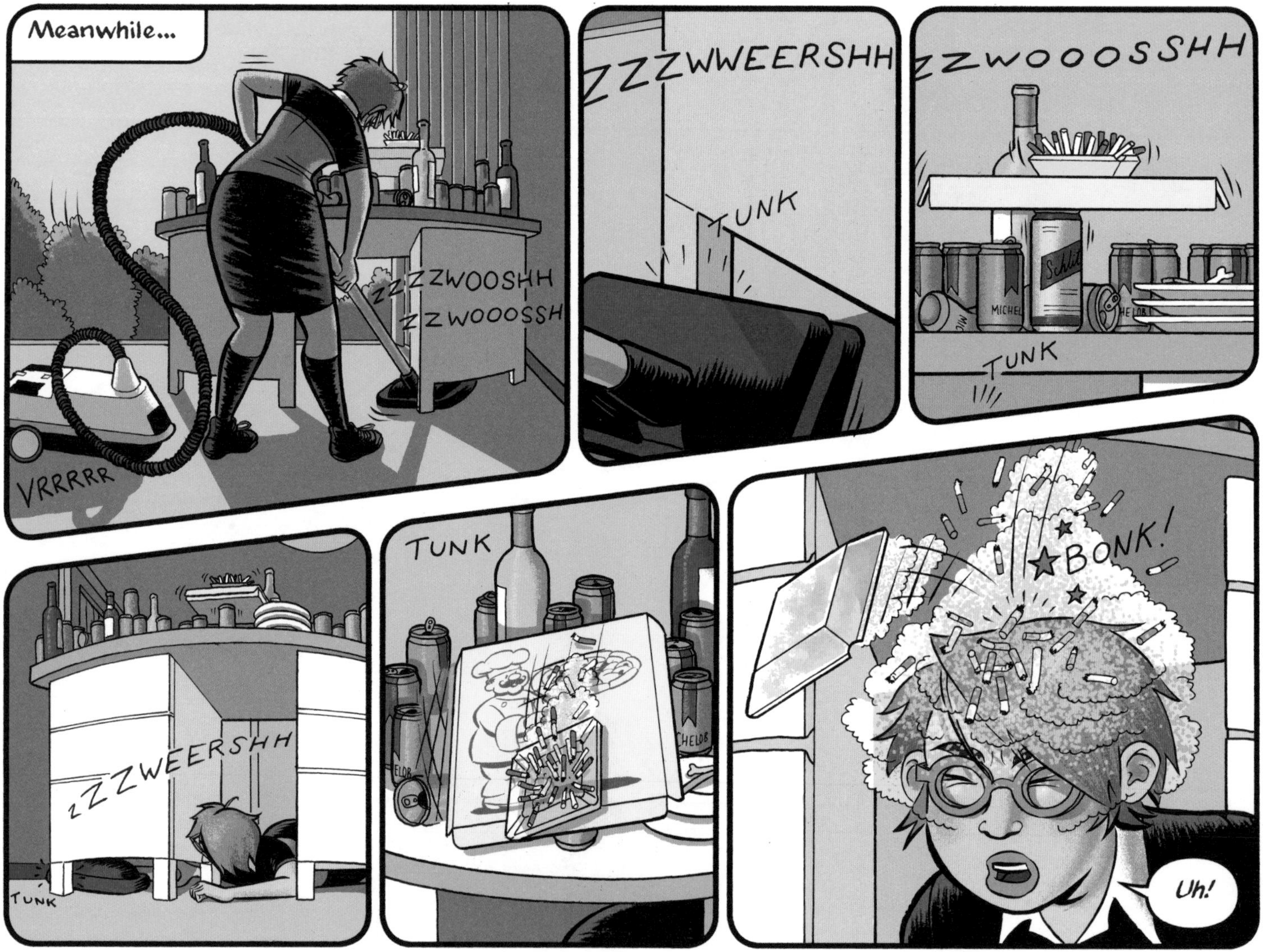
Meanwhile...
VRRRRR
ZZZZWOOSHH
ZZWOOOSSH
ZZZWWEERSHH
TUNK
ZZWOOOSSHH
TUNK
TUNK
ZZZWEERSHH
TUNK
BONK!
Uh!

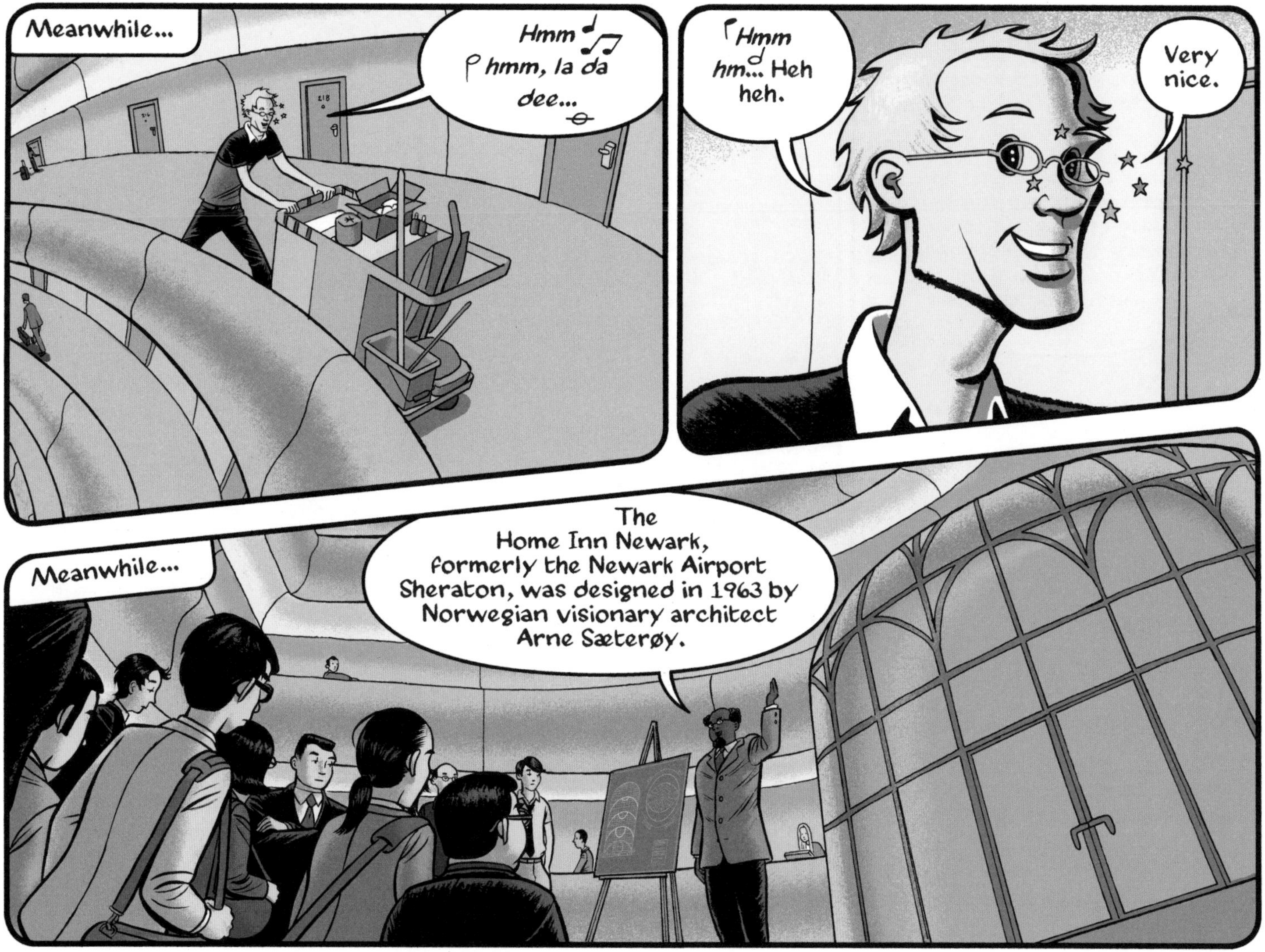
Meanwhile...
Hmm hmm, la da dee...
Hmm hm... Heh heh.
Very nice.
Meanwhile...
The Home Inn Newark, formerly the Newark Airport Sheraton, was designed in 1963 by Norwegian visionary architect Arne Sæterøy.

All of Sæterøy's buildings incorporate motifs inspired by the architect's deeply held religious beliefs. In our building, the human eye is a constantly recurring shape. In the elevation view, we see a rising eye rolling up, symbolizing the transfer of the consciousness from the material world to the inner world of the soul.

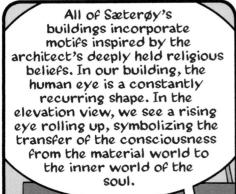

Here, in the plan view, we see the roof dome. The internal eye has emerged and gazes up at heaven.

Now we'll visit one of the suites.

Carol, what suite can I show these folks?

Suite number 217 is unoccupied. Mr. Perez.

Meanwhile...

Deé da dee, ♩ tum tum, ♪ yadda dum, ♩♫ da da... ♩ ♪ ♩

217

♫ Da da daa ♩♪, hmm hm, da ♩ dum... ♩♪ ♩♪

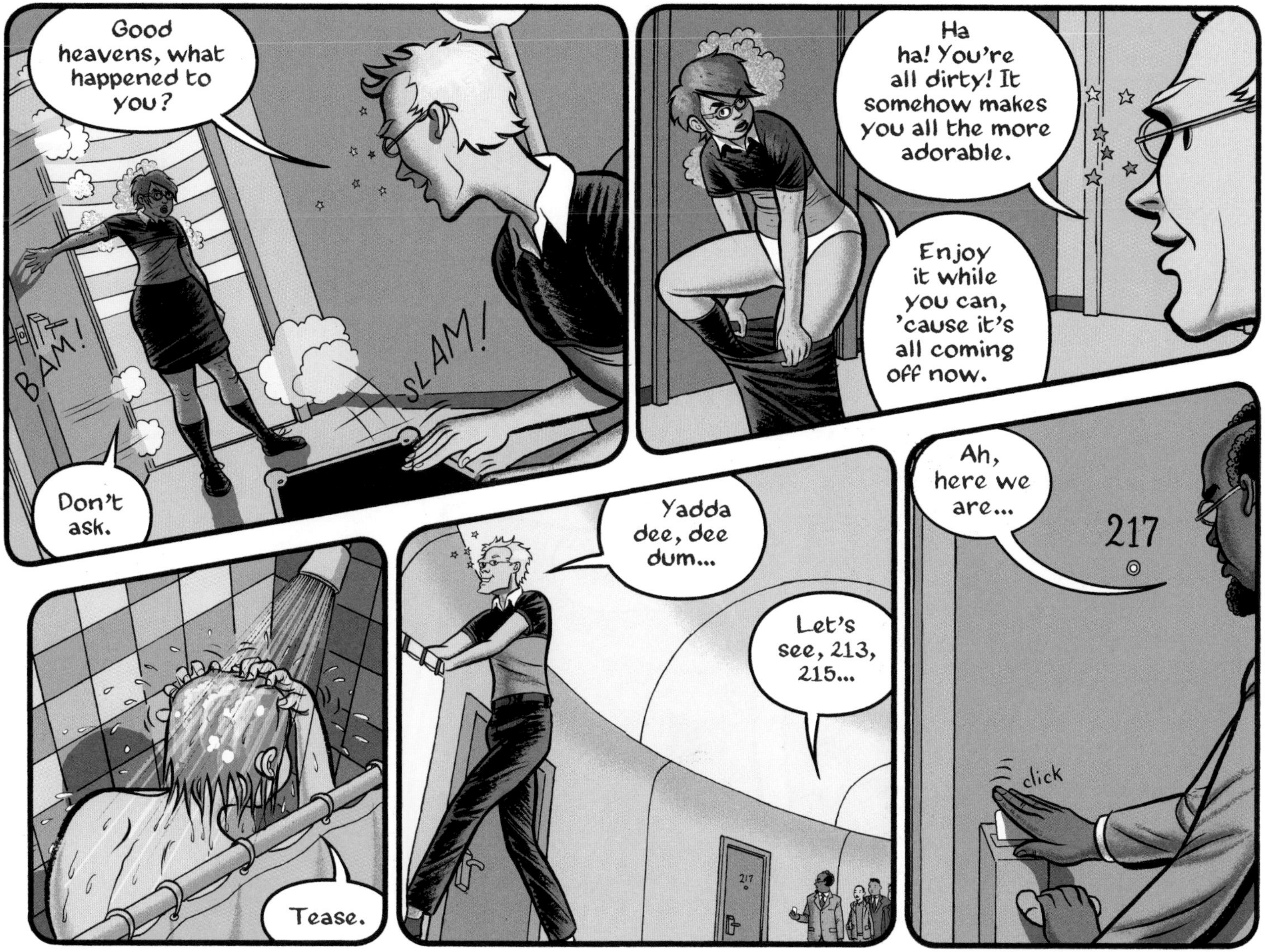
Good heavens, what happened to you?
BAM!
SLAM!
Don't ask.
Ha ha! You're all dirty! It somehow makes you all the more adorable.
Enjoy it while you can, 'cause it's all coming off now.
Ah, here we are...
217
click
Yadda dee, dee dum...
Let's see, 213, 215...
Tease.

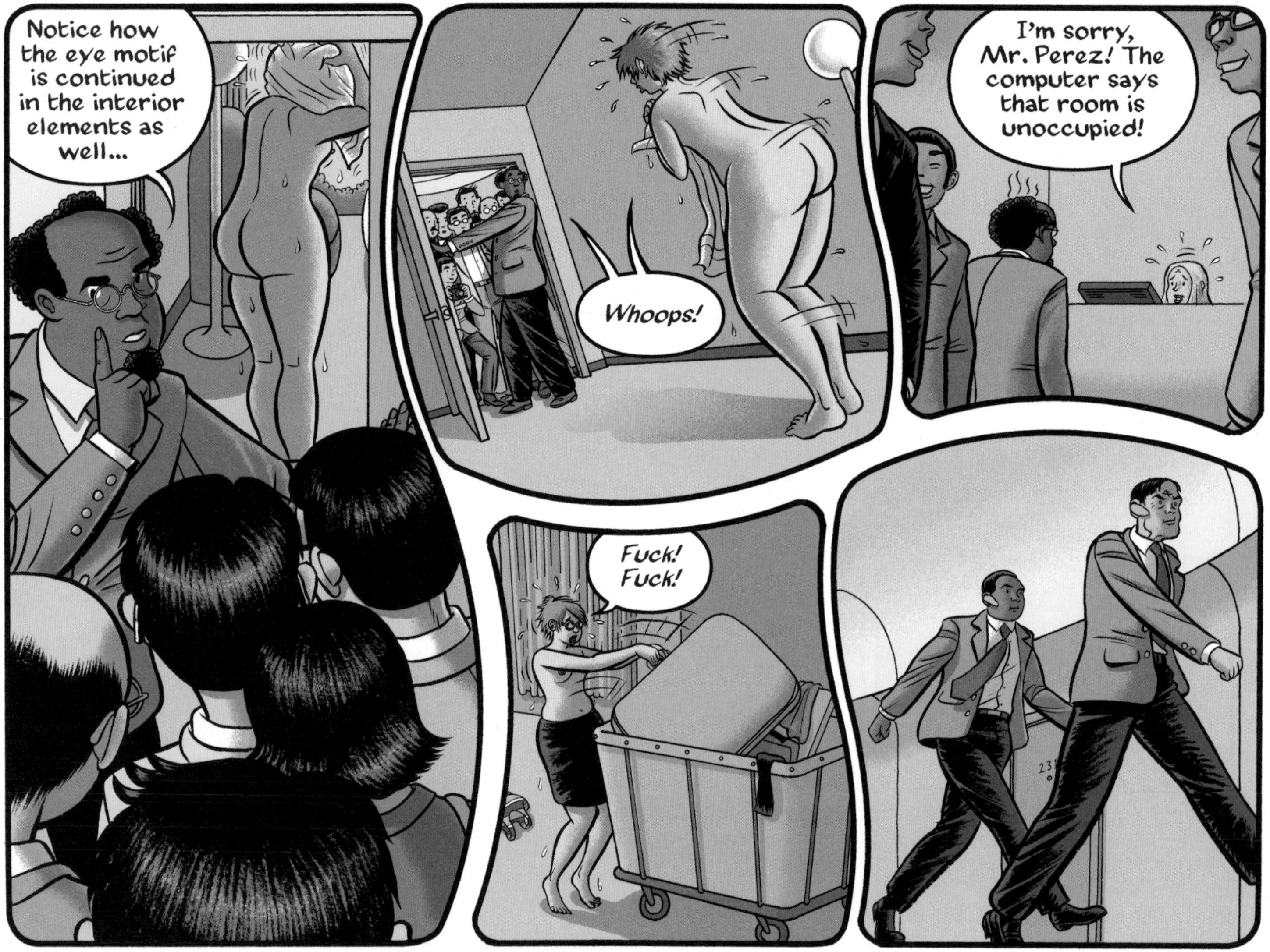
Notice how the eye motif is continued in the interior elements as well...
Whoops!
I'm sorry, Mr. Perez! The computer says that room is unoccupied!
Fuck! Fuck!

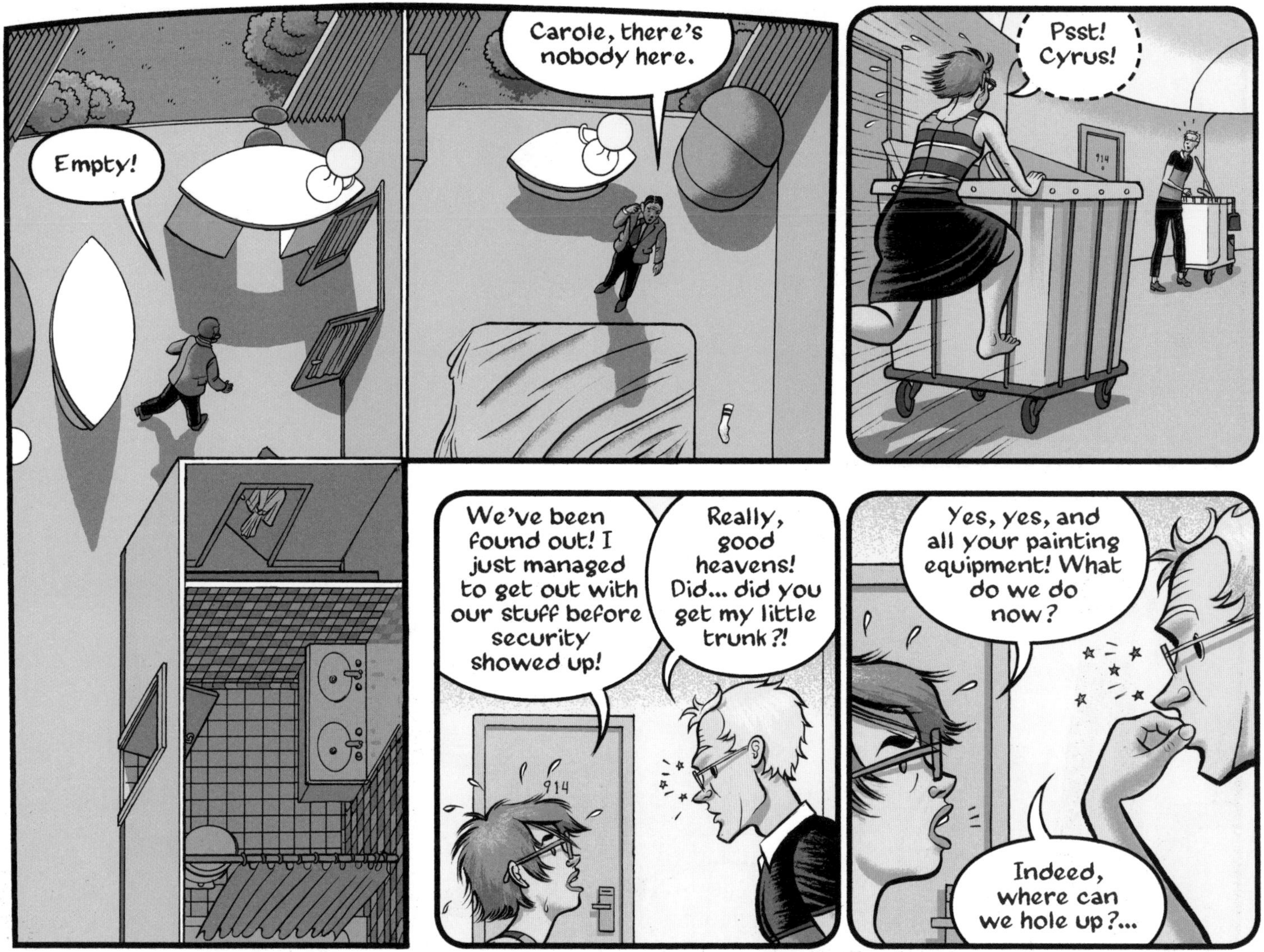

Empty!
Carole, there's nobody here.
Psst! Cyrus!
914
We've been found out! I just managed to get out with our stuff before security showed up!
Really, good heavens! Did... did you get my little trunk?!
Yes, yes, and all your painting equipment! What do we do now?
Indeed, where can we hole up?...

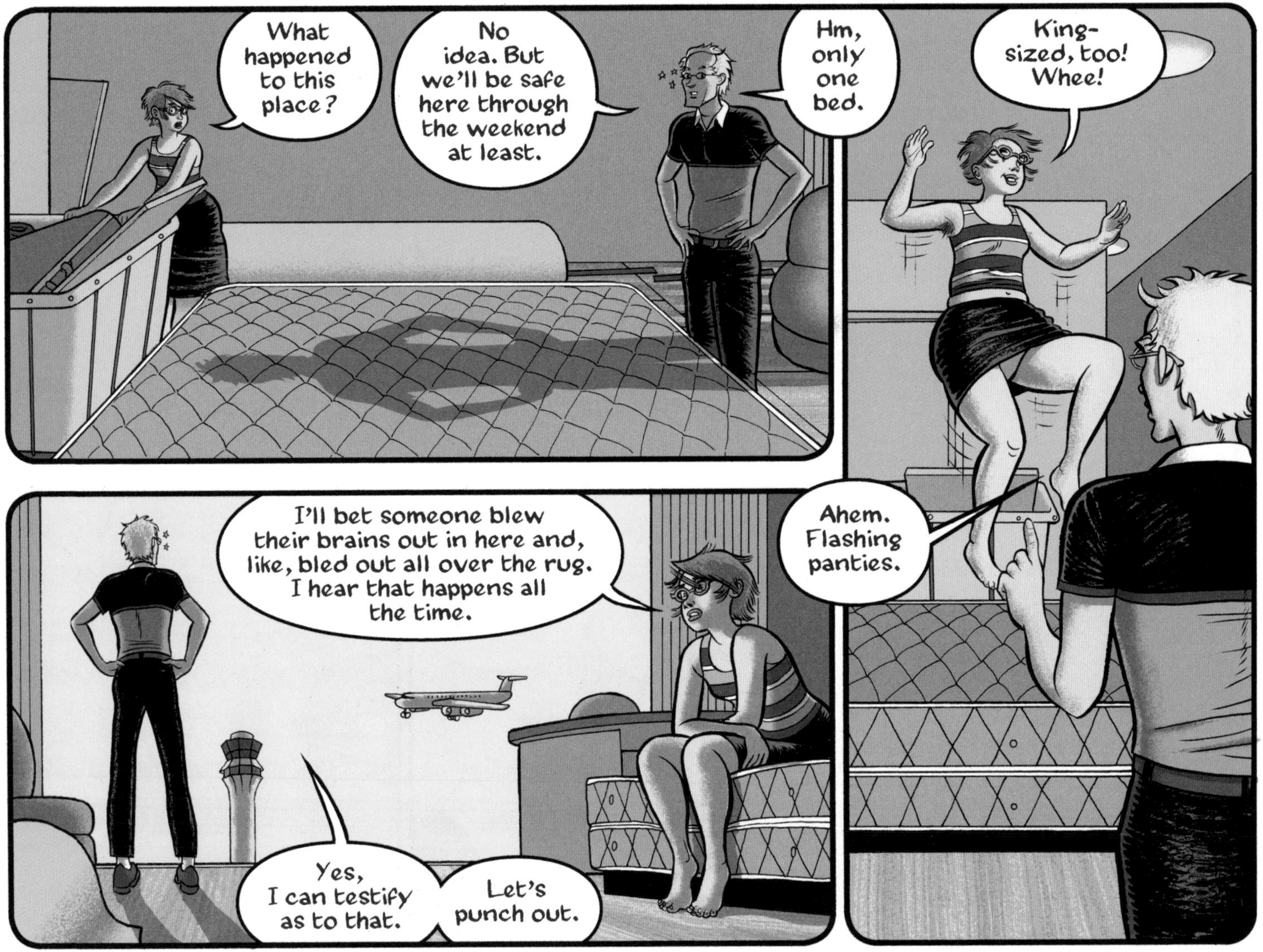
What happened to this place?
No idea. But we'll be safe here through the weekend at least.
Hm, only one bed.
King-sized, too! Whee!
Ahem. Flashing panties.
I'll bet someone blew their brains out in here and, like, bled out all over the rug. I hear that happens all the time.
Yes, I can testify as to that.
Let's punch out.

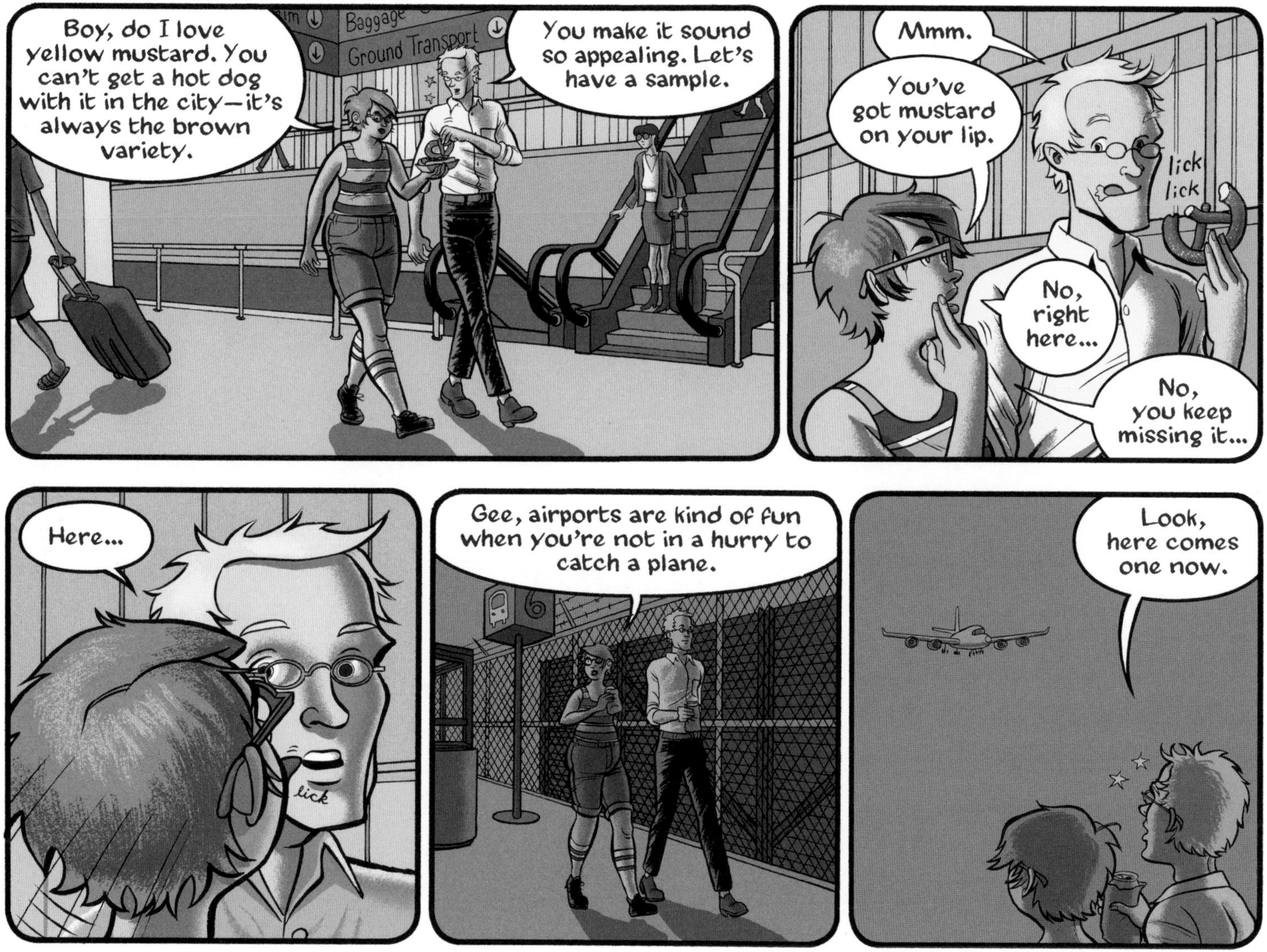
Baggage
Ground Transport
Boy, do I love yellow mustard. You can't get a hot dog with it in the city—it's always the brown variety.
You make it sound so appealing. Let's have a sample.
Mmm.
You've got mustard on your lip.
lick lick
No, right here...
No, you keep missing it...
Here...
lick
Gee, airports are kind of fun when you're not in a hurry to catch a plane.
Look, here comes one now.

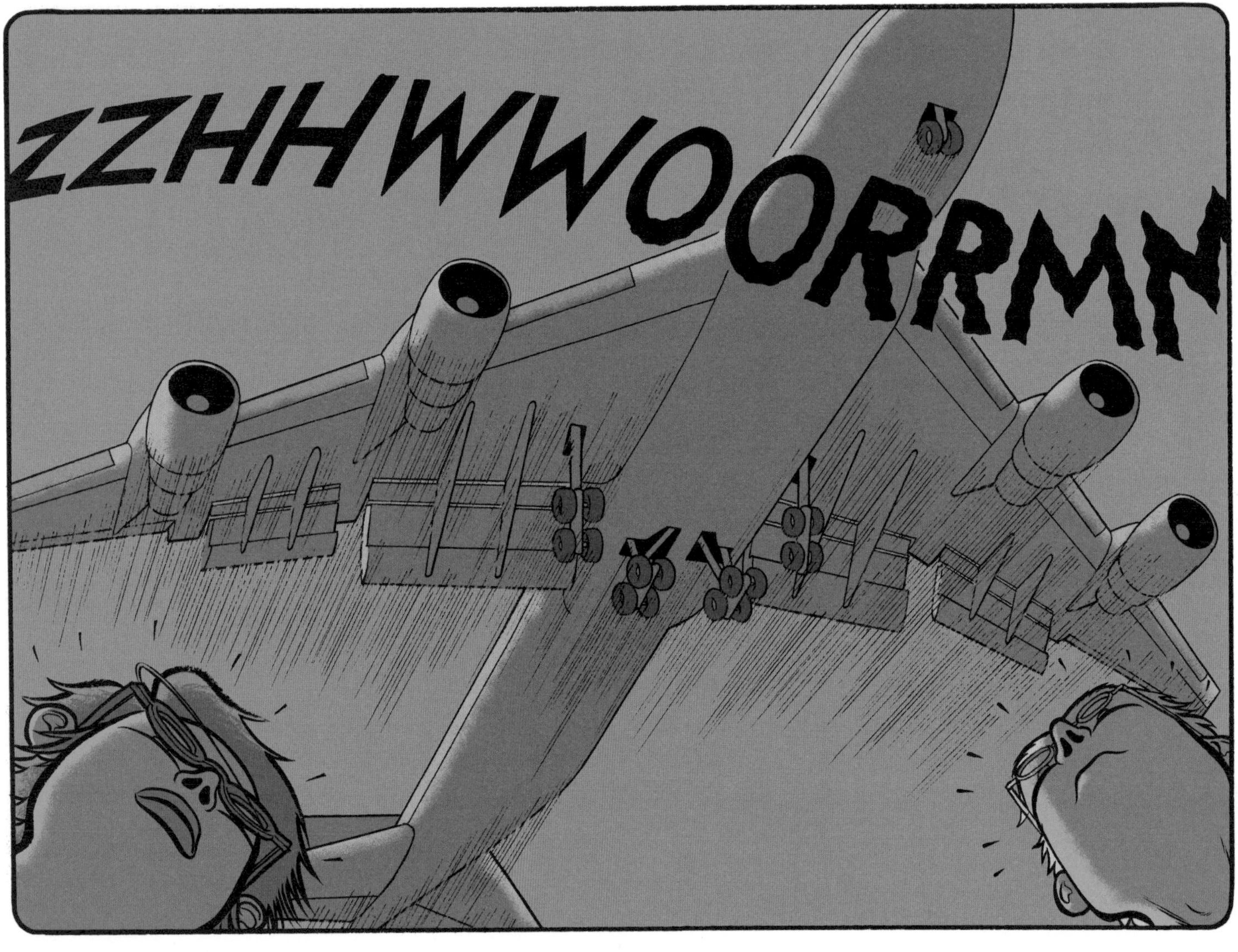
ZZHHWWOORRMN

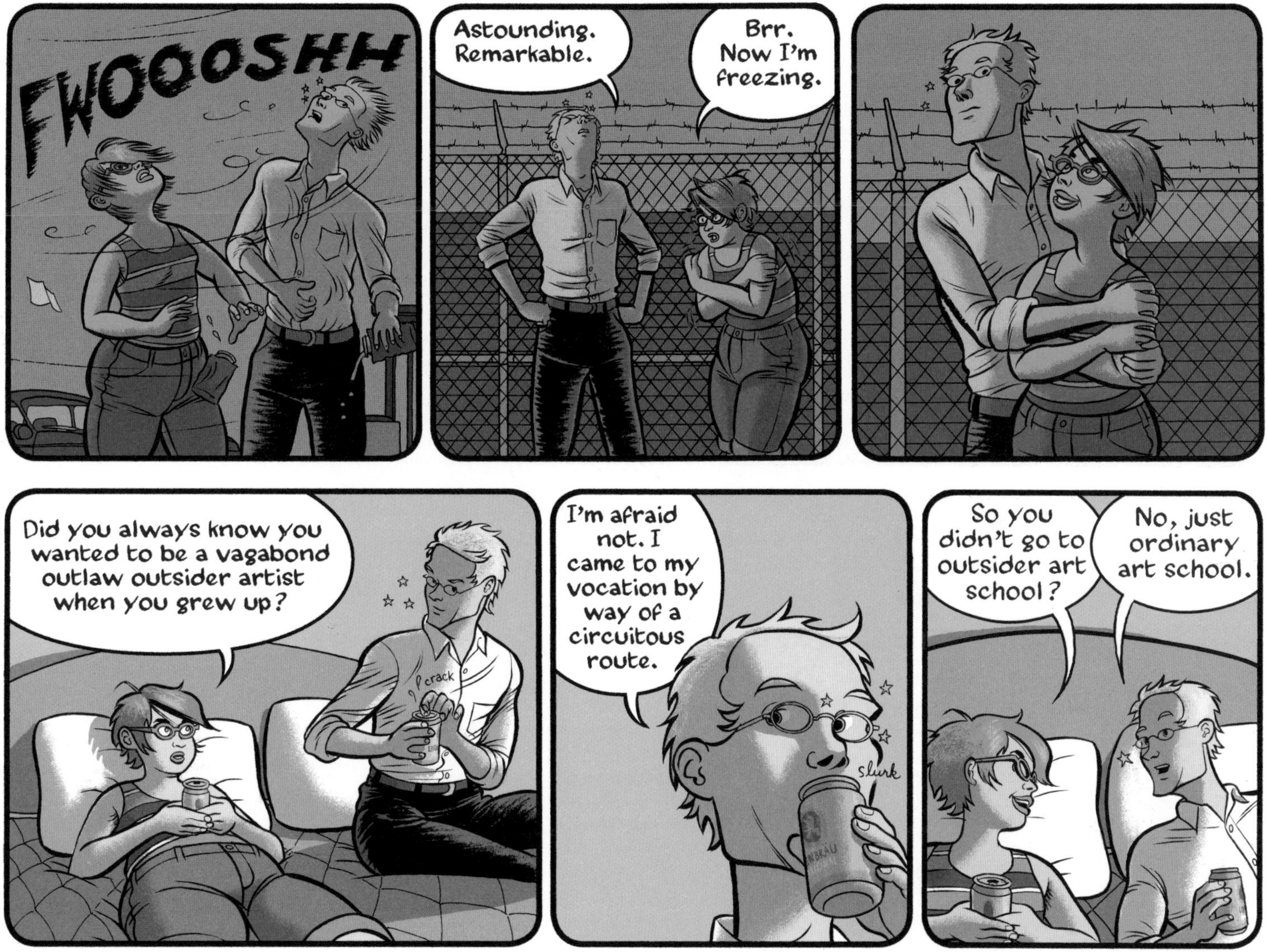
FWOOOSHH
Astounding. Remarkable.
Brr. Now I'm freezing.
Did you always know you wanted to be a vagabond outlaw outsider artist when you grew up?
crack
I'm afraid not. I came to my vocation by way of a circuitous route.
slurk
So you didn't go to outsider art school?
No, just ordinary art school.

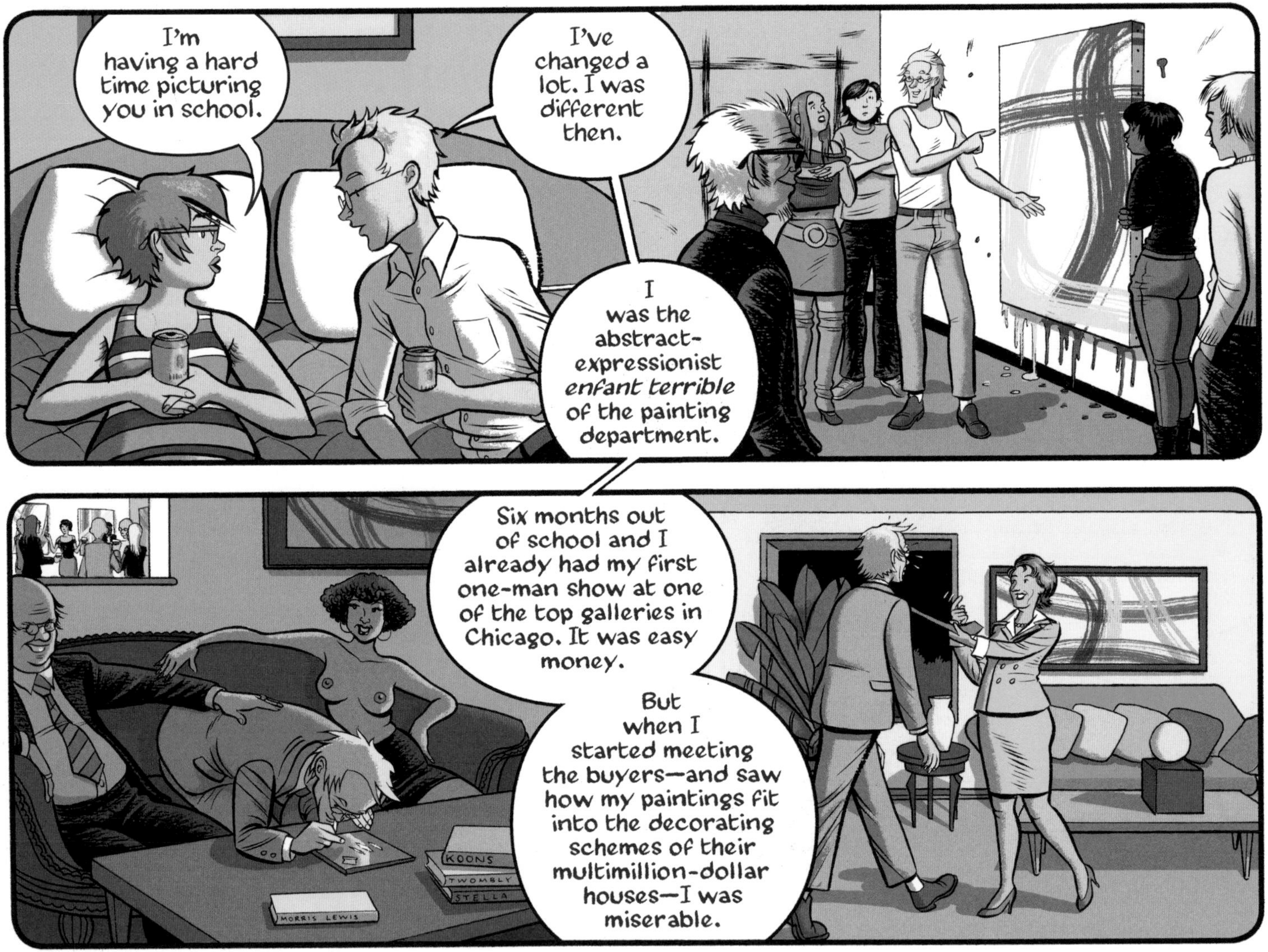
I'm having a hard time picturing you in school.
I've changed a lot. I was different then.
I was the abstract-expressionist *enfant terrible* of the painting department.
Six months out of school and I already had my first one-man show at one of the top galleries in Chicago. It was easy money.
But when I started meeting the buyers—and saw how my paintings fit into the decorating schemes of their multimillion-dollar houses—I was miserable.
KOONS
TWOMBLY
STELLA
MORRIS LEWIS

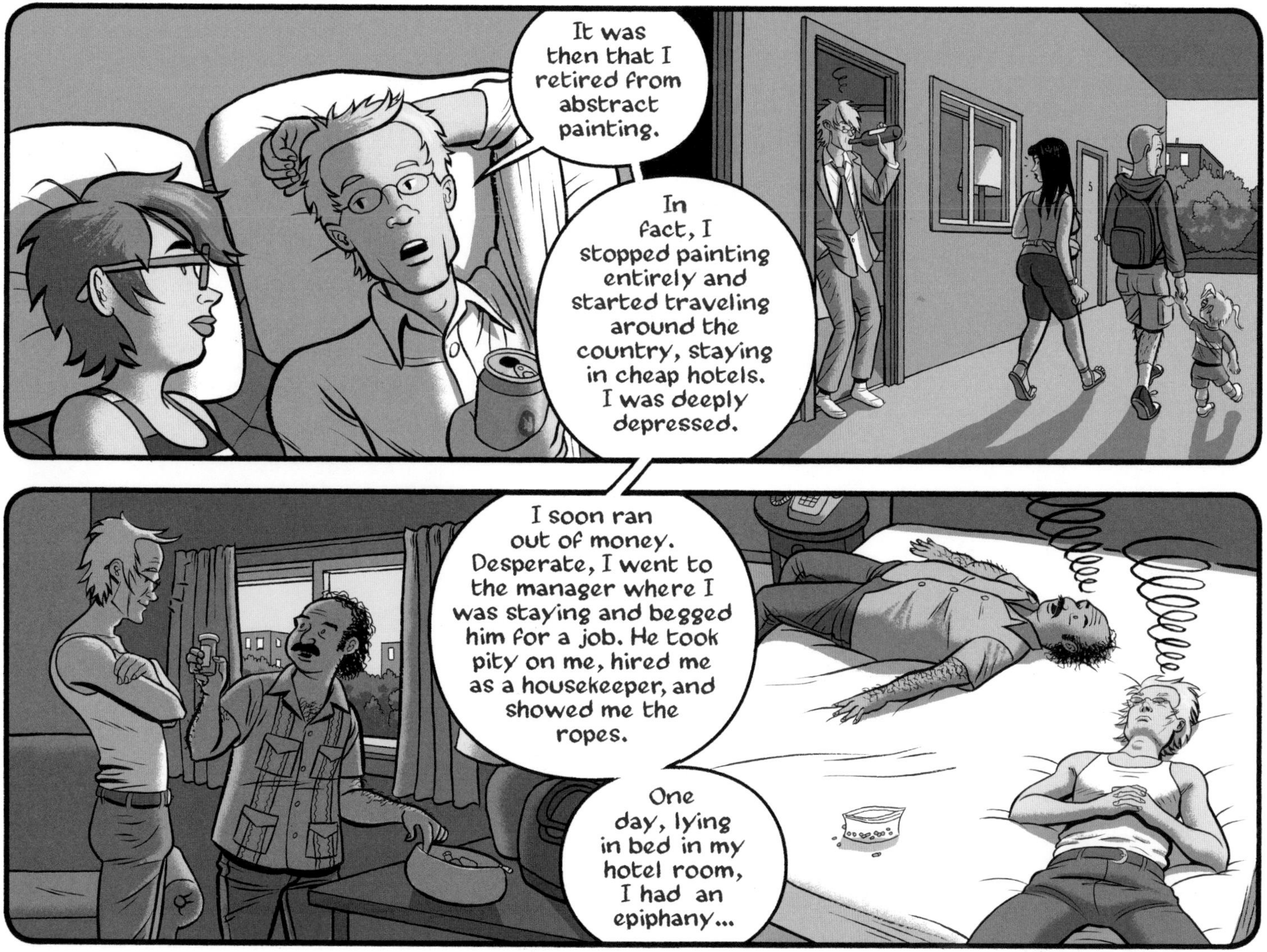

It was then that I retired from abstract painting.
In fact, I stopped painting entirely and started traveling around the country, staying in cheap hotels. I was deeply depressed.
I soon ran out of money. Desperate, I went to the manager where I was staying and begged him for a job. He took pity on me, hired me as a housekeeper, and showed me the ropes.
One day, lying in bed in my hotel room, I had an epiphany...

I realized how many eyes see the pathetic, tacky artwork that hangs in hotel rooms.

And I realized that I hadn't learned a single thing in art school.

I immediately started painting again, and haven't stopped since.

So you had your moment in the spotlight, and you were like, "Forget it."

Indeed. I could not tolerate being commodified.

No fame? No fortune? No recognition?

No thank you.

nudge

I sure do admire your antimaterialism.

It's very... attractive.

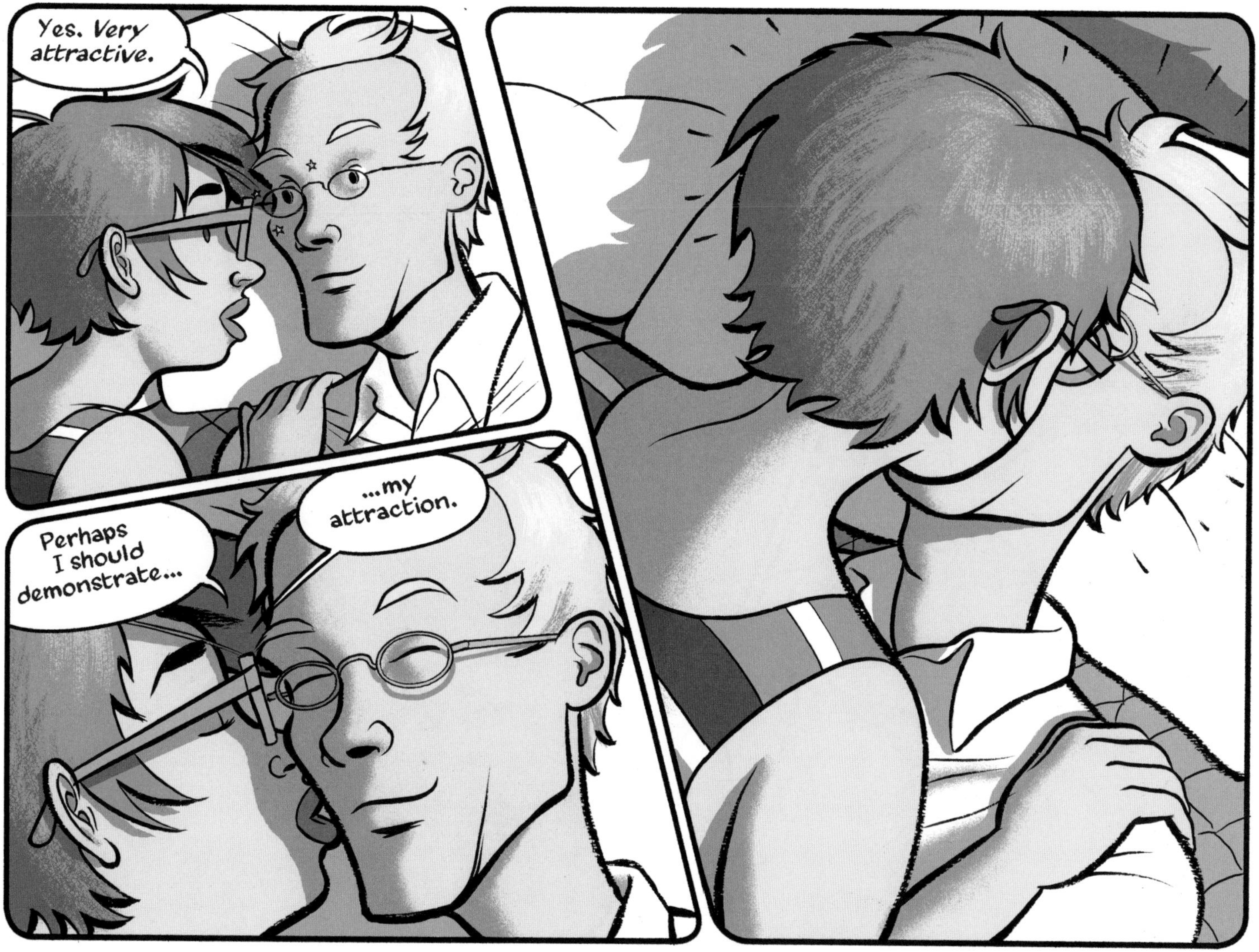
Yes. Very attractive.
Perhaps I should demonstrate...
...my attraction.

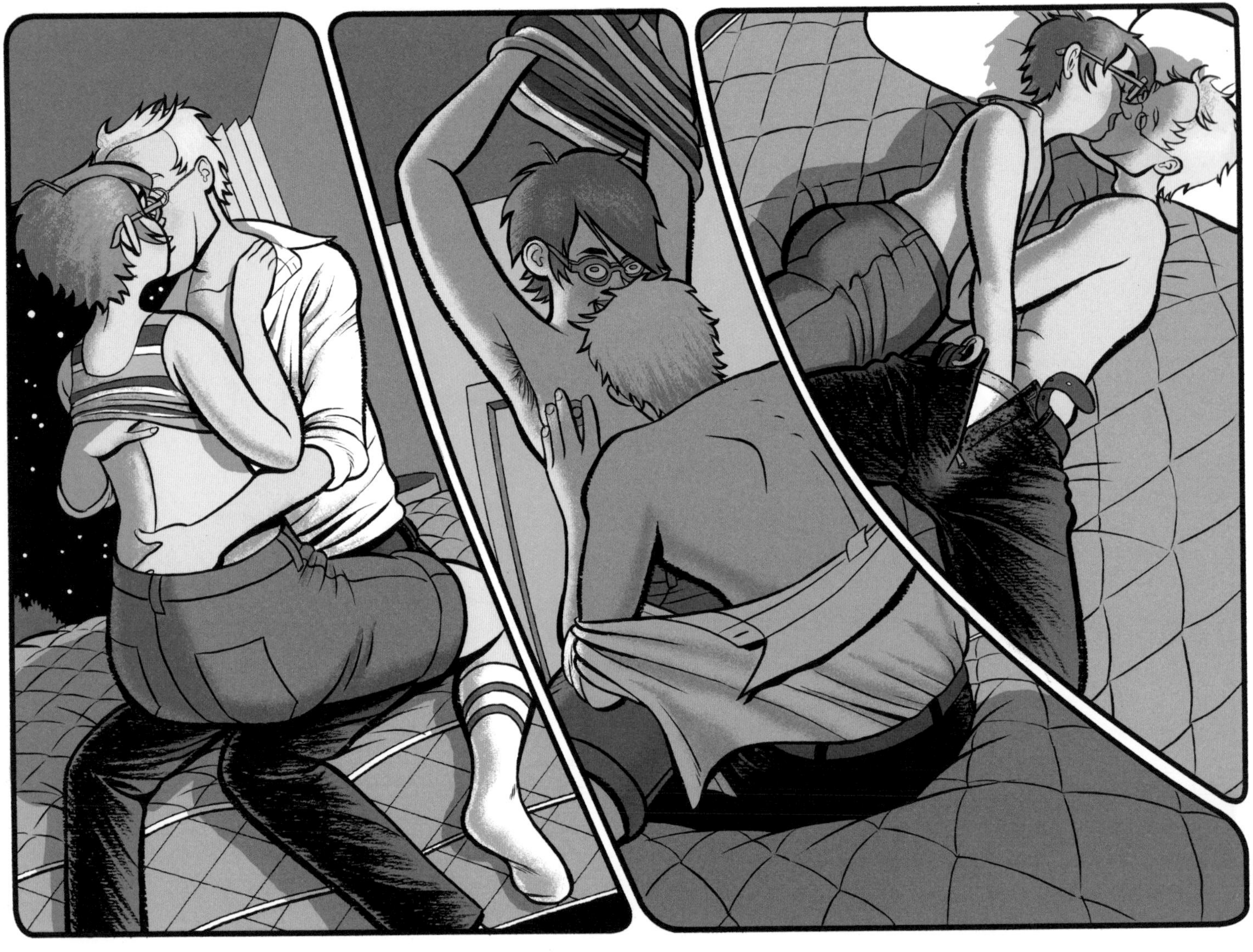

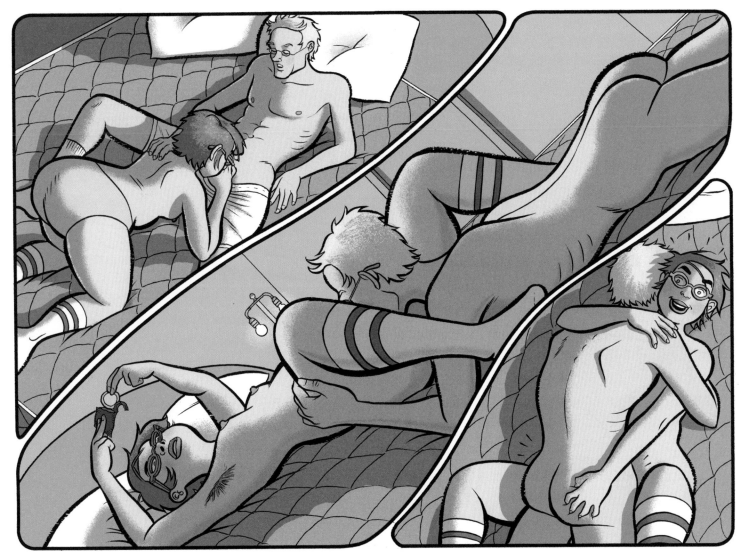

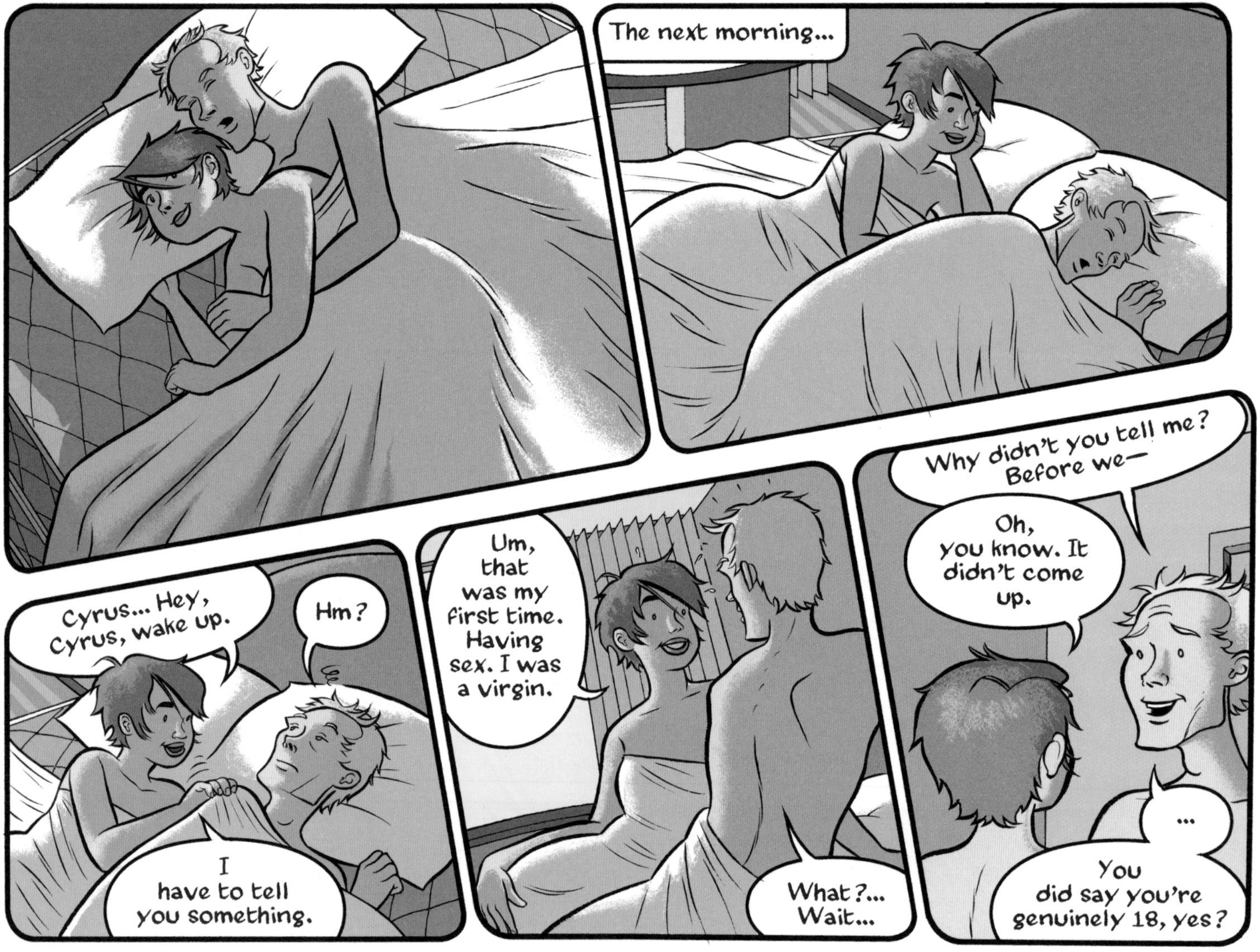
The next morning...
Cyrus... Hey, Cyrus, wake up.
Hm?
I have to tell you something.
Um, that was my first time. Having sex. I was a virgin.
What?... Wait...
Why didn't you tell me? Before we—
Oh, you know. It didn't come up.
...
You did say you're genuinely 18, yes?

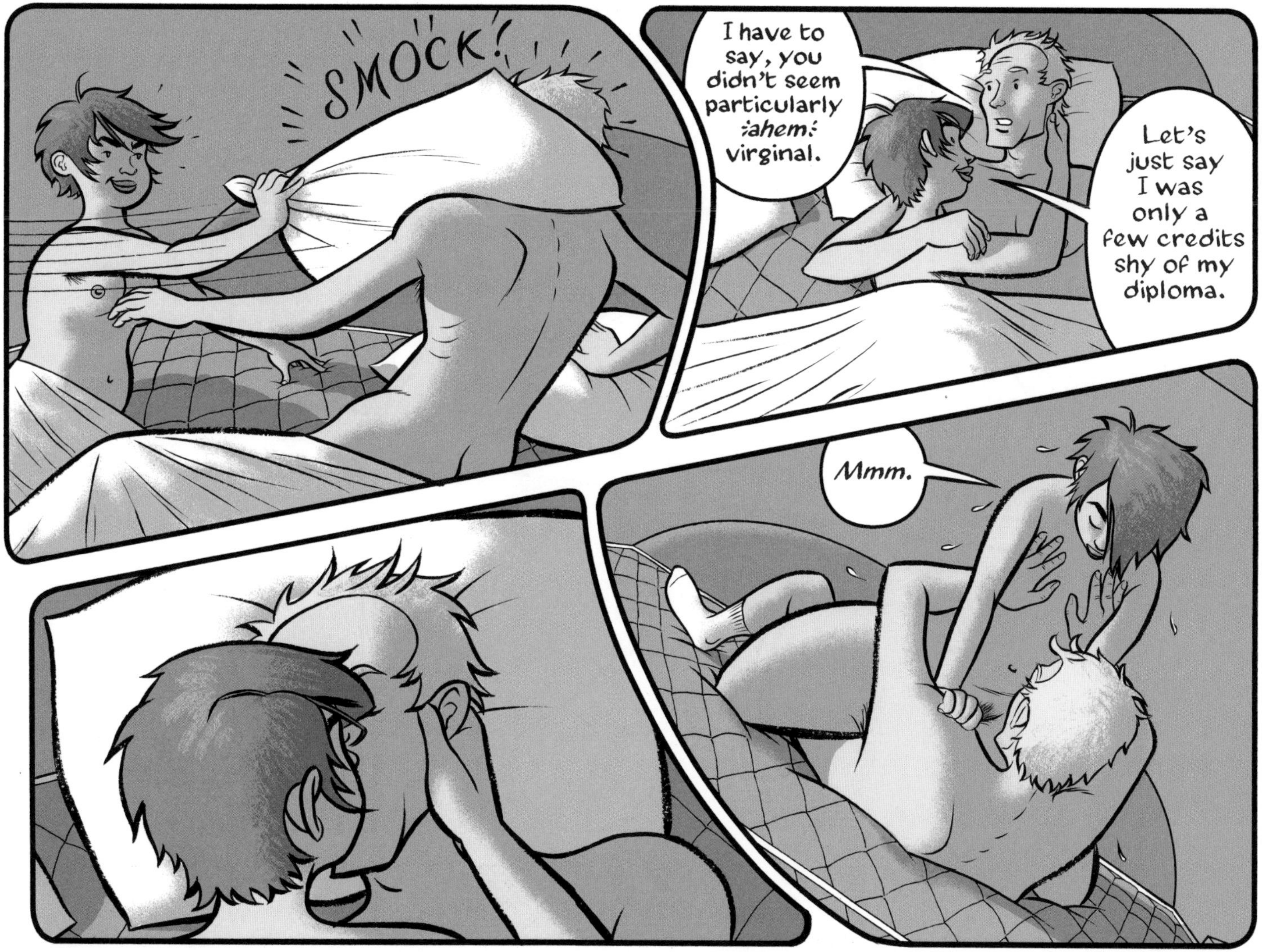
SMOCK!
I have to say, you didn't seem particularly :ahem: virginal.
Let's just say I was only a few credits shy of my diploma.
Mmm.

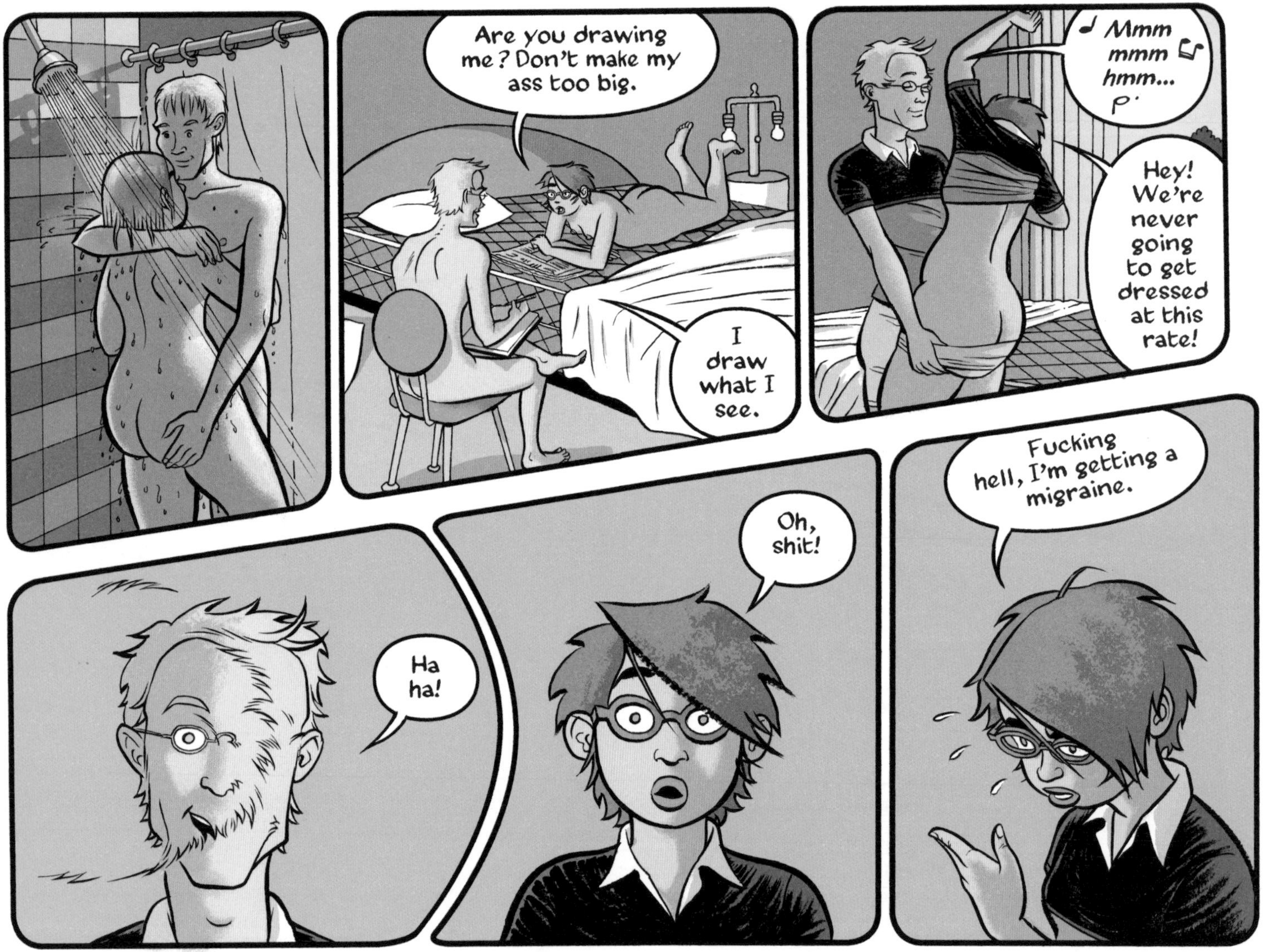

Are you drawing me? Don't make my ass too big.
I draw what I see.
Mmm mmm hmm...
Hey! We're never going to get dressed at this rate!
Ha ha!
Oh, shit!
Fucking hell, I'm getting a migraine.

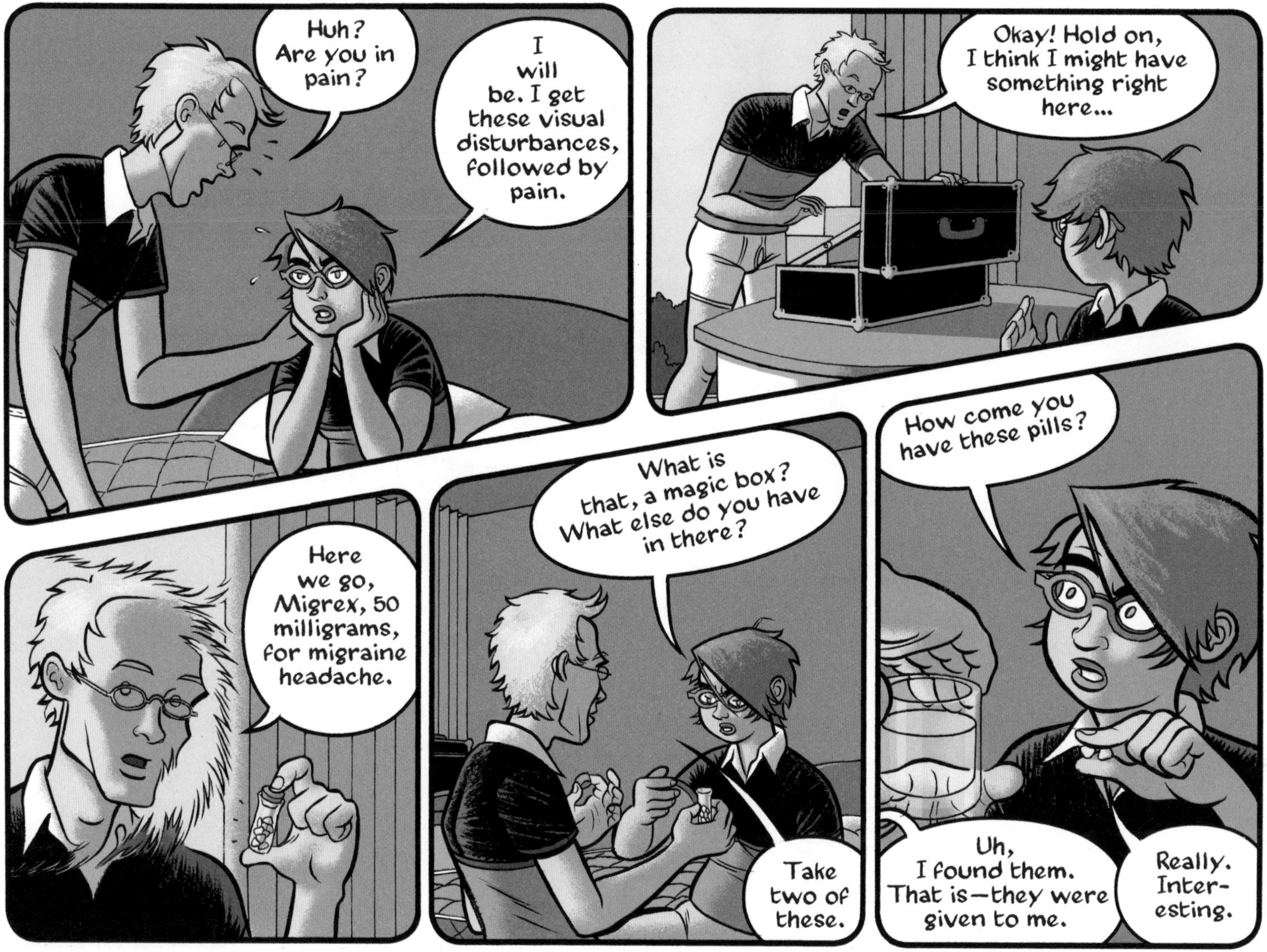

Huh? Are you in pain?
I will be. I get these visual disturbances, followed by pain.
Okay! Hold on, I think I might have something right here...
Here we go, Migrex, 50 milligrams, for migraine headache.
What is that, a magic box? What else do you have in there?
Take two of these.
How come you have these pills?
Uh, I found them. That is—they were given to me.
Really. Inter-esting.

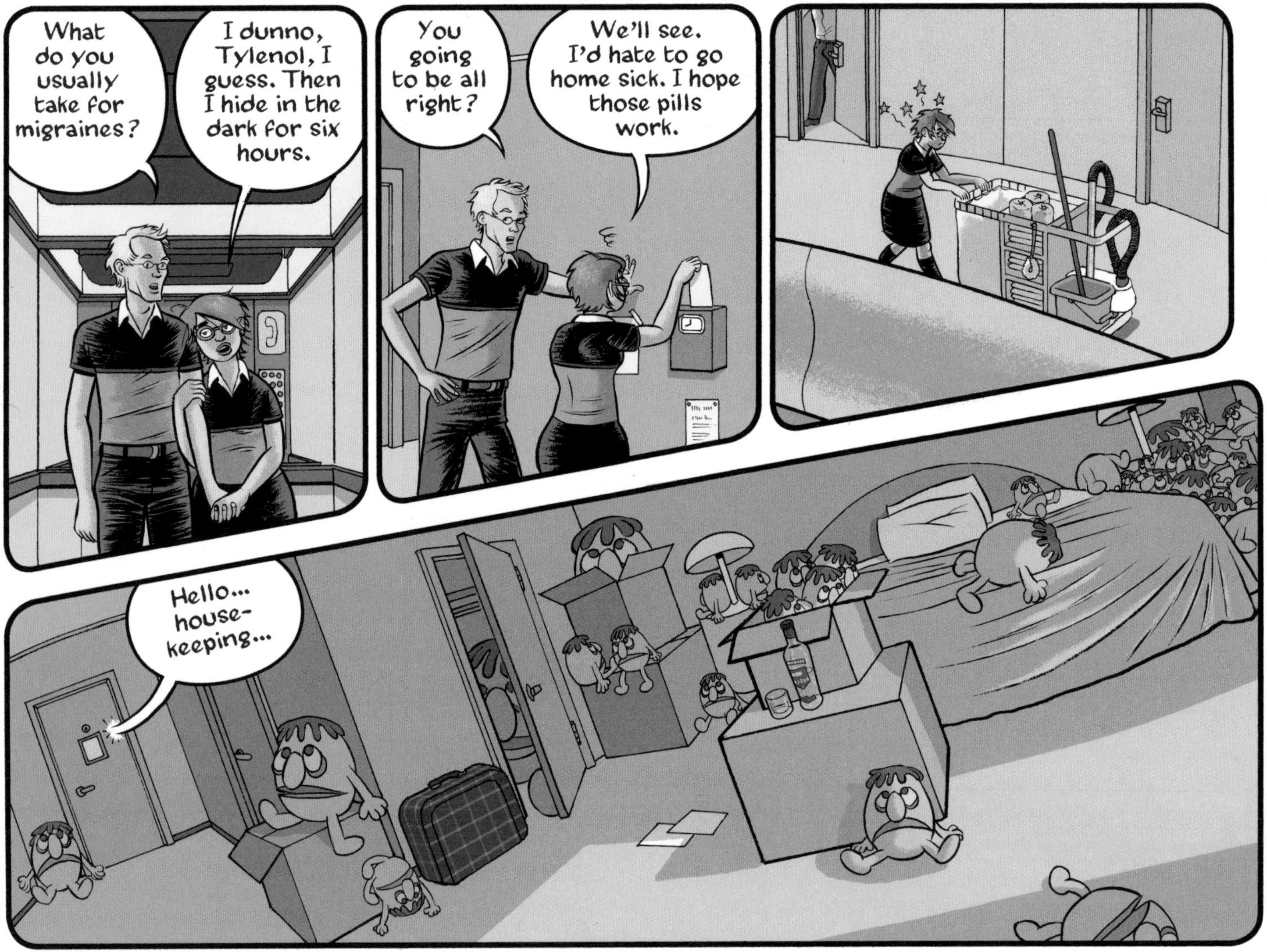
What do you usually take for migraines?
I dunno, Tylenol, I guess. Then I hide in the dark for six hours.
You going to be all right?
We'll see. I'd hate to go home sick. I hope those pills work.
Hello... house-keeping...

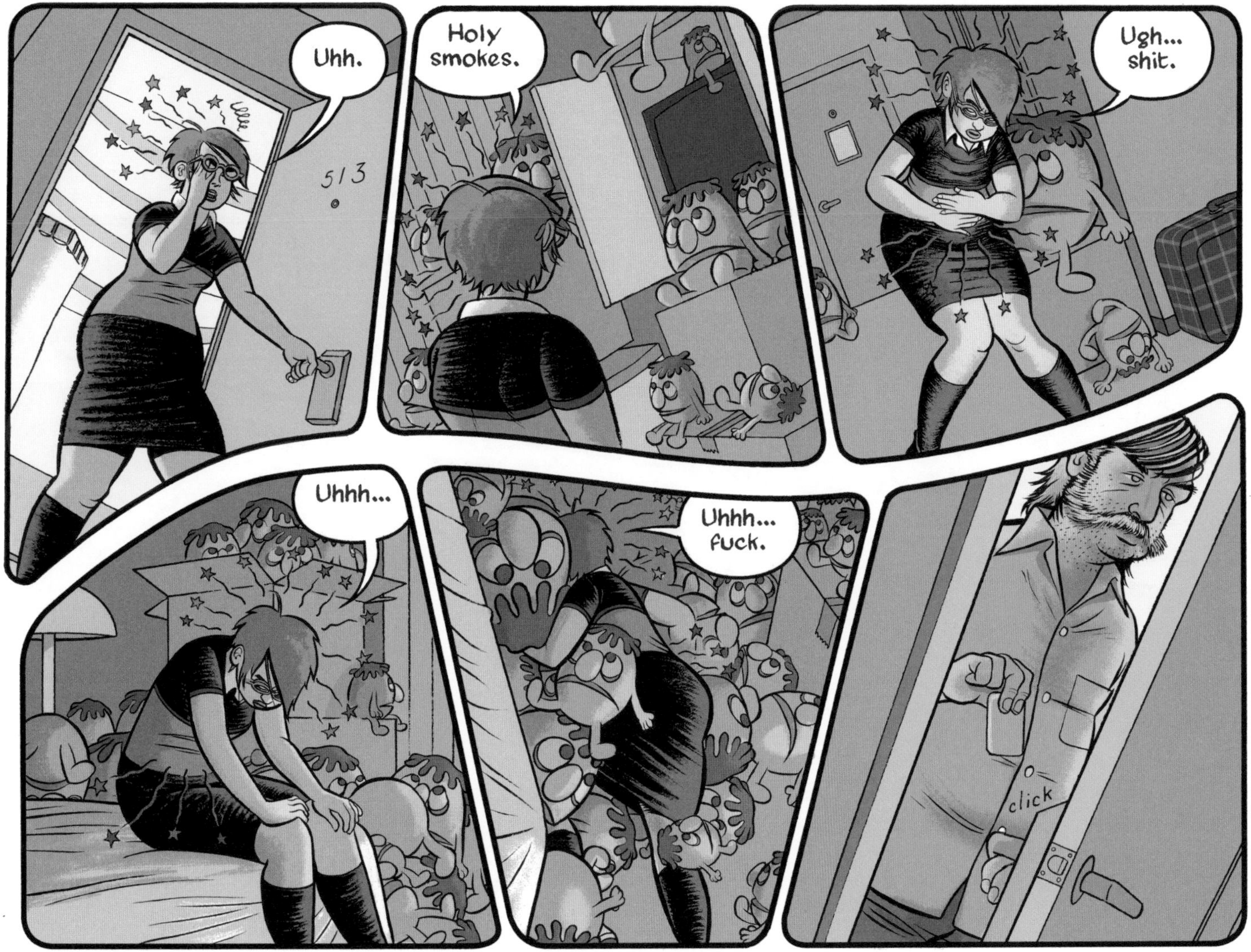
Uhh.
513
Holy smokes.
Ugh... shit.
Uhhh...
Uhhh... fuck.
click

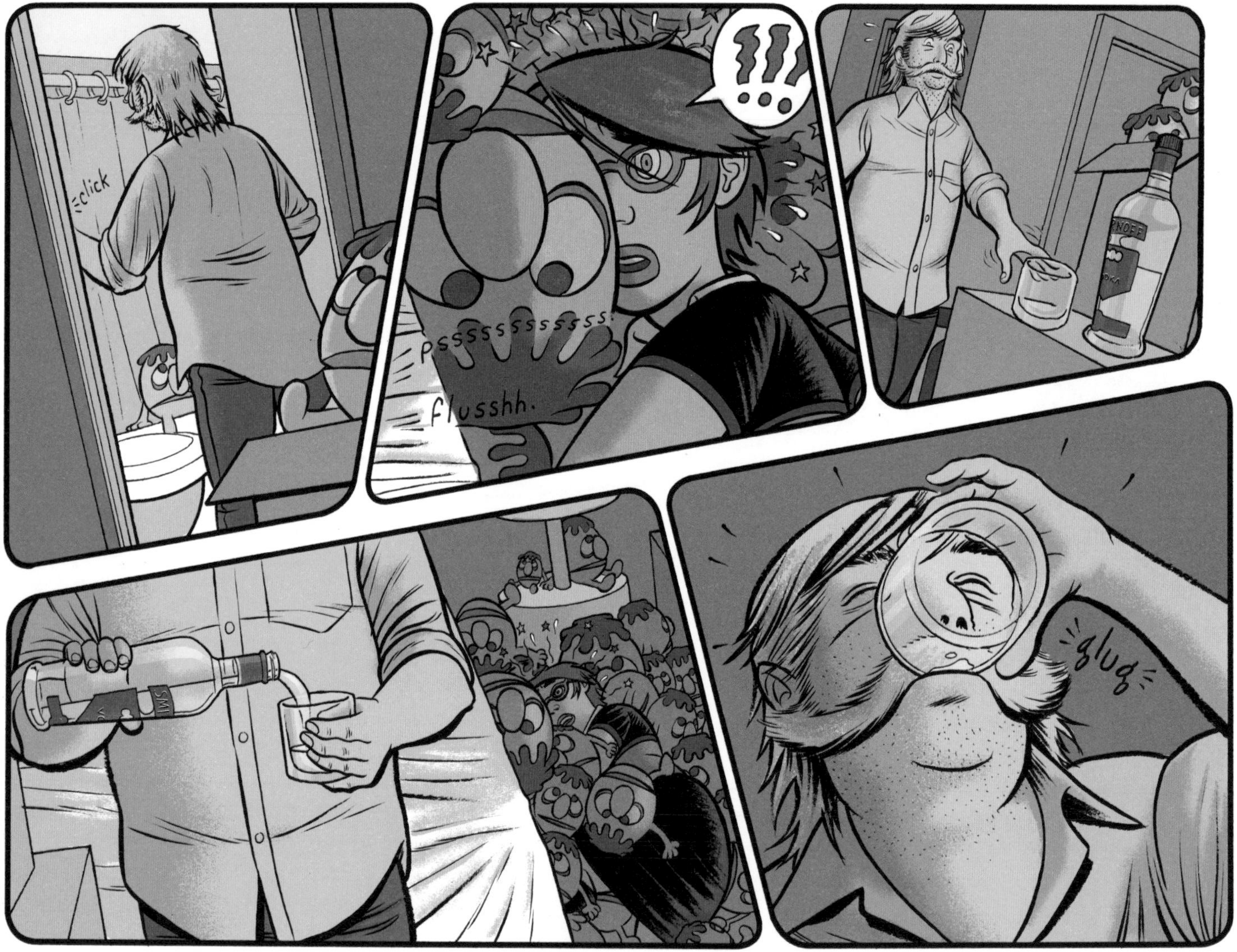
click
!!!
psssssssssssss
flusshh.
glug

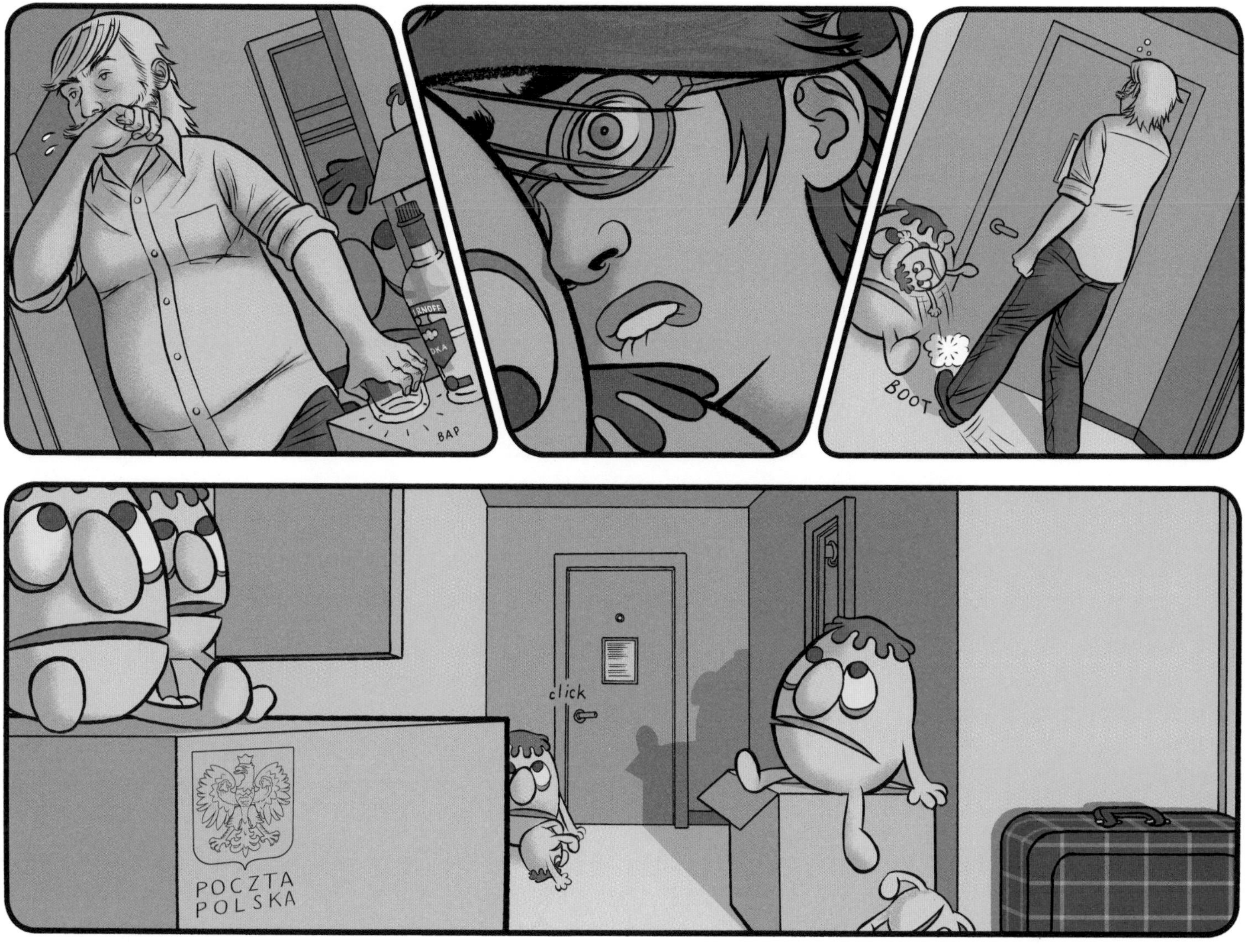
BAP
BOOT
click
POCZTA
POLSKA

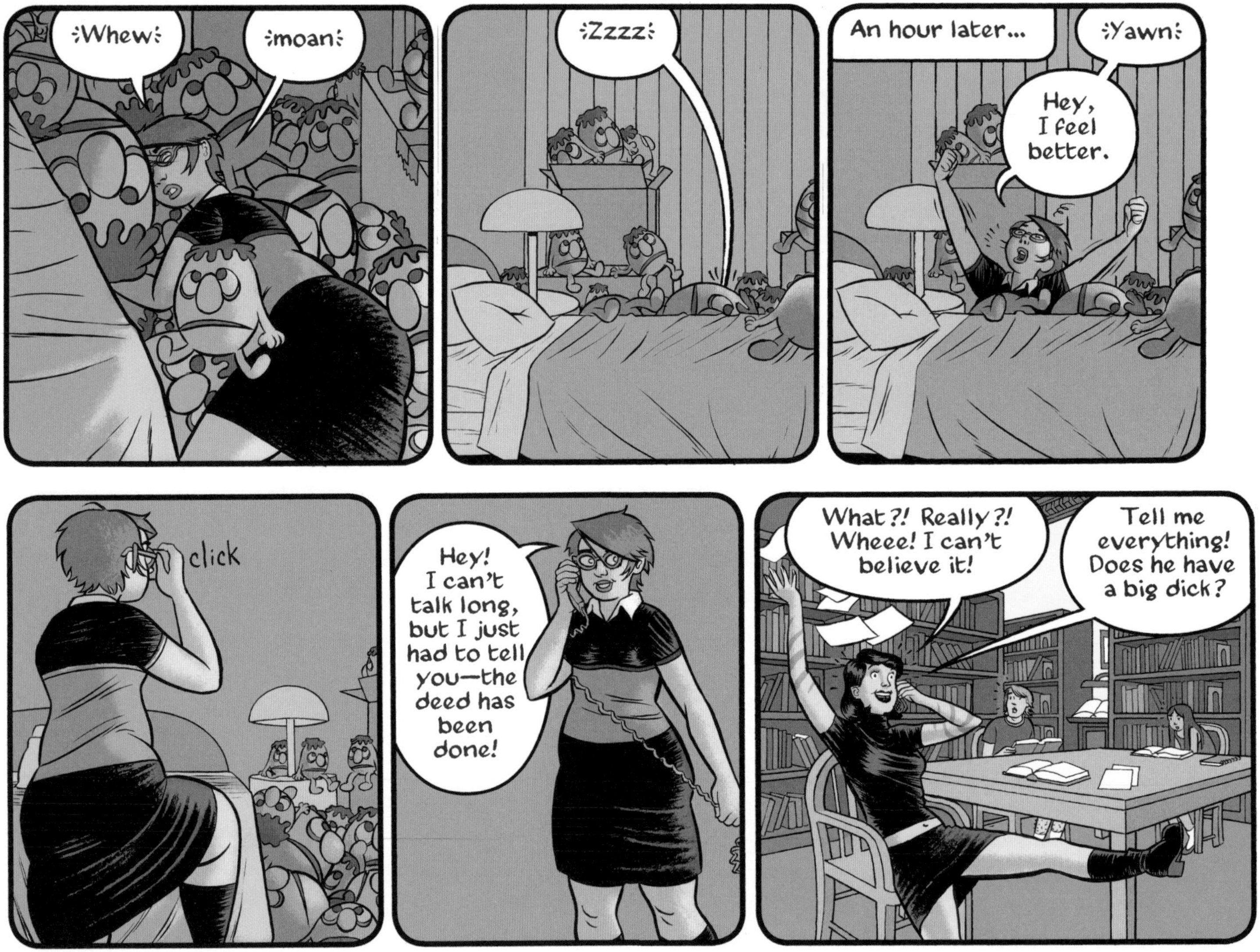
Whew
moan
Zzzz
An hour later...
Yawn
Hey, I feel better.
click
Hey! I can't talk long, but I just had to tell you—the deed has been done!
What?! Really?! Wheee! I can't believe it!
Tell me everything! Does he have a big dick?

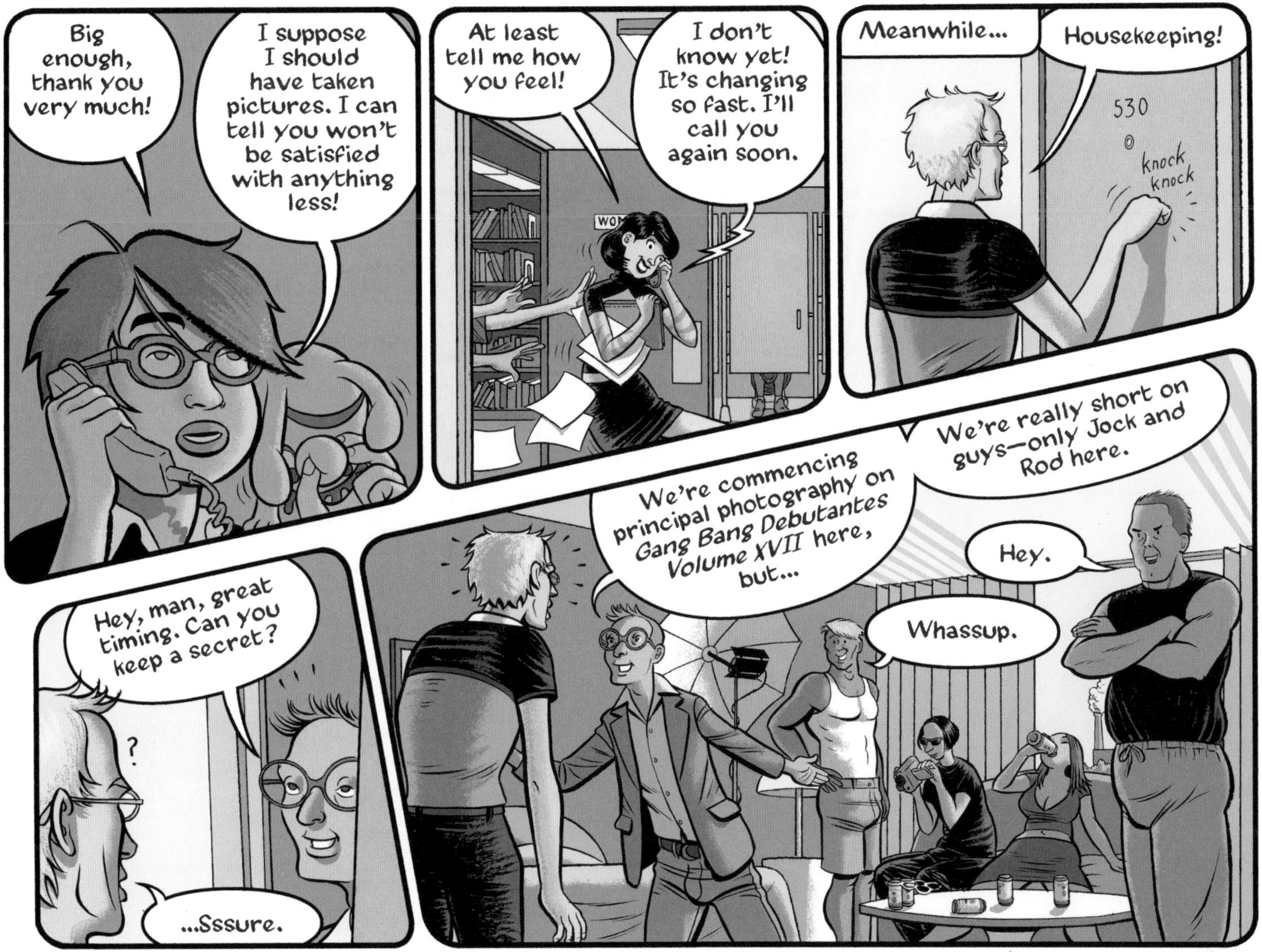
Big enough, thank you very much!
I suppose I should have taken pictures. I can tell you won't be satisfied with anything less!
At least tell me how you feel!
I don't know yet! It's changing so fast. I'll call you again soon.
Meanwhile...
Housekeeping!
530
knock knock
Hey, man, great timing. Can you keep a secret?
?
...Sssure.
We're commencing principal photography on Gang Bang Debutantes Volume XVII here, but...
We're really short on guys—only Jock and Rod here.
Hey.
Whassup.

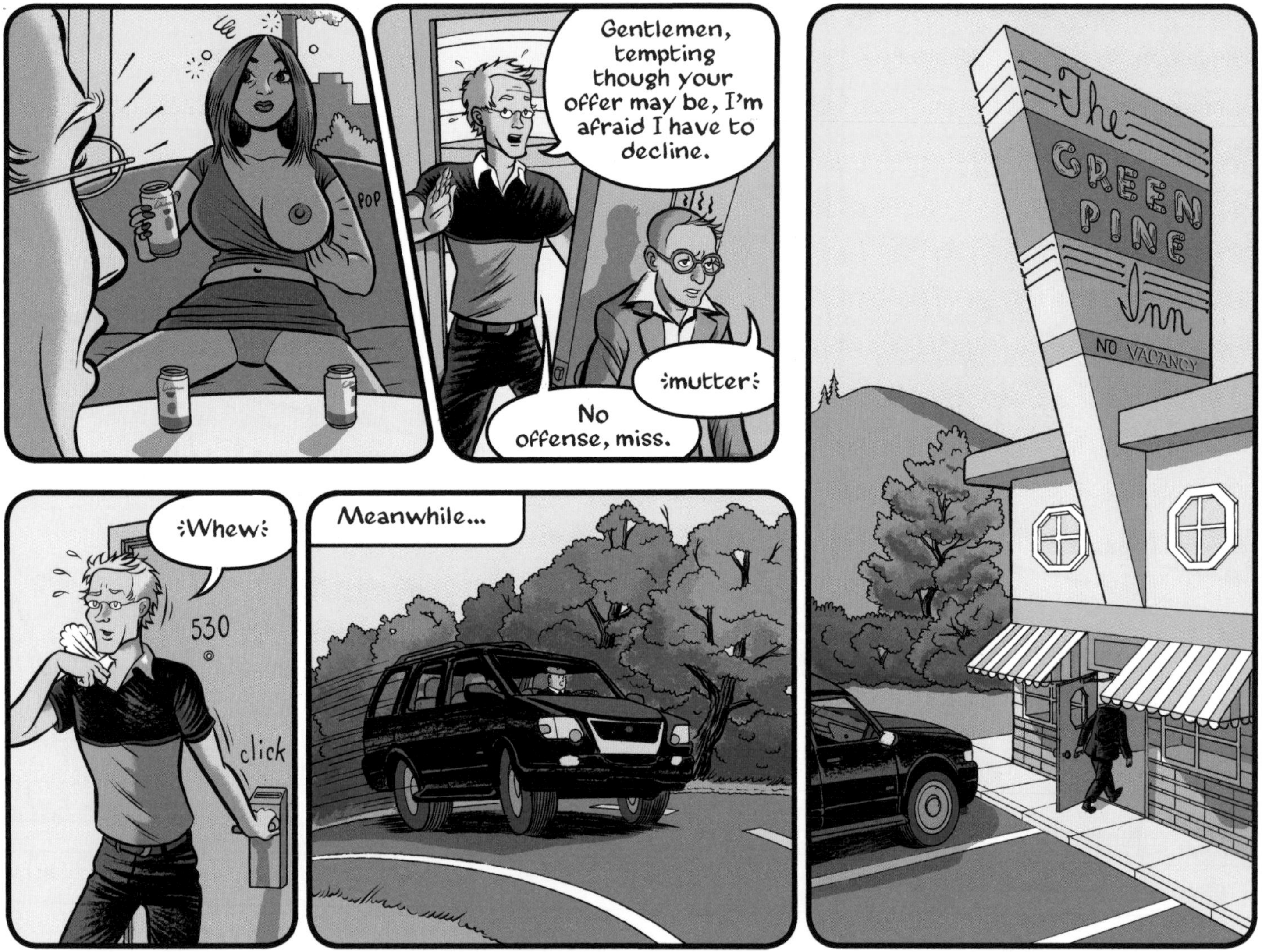
POP
Gentlemen, tempting though your offer may be, I'm afraid I have to decline.
:mutter:
No offense, miss.
The GREEN PINE Inn
NO VACANCY
:Whew:
530
click
Meanwhile...

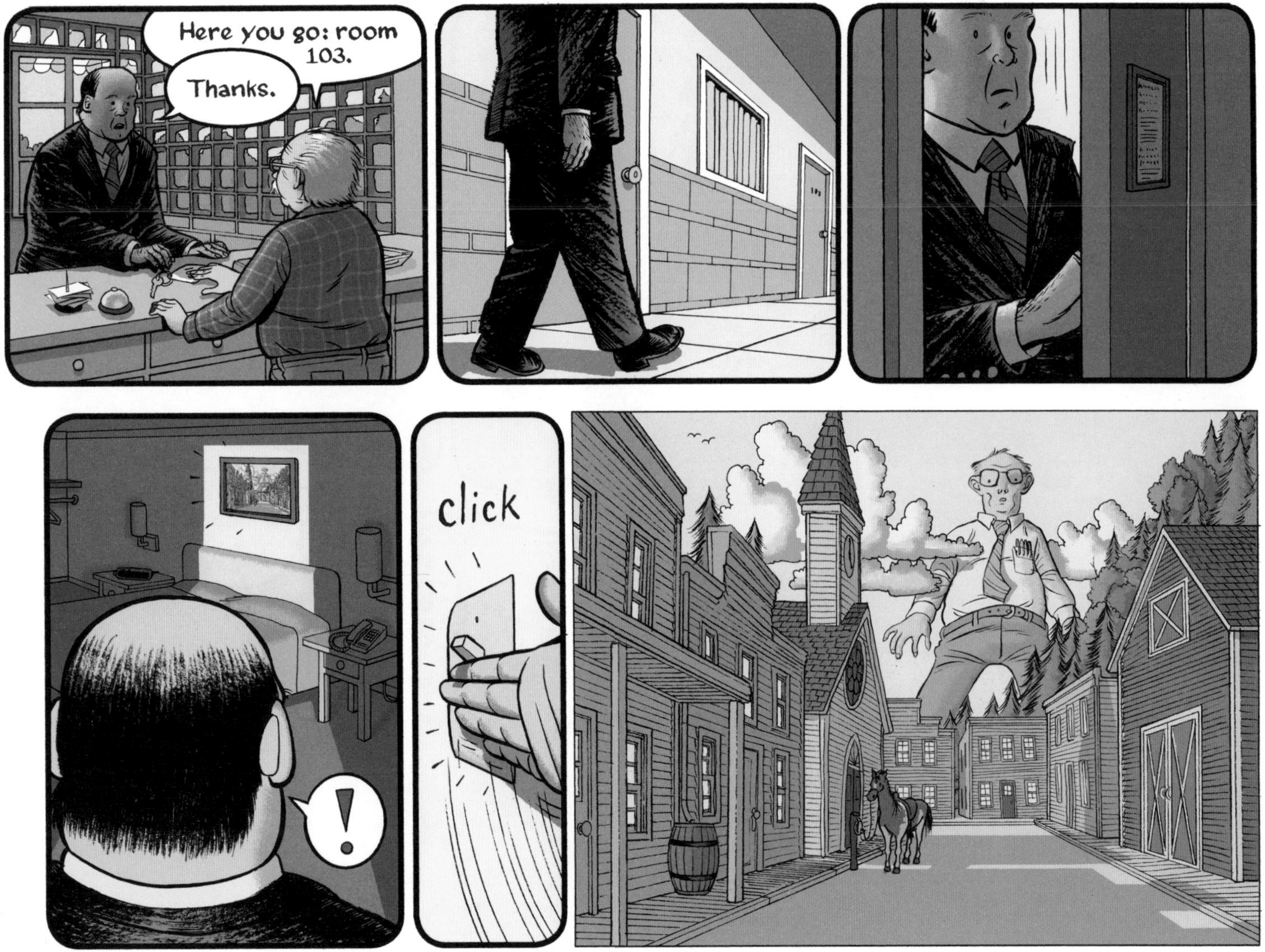

Here you go: room 103.
Thanks.
!
click

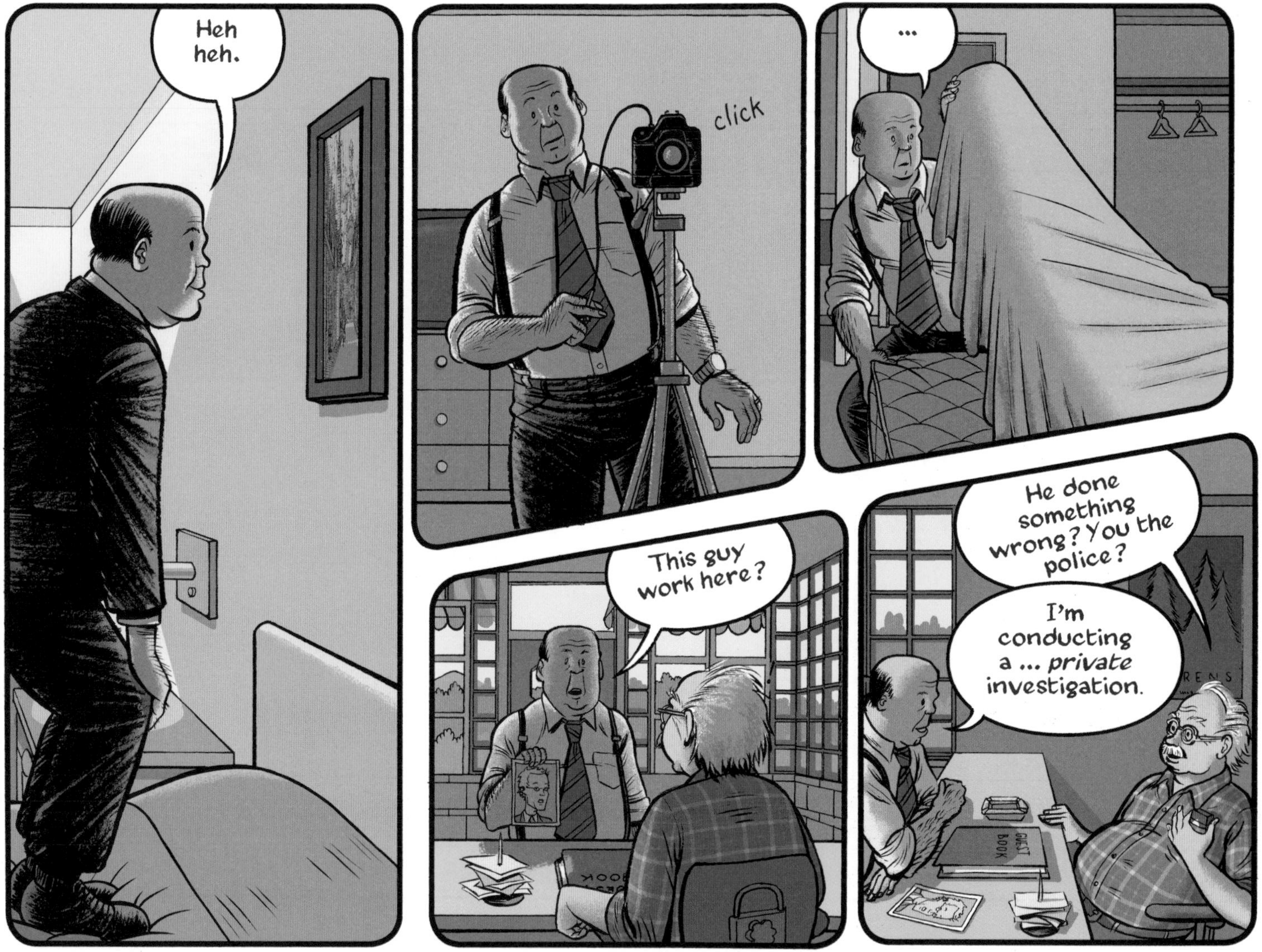
Heh heh.
click
...
This guy work here?
He done something wrong? You the police?
I'm conducting a ... *private* investigation.
GUEST BOOK

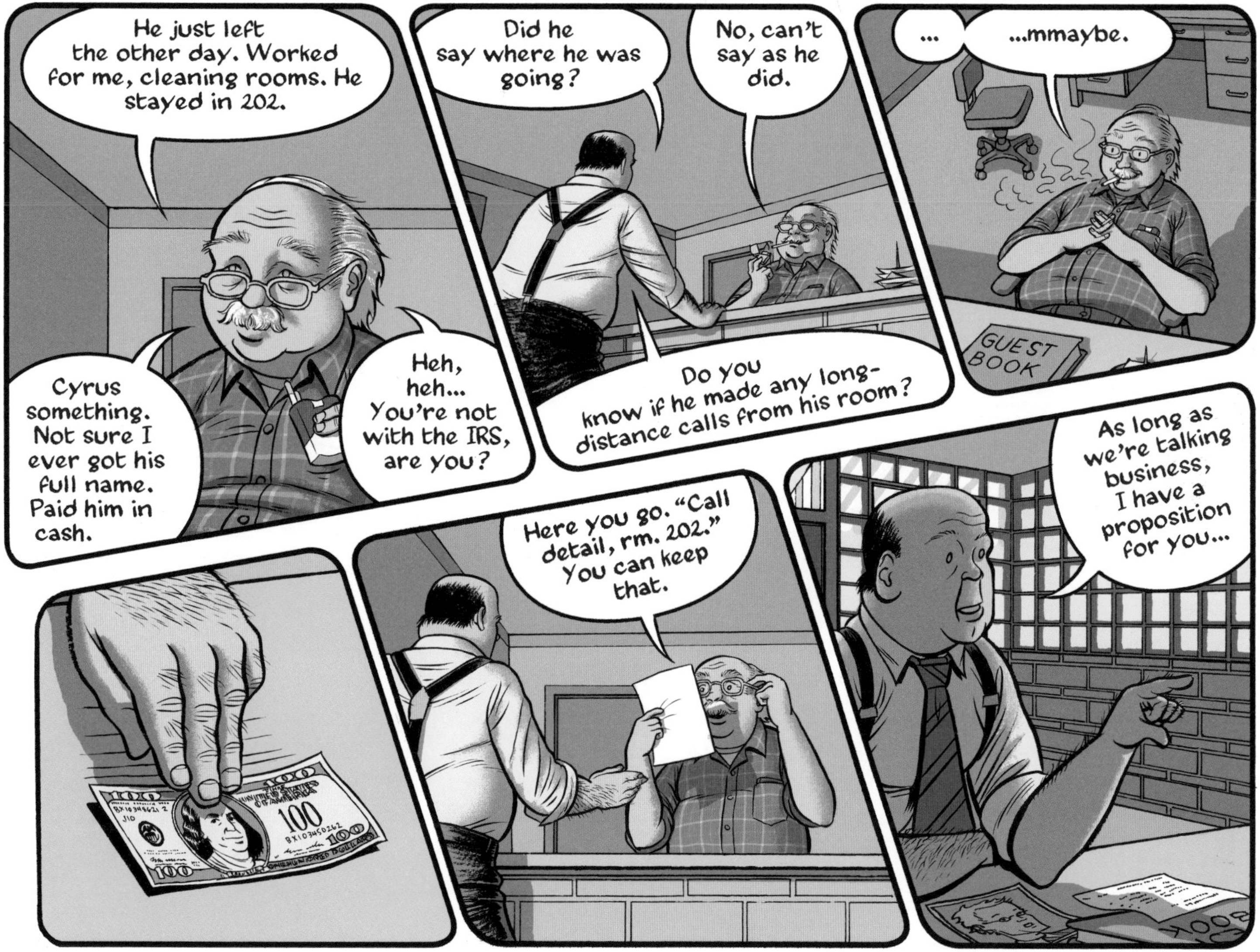
He just left the other day. Worked for me, cleaning rooms. He stayed in 202.
Cyrus something. Not sure I ever got his full name. Paid him in cash.
Heh, heh... You're not with the IRS, are you?
Did he say where he was going?
No, can't say as he did.
Do you know if he made any long-distance calls from his room?
...
...mmaybe.
GUEST BOOK
Here you go. "Call detail, rm. 202." You can keep that.
As long as we're talking business, I have a proposition for you...

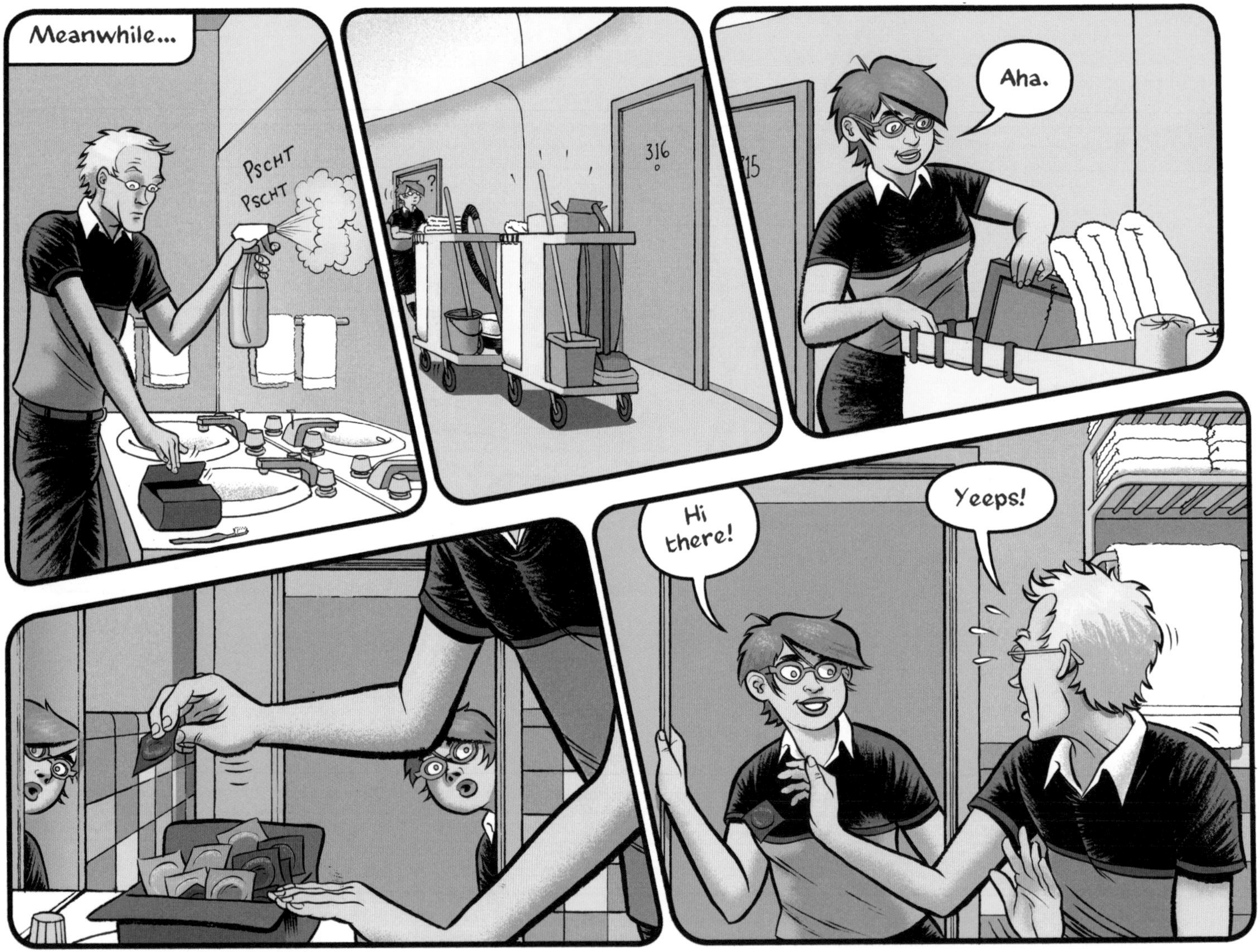
Meanwhile...
PSCHT
PSCHT
316
315
Aha.
Hi there!
Yeeps!

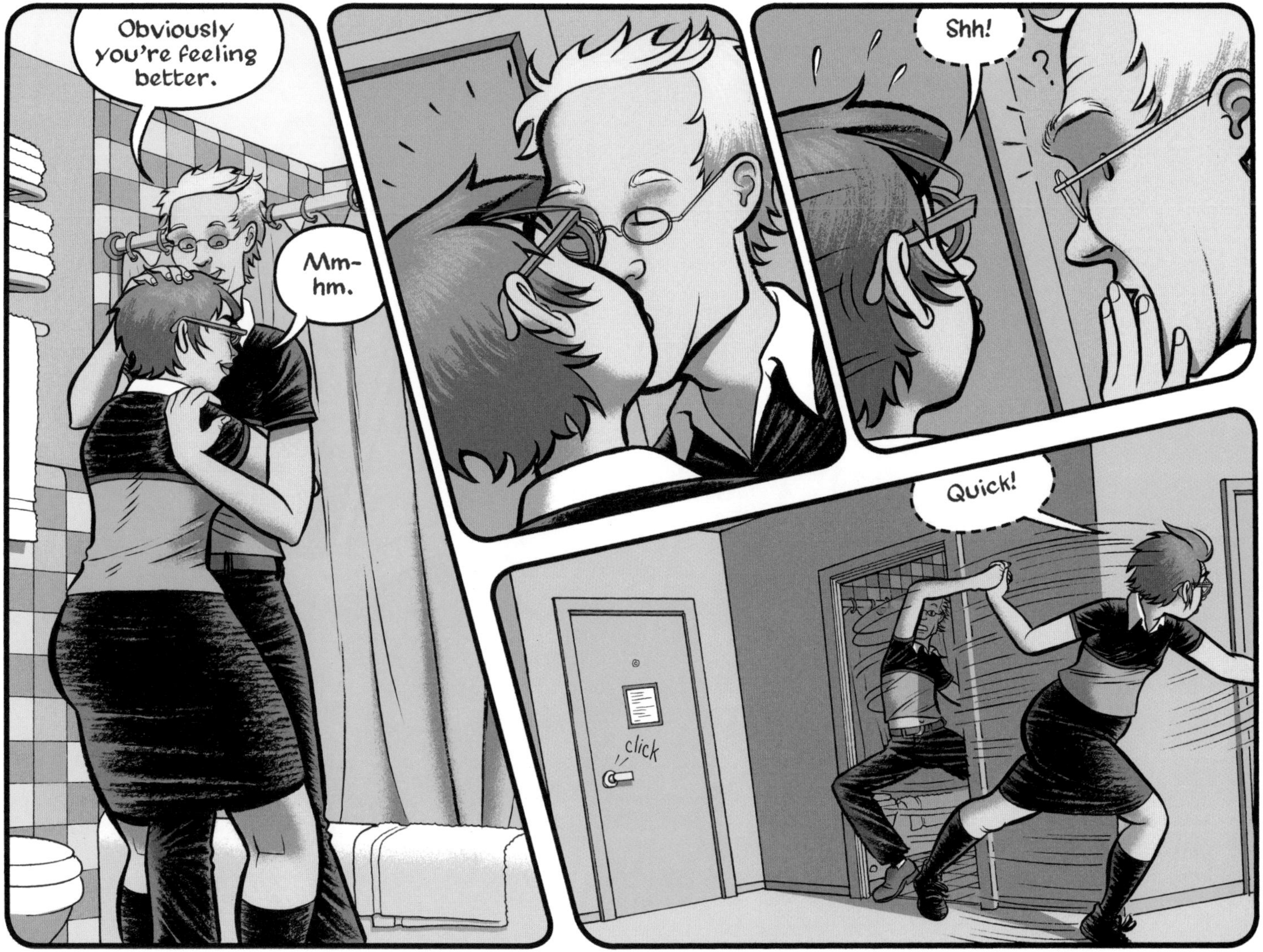
Obviously you're feeling better.
Mm-hm.
Shh!
?
Quick!
click

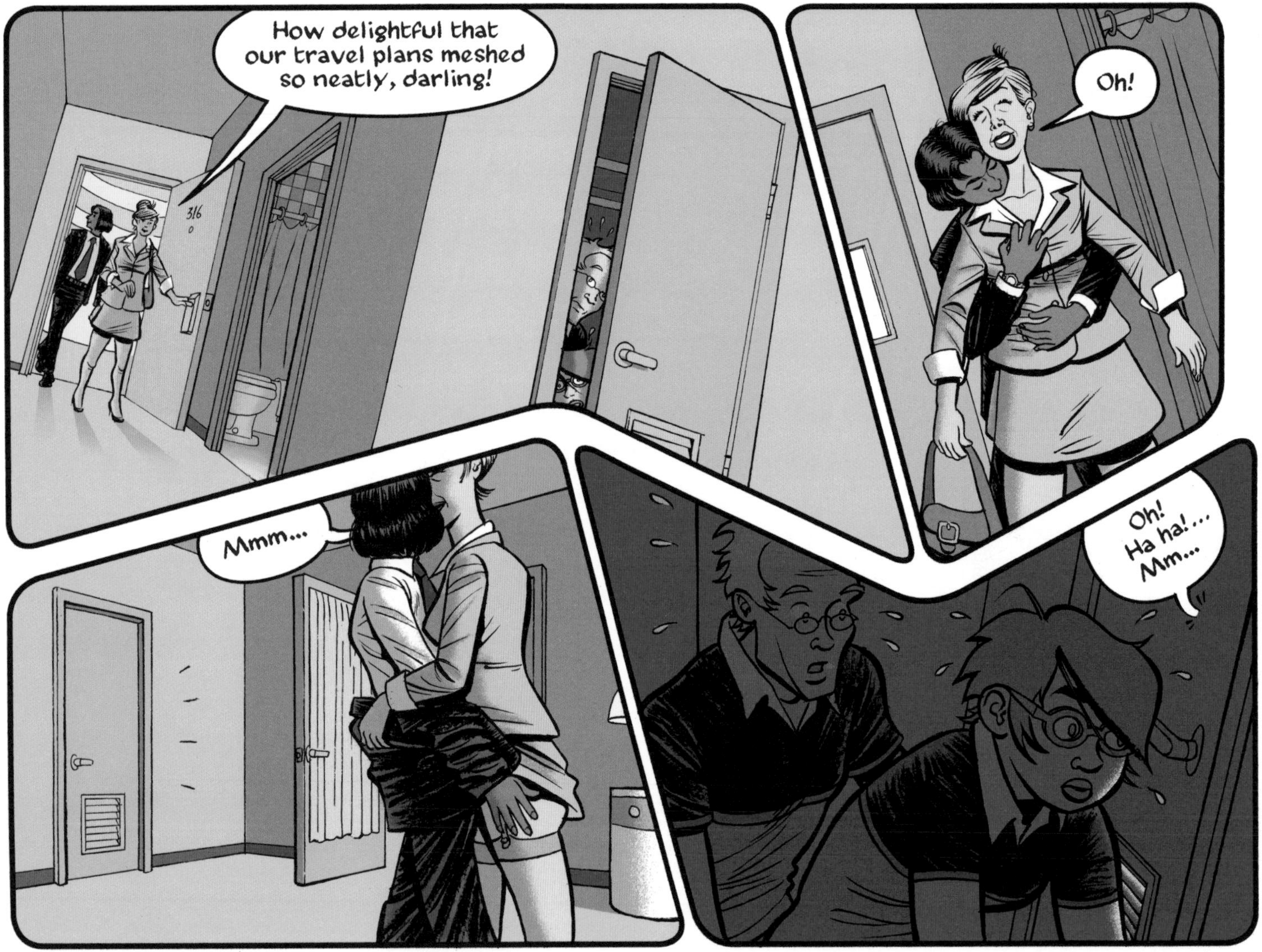
How delightful that our travel plans meshed so neatly, darling!
Oh!
Mmm...
Oh! Ha ha!... Mm...

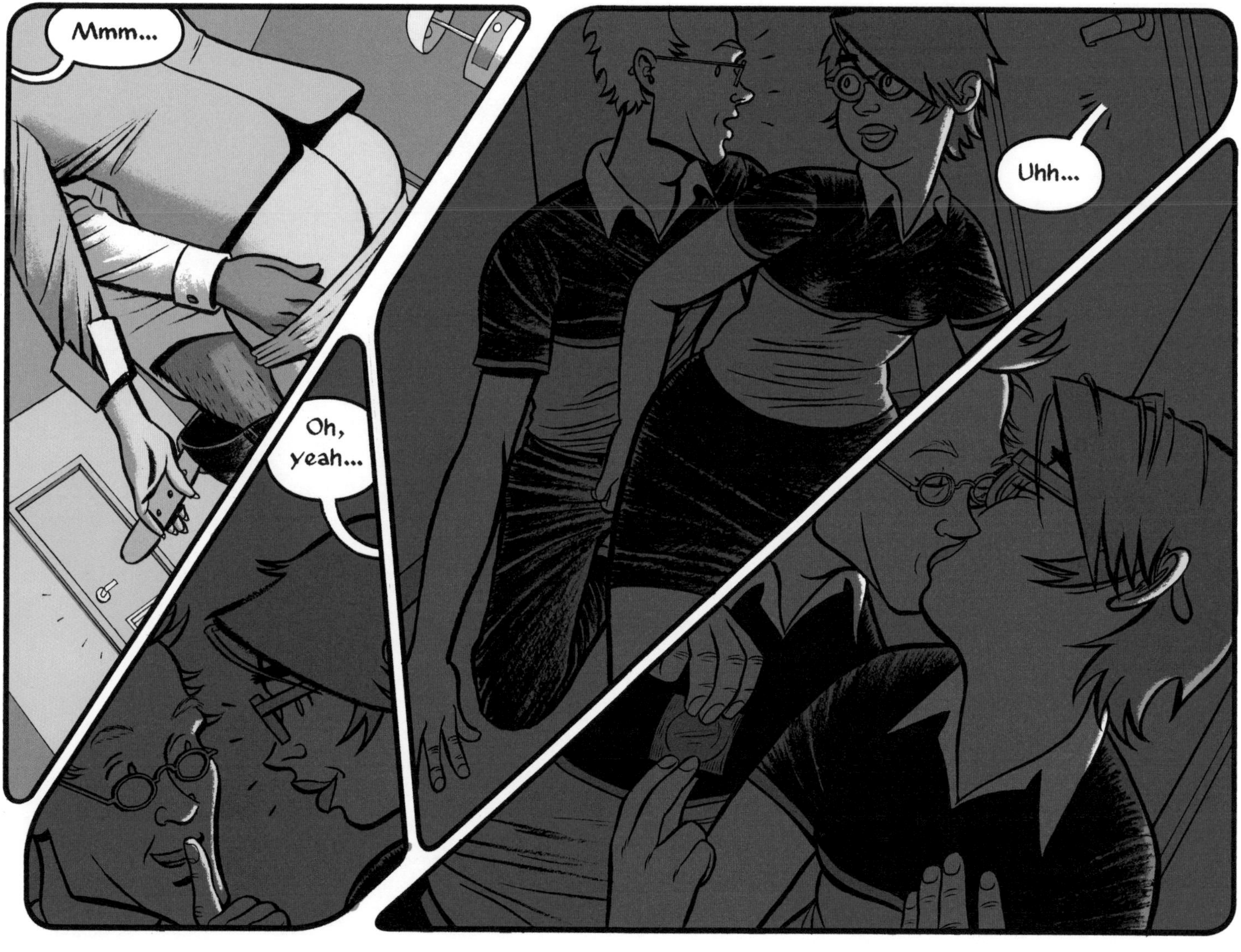
Mmm...
Oh, yeah...
Uhh...

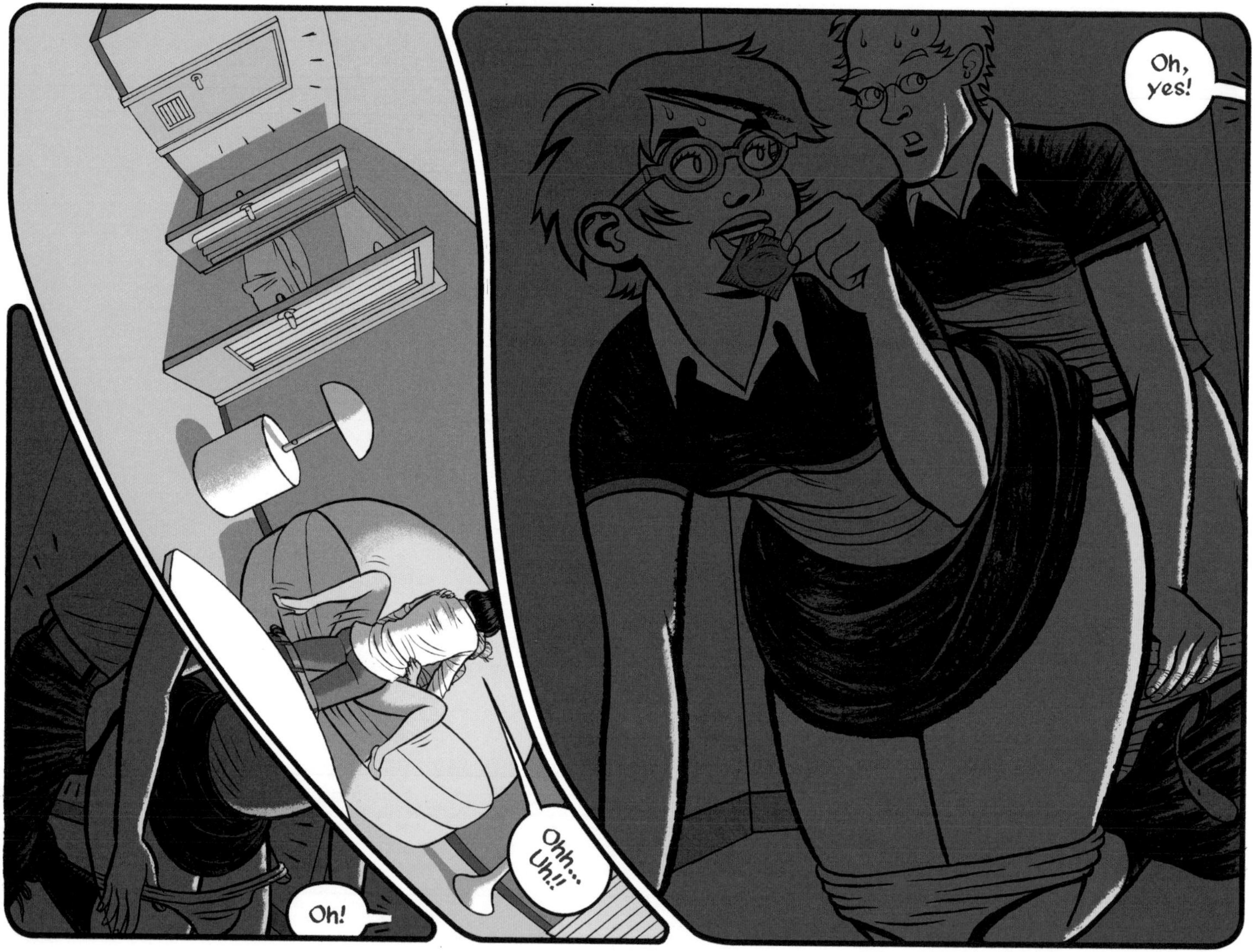
Oh!
Ohh... Uh!!
Oh, yes!

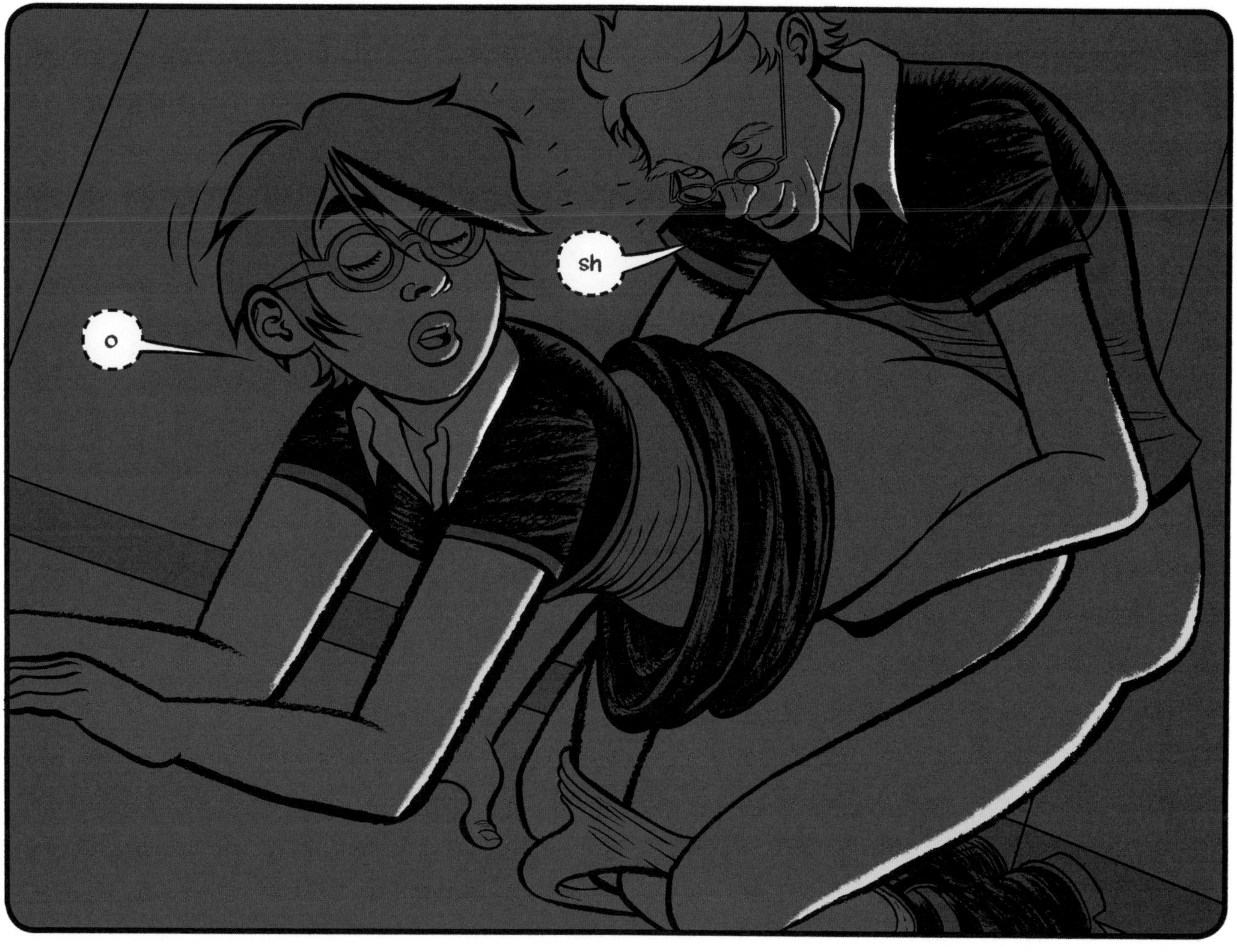
o
sh

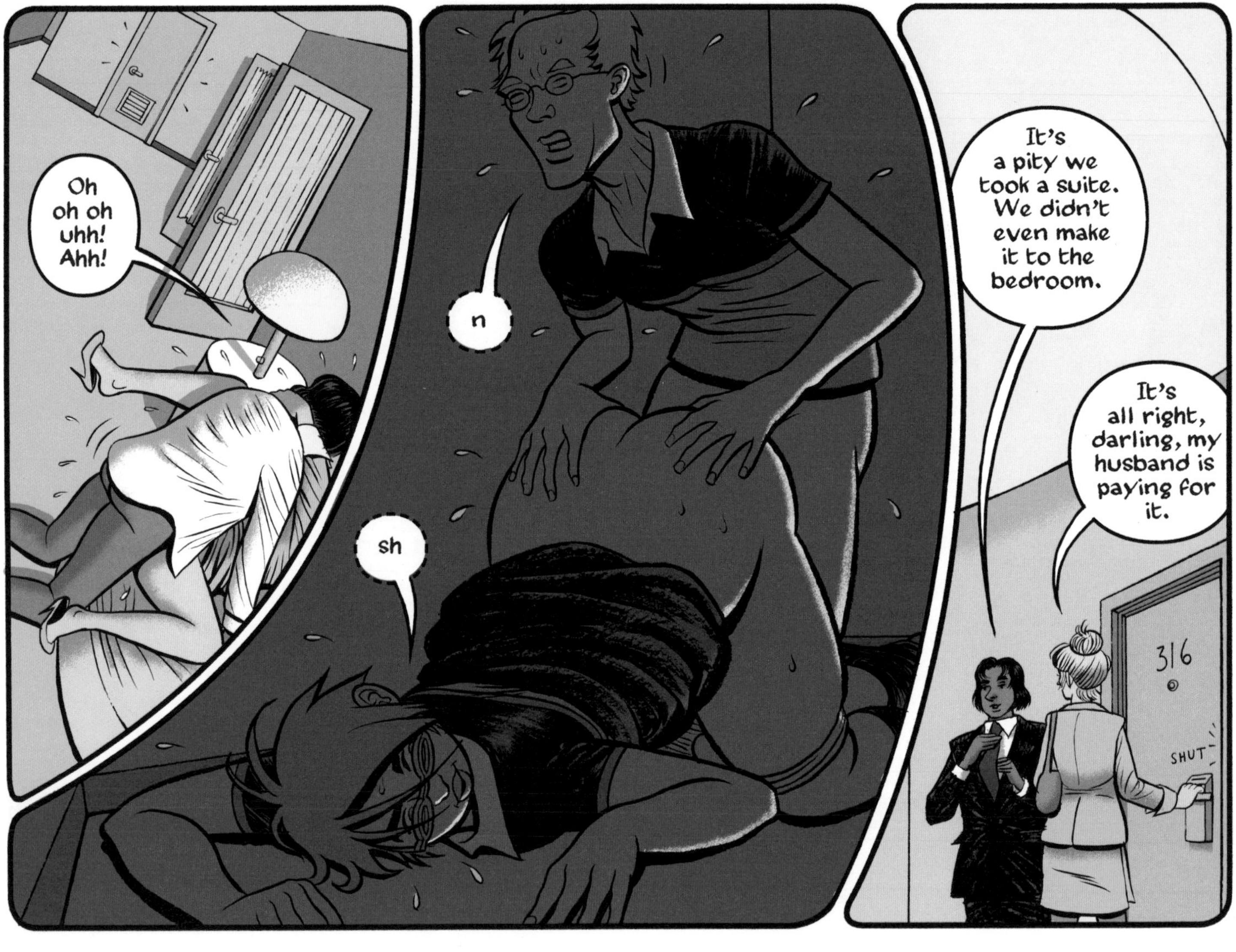
Oh oh oh uhh! Ahh!
n
sh
It’s a pity we took a suite. We didn’t even make it to the bedroom.
It’s all right, darling, my husband is paying for it.
316
SHUT

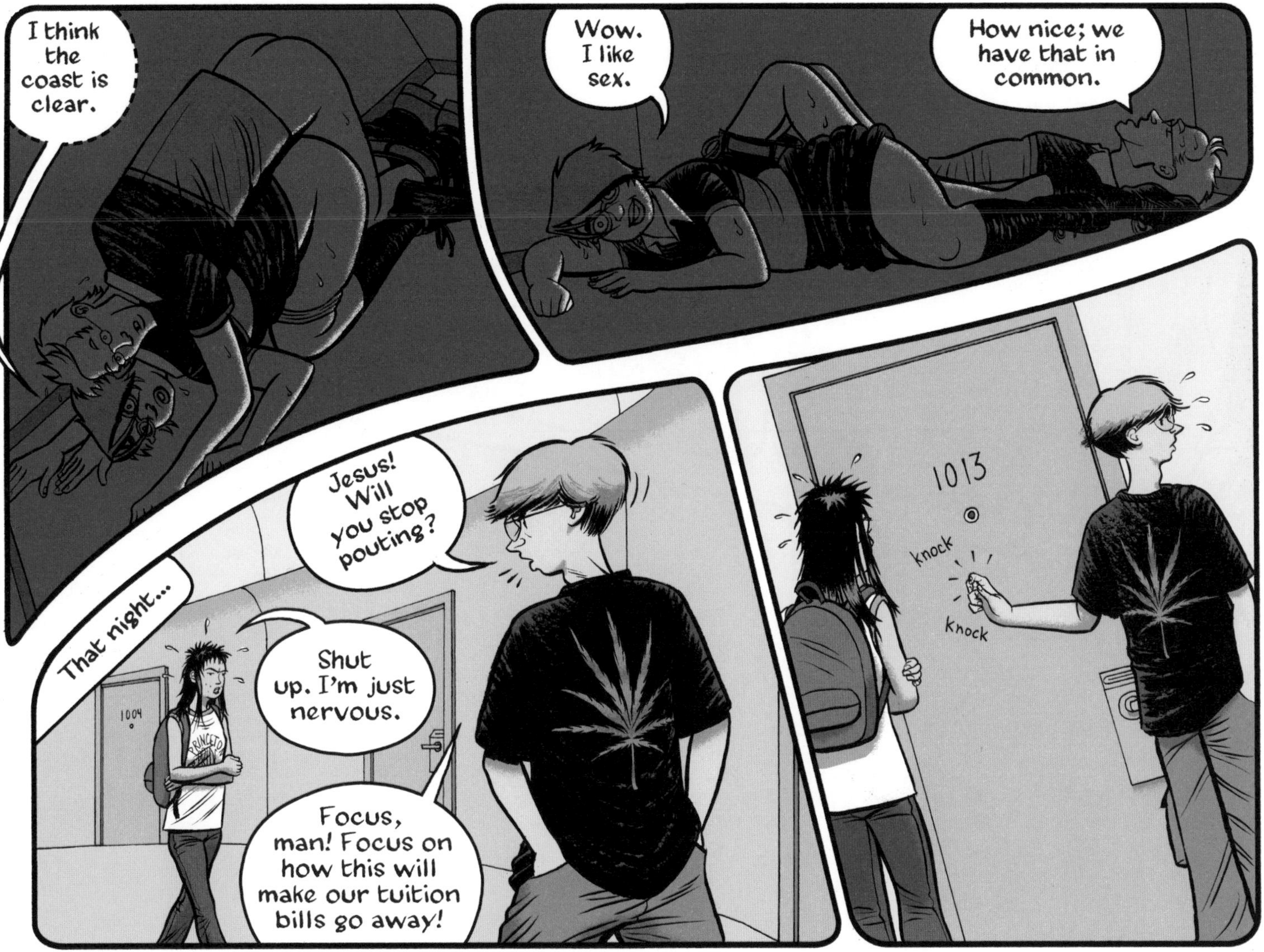

I think the coast is clear.
Wow. I like sex.
How nice; we have that in common.
That night...
Jesus! Will you stop pouting?
Shut up. I'm just nervous.
Focus, man! Focus on how this will make our tuition bills go away!
1004
1013
knock
knock

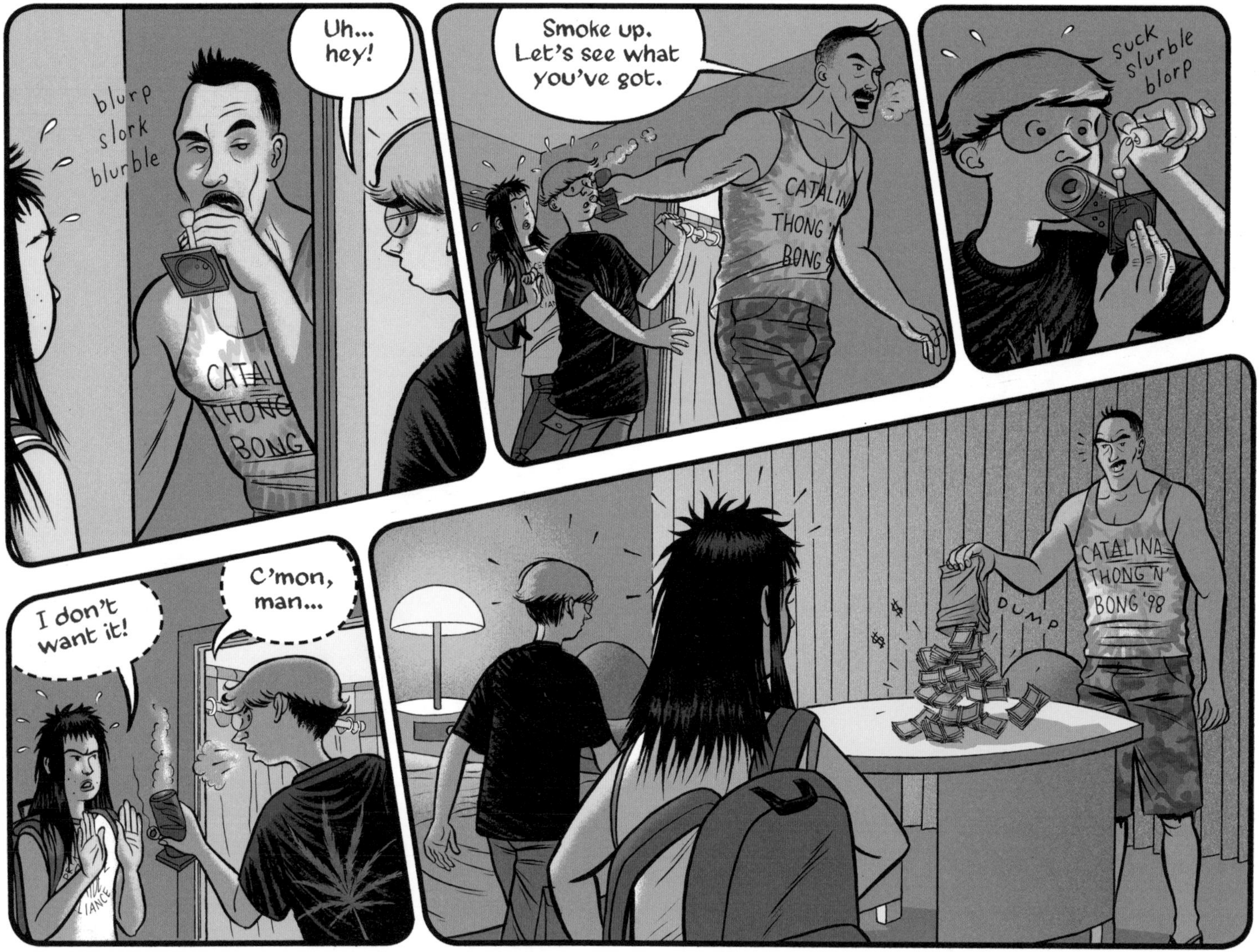
blurp
slork
blurble
Uh... hey!
CATAL
THONG
BONG
Smoke up. Let's see what you've got.
CATALIN
THONG 'N'
BONG
Suck
slurble
blorp
I don't want it!
C'mon, man...
DUMP
CATALINA
THONG 'N'
BONG '98

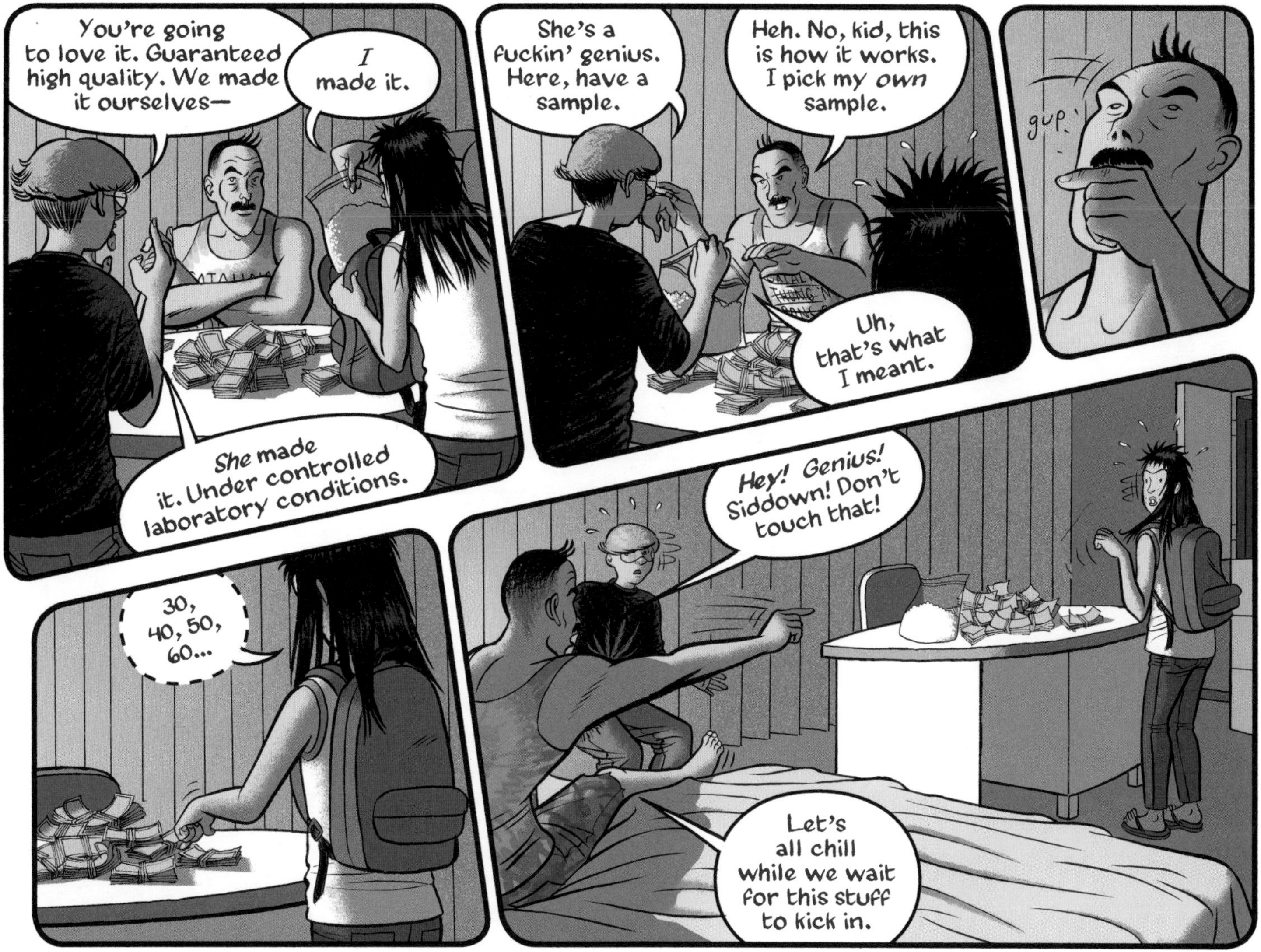
You're going to love it. Guaranteed high quality. We made it ourselves—
I made it.
She made it. Under controlled laboratory conditions.
She's a fuckin' genius. Here, have a sample.
Heh. No, kid, this is how it works. I pick my own sample.
Uh, that's what I meant.
gup
30, 40, 50, 60...
Hey! Genius! Siddown! Don't touch that!
Let's all chill while we wait for this stuff to kick in.

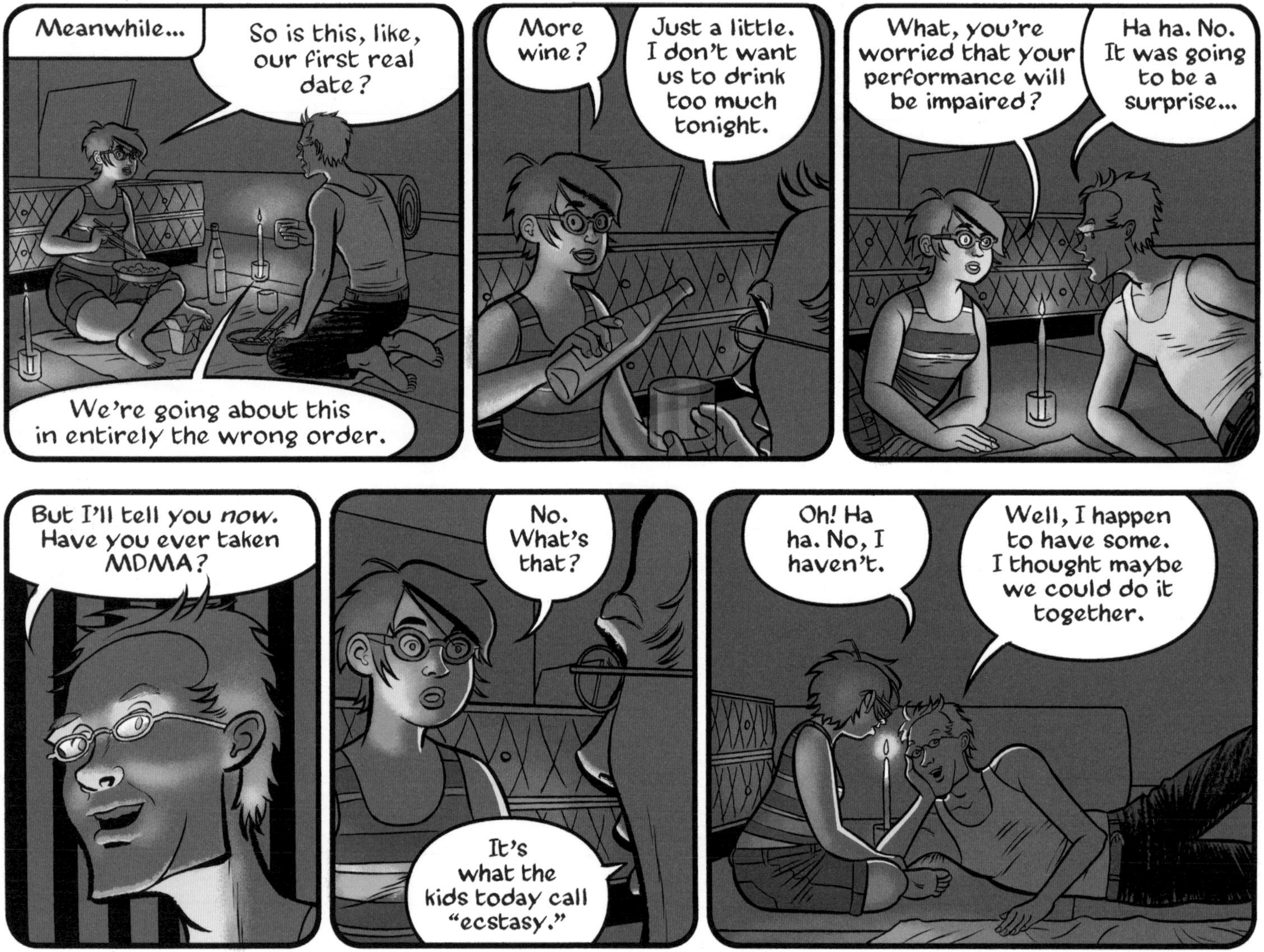
Meanwhile...
So is this, like, our first real date?
We're going about this in entirely the wrong order.
More wine?
Just a little. I don't want us to drink too much tonight.
What, you're worried that your performance will be impaired?
Ha ha. No. It was going to be a surprise...
But I'll tell you *now*. Have you ever taken MDMA?
No. What's that?
It's what the kids today call "ecstasy."
Oh! Ha ha. No, I haven't.
Well, I happen to have some. I thought maybe we could do it together.

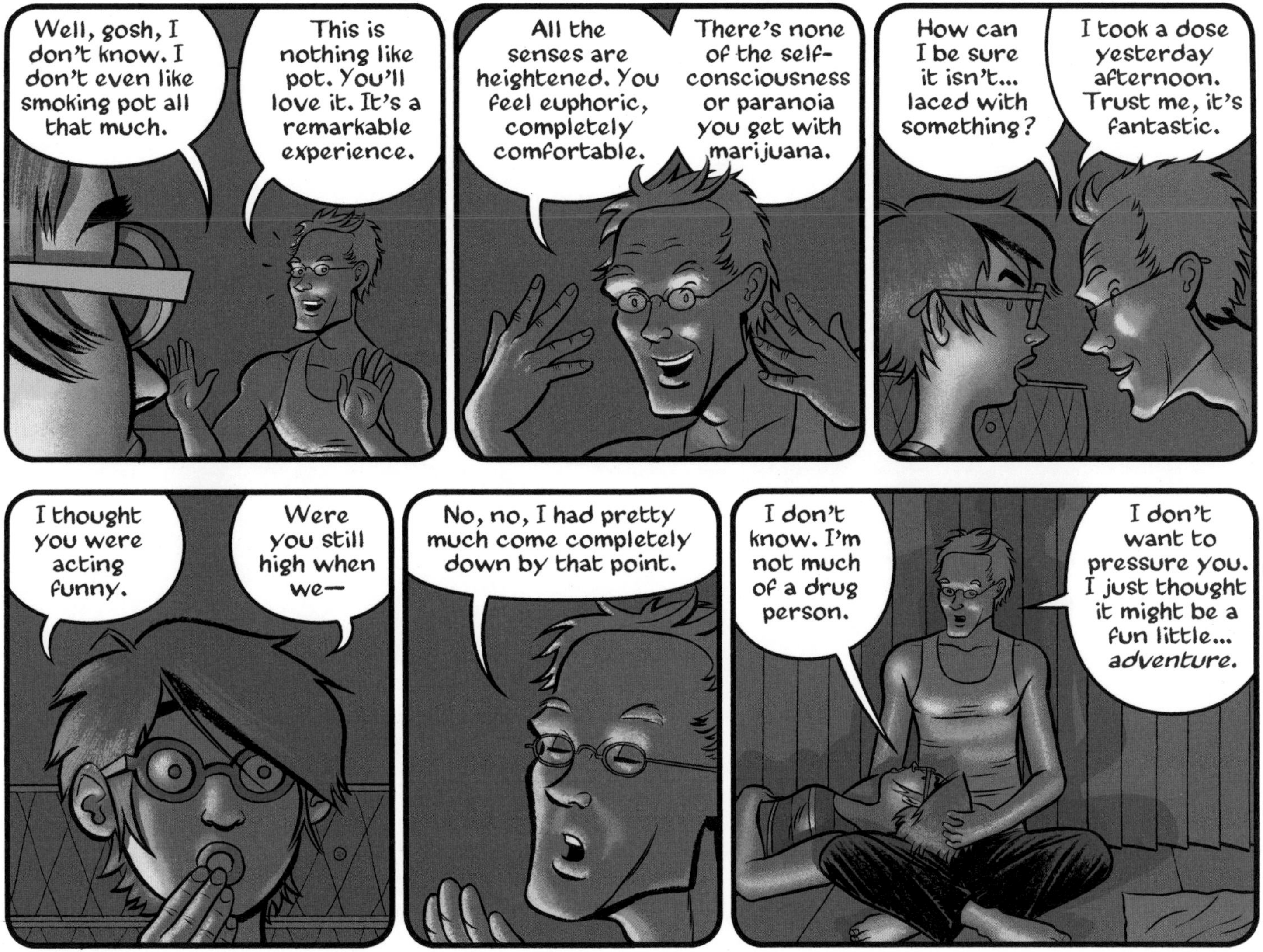
Well, gosh, I don't know. I don't even like smoking pot all that much.
This is nothing like pot. You'll love it. It's a remarkable experience.
All the senses are heightened. You feel euphoric, completely comfortable.
There's none of the self-consciousness or paranoia you get with marijuana.
How can I be sure it isn't... laced with something?
I took a dose yesterday afternoon. Trust me, it's fantastic.
I thought you were acting funny.
Were you still high when we—
No, no, I had pretty much come completely down by that point.
I don't know. I'm not much of a drug person.
I don't want to pressure you. I just thought it might be a fun little... *adventure.*

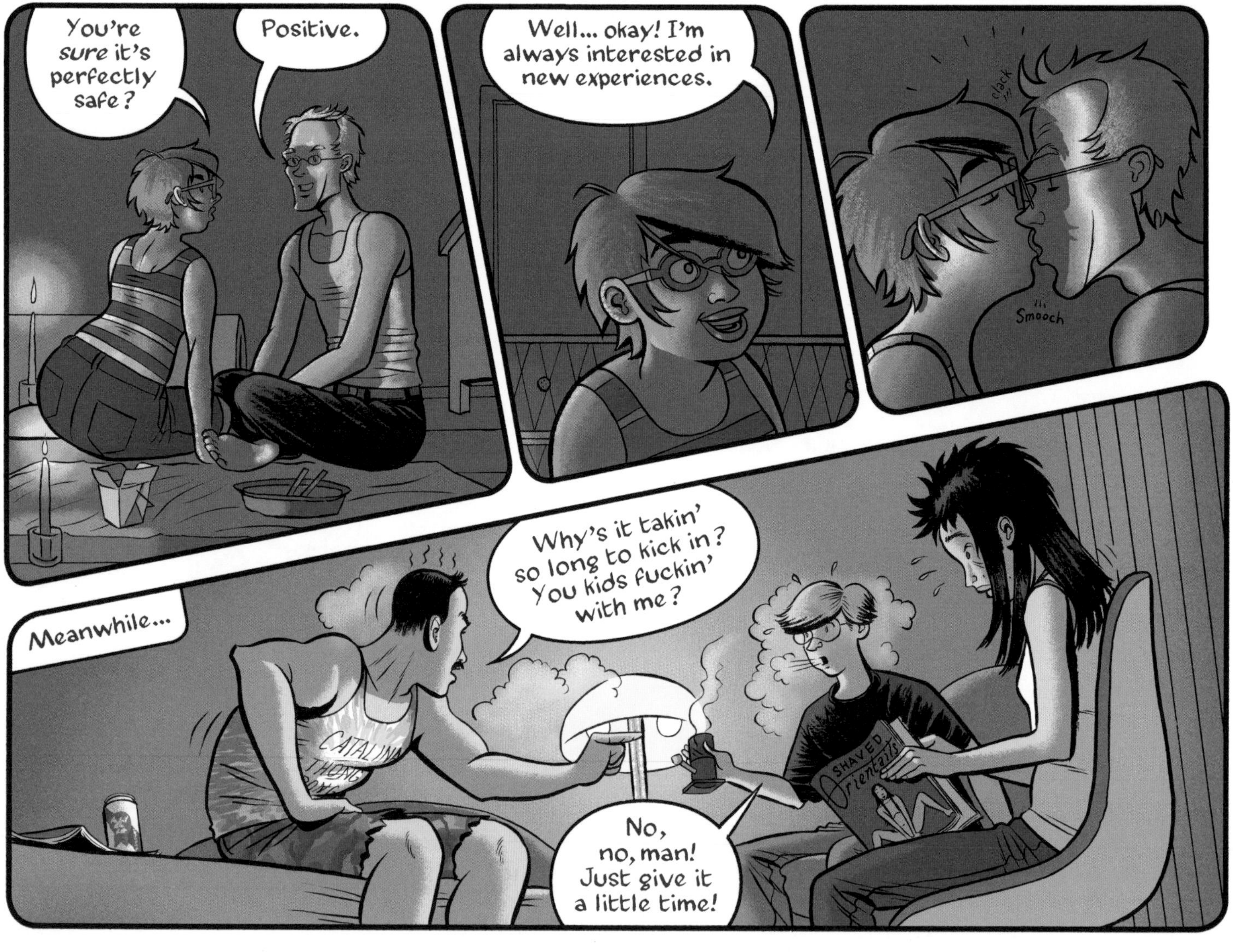
You're sure it's perfectly safe?
Positive.
Well... okay! I'm always interested in new experiences.
clack
Smooch
Meanwhile...
Why's it takin' so long to kick in? You kids fuckin' with me?
CATALINA THONG
SHAVED Orientails
No, no, man! Just give it a little time!

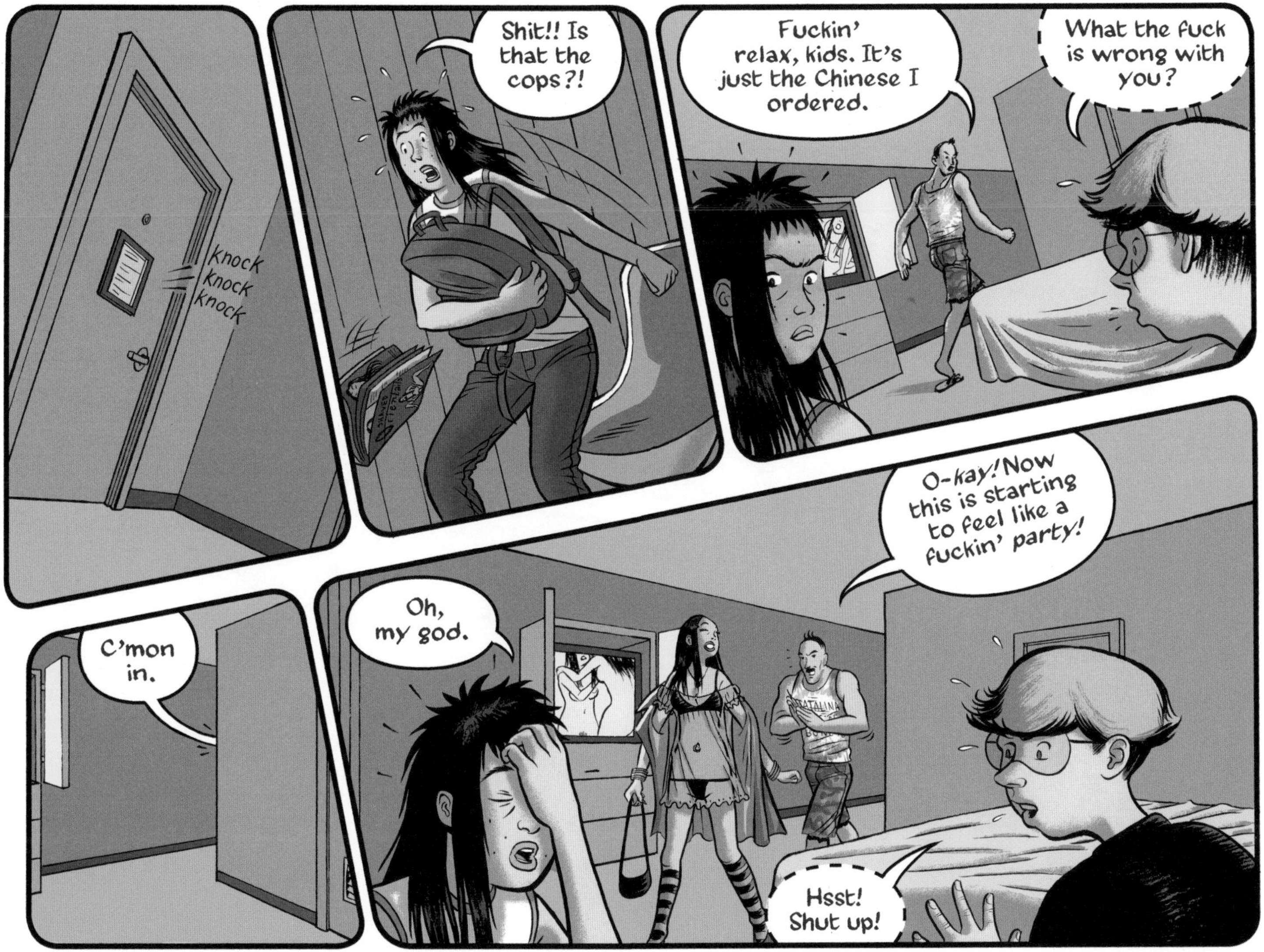
knock knock knock
Shit!! Is that the cops?!
Fuckin' relax, kids. It's just the Chinese I ordered.
What the fuck is wrong with you?
O-kay! Now this is starting to feel like a fuckin' party!
C'mon in.
Oh, my god.
Hsst! Shut up!

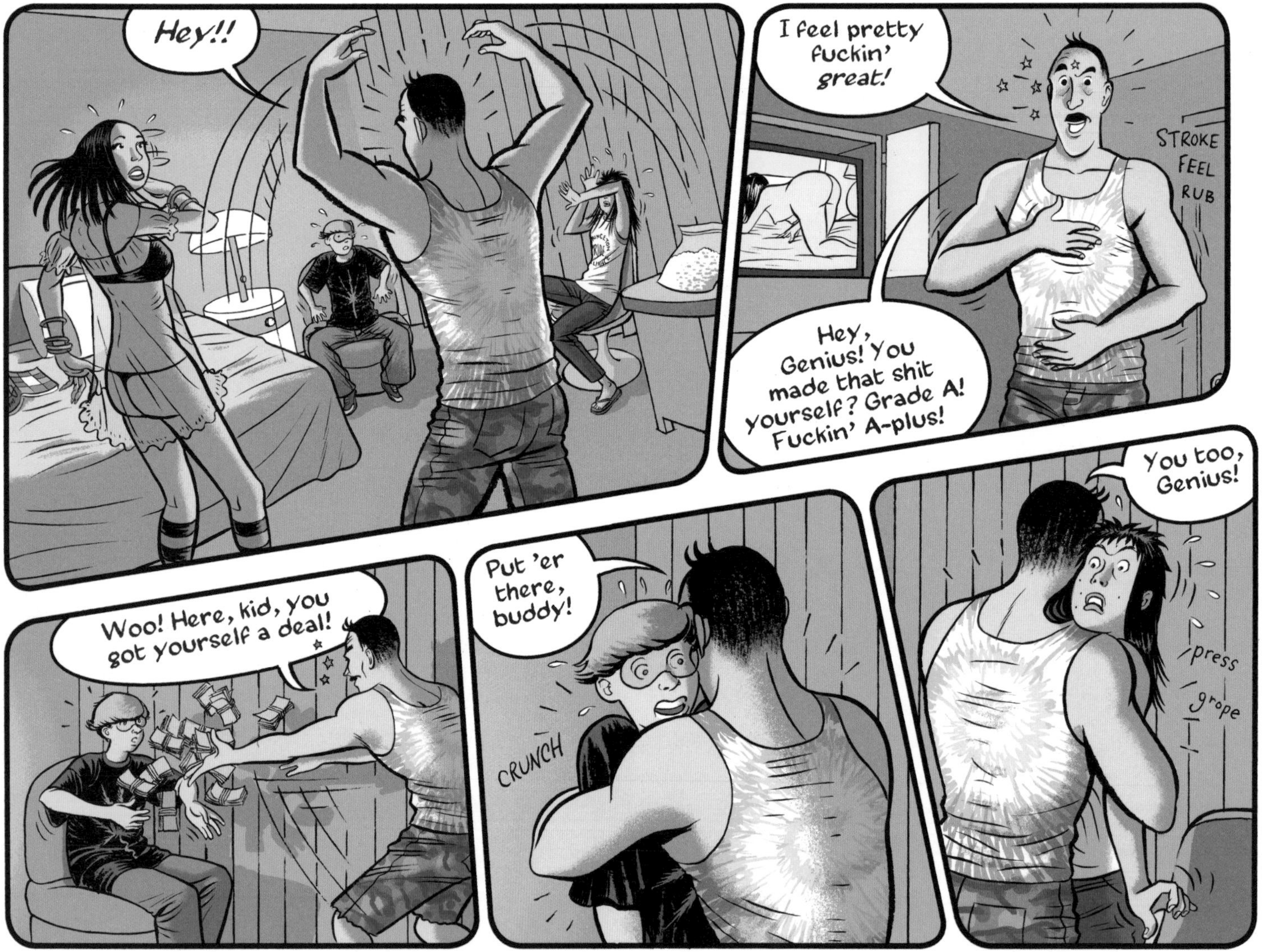
Hey!!
I feel pretty fuckin' great!
STROKE
FEEL
RUB
Hey, Genius! You made that shit yourself? Grade A! Fuckin' A-plus!
Woo! Here, kid, you got yourself a deal!
Put 'er there, buddy!
CRUNCH
You too, Genius!
press
grope

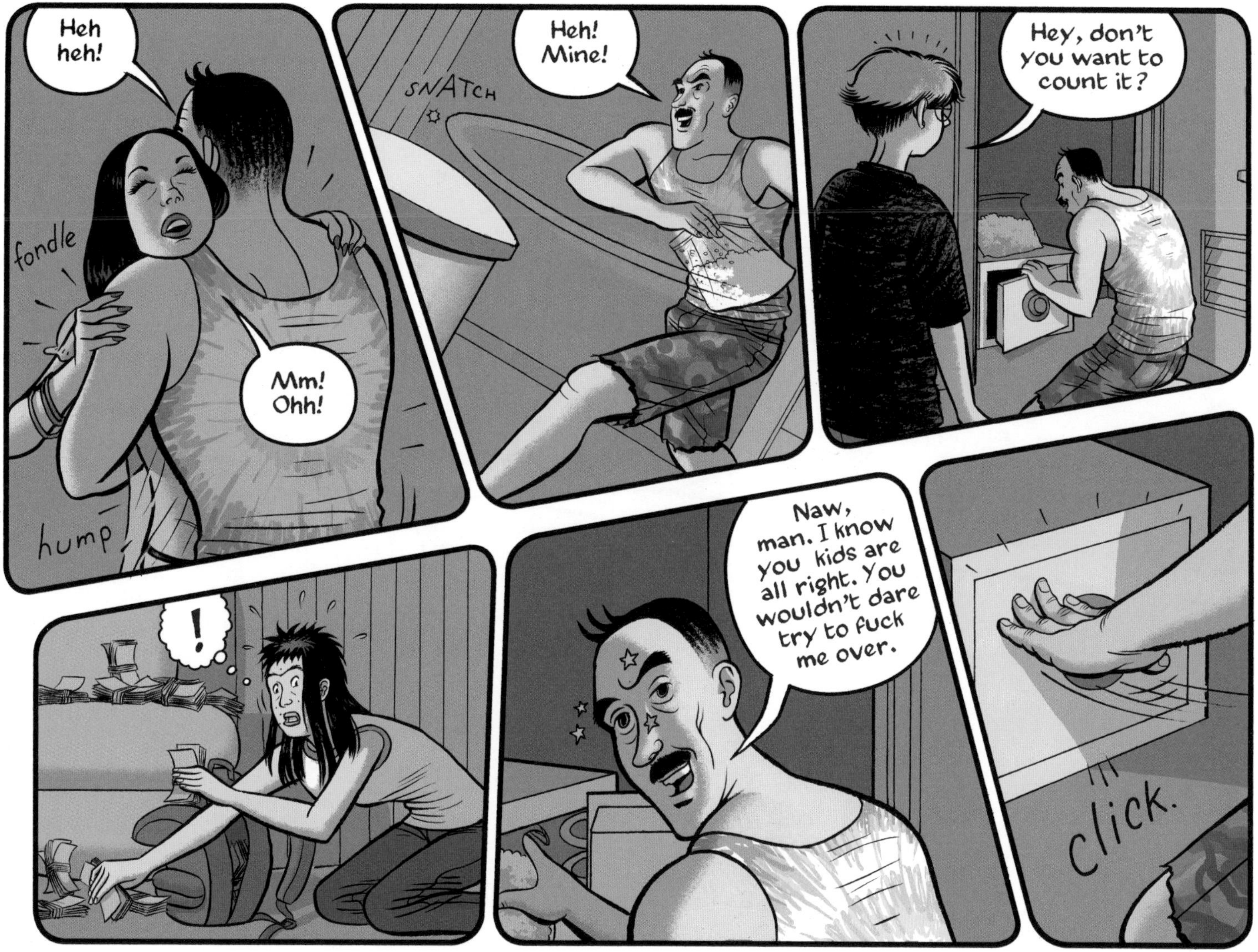

Heh heh!
fondle
Mm! Ohh!
hump
SNATCH
Heh! Mine!
Hey, don't you want to count it?
!
Naw, man. I know you kids are all right. You wouldn't dare try to fuck me over.
click.

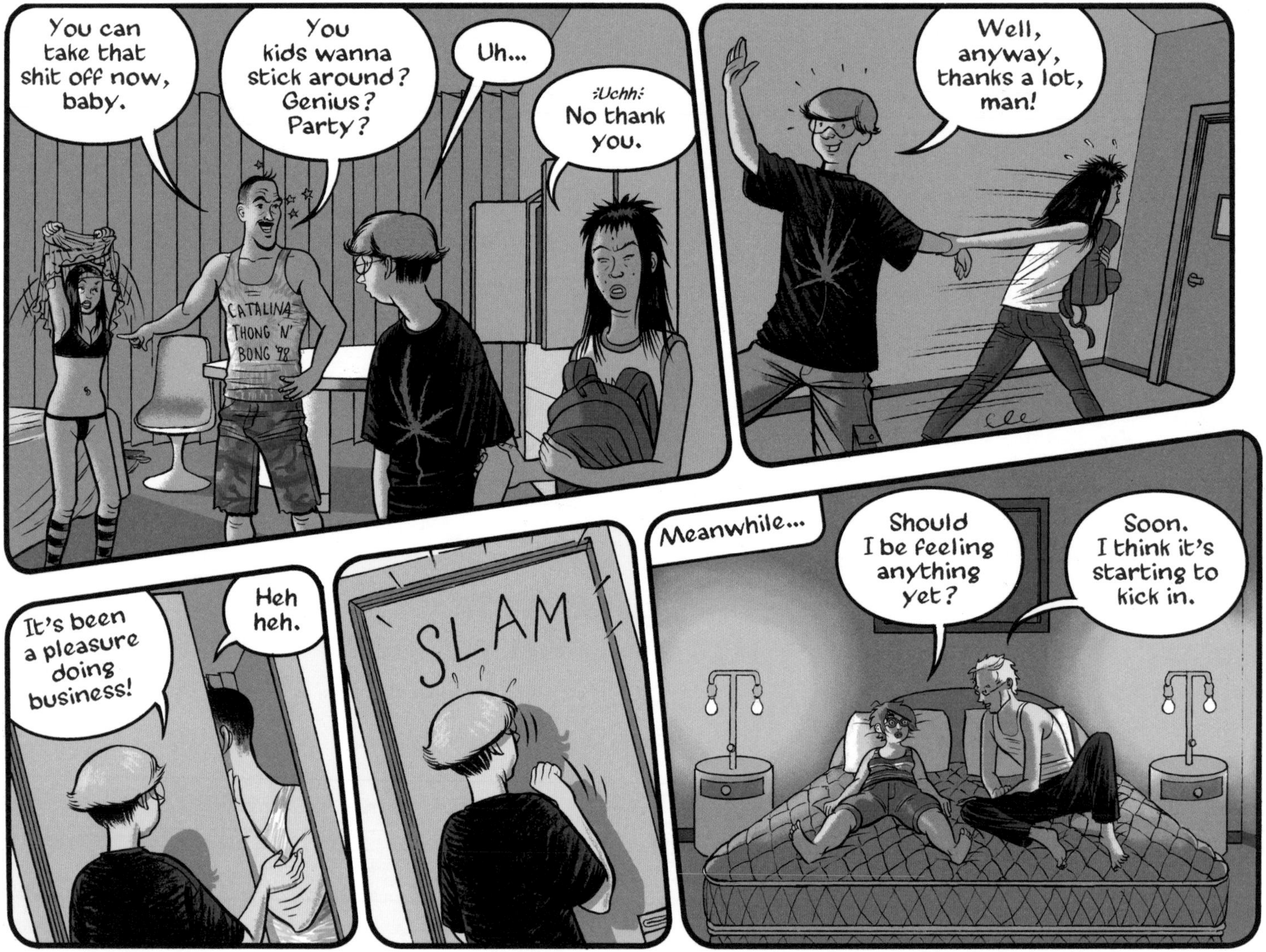
You can take that shit off now, baby.
You kids wanna stick around? Genius? Party?
Uh...
:Uchh: No thank you.
CATALINA THONG 'N' BONG '98
Well, anyway, thanks a lot, man!
It's been a pleasure doing business!
Heh heh.
SLAM
Meanwhile...
Should I be feeling anything yet?
Soon. I think it's starting to kick in.

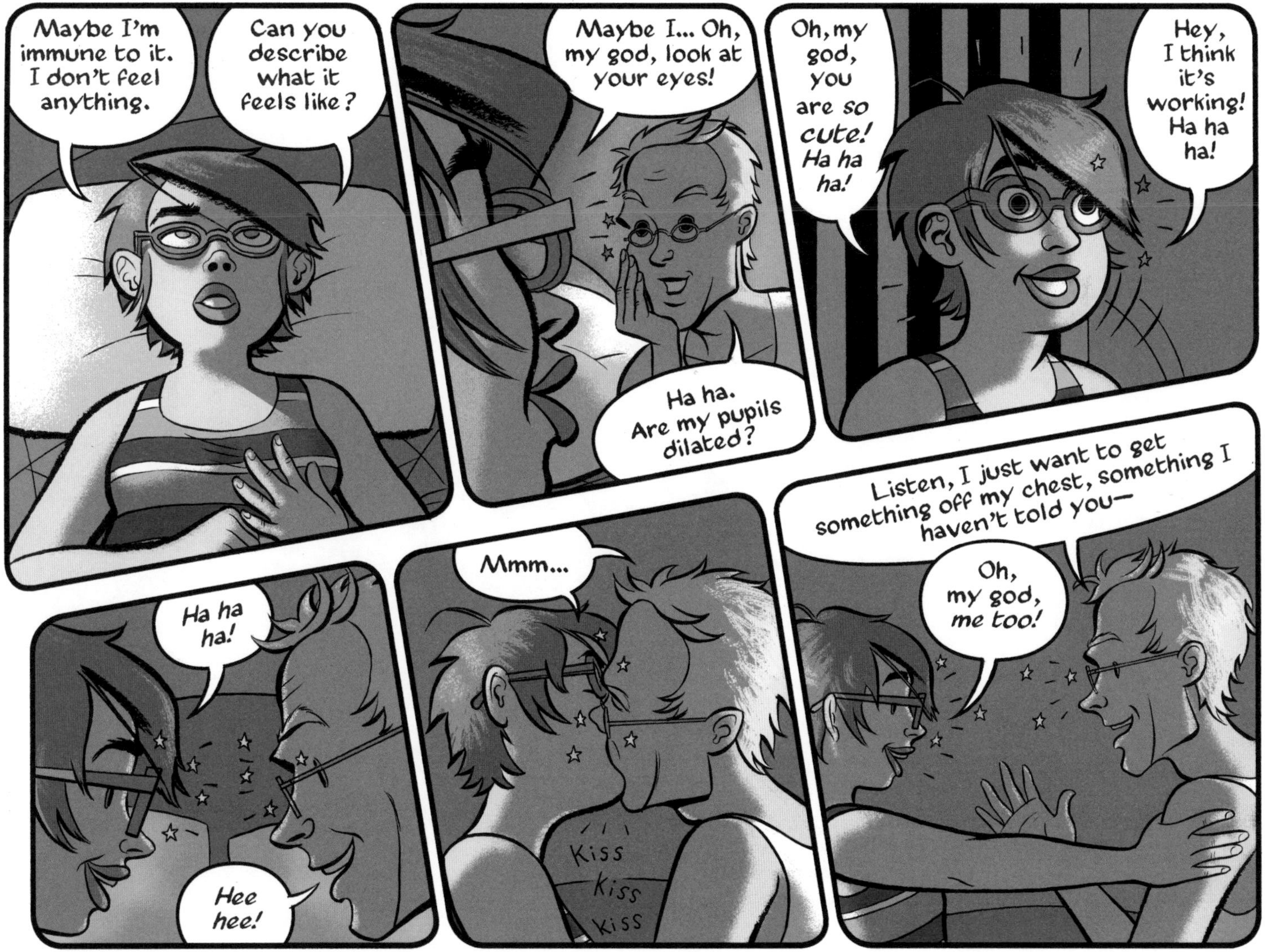
Maybe I'm immune to it. I don't feel anything.
Can you describe what it feels like?
Maybe I... Oh, my god, look at your eyes!
Ha ha. Are my pupils dilated?
Oh, my god, you are so cute! Ha ha ha!
Hey, I think it's working! Ha ha ha!
Ha ha ha!
Hee hee!
Mmm...
Kiss
Kiss
Kiss
Listen, I just want to get something off my chest, something I haven't told you—
Oh, my god, me too!

But I interrupted you, sorry. You go first!

No, no, you go first!

Okay! Okay! Like, so I've totally figured out that you're into stealing a little bit of this and that, like, *drug-wise*, and that you've amassed this, like, *giant* collection of pharmaceuticals in that little trunk, *but* I'm totally cool with it because you seem to, I'm guessing, have a totally level head about the whole thing, and plus, I have to admit, it's a total enhancement to your, um, sexiness.

But anyway, sorry, go ahead, your turn!

Here's valium... this is an ordinary non-sedating antihistamine... this one's a MAOI inhibitor...

Here's a garden-variety selective serotonin reuptake inhibitor... here's Viagra—I think you know what that does.

Hee hee! Boner!

THE PILL BOOK

THE PILL BOOK

PHYSICIAN'S PK REFERENCE

THE MERCK INDEX

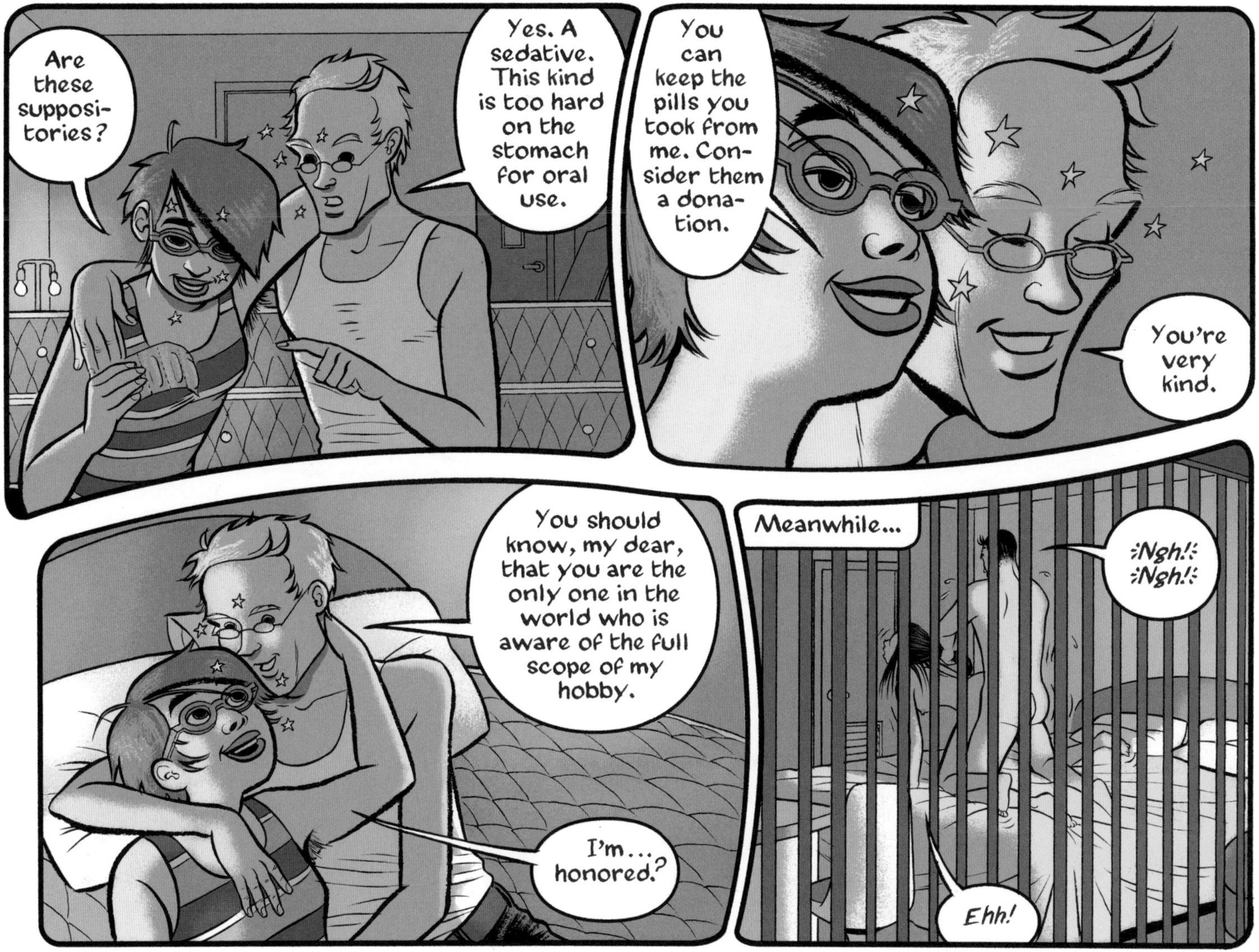
Are these suppositories?
Yes. A sedative. This kind is too hard on the stomach for oral use.
You can keep the pills you took from me. Consider them a donation.
You're very kind.
You should know, my dear, that you are the only one in the world who is aware of the full scope of my hobby.
I'm... honored.?
Meanwhile...
Ngh! Ngh!
Ehh!

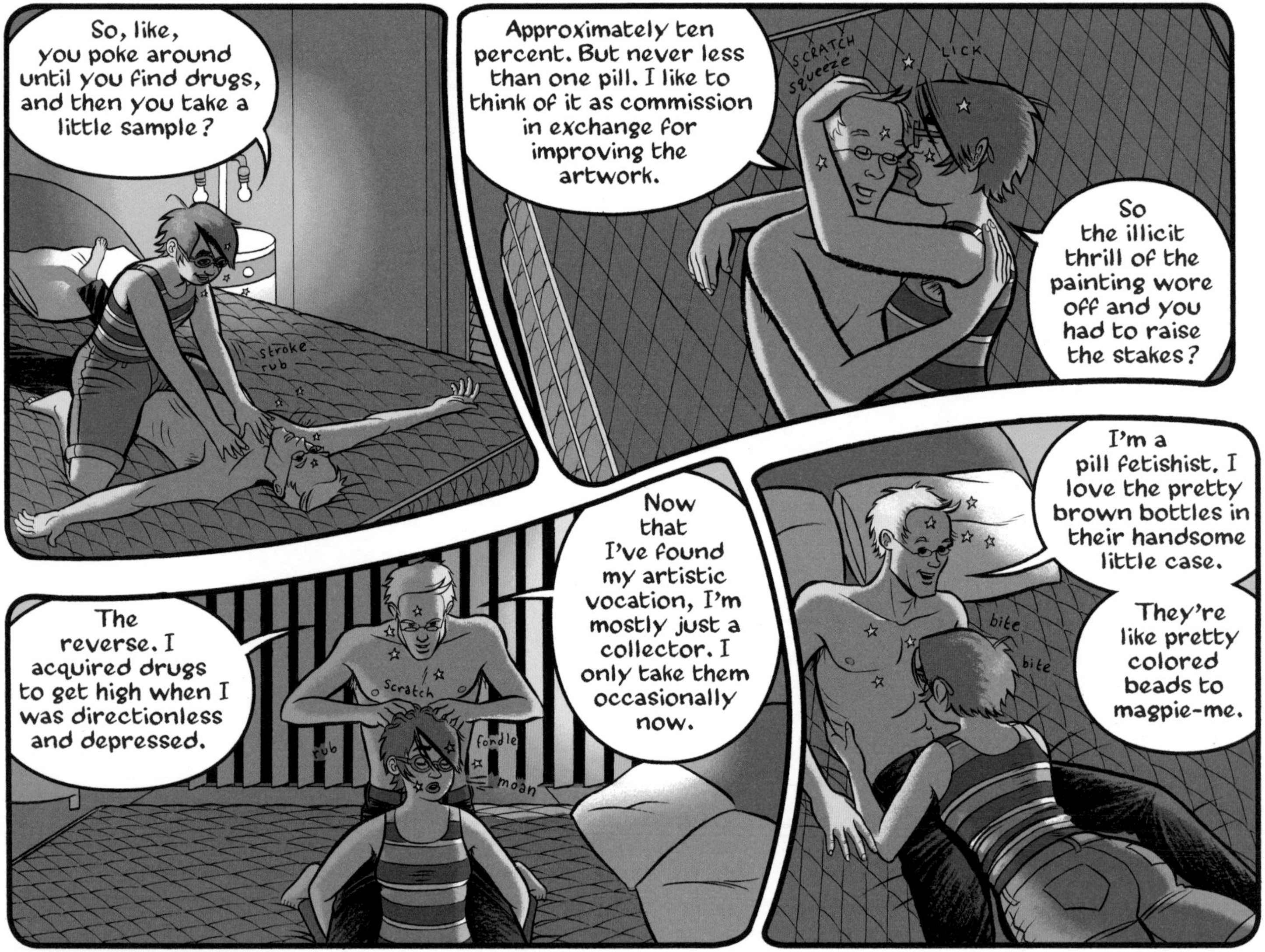
So, like, you poke around until you find drugs, and then you take a little sample?
stroke
rub
Approximately ten percent. But never less than one pill. I like to think of it as commission in exchange for improving the artwork.
SCRATCH
squeeze
LICK
So the illicit thrill of the painting wore off and you had to raise the stakes?
The reverse. I acquired drugs to get high when I was directionless and depressed.
Now that I've found my artistic vocation, I'm mostly just a collector. I only take them occasionally now.
scratch
rub
fondle
moan
I'm a pill fetishist. I love the pretty brown bottles in their handsome little case.
They're like pretty colored beads to magpie-me.
bite
bite

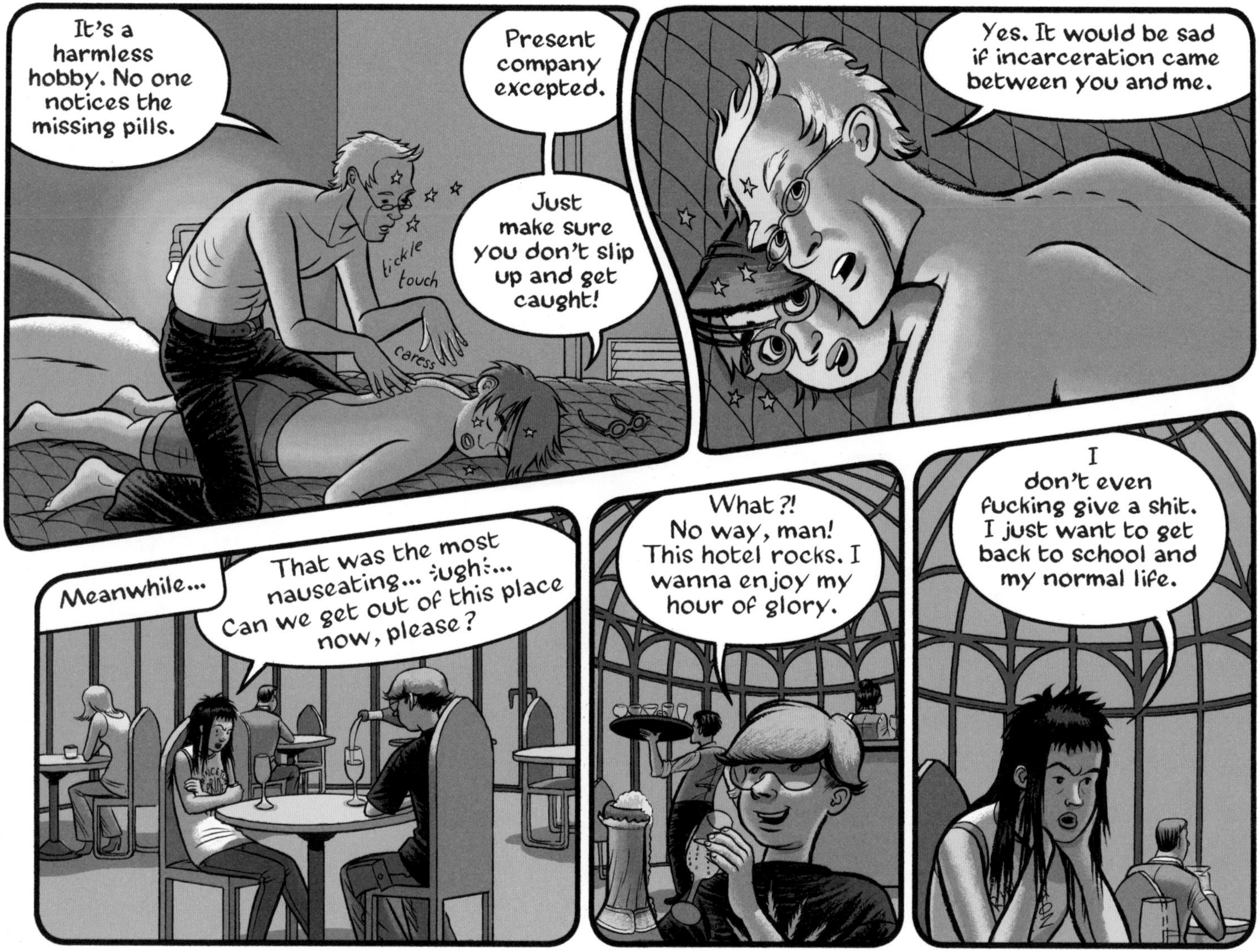
It's a harmless hobby. No one notices the missing pills.
Present company excepted.
Just make sure you don't slip up and get caught!
tickle
touch
caress
Yes. It would be sad if incarceration came between you and me.
Meanwhile...
That was the most nauseating... ⁝ugh⁝... Can we get out of this place now, please?
What?! No way, man! This hotel rocks. I wanna enjoy my hour of glory.
I don't even fucking give a shit. I just want to get back to school and my normal life.

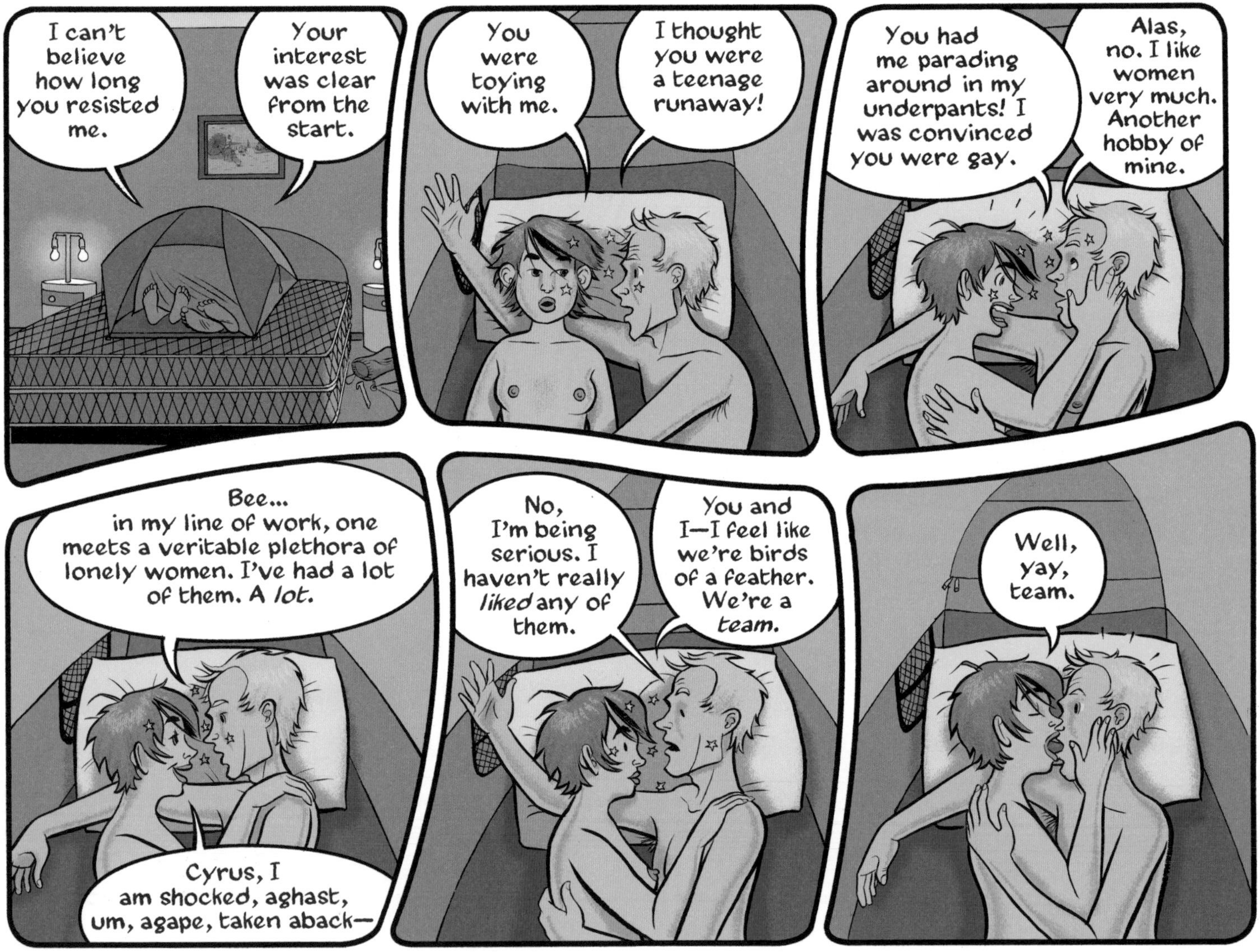
I can't believe how long you resisted me.
Your interest was clear from the start.
You were toying with me.
I thought you were a teenage runaway!
You had me parading around in my underpants! I was convinced you were gay.
Alas, no. I like women very much. Another hobby of mine.
Bee... in my line of work, one meets a veritable plethora of lonely women. I've had a lot of them. A *lot*.
Cyrus, I am shocked, aghast, um, agape, taken aback—
No, I'm being serious. I haven't really *liked* any of them.
You and I—I feel like we're birds of a feather. We're a *team*.
Well, yay, team.

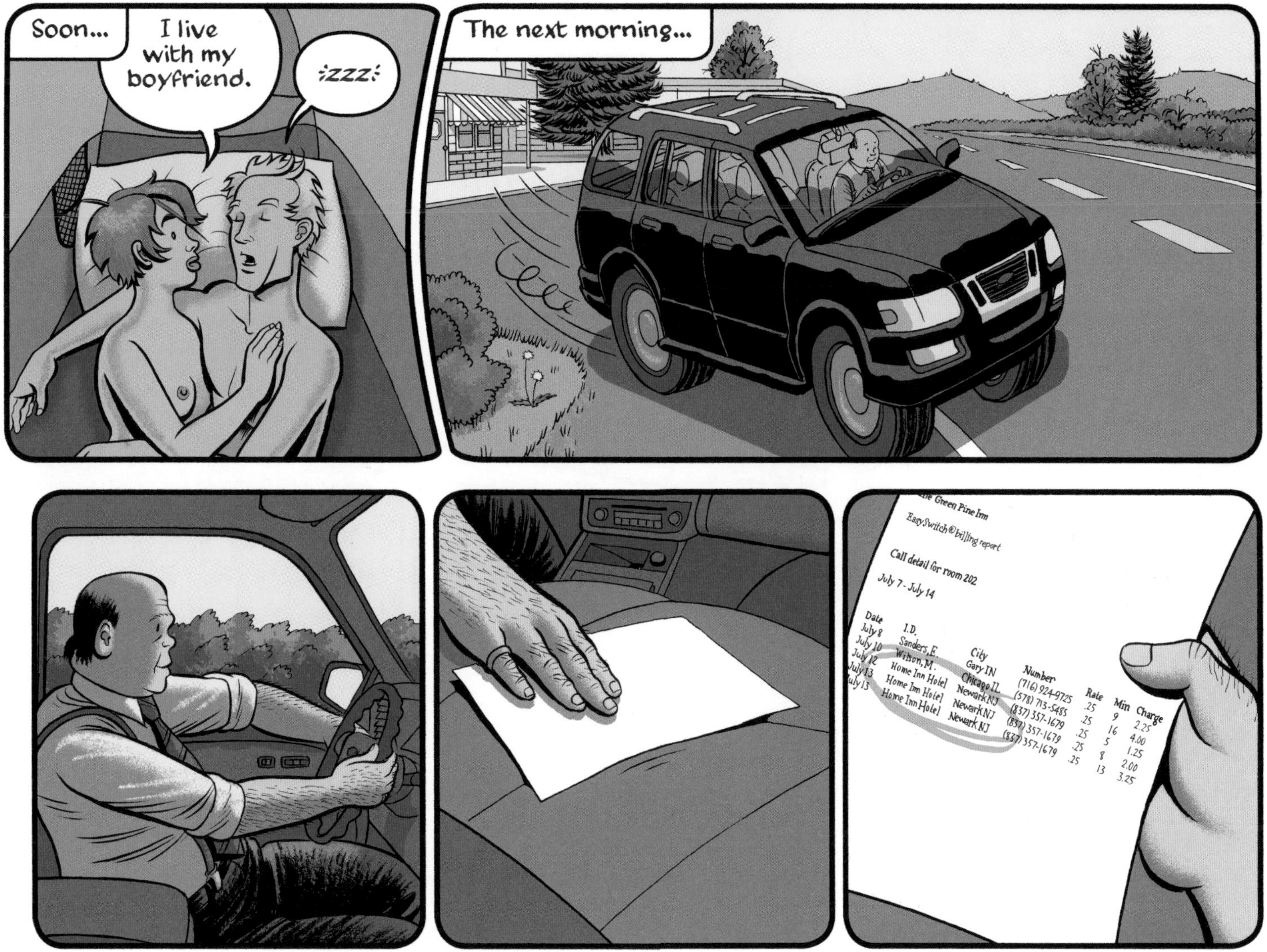

Soon...
I live with my boyfriend.
:zzz:
The next morning...
Green Pine Inn
EasySwitch® billing report
Call detail for room 202
July 7 - July 14
Date I.D. City Number Rate Min Charge
July 8 Sanders, E. Gary IN (716) 924-9725 .25 9 2.25
July 10 Wilson, M. Chicago IL (578) 713-5485 .25 16 4.00
July 12 Home Inn Hotel Newark NJ (837) 357-1679 .25 5 1.25
July 13 Home Inn Hotel Newark NJ (837) 357-1679 .25 8 2.00
July 13 Home Inn Hotel Newark NJ (837) 357-1679 .25 13 3.25

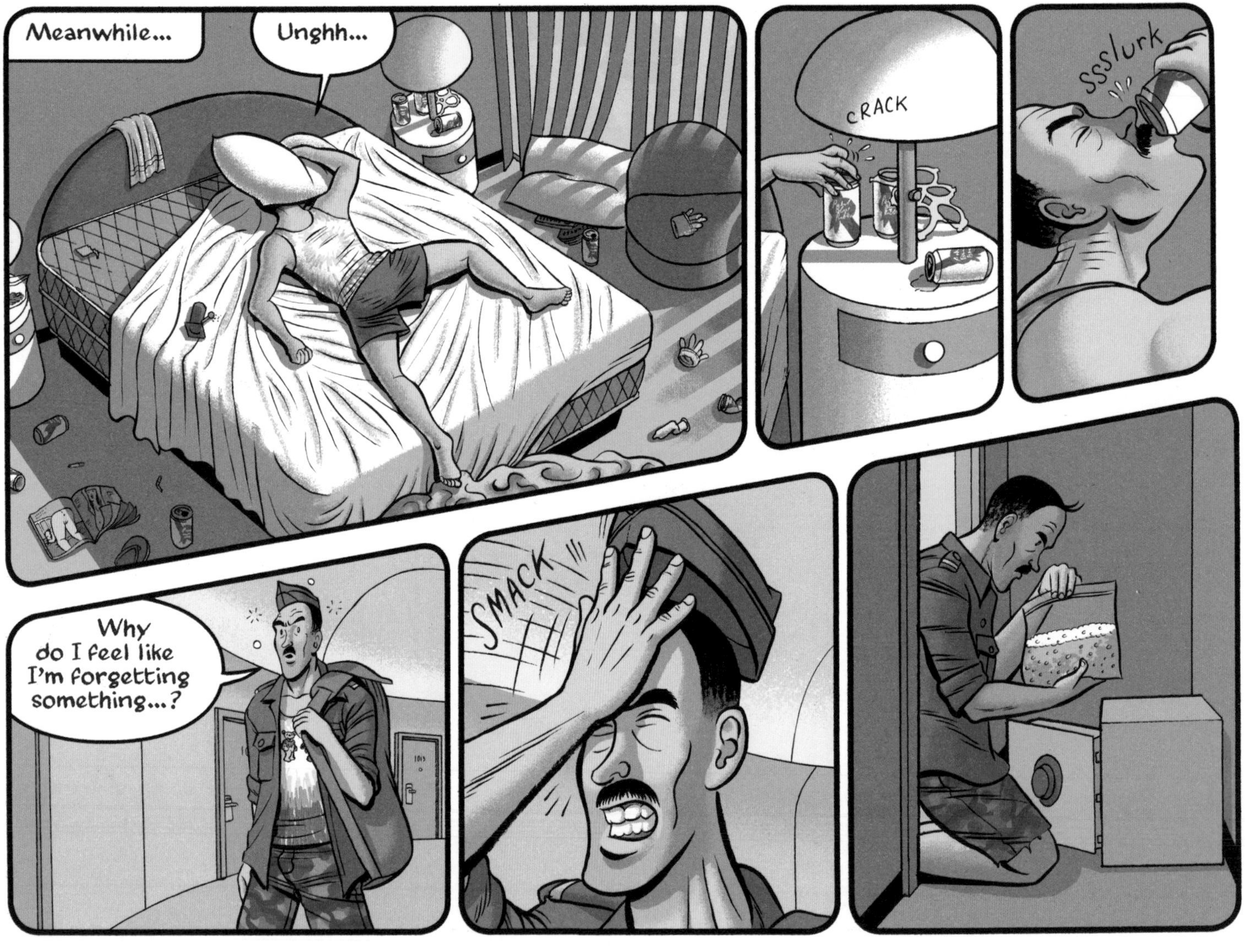
Meanwhile...
Unghh...
CRACK
SSSlurk
Why do I feel like I'm forgetting something...?
SMACK

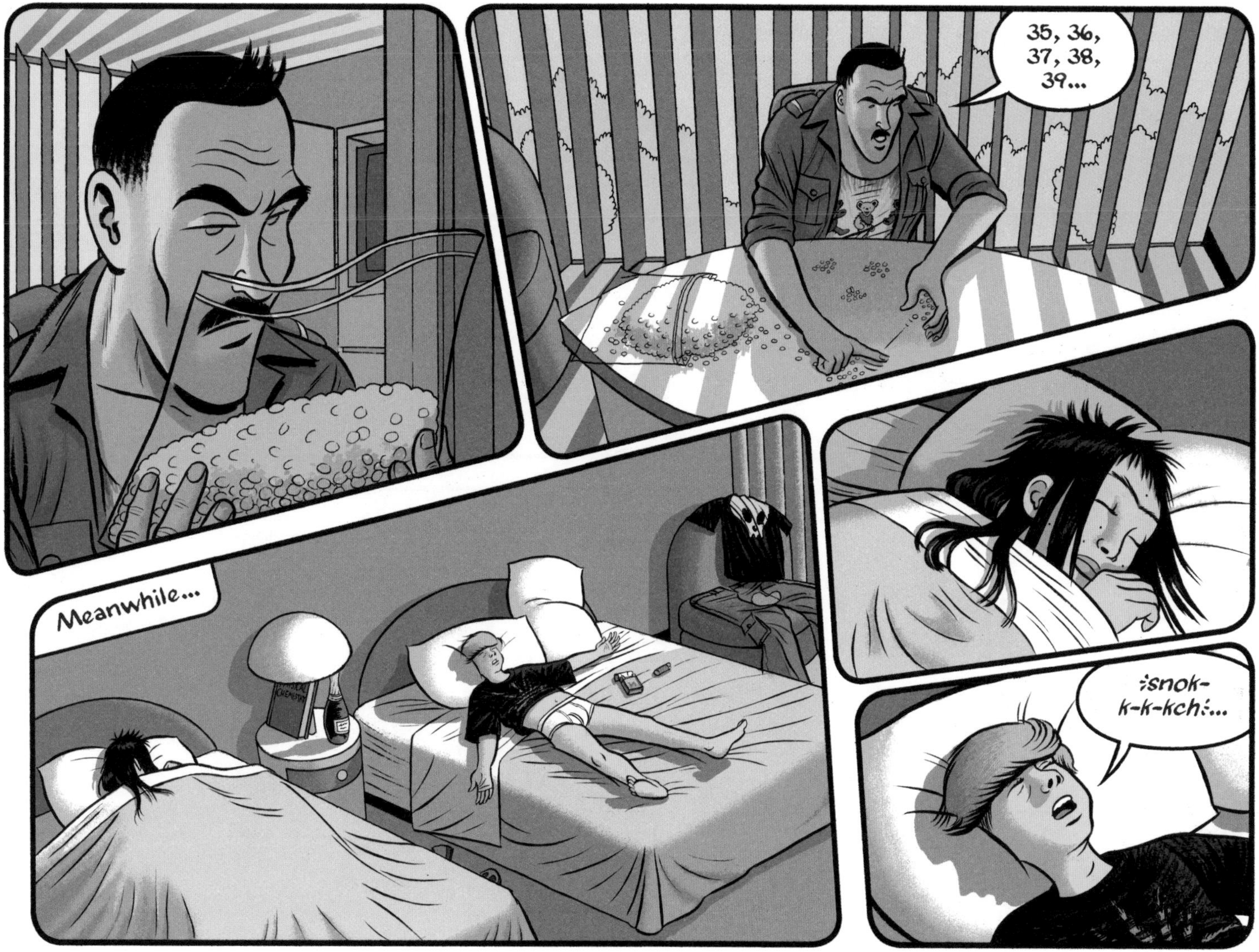
35, 36, 37, 38, 39...
Meanwhile...
:snok-k-k-kch:...

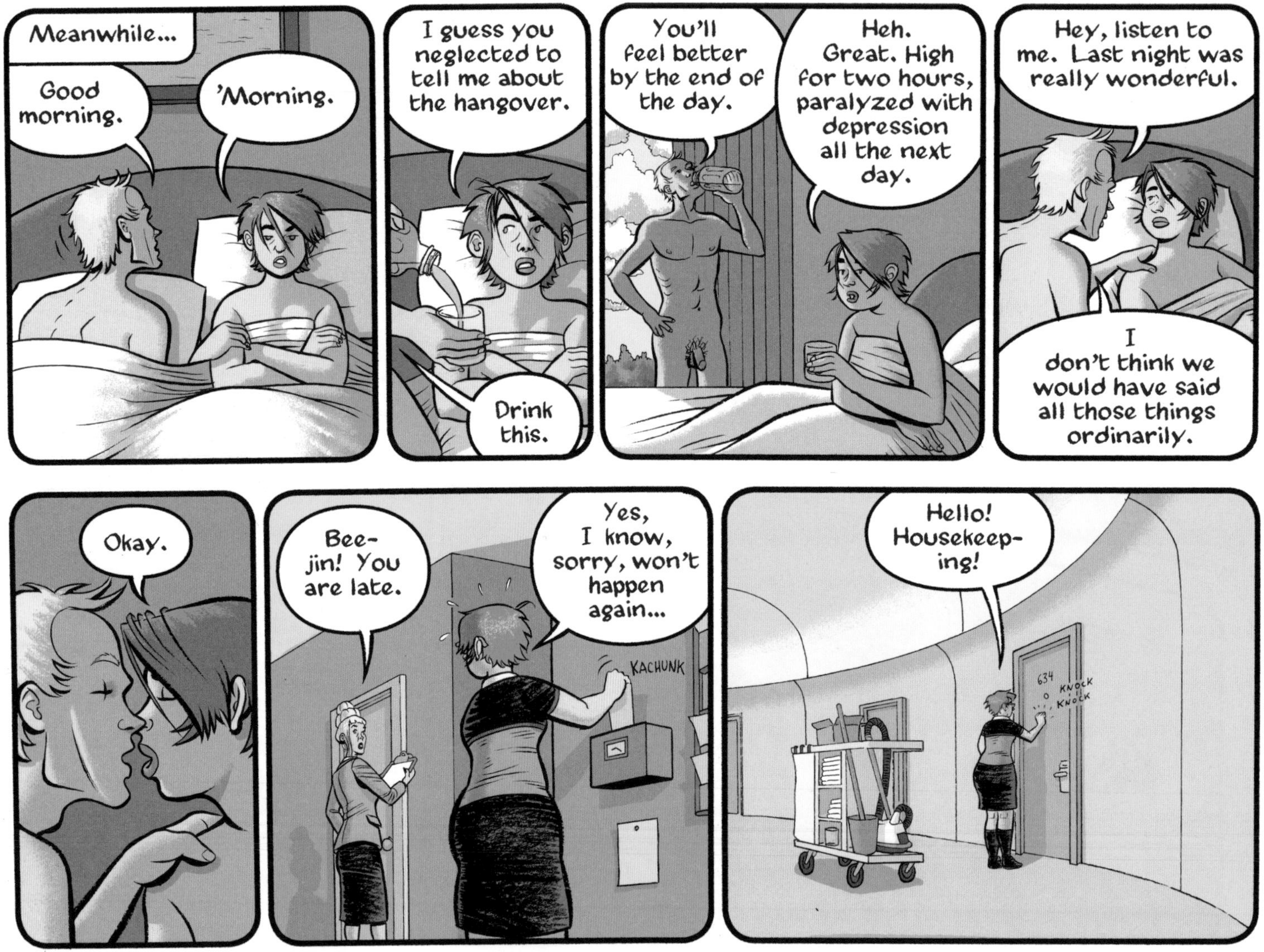
Meanwhile...
Good morning.
'Morning.
I guess you neglected to tell me about the hangover.
Drink this.
You'll feel better by the end of the day.
Heh. Great. High for two hours, paralyzed with depression all the next day.
Hey, listen to me. Last night was really wonderful.
I don't think we would have said all those things ordinarily.
Okay.
Bee-jin! You are late.
Yes, I know, sorry, won't happen again...
KACHUNK
Hello! Housekeeping!
634
KNOCK KNOCK

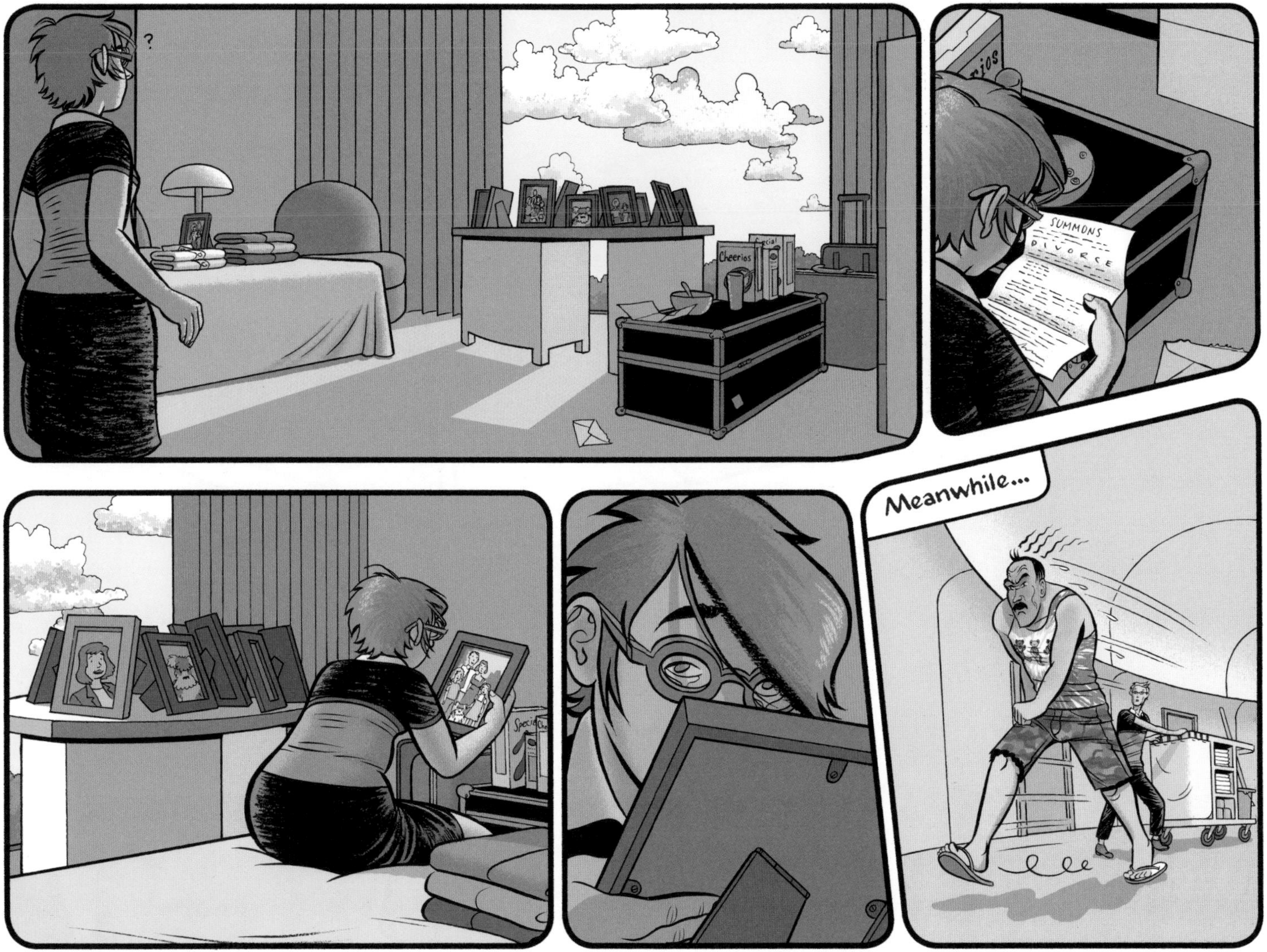
?
Cheerios
SUMMONS
DIVORCE
Meanwhile...

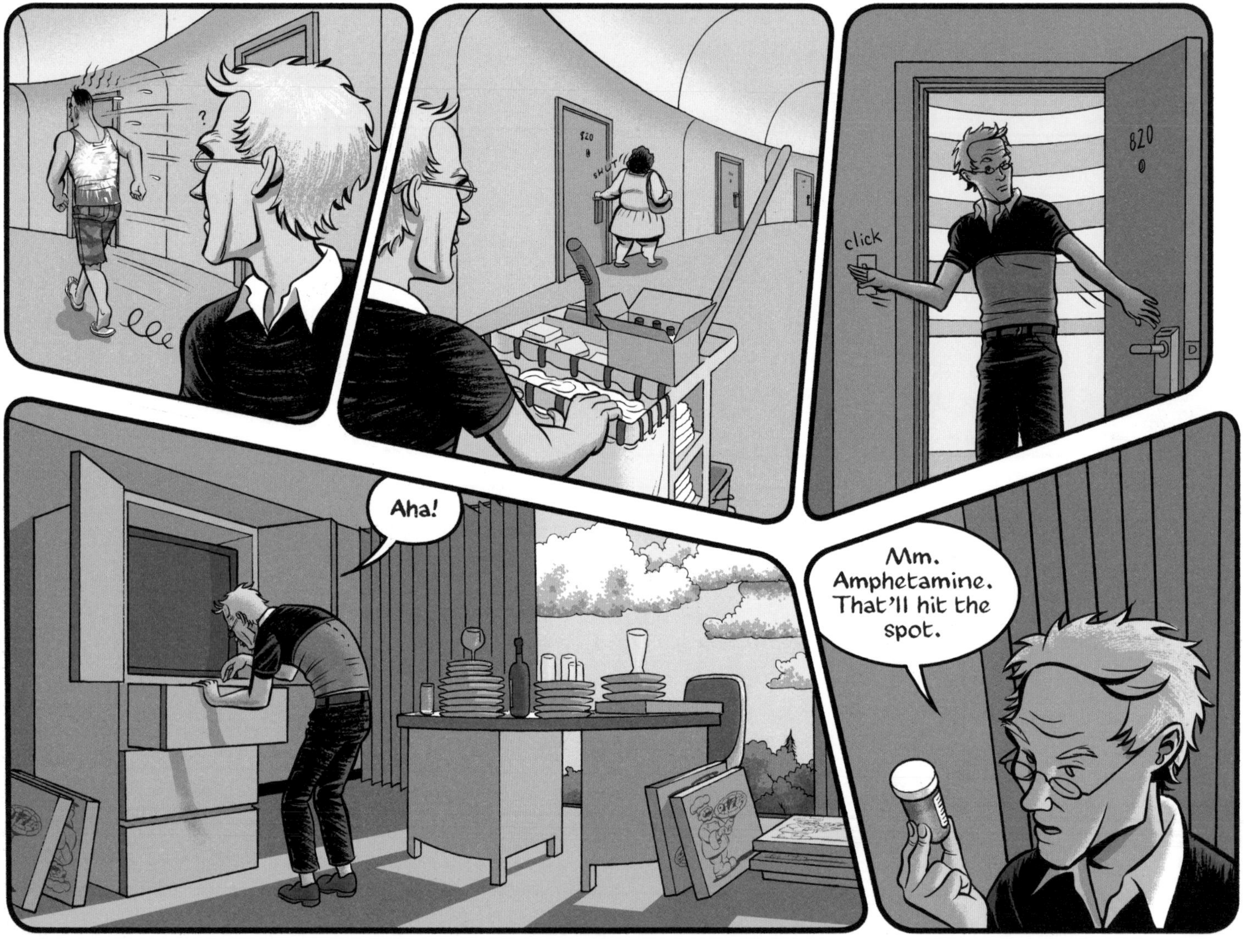
?
820
SHUT
820
click
Aha!
Mm. Amphetamine. That'll hit the spot.

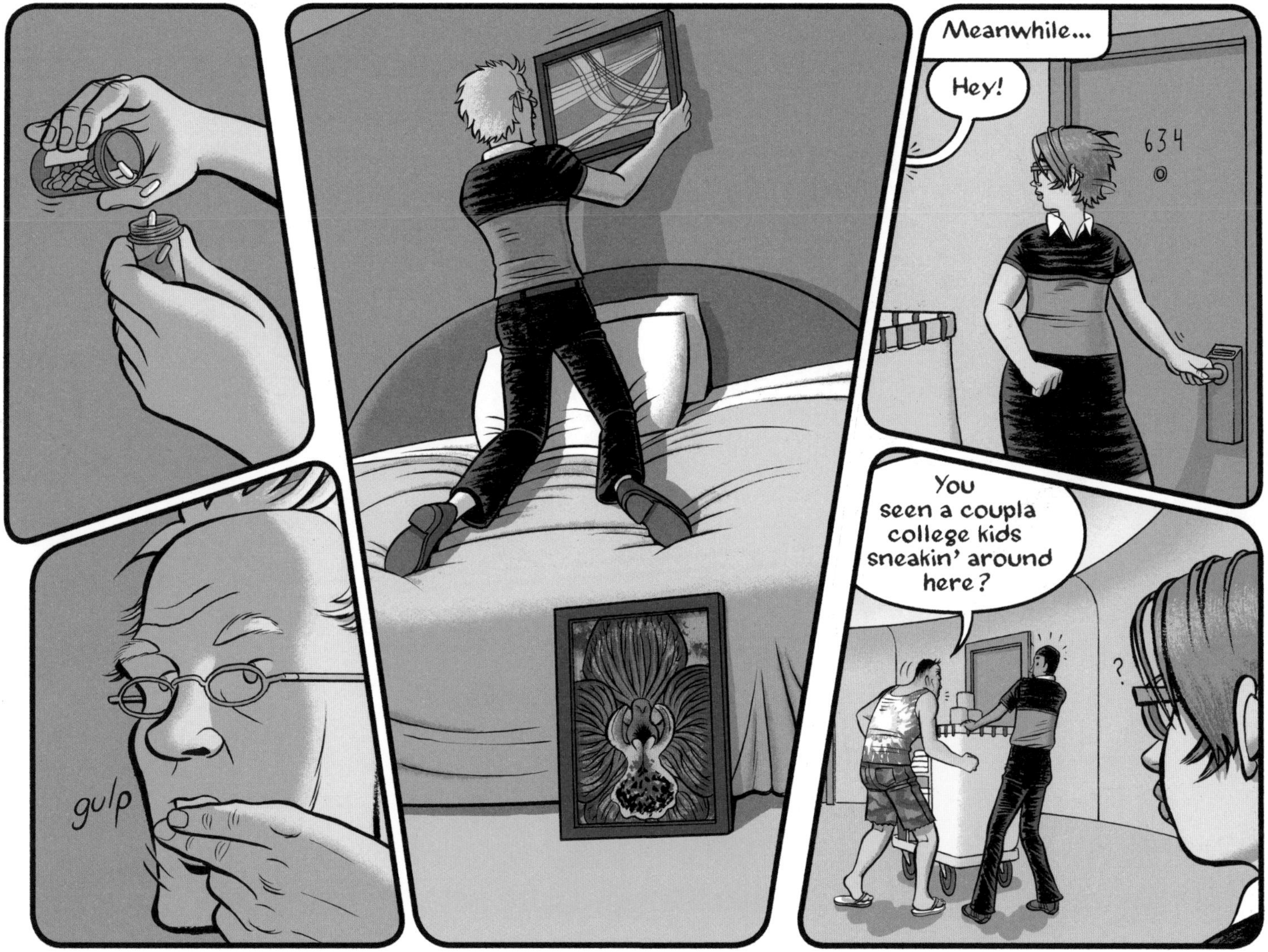
gulp
Meanwhile...
Hey!
634
You seen a coupla college kids sneakin' around here?
?

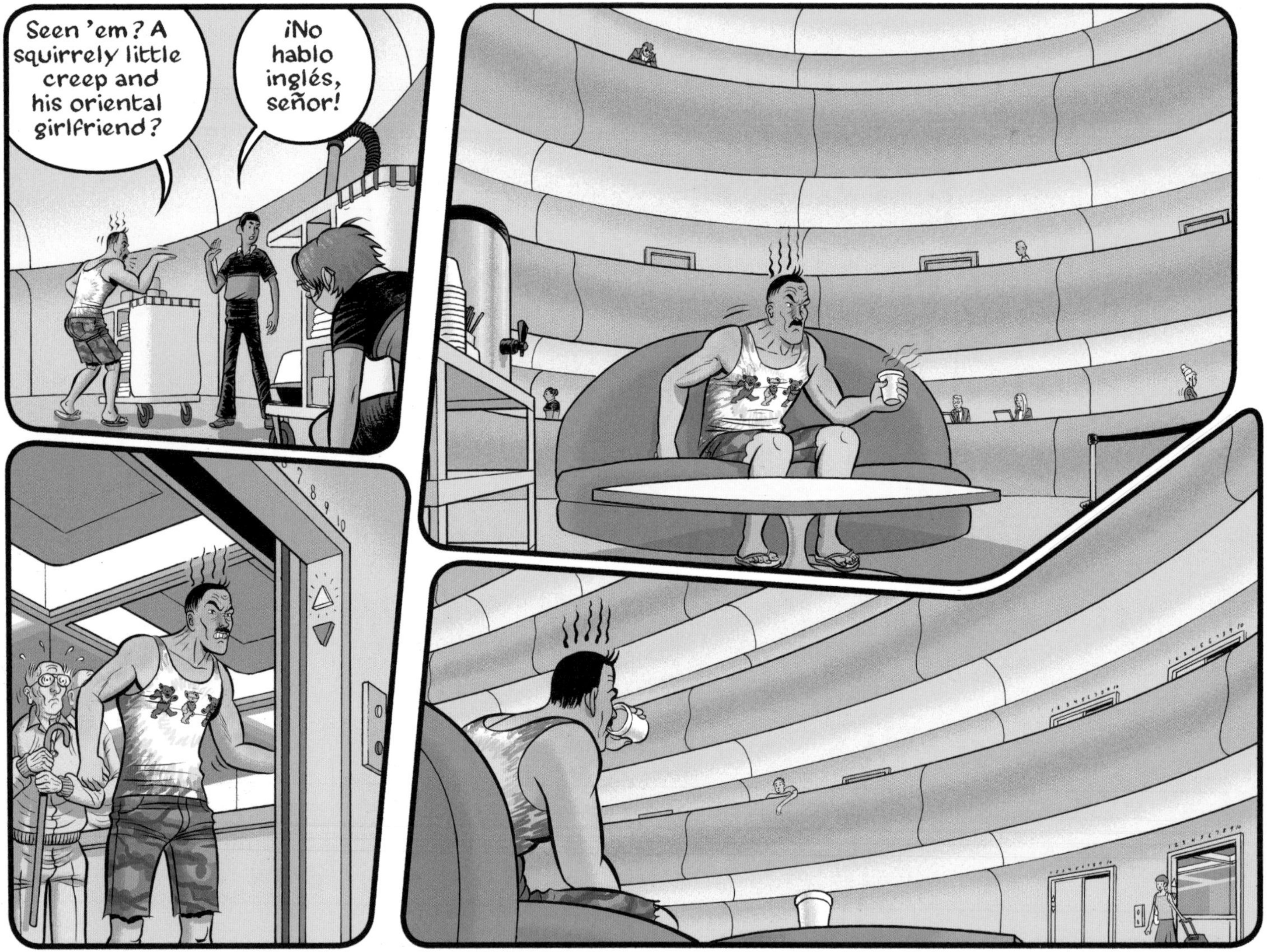
Seen 'em? A squirrely little creep and his oriental girlfriend?
¡No hablo inglés, señor!

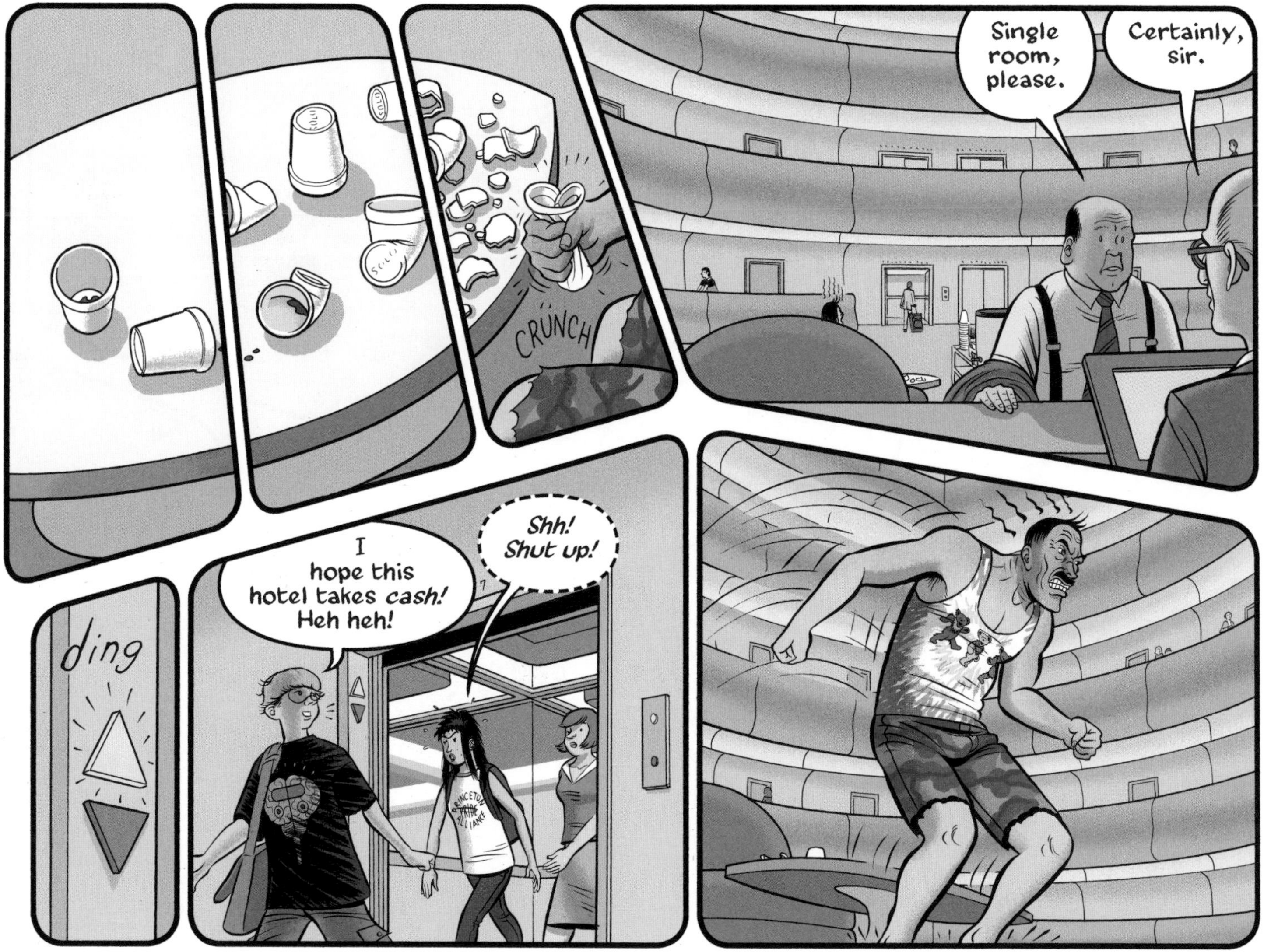
CRUNCH
Single room, please.
Certainly, sir.
ding
I hope this hotel takes cash! Heh heh!
Shh! Shut up!

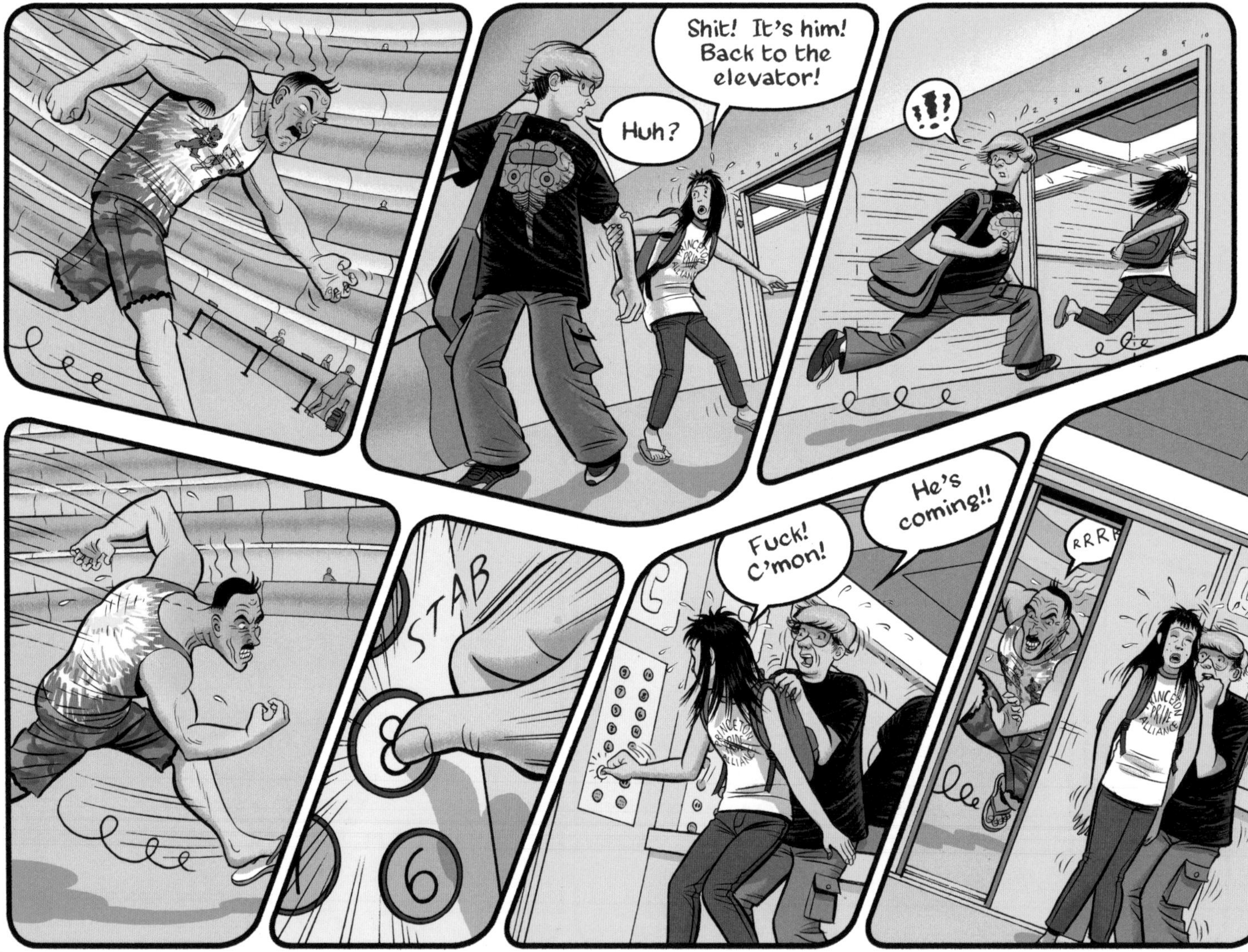
Huh?
Shit! It's him! Back to the elevator!
!!?!
STAB
Fuck! C'mon!
He's coming!!
RRRR

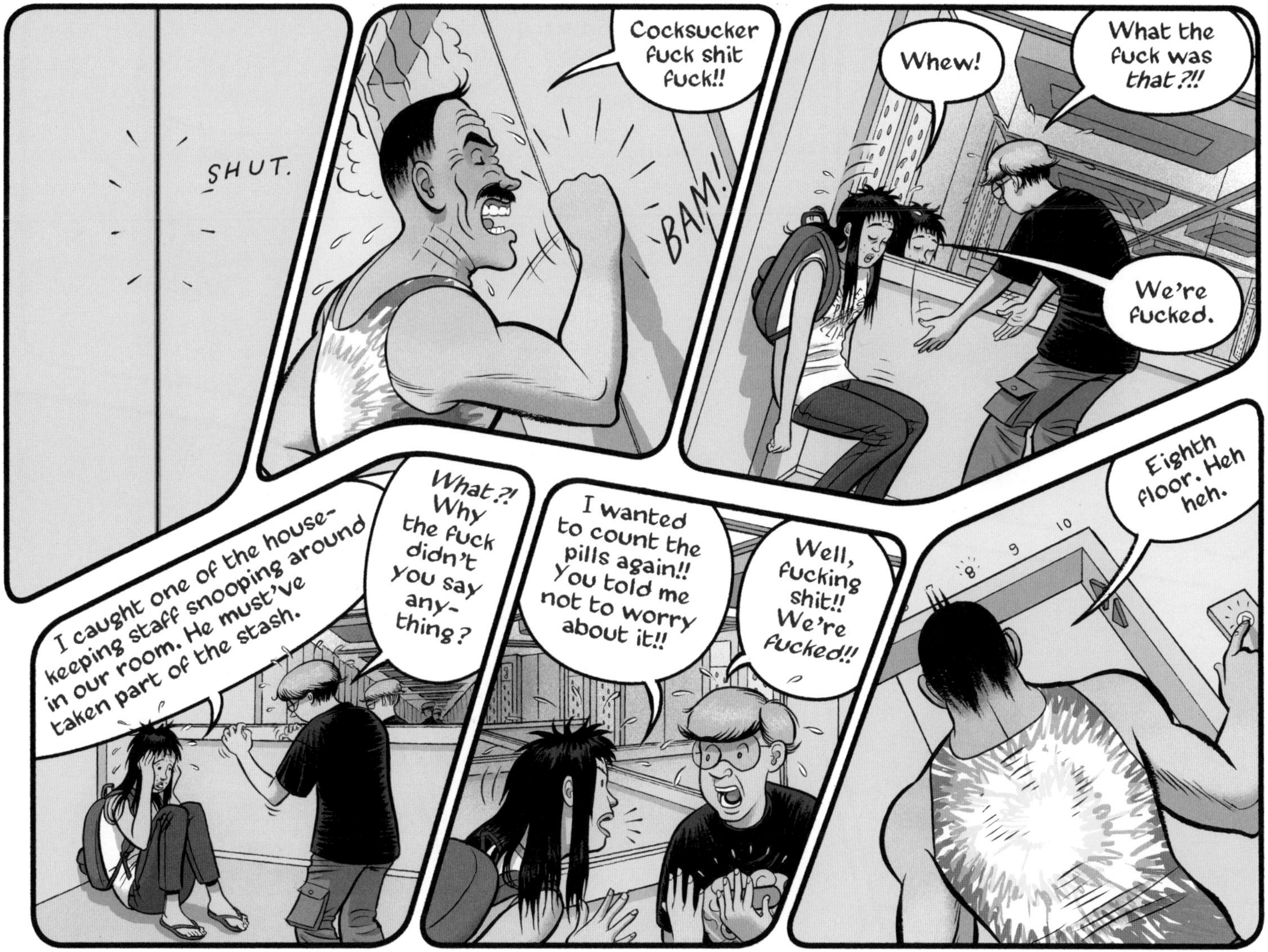
SHUT.
Cocksucker fuck shit fuck!!
BAM!!
Whew!
What the fuck was *that?!!*
We're fucked.
I caught one of the house-keeping staff snooping around in our room. He must've taken part of the stash.
What?! Why the fuck didn't you say any-thing?
I wanted to count the pills again!! You told me not to worry about it!!
Well, fucking shit!! We're fucked!!
10
9
8
Eighth floor. Heh heh.

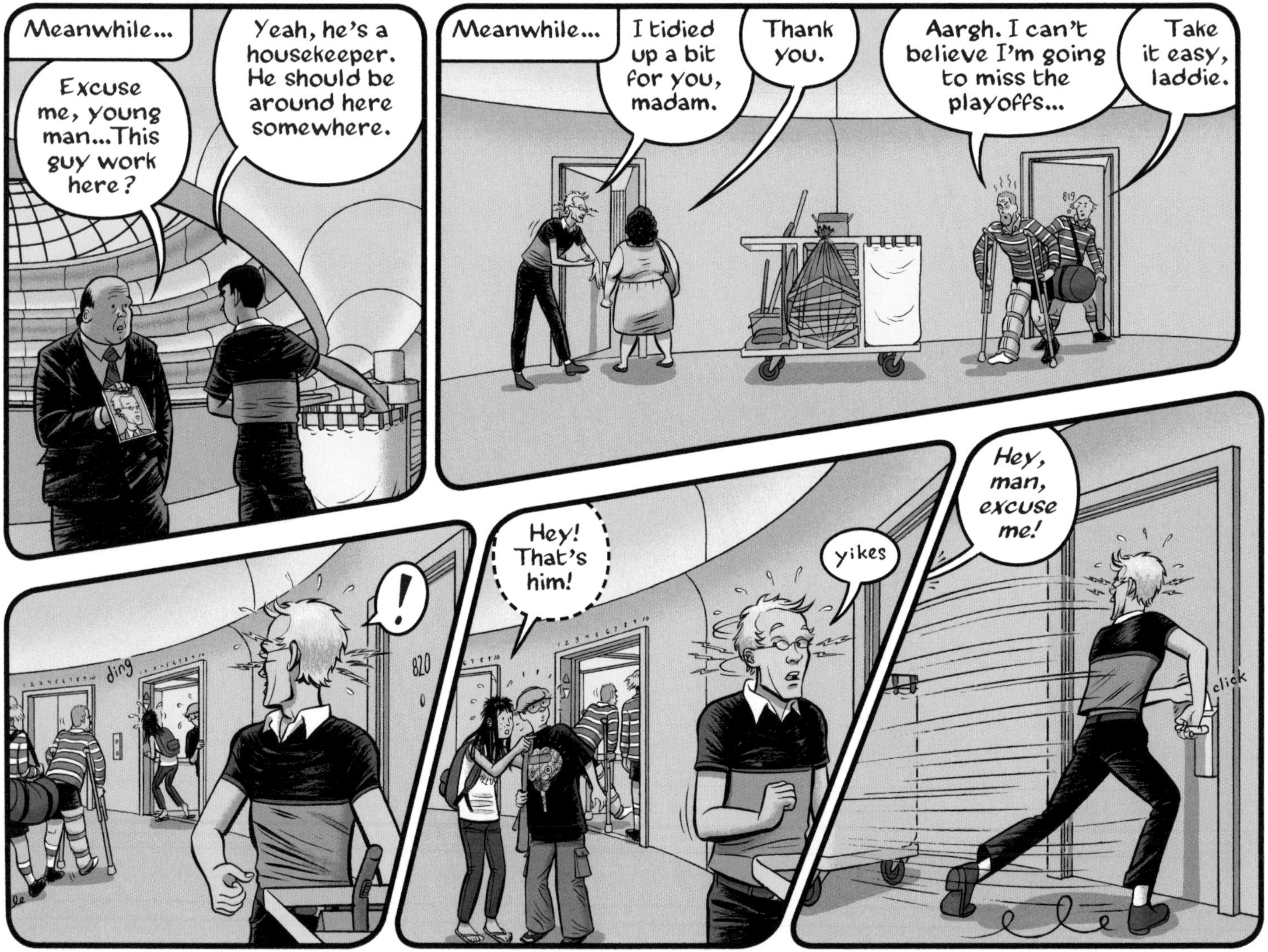

Meanwhile...
Excuse me, young man...This guy work here?
Yeah, he's a housekeeper. He should be around here somewhere.
Meanwhile...
I tidied up a bit for you, madam.
Thank you.
Aargh. I can't believe I'm going to miss the playoffs...
Take it easy, laddie.
819
ding
820
!
Hey! That's him!
yikes
Hey, man, excuse me!
click

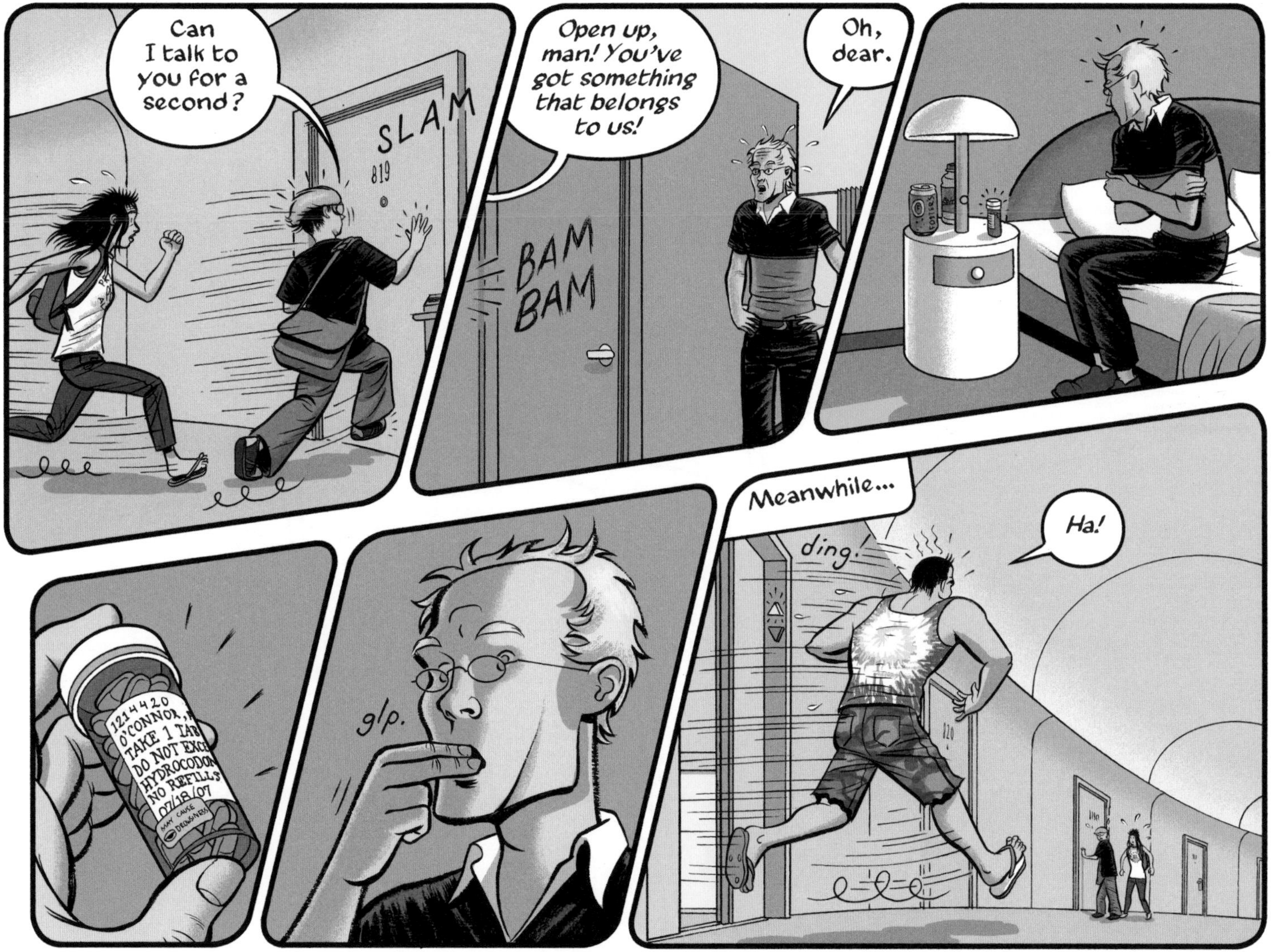
Can I talk to you for a second?
SLAM
819
Open up, man! You've got something that belongs to us!
BAM BAM
Oh, dear.
1214420
NO REFILLS
07/18/07
MAY CAUSE DROWSINESS
glp.
Meanwhile...
ding!
Ha!

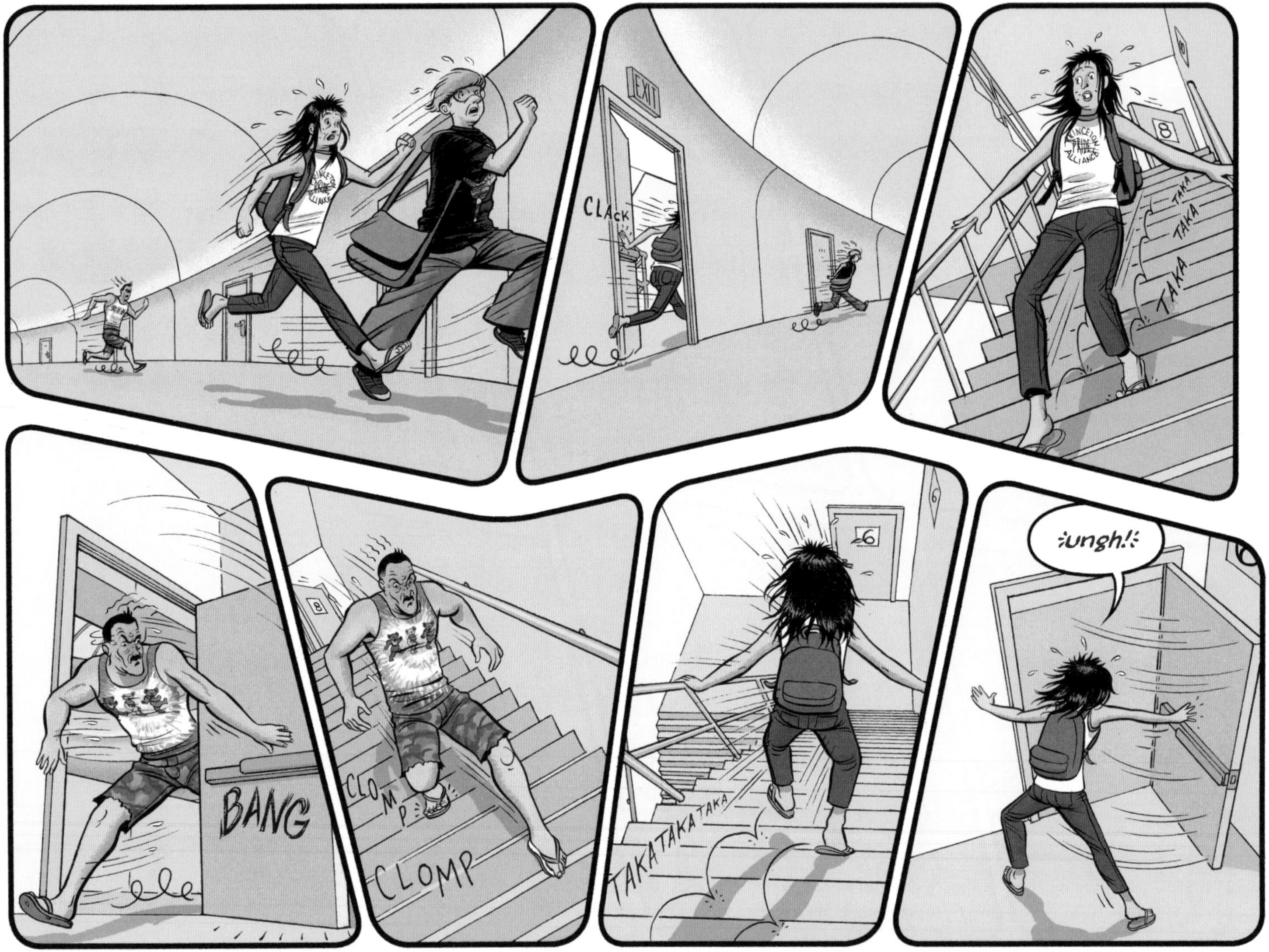
EXIT
CLACK
PRINCETON PRIDE ALLIANCE
8
TAKA TAKA TAKA
BANG
8
CLOMP
CLOMP
6
TAKATAKATAKA
ungh!

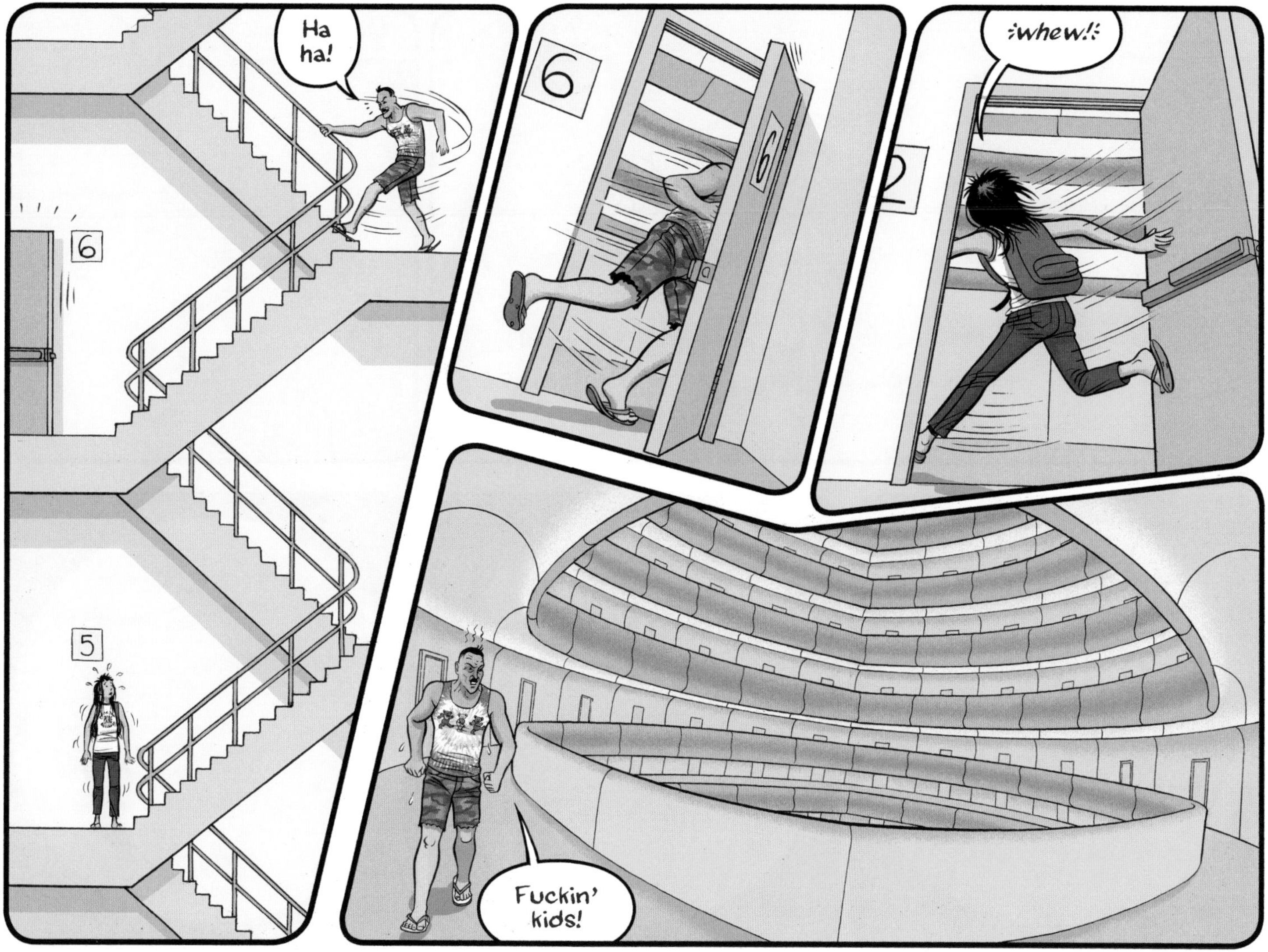
Ha ha!
6
5
6
6
:whew!:
2
Fuckin' kids!

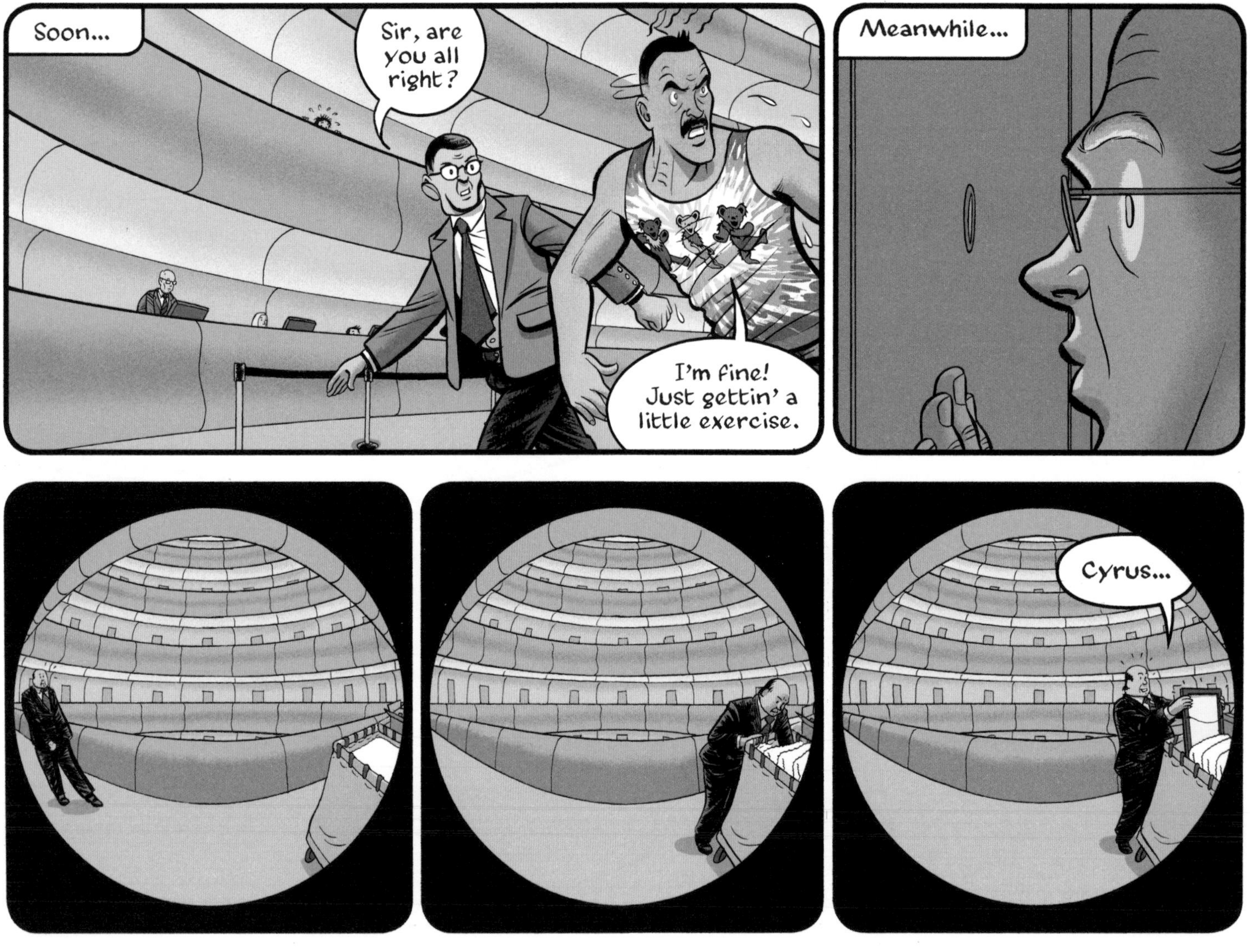

Soon...
Sir, are you all right?
I'm fine! Just gettin' a little exercise.
Meanwhile...
Cyrus...

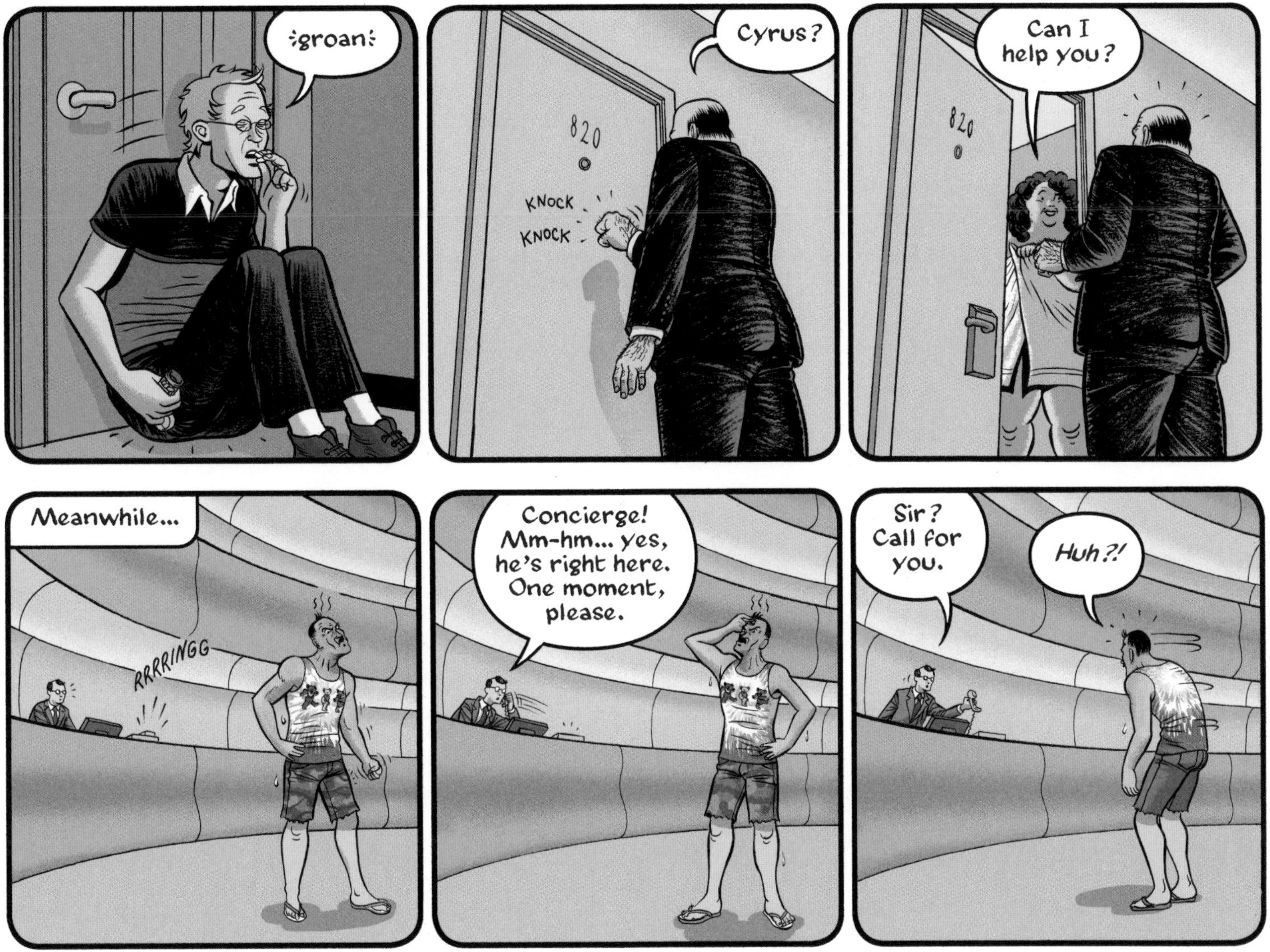
groan
Cyrus?
820
KNOCK
KNOCK
Can I help you?
820
Meanwhile...
RRRRINGG
Concierge! Mm-hm... yes, he's right here. One moment, please.
Sir? Call for you.
Huh?!

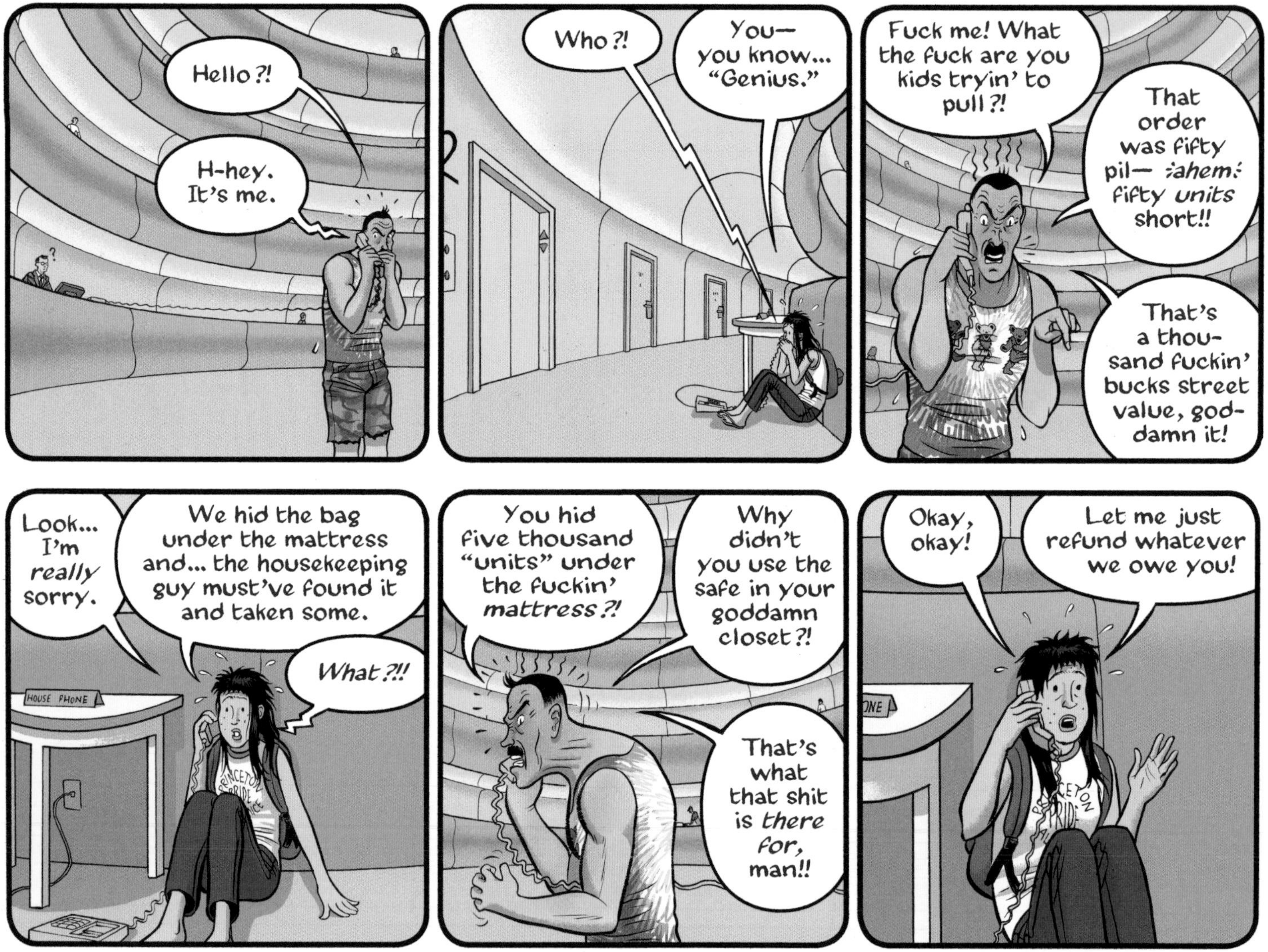
Hello?!
H-hey. It's me.
Who?!
You— you know... "Genius."
Fuck me! What the fuck are you kids tryin' to pull?!
That order was fifty pil— :ahem: fifty *units* short!!
That's a thousand fuckin' bucks street value, goddamn it!
Look... I'm *really* sorry.
We hid the bag under the mattress and... the housekeeping guy must've found it and taken some.
What?!!
HOUSE PHONE
You hid five thousand "units" under the fuckin' *mattress?!*
Why didn't you use the safe in your goddamn closet?!
That's what that shit is *there* for, man!!
Okay, okay!
Let me just refund whatever we owe you!

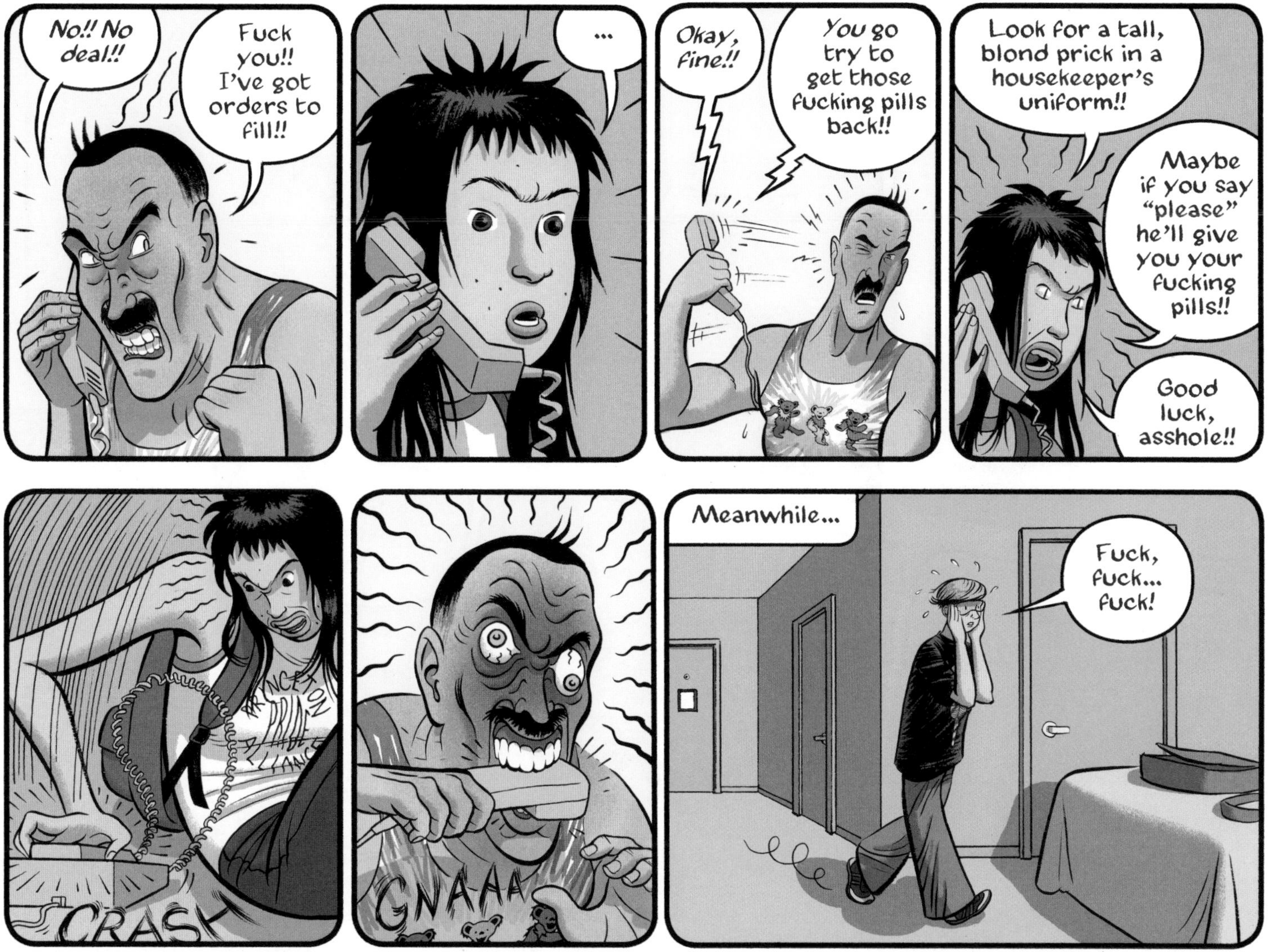

No!! No deal!!
Fuck you!! I've got orders to fill!!
...
Okay, fine!!
You go try to get those fucking pills back!!
Look for a tall, blond prick in a housekeeper's uniform!!
Maybe if you say "please" he'll give you your fucking pills!!
Good luck, asshole!!
CRASH
GNAAA
Meanwhile...
Fuck, fuck... fuck!

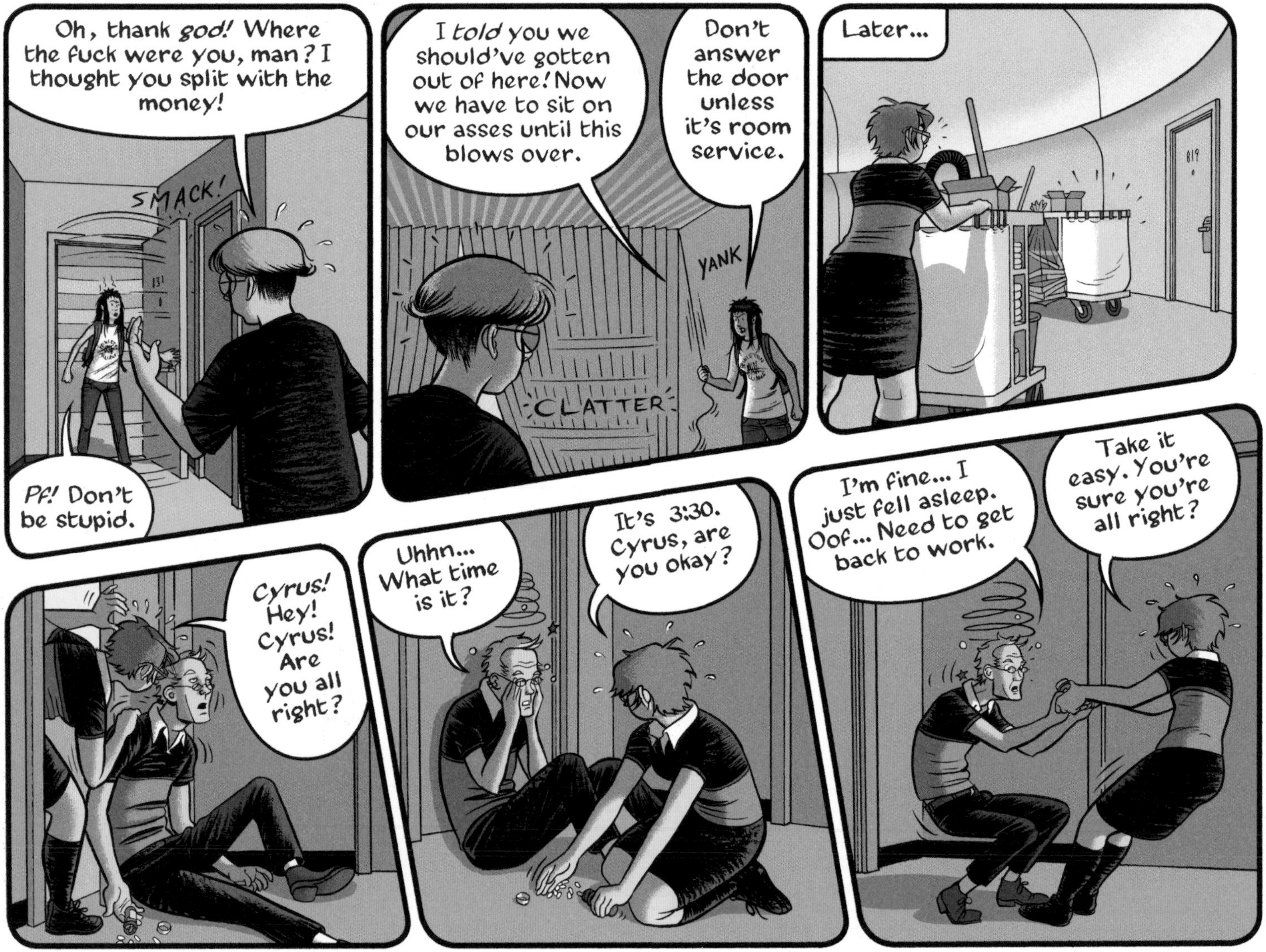

Oh, thank god! Where the fuck were you, man? I thought you split with the money!
SMACK!
131
Pf! Don't be stupid.
I told you we should've gotten out of here! Now we have to sit on our asses until this blows over.
Don't answer the door unless it's room service.
YANK
CLATTER
Later...
819
Cyrus! Hey! Cyrus! Are you all right?
Uhhn... What time is it?
It's 3:30. Cyrus, are you okay?
I'm fine... I just fell asleep. Oof... Need to get back to work.
Take it easy. You're sure you're all right?

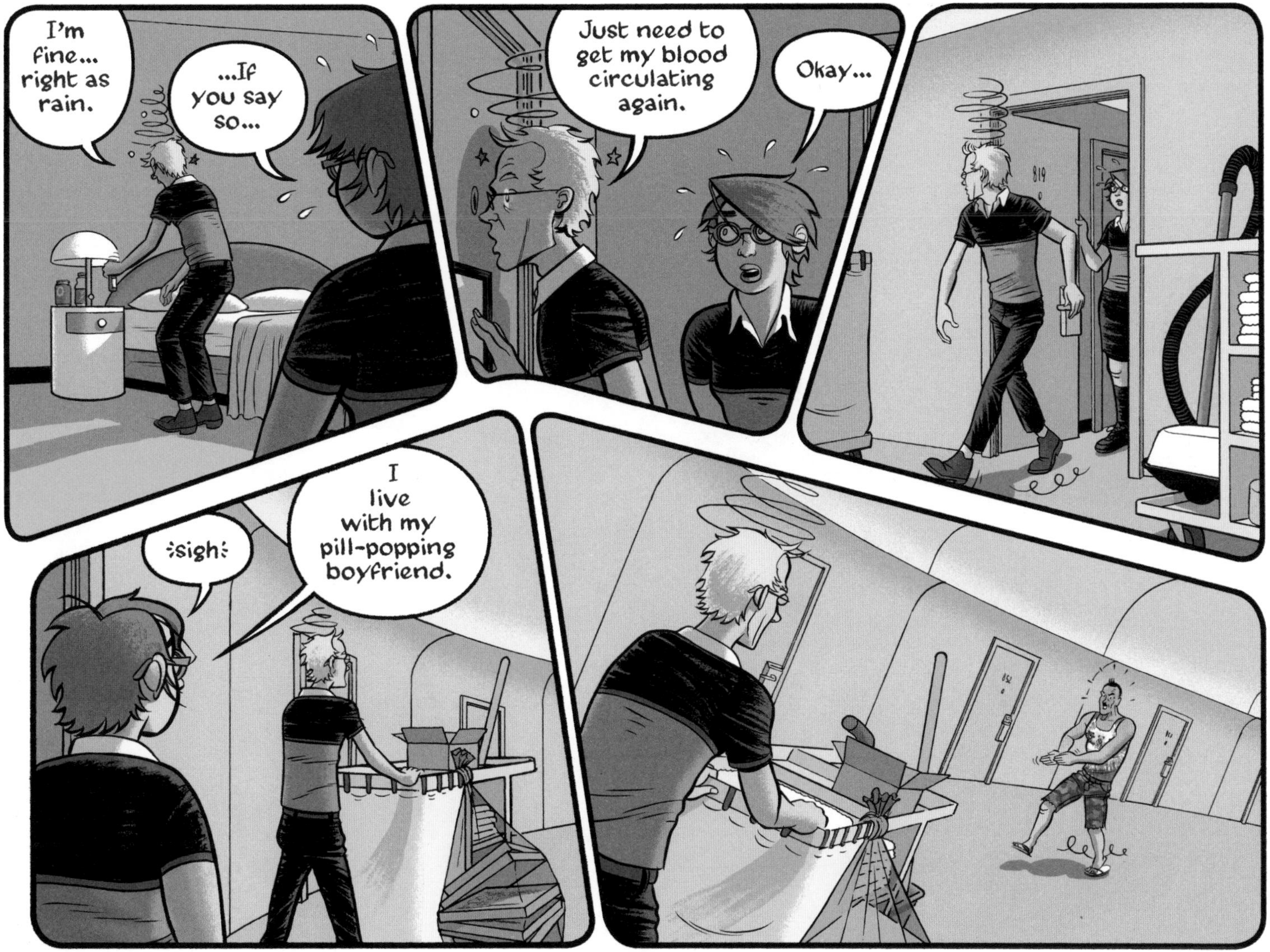
I'm fine... right as rain.
...If you say so...
Just need to get my blood circulating again.
Okay...
819
:sigh:
I live with my pill-popping boyfriend.

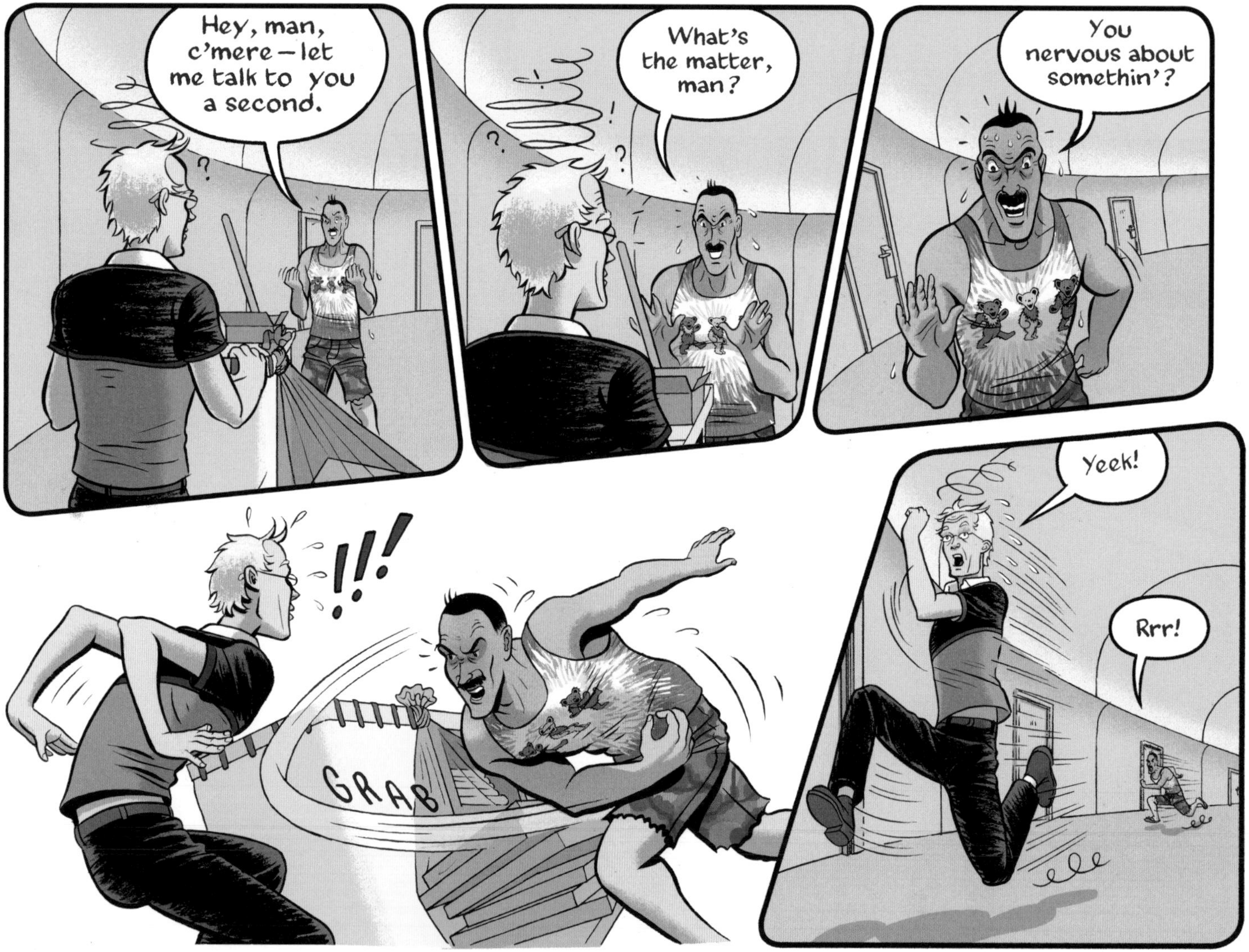
Hey, man, c'mere—let me talk to you a second.
What's the matter, man?
You nervous about somethin'?
!!!
GRAB
Yeek!
Rrr!

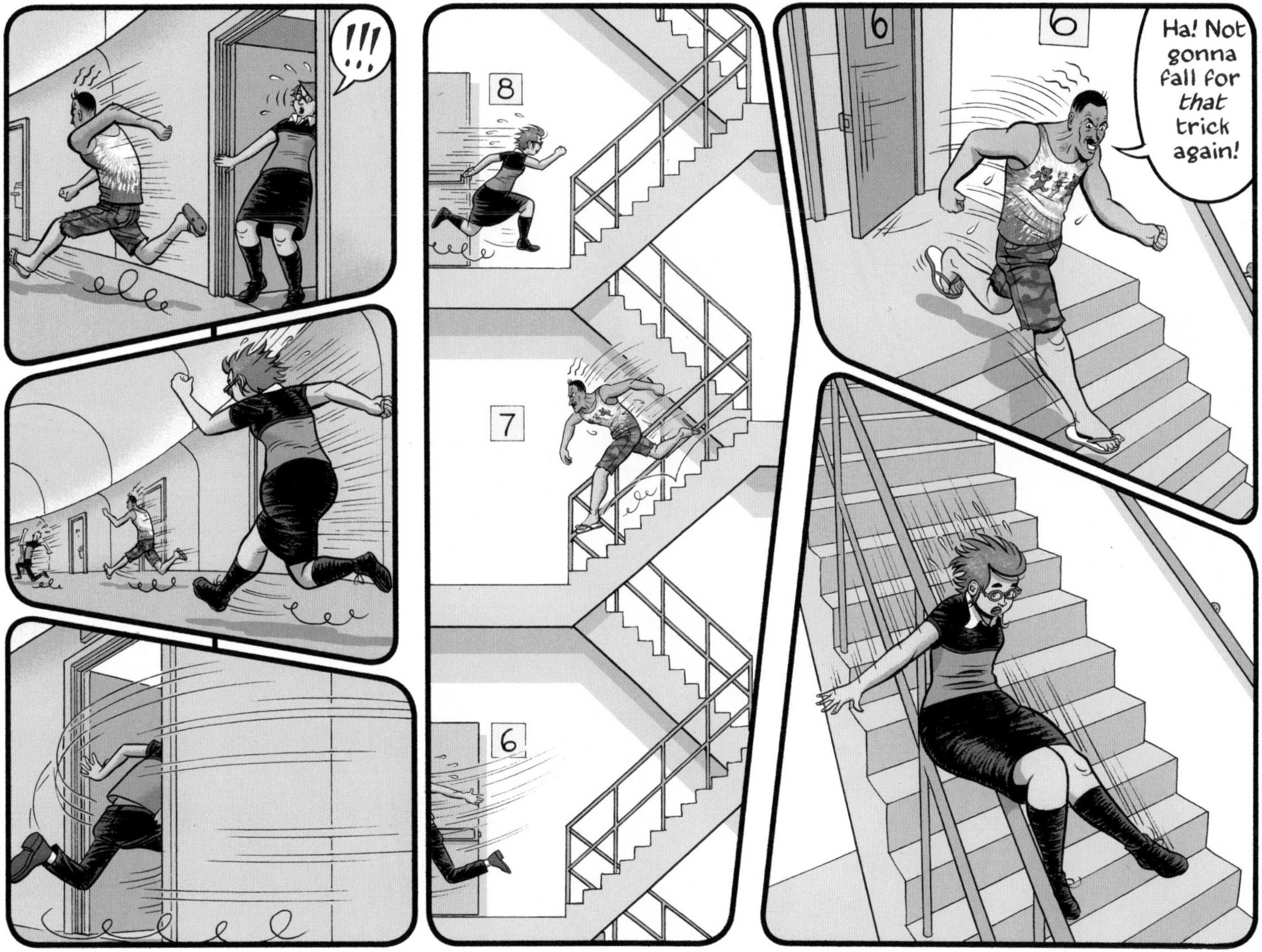
!!!
8
7
6
6
6
Ha! Not gonna fall for *that* trick again!

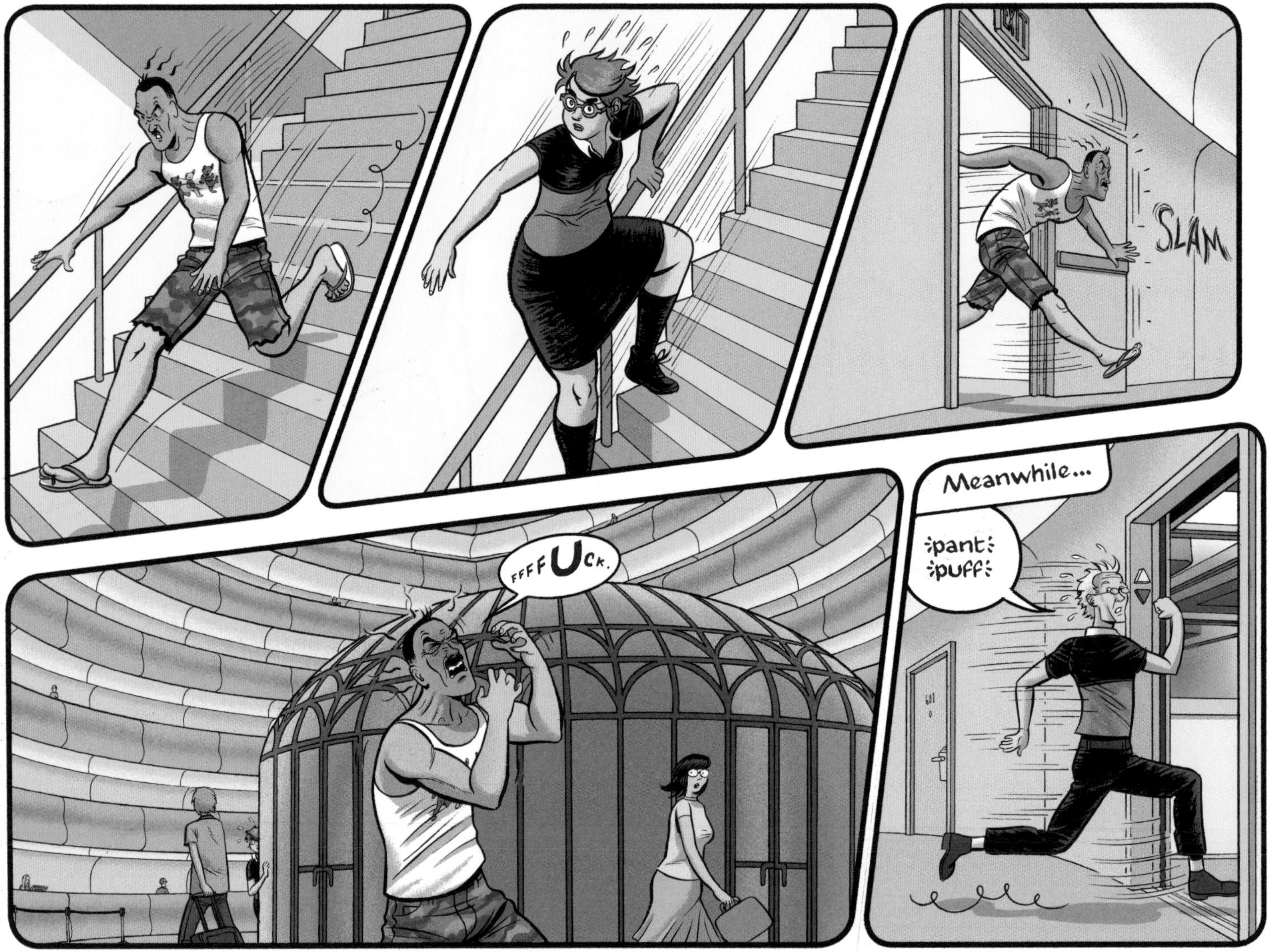
SLAM
FFFFUCK.
Meanwhile...
:pant:
:puff:

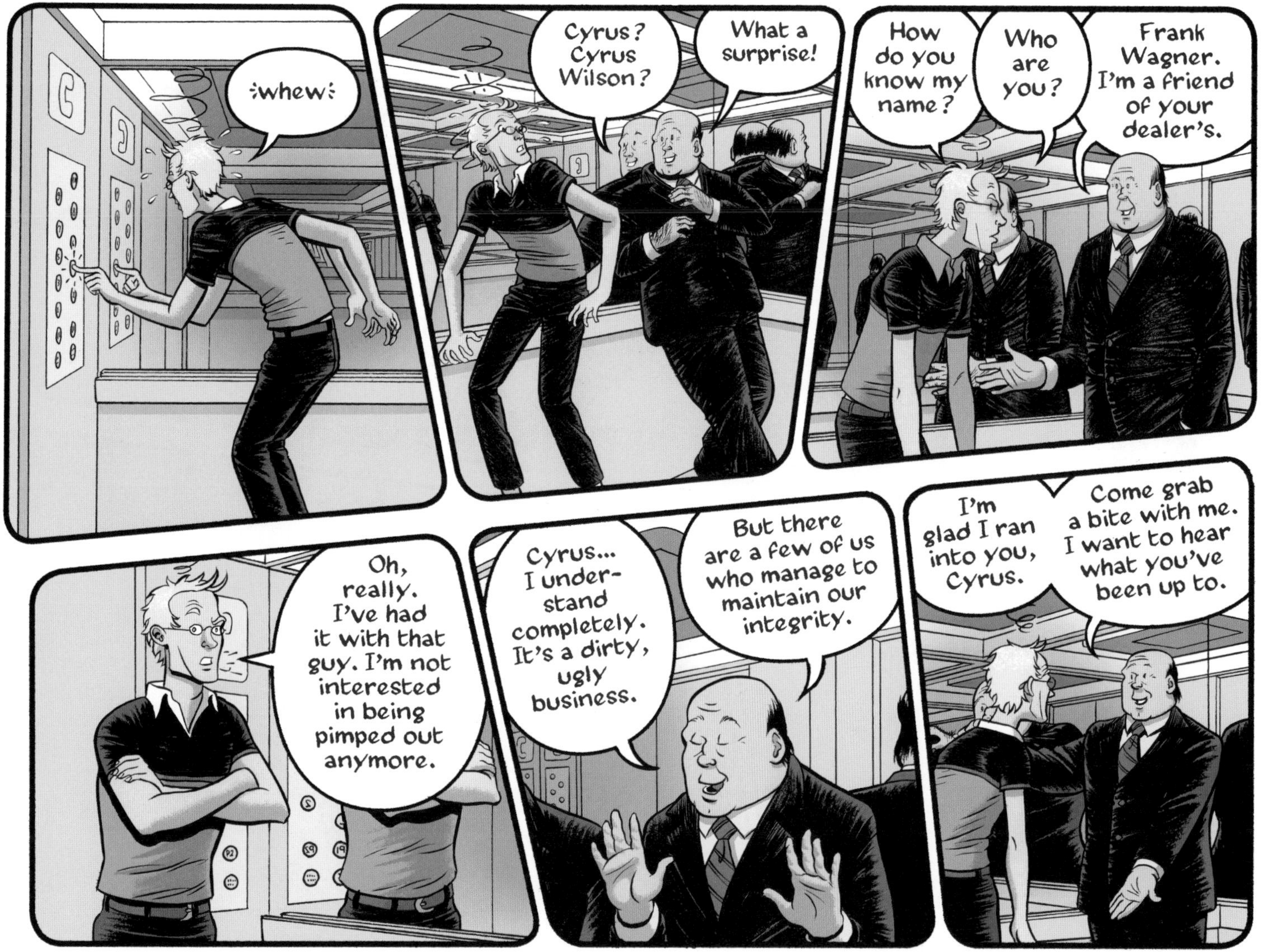
whew
Cyrus? Cyrus Wilson?
What a surprise!
How do you know my name?
Who are you?
Frank Wagner. I'm a friend of your dealer's.
Oh, really. I've had it with that guy. I'm not interested in being pimped out anymore.
Cyrus... I understand completely. It's a dirty, ugly business.
But there are a few of us who manage to maintain our integrity.
I'm glad I ran into you, Cyrus.
Come grab a bite with me. I want to hear what you've been up to.

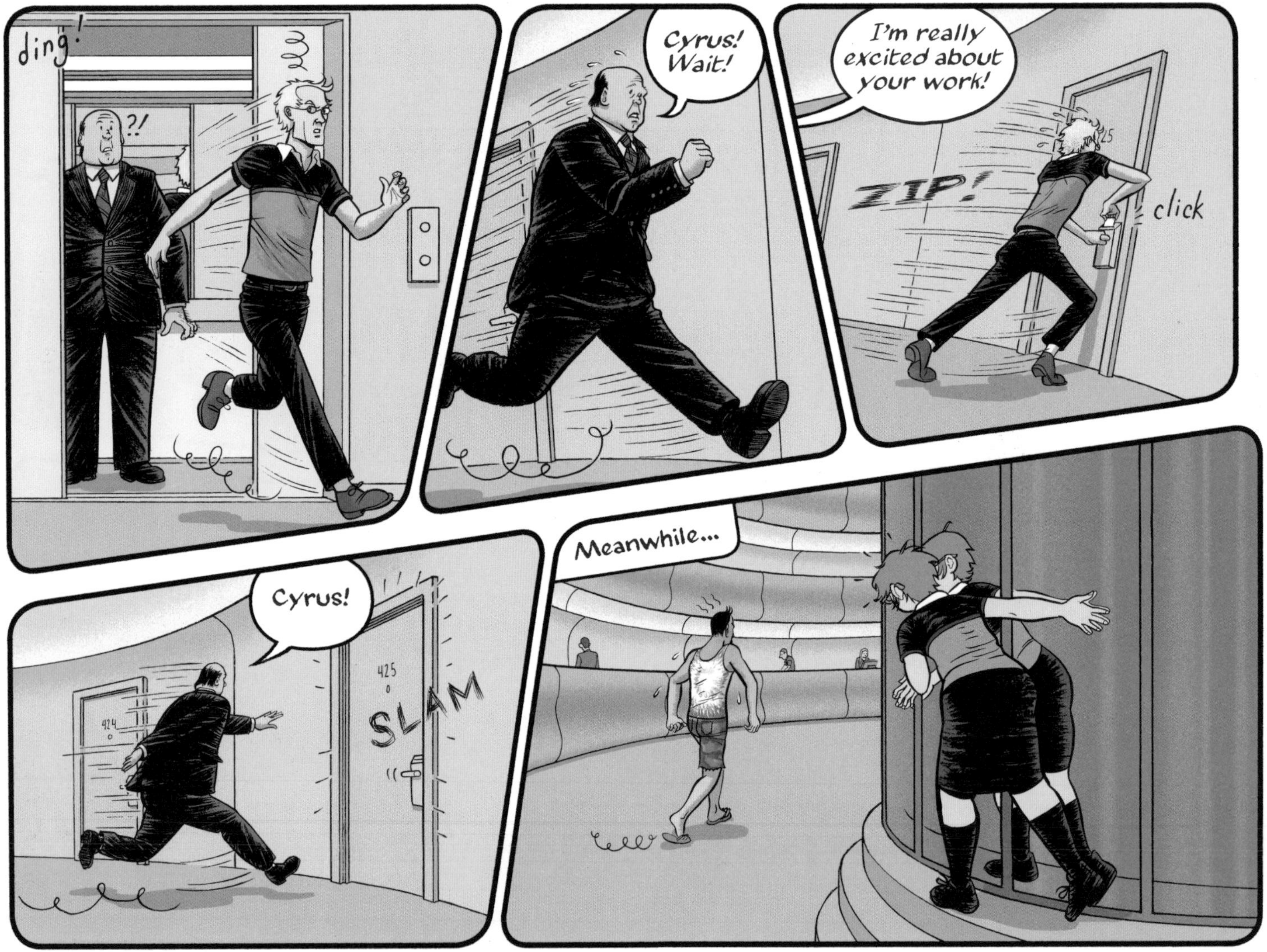
ding!
?!
Cyrus! Wait!
I'm really excited about your work!
ZIP!
click
Cyrus!
425
424
SLAM
Meanwhile...

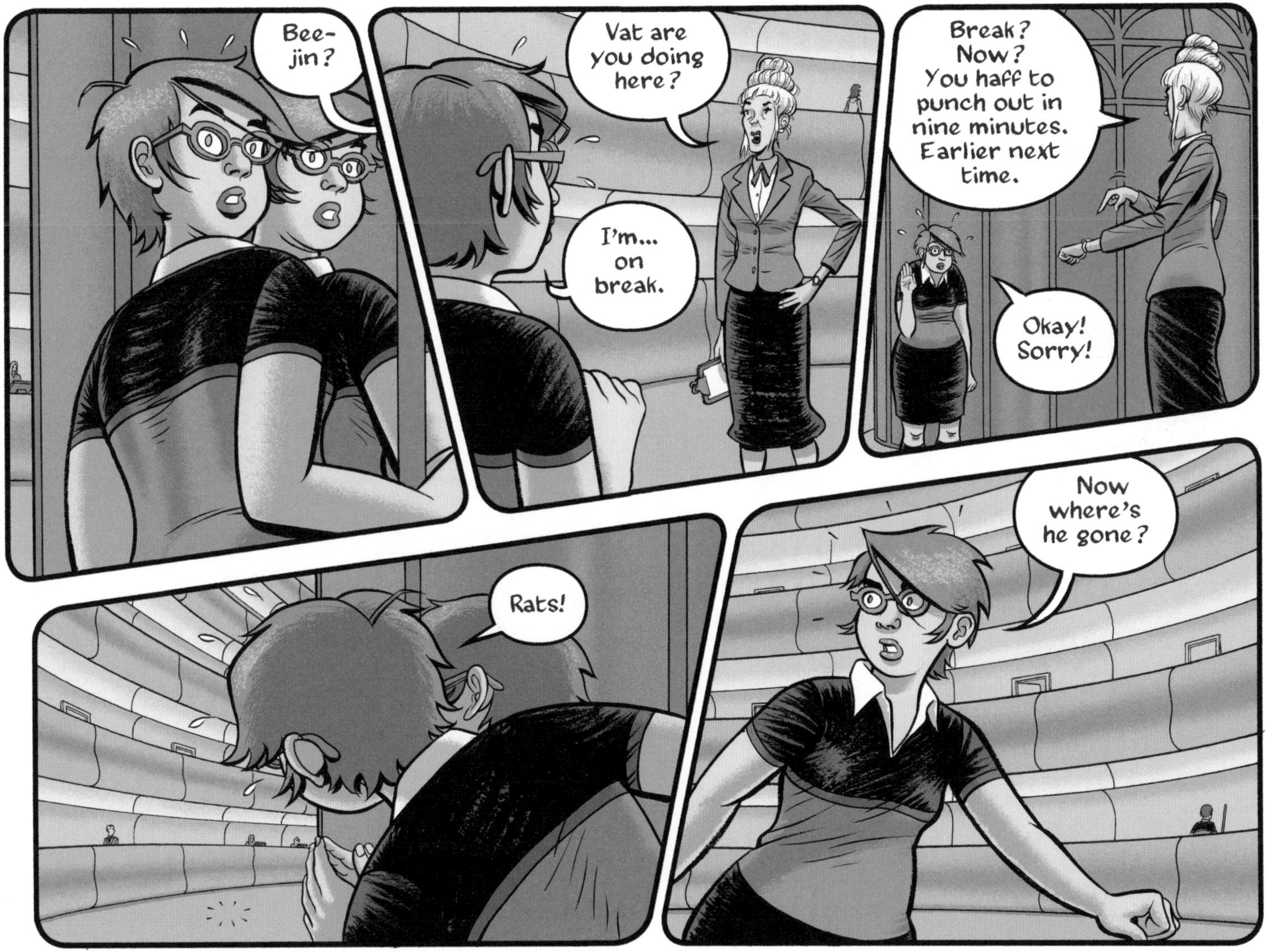
Bee-jin?
Vat are you doing here?
I'm... on break.
Break? Now? You haff to punch out in nine minutes. Earlier next time.
Okay! Sorry!
Rats!
Now where's he gone?

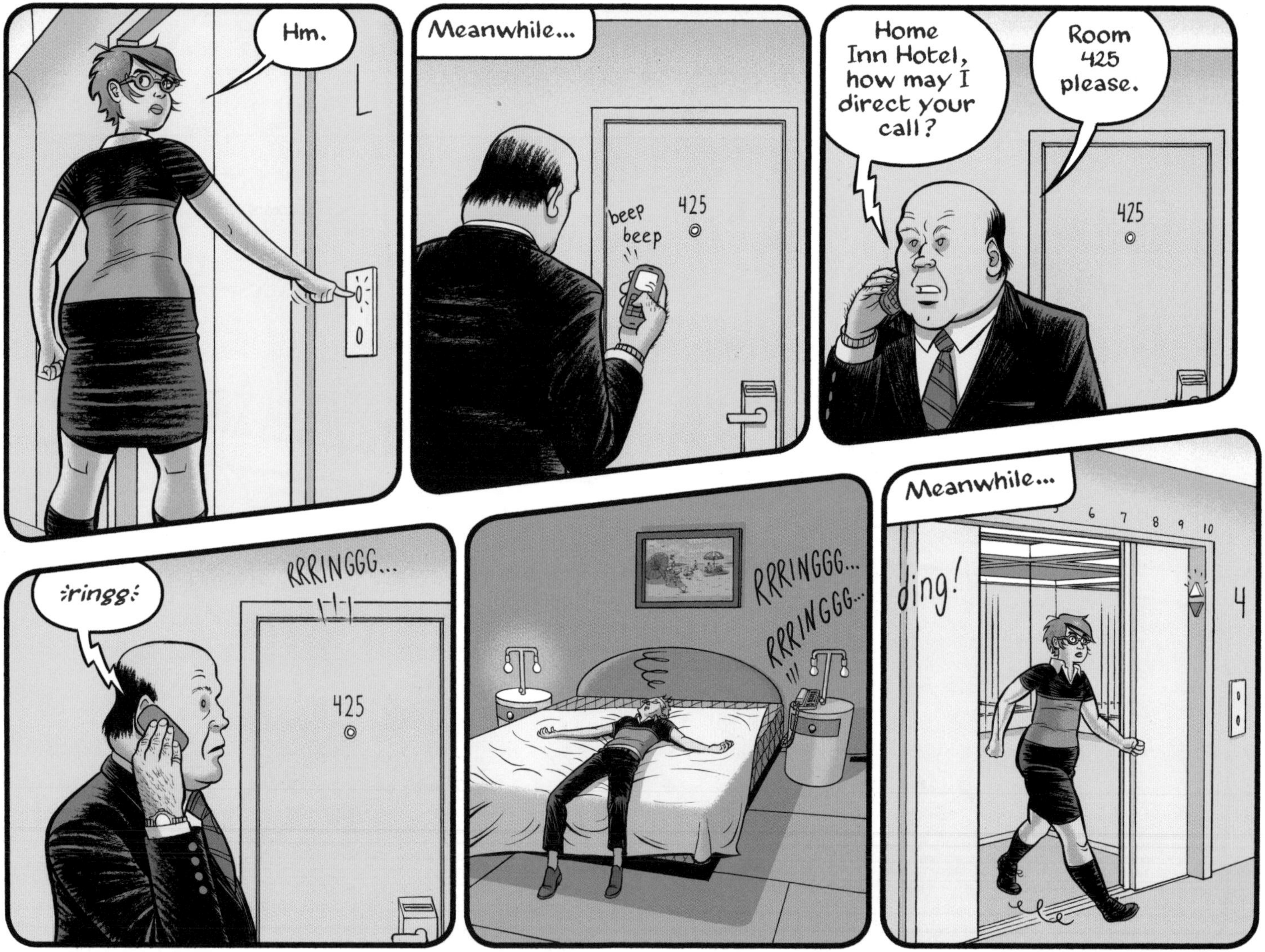
Hm.
Meanwhile...
beep beep
425
Home Inn Hotel, how may I direct your call?
Room 425 please.
425
:ringg:
RRRINGGG...
425
RRRINGGG...
RRRINGGG...
Meanwhile...
6 7 8 9 10
ding!
4

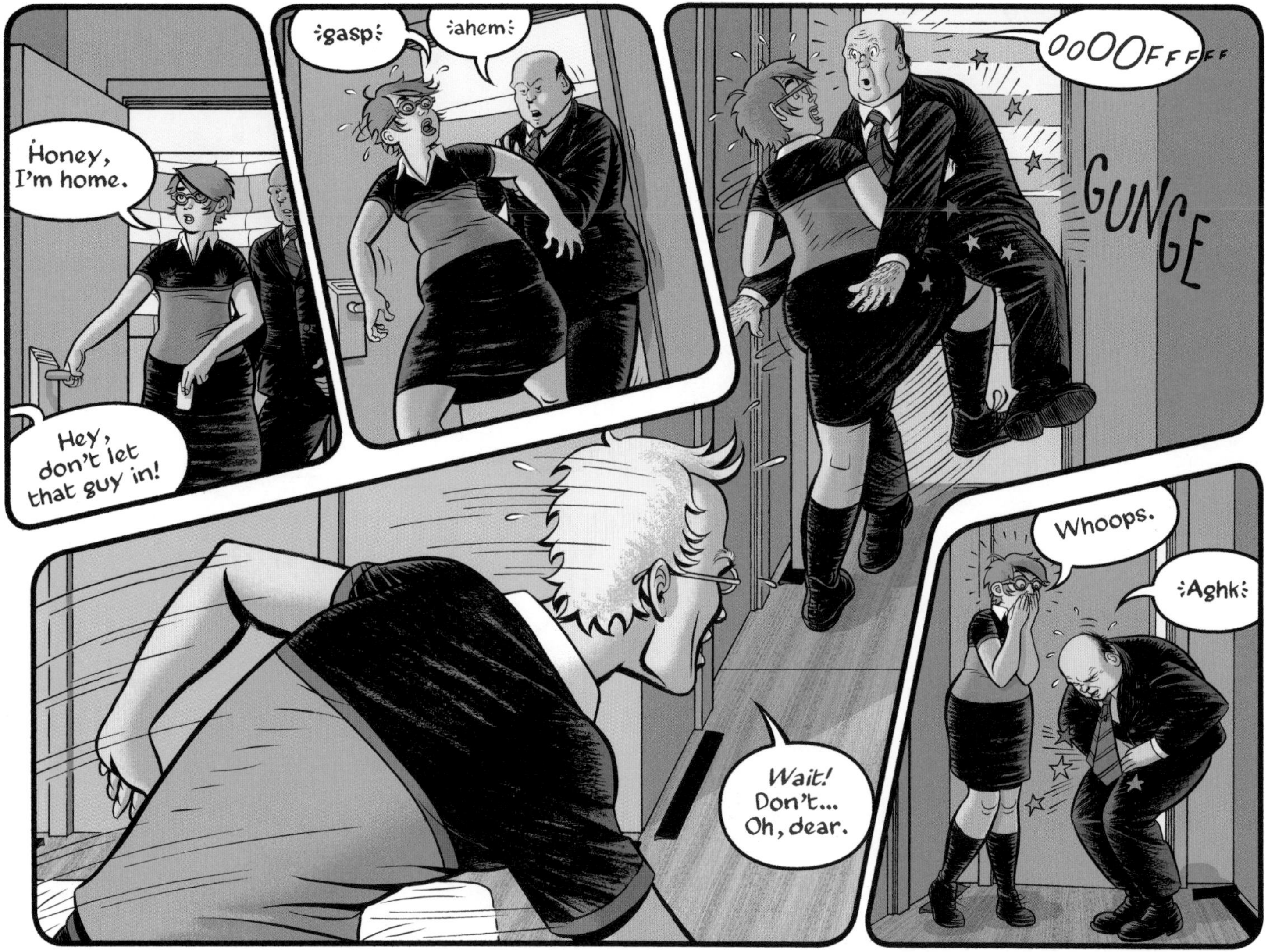

Honey, I'm home.
Hey, don't let that guy in!
gasp
ahem
OOOOFFFFF
GUNGE
Wait! Don't... Oh, dear.
Whoops.
Aghk

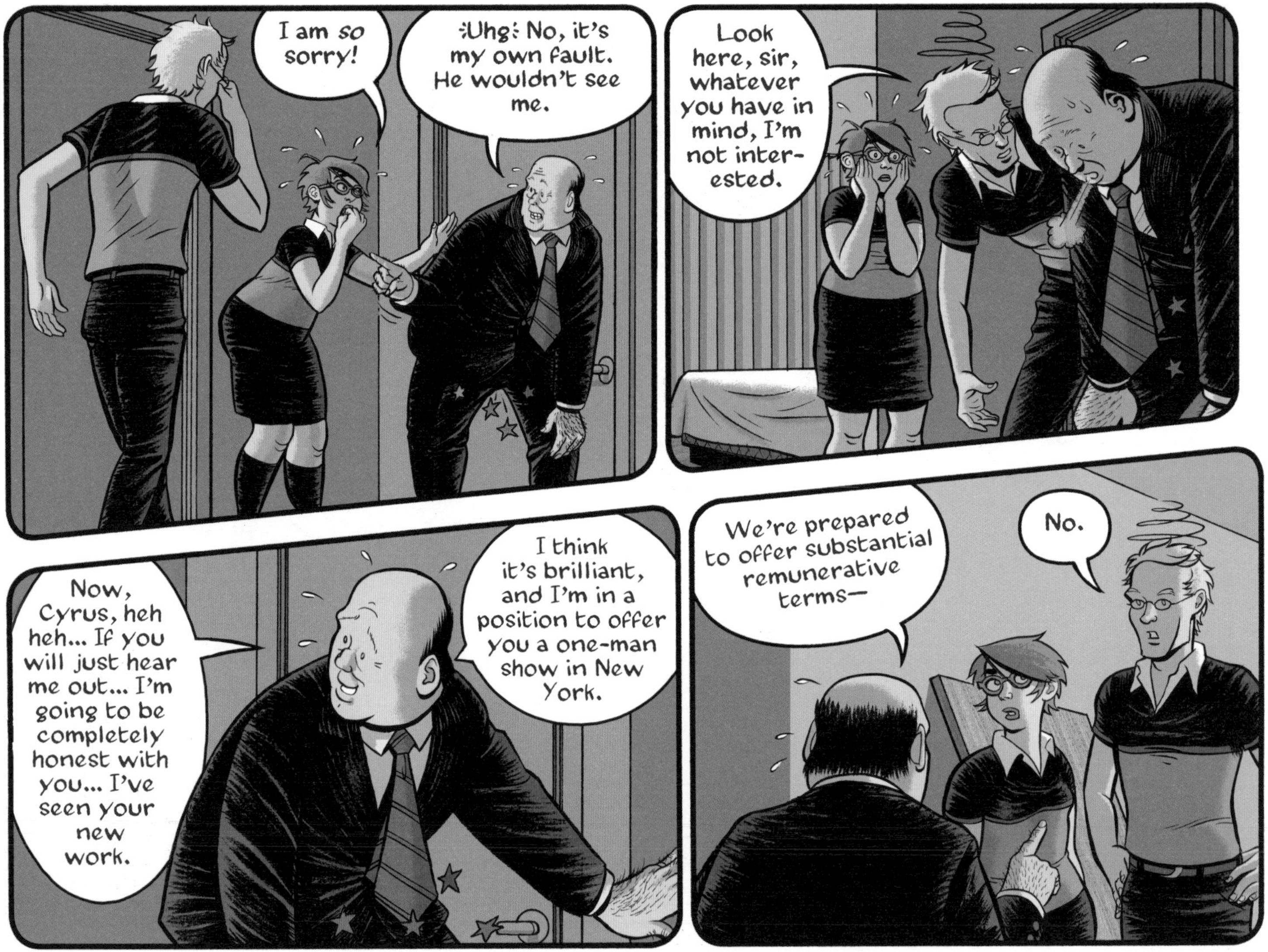
I am so sorry!
:Uhg: No, it's my own fault. He wouldn't see me.
Look here, sir, whatever you have in mind, I'm not interested.
Now, Cyrus, heh heh... If you will just hear me out... I'm going to be completely honest with you... I've seen your new work.
I think it's brilliant, and I'm in a position to offer you a one-man show in New York.
We're prepared to offer substantial remunerative terms—
No.

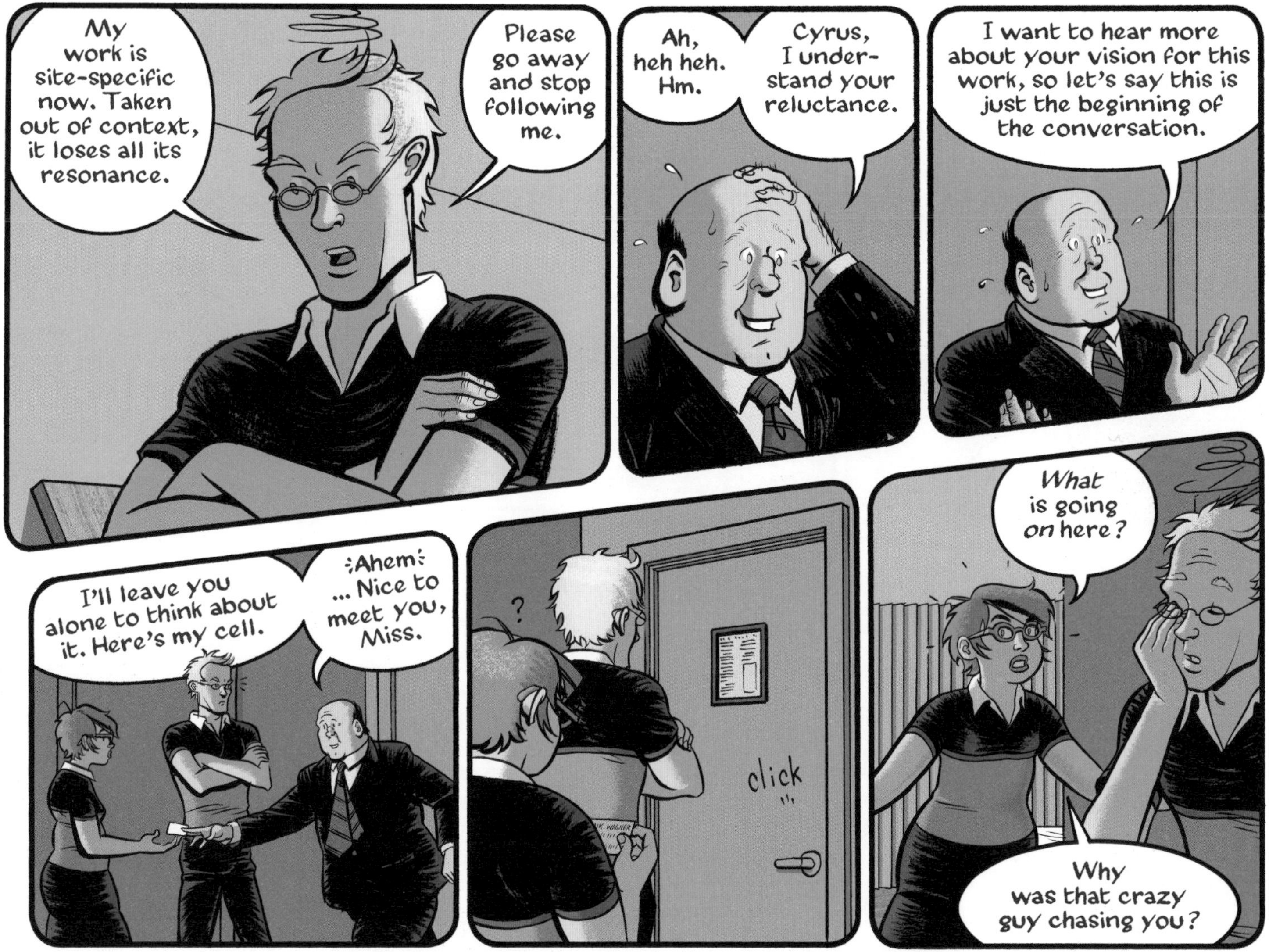
My work is site-specific now. Taken out of context, it loses all its resonance.
Please go away and stop following me.
Ah, heh heh. Hm.
Cyrus, I under-stand your reluctance.
I want to hear more about your vision for this work, so let's say this is just the beginning of the conversation.
I'll leave you alone to think about it. Here's my cell.
Ahem ... Nice to meet you, Miss.
?
click
What is going on here?
Why was that crazy guy chasing you?

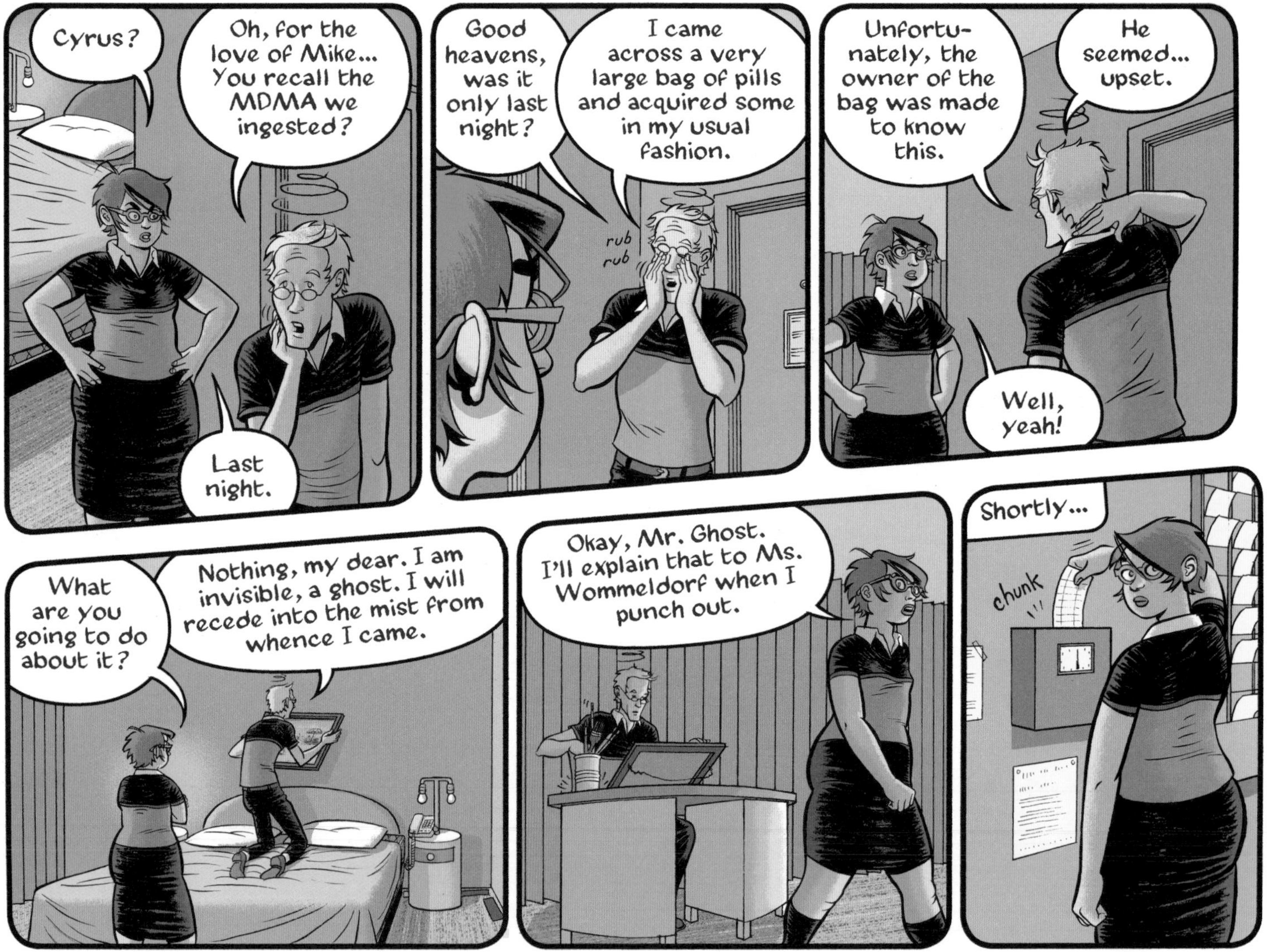

Cyrus?
Oh, for the love of Mike... You recall the MDMA we ingested?
Last night.
Good heavens, was it only last night?
I came across a very large bag of pills and acquired some in my usual fashion.
rub rub
Unfortunately, the owner of the bag was made to know this.
He seemed... upset.
Well, yeah!
What are you going to do about it?
Nothing, my dear. I am invisible, a ghost. I will recede into the mist from whence I came.
Okay, Mr. Ghost. I'll explain that to Ms. Wommeldorf when I punch out.
Shortly...
chunk

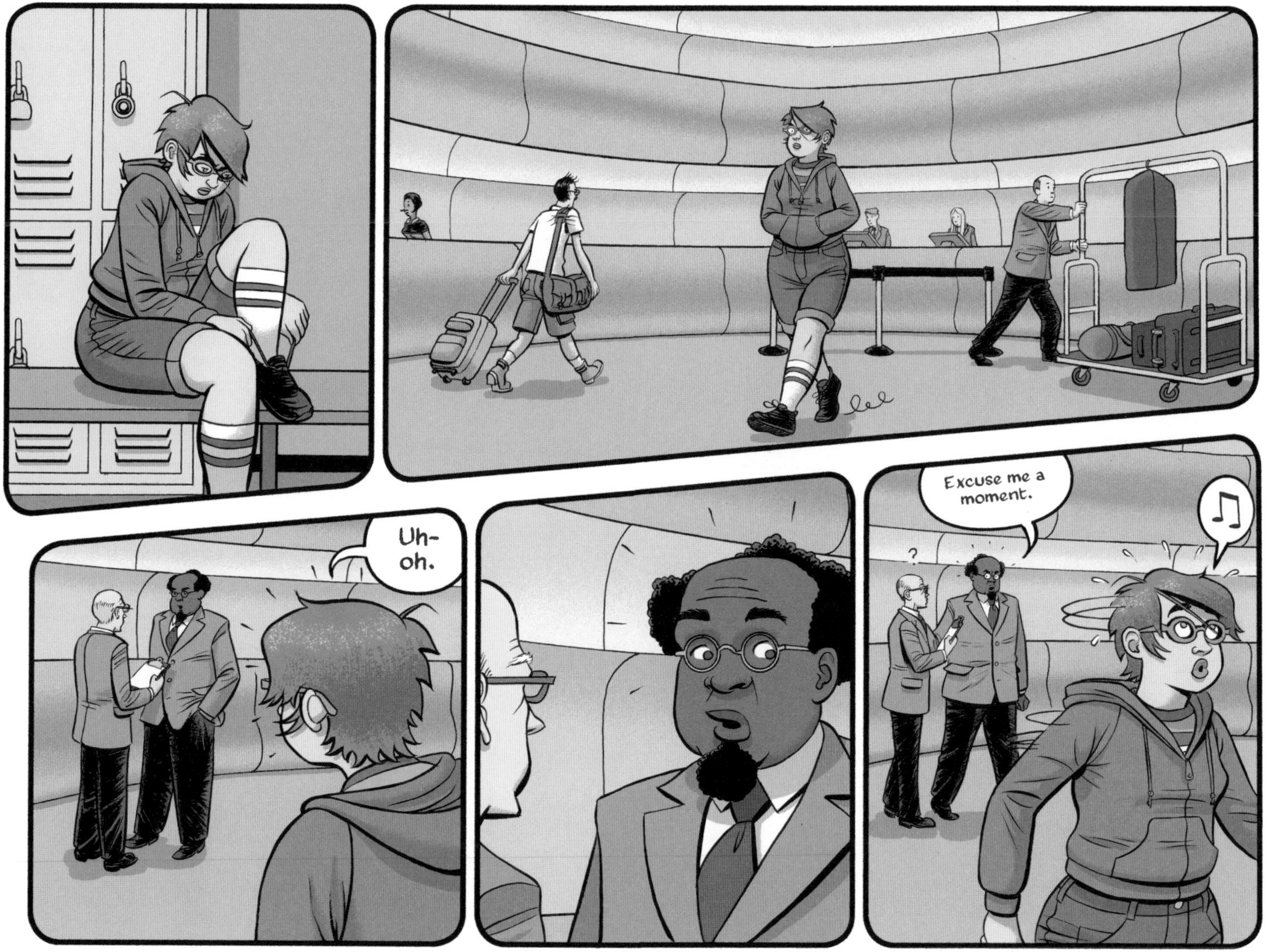
Uh-
oh.
?
Excuse me a
moment.
♫

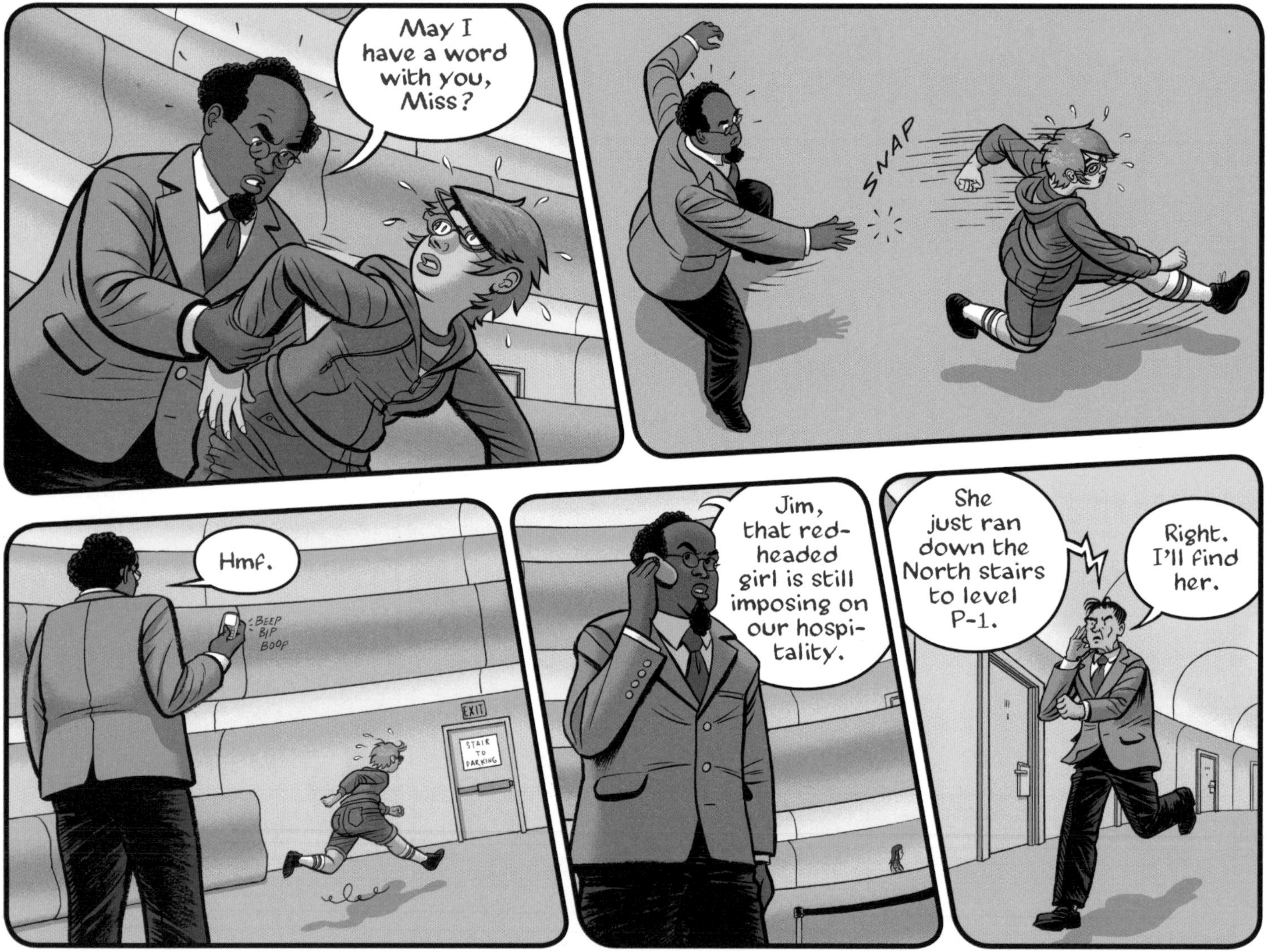
May I have a word with you, Miss?
SNAP
Hmf.
BEEP BIP BOOP
EXIT
STAIR TO PARKING
Jim, that red-headed girl is still imposing on our hospitality.
She just ran down the North stairs to level P-1.
Right. I'll find her.

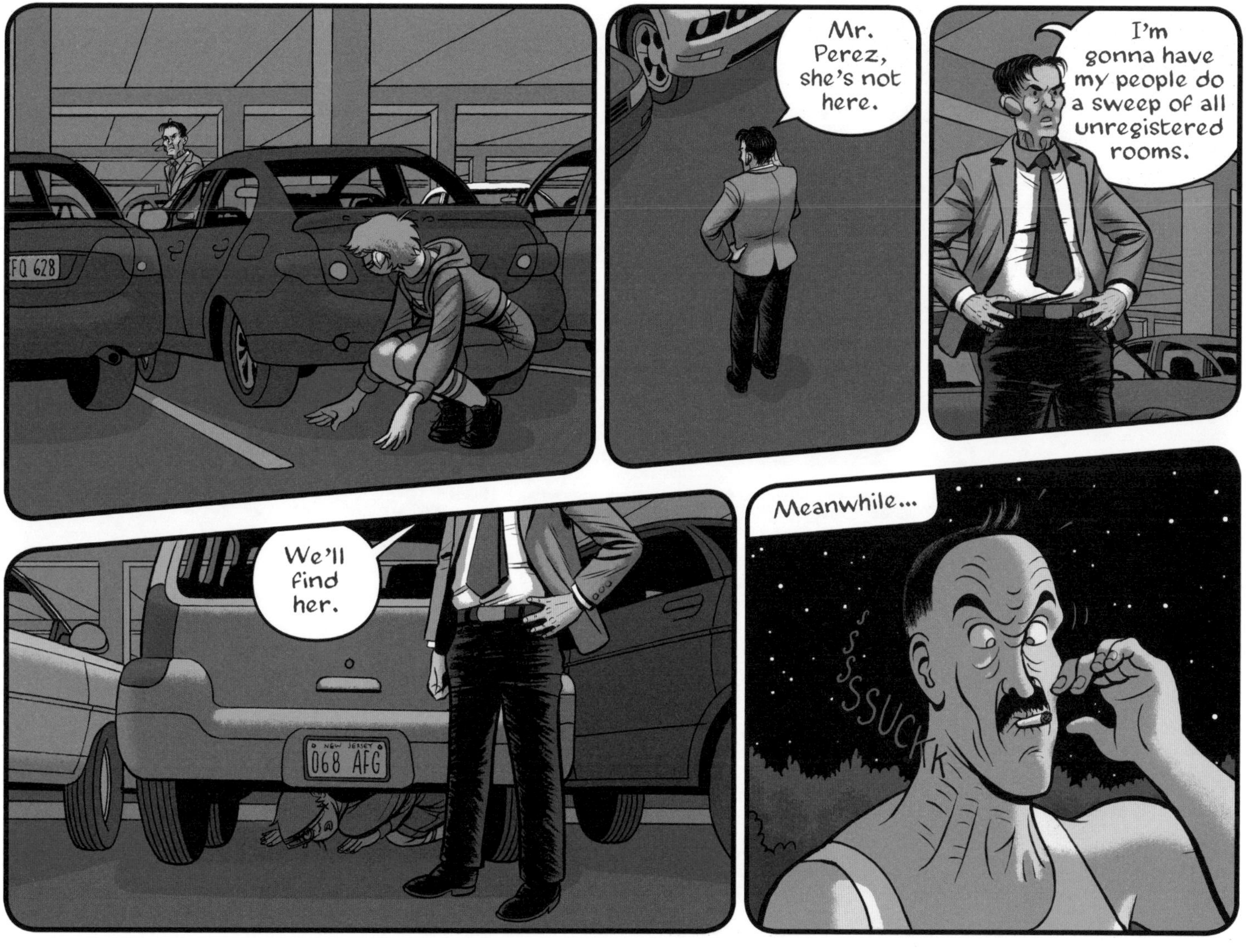
FQ 628
Mr. Perez, she's not here.
I'm gonna have my people do a sweep of all unregistered rooms.
We'll find her.
NEW JERSEY
068 AFG
Meanwhile...
SSSSUCKK

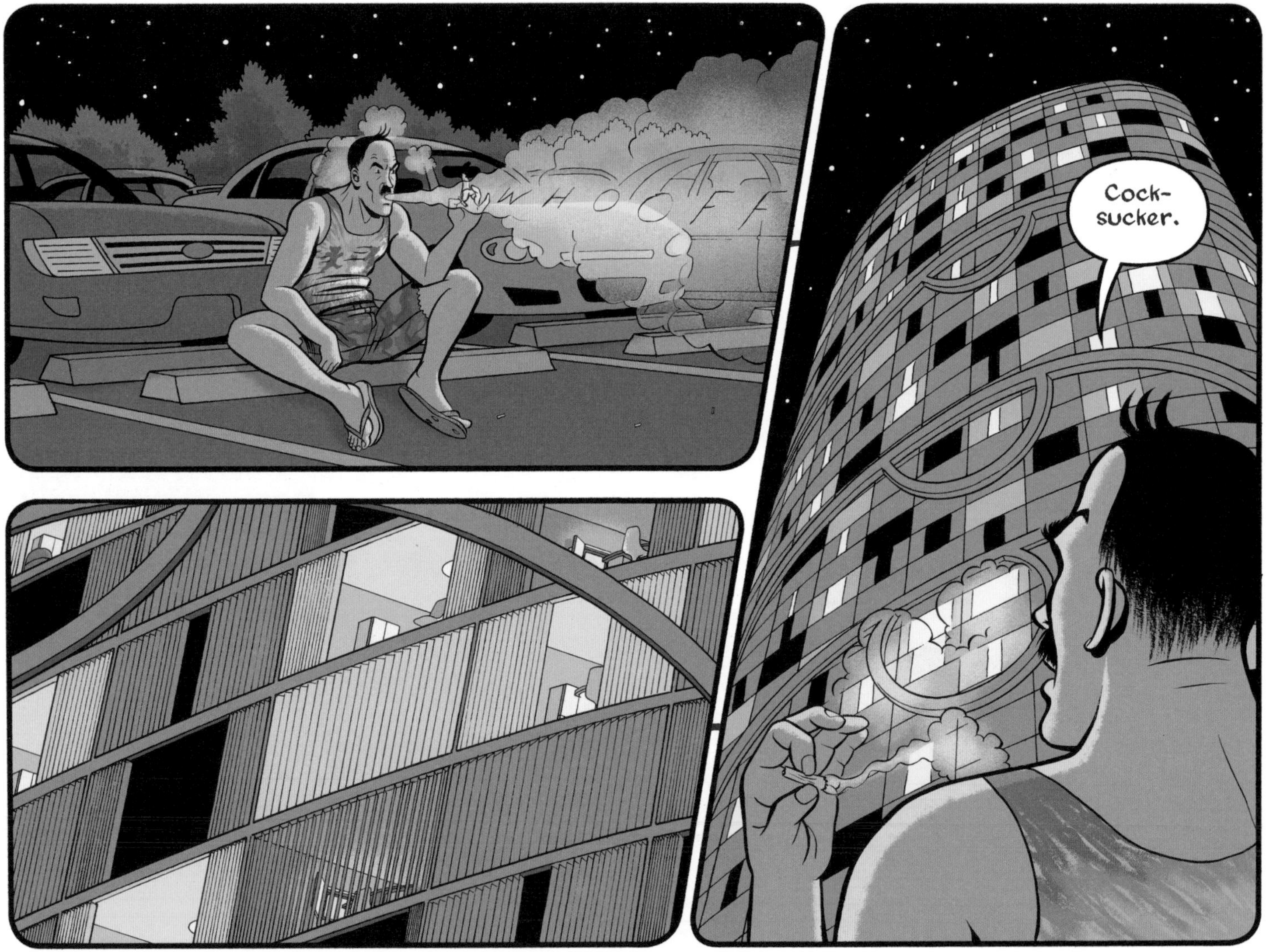
WHOOFF
Cock-sucker.

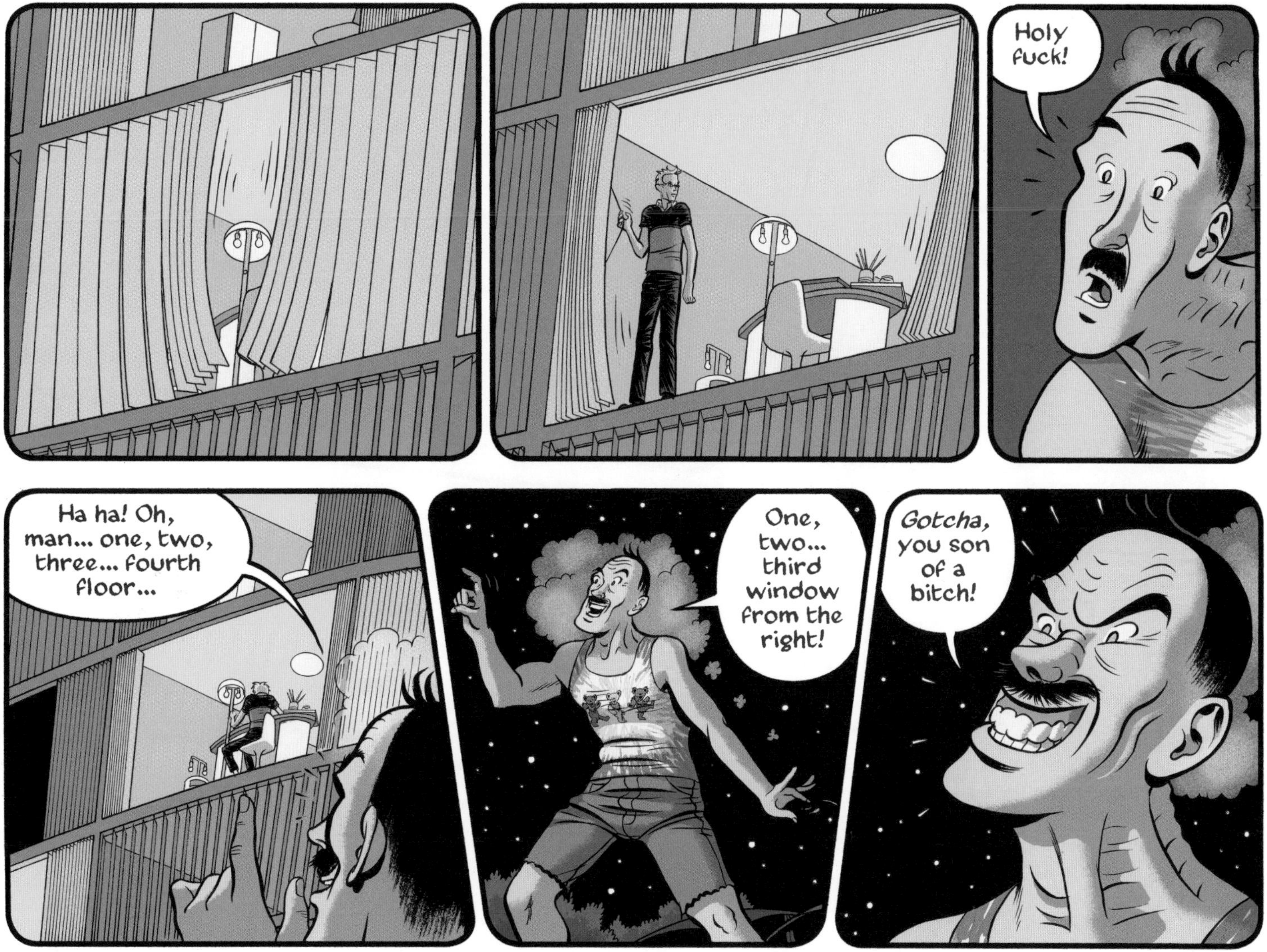
Holy fuck!
Ha ha! Oh, man... one, two, three... fourth floor...
One, two... third window from the right!
Gotcha, you son of a bitch!

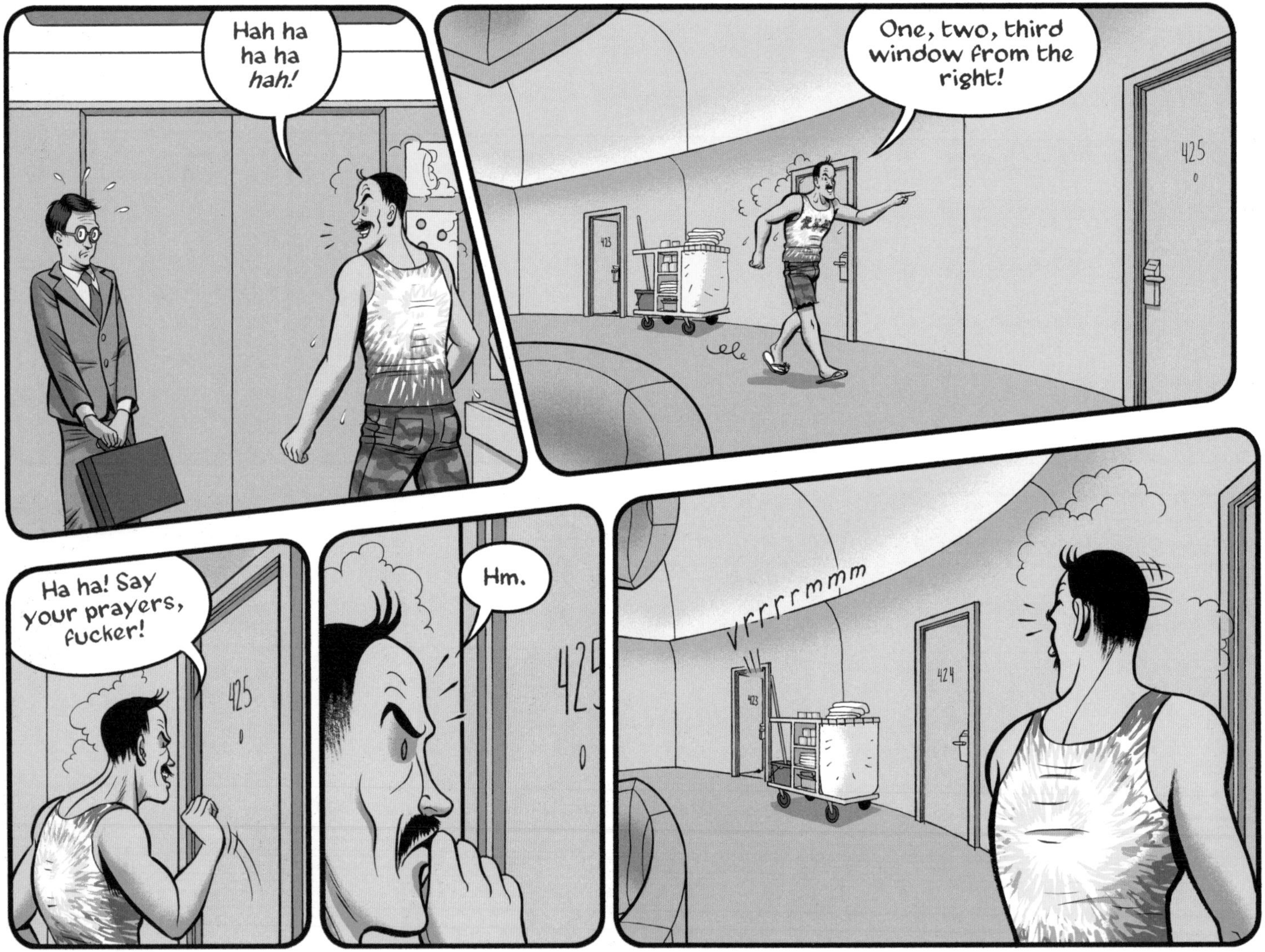

Hah ha ha ha *hah!*
One, two, third window from the right!
425
Ha ha! Say your prayers, fucker!
425
Hm.
425
vrrrrmmm
424

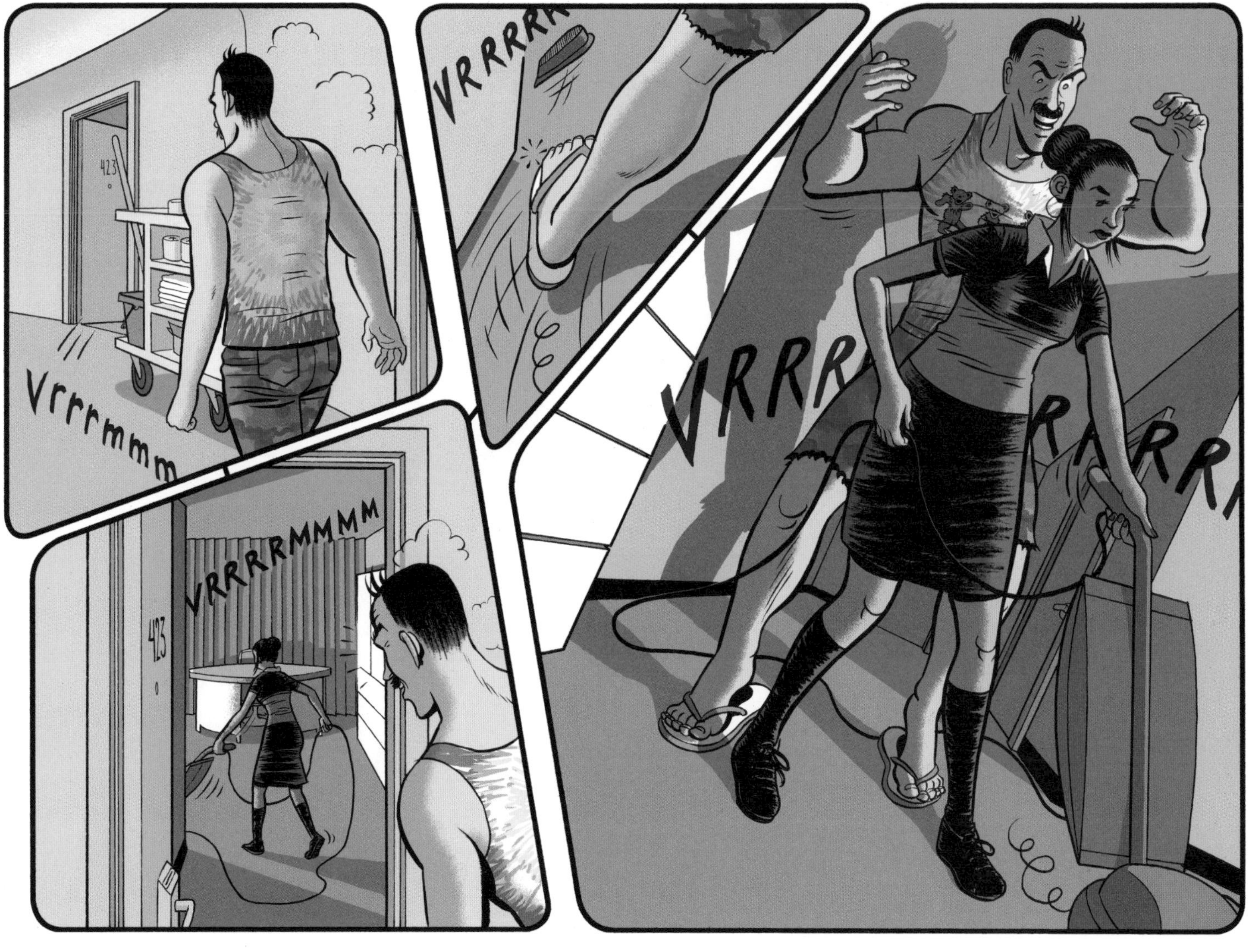
Vrrrmmm
VRRRR
VRRRRMMMM
VRRRRRRRRR

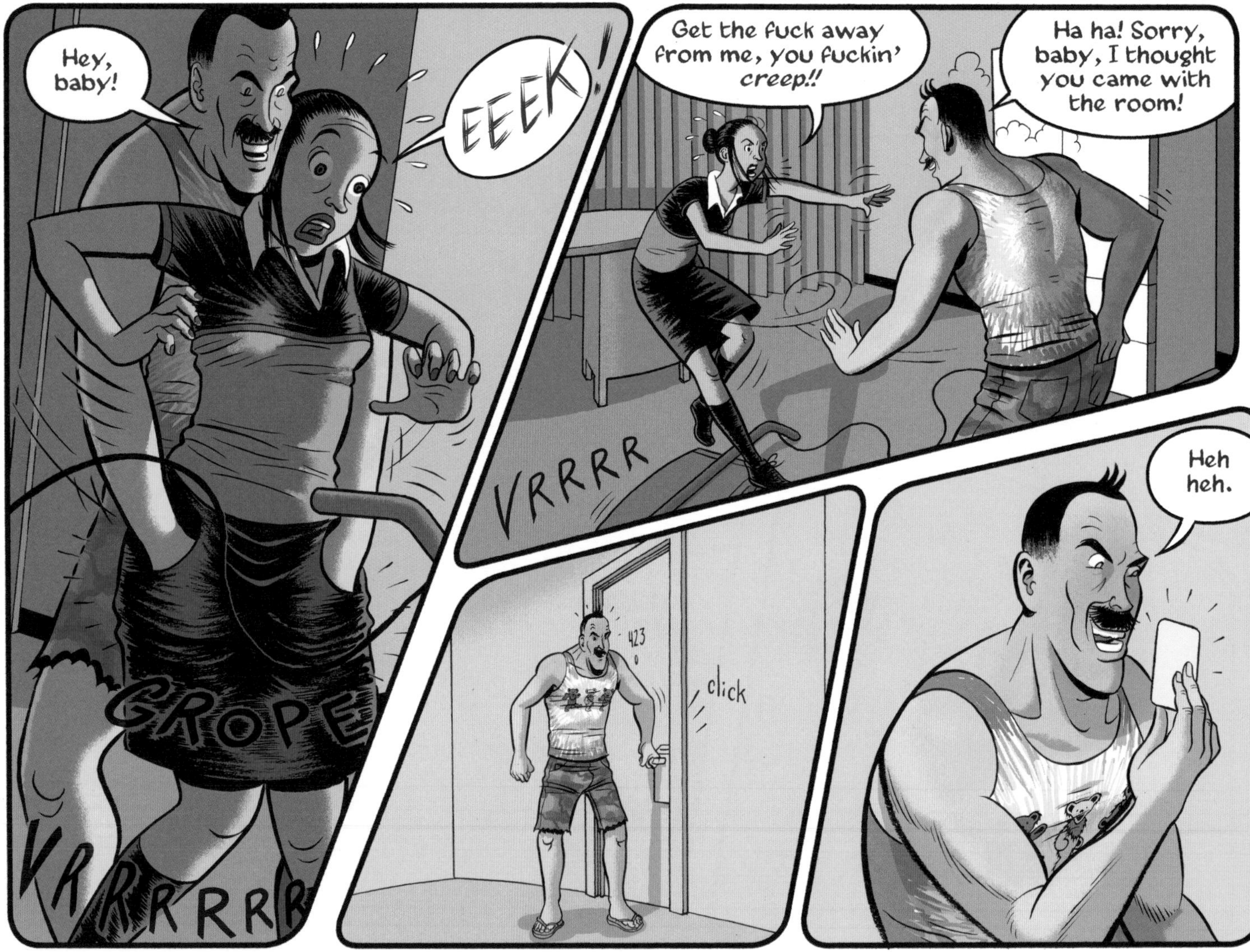
Hey, baby!
EEEK!
GROPE
VRRRRRR
Get the fuck away from me, you fuckin' creep!!
Ha ha! Sorry, baby, I thought you came with the room!
VRRRR
423
click
Heh heh.

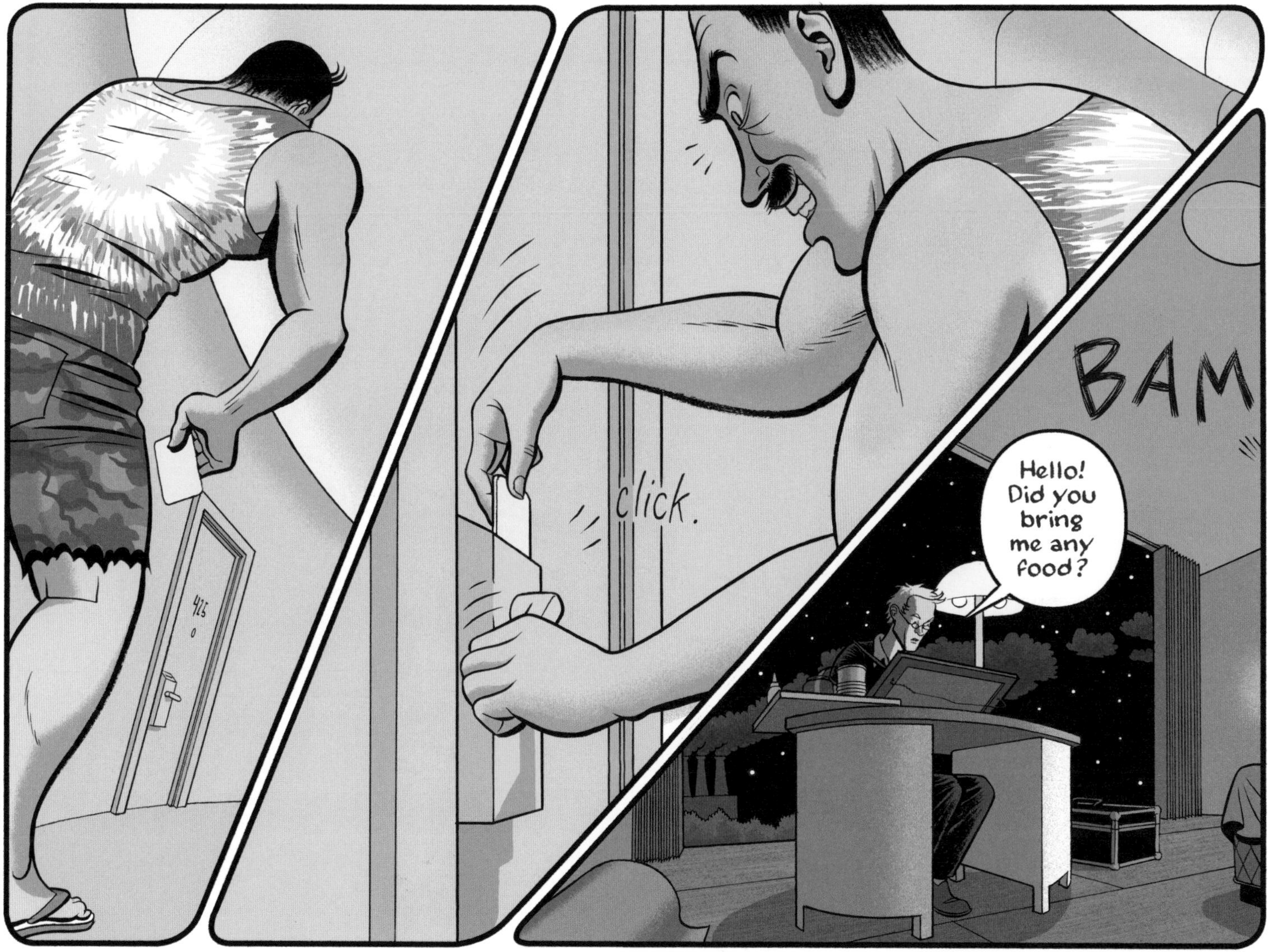

425
click.
BAM
Hello! Did you bring me any food?

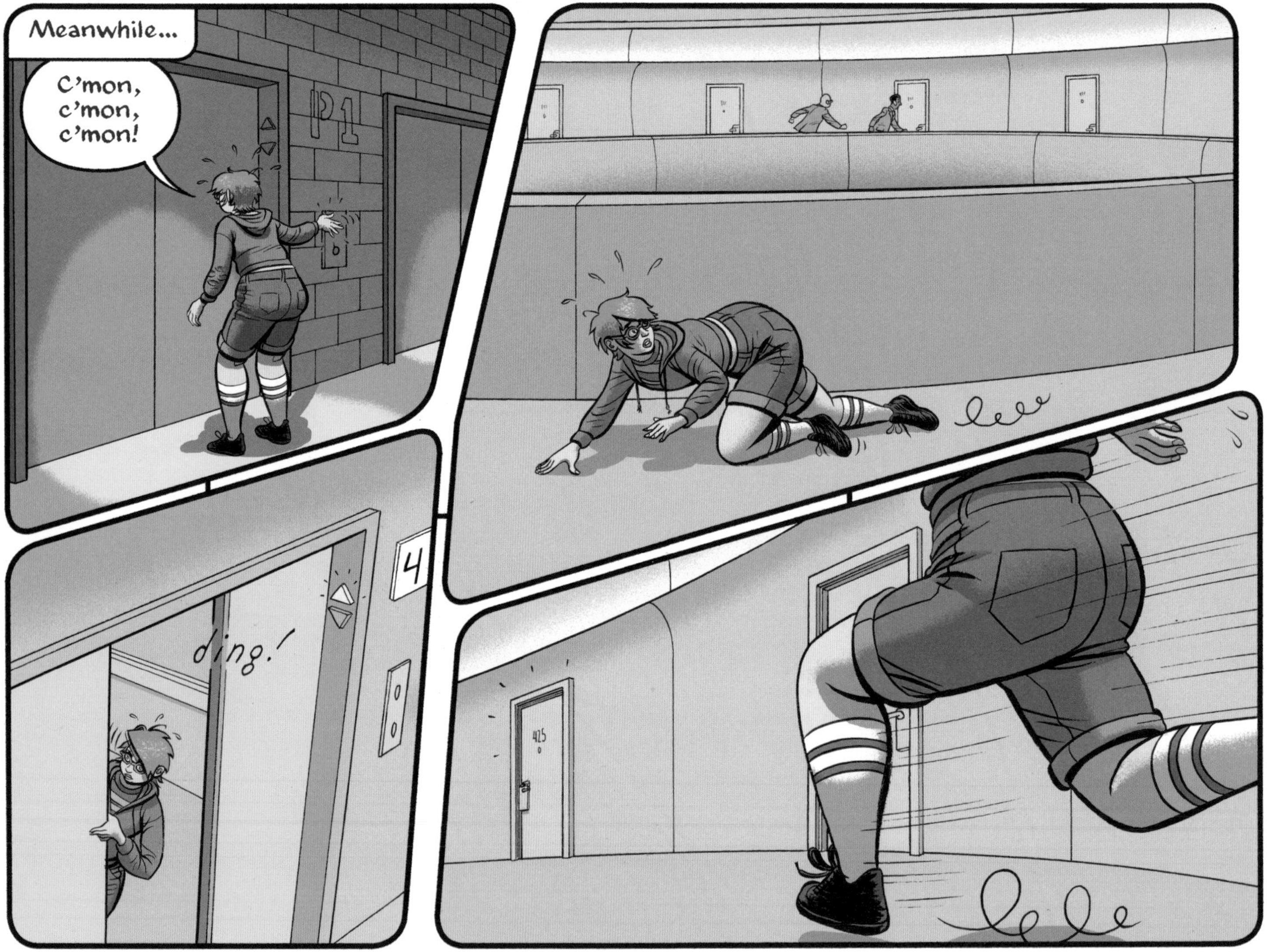
Meanwhile...
C'mon, c'mon, c'mon!
P1
4
ding.!
425

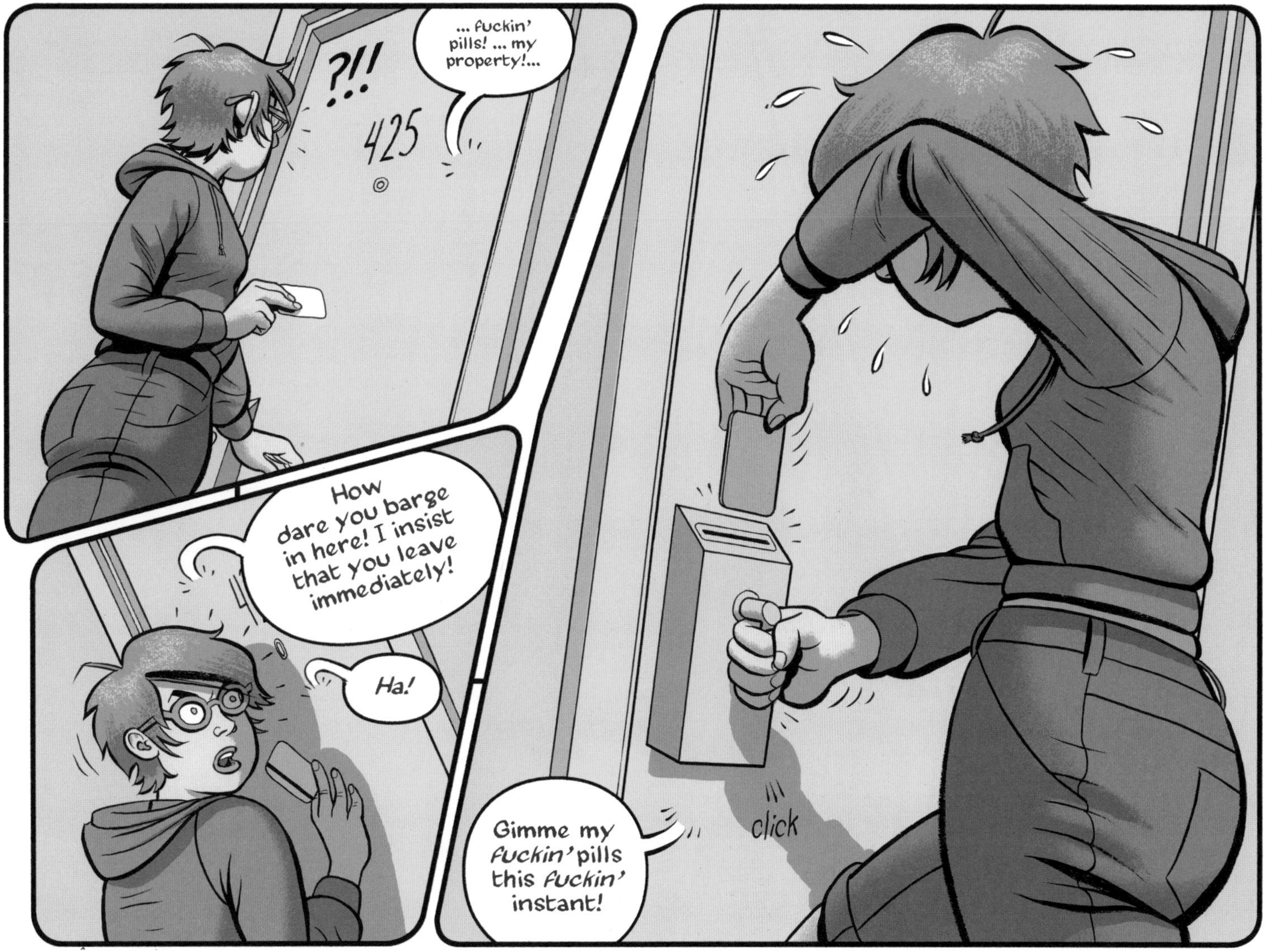

... fuckin' pills! ... my property!...
?!!
425
How dare you barge in here! I insist that you leave immediately!
Ha!
Gimme my *fuckin'* pills this *fuckin'* instant!
click

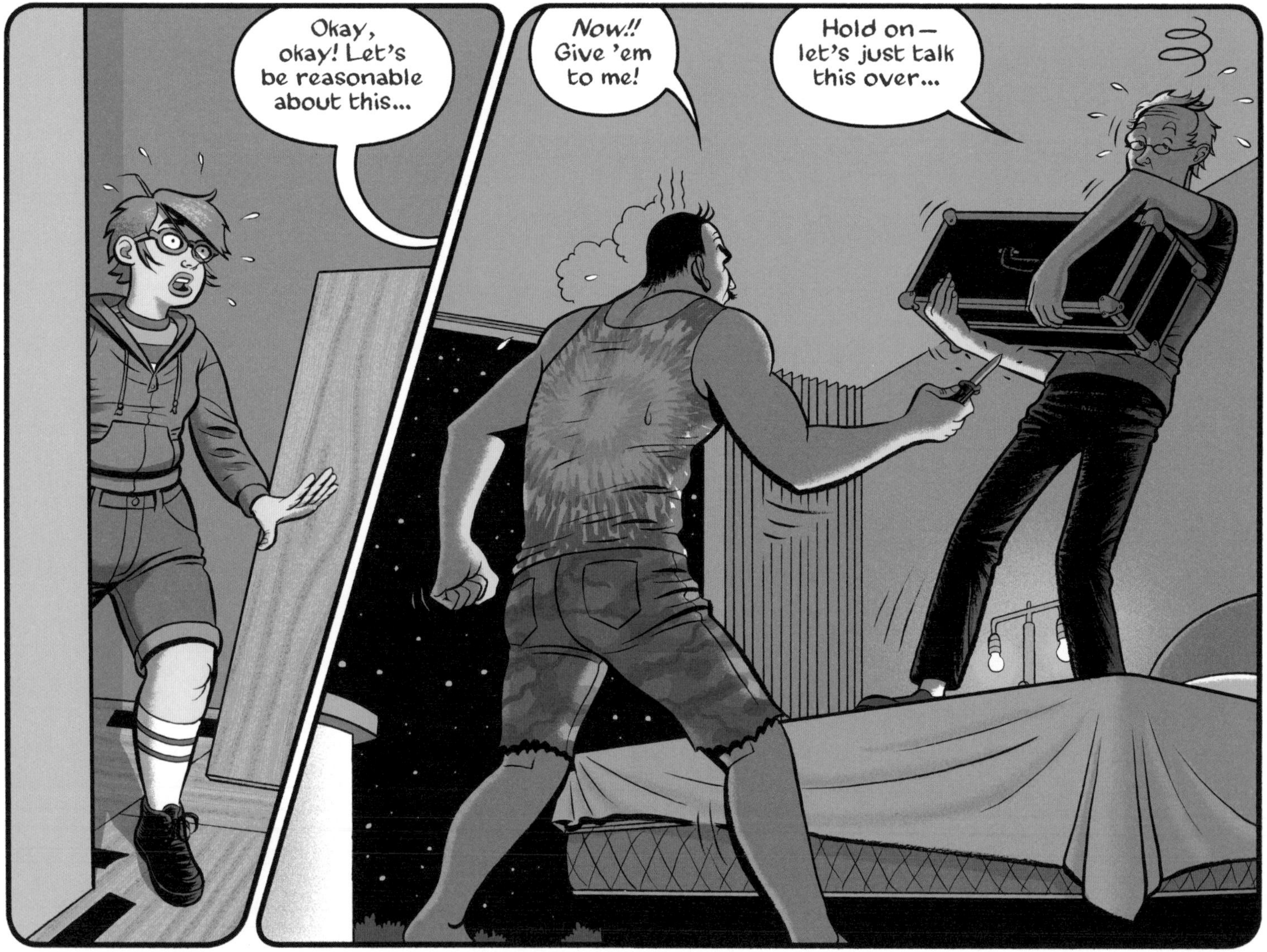
Okay, okay! Let's be reasonable about this...
Now!! Give 'em to me!
Hold on— let's just talk this over...

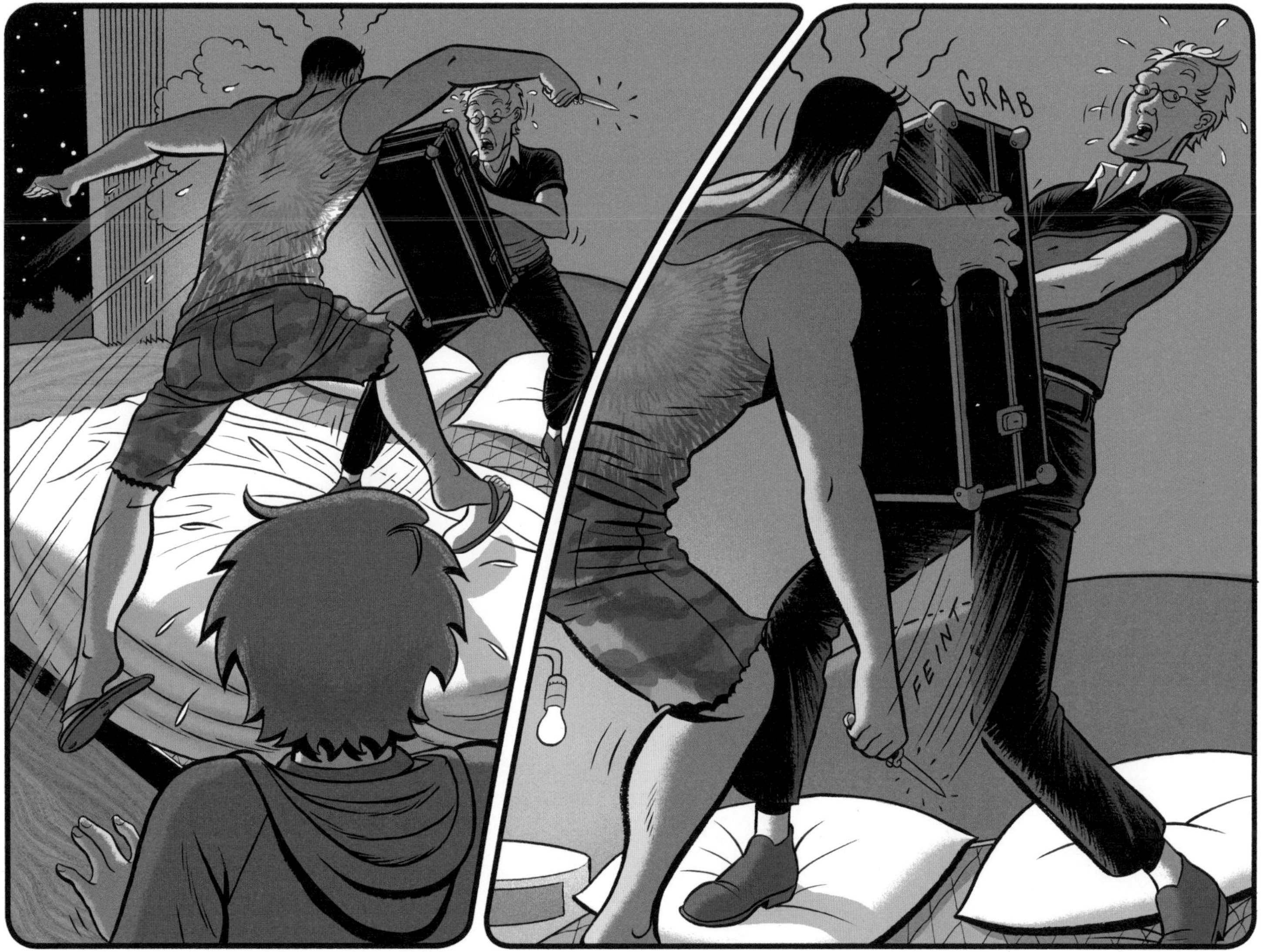
GRAB
FEINT

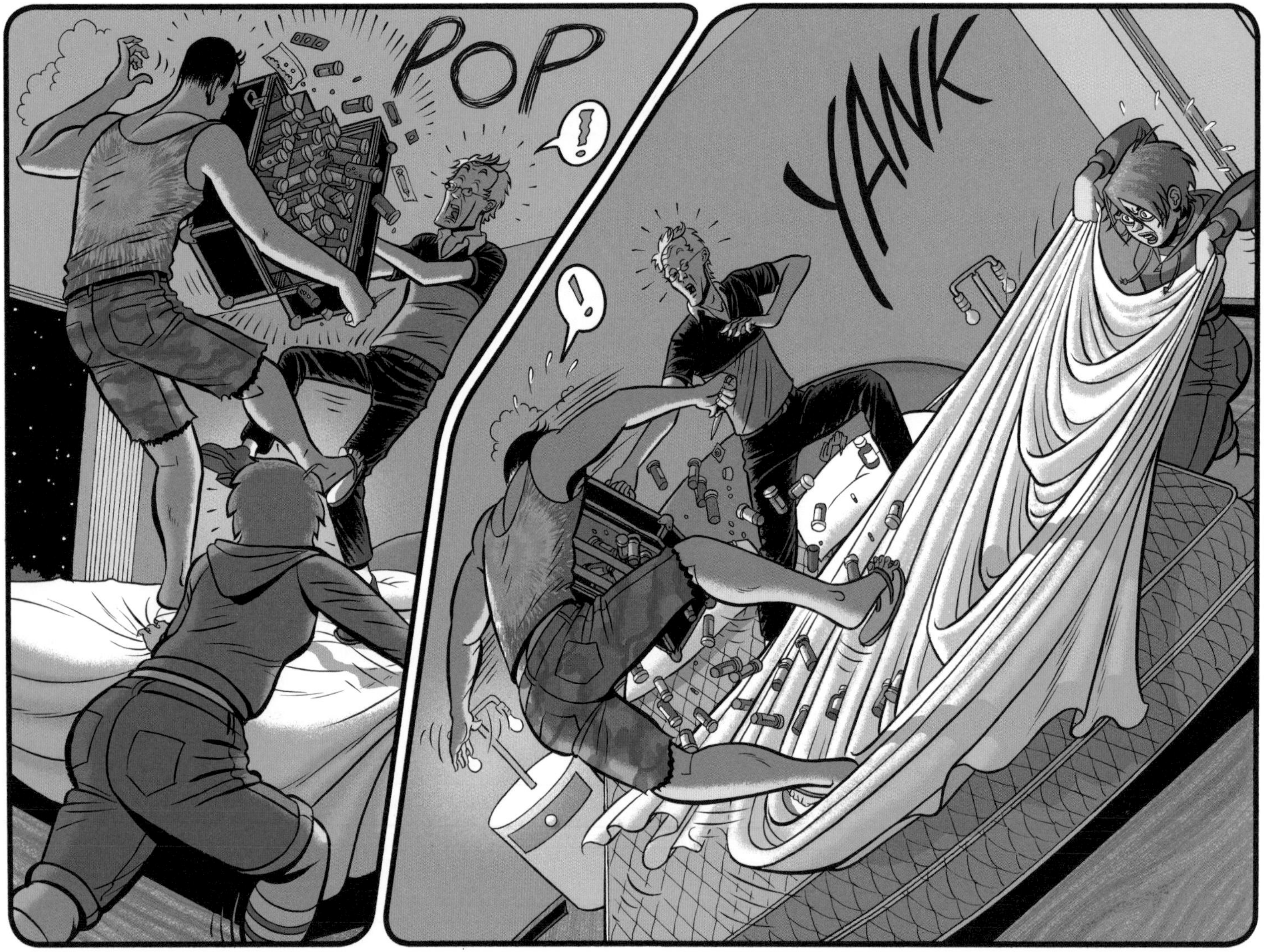
POP
!
YANK
!

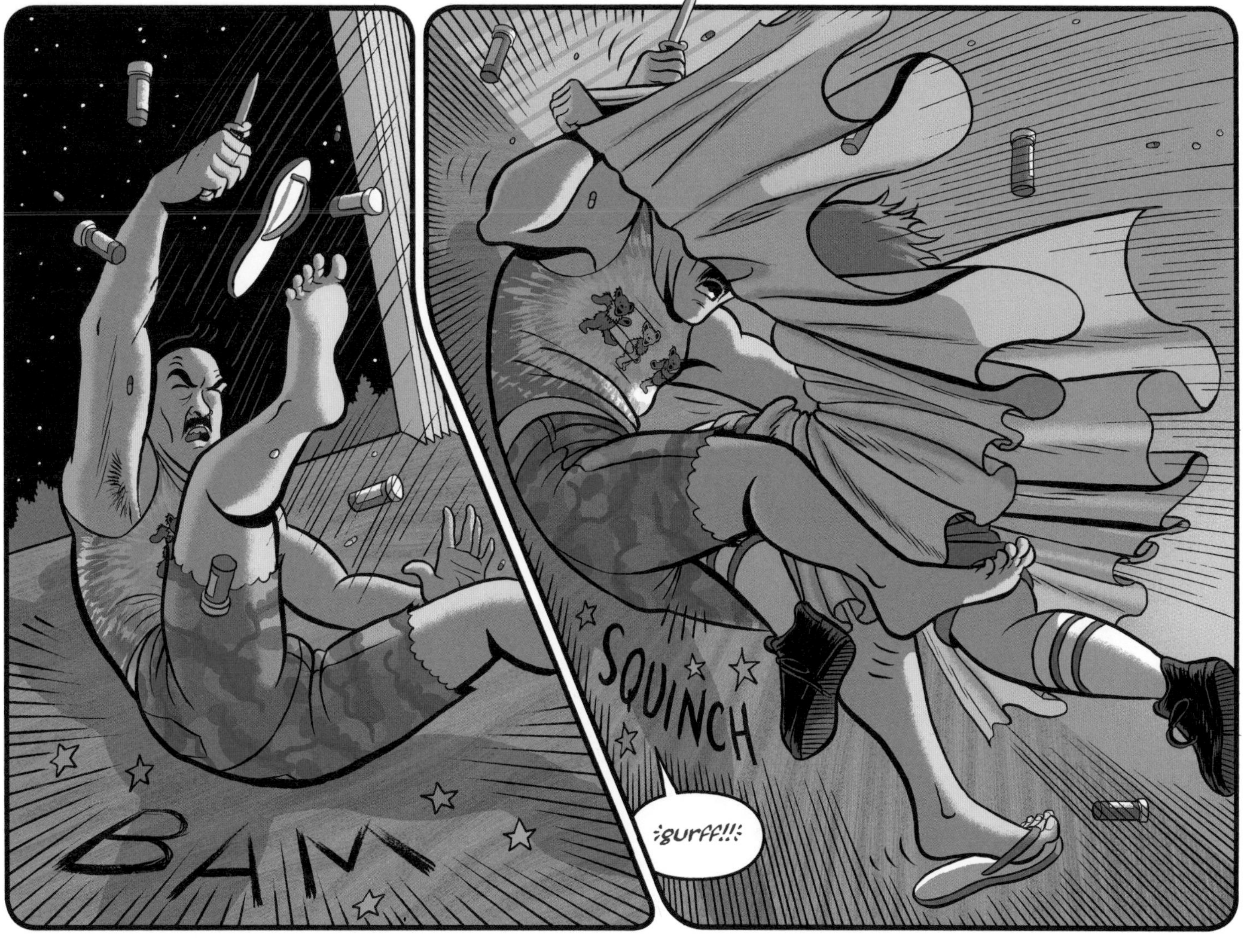
BAM
SQUINCH
:gurff!!:

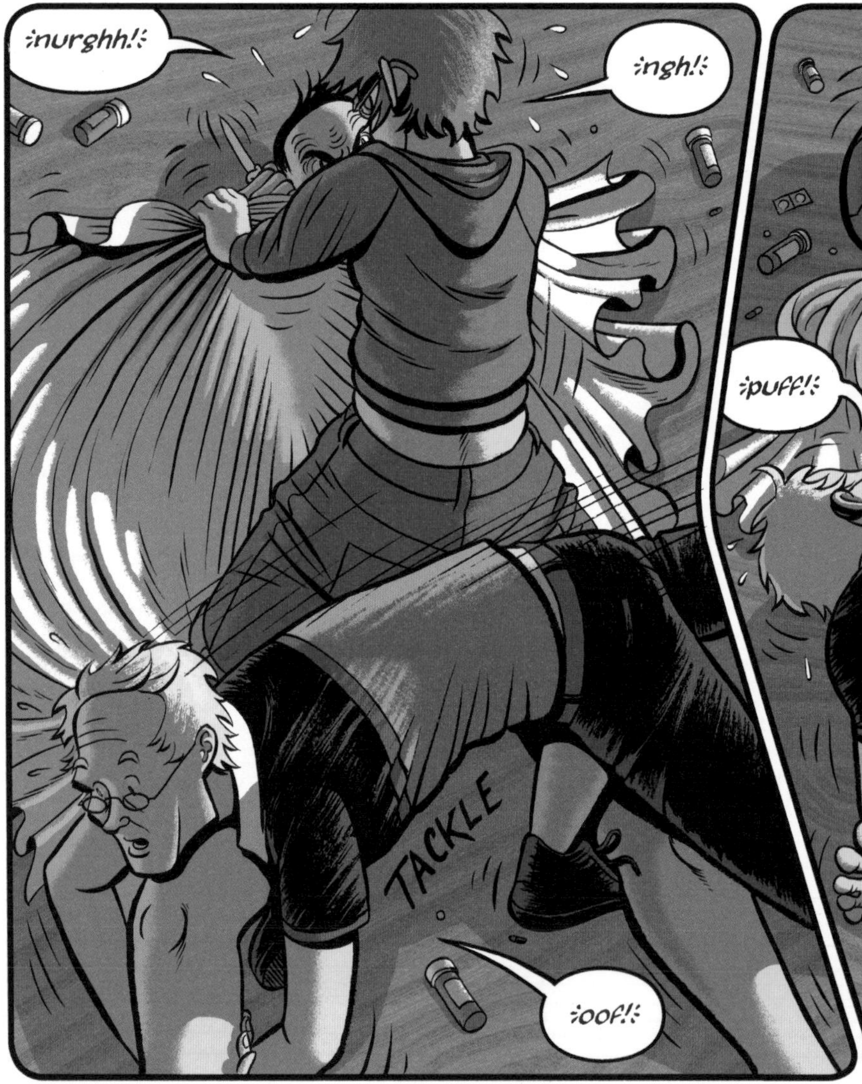
:nurghh!:
:ngh!:
TACKLE
:oof!:

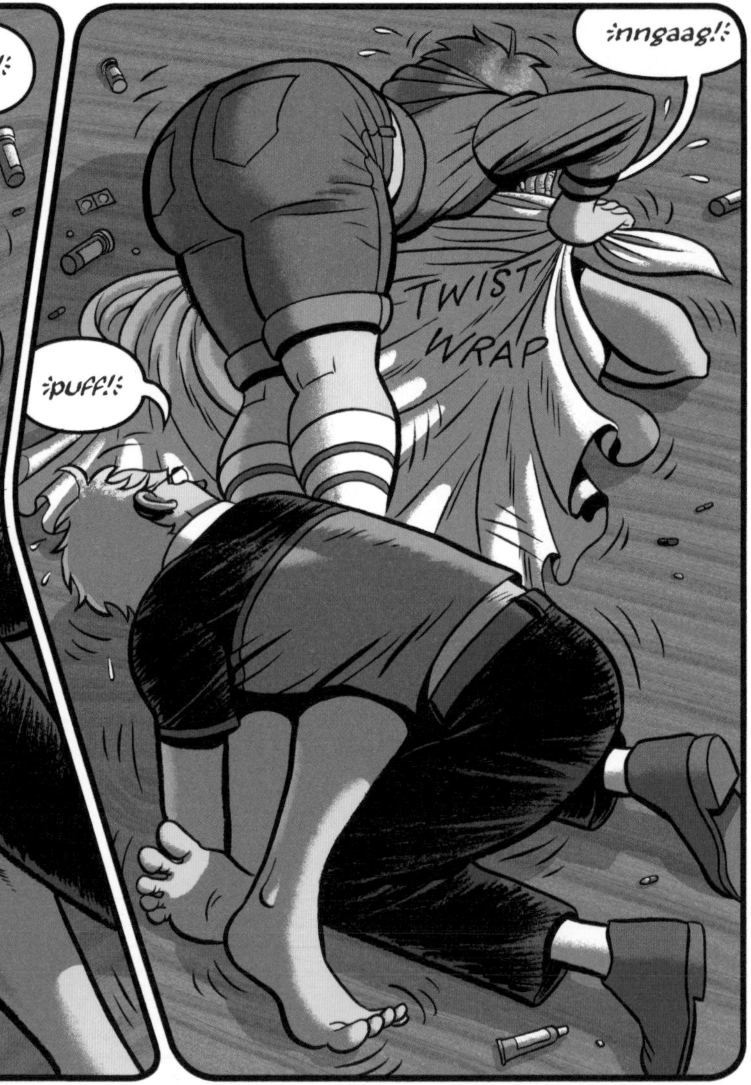
:nngaag!:
TWIST
WRAP
:puff!:

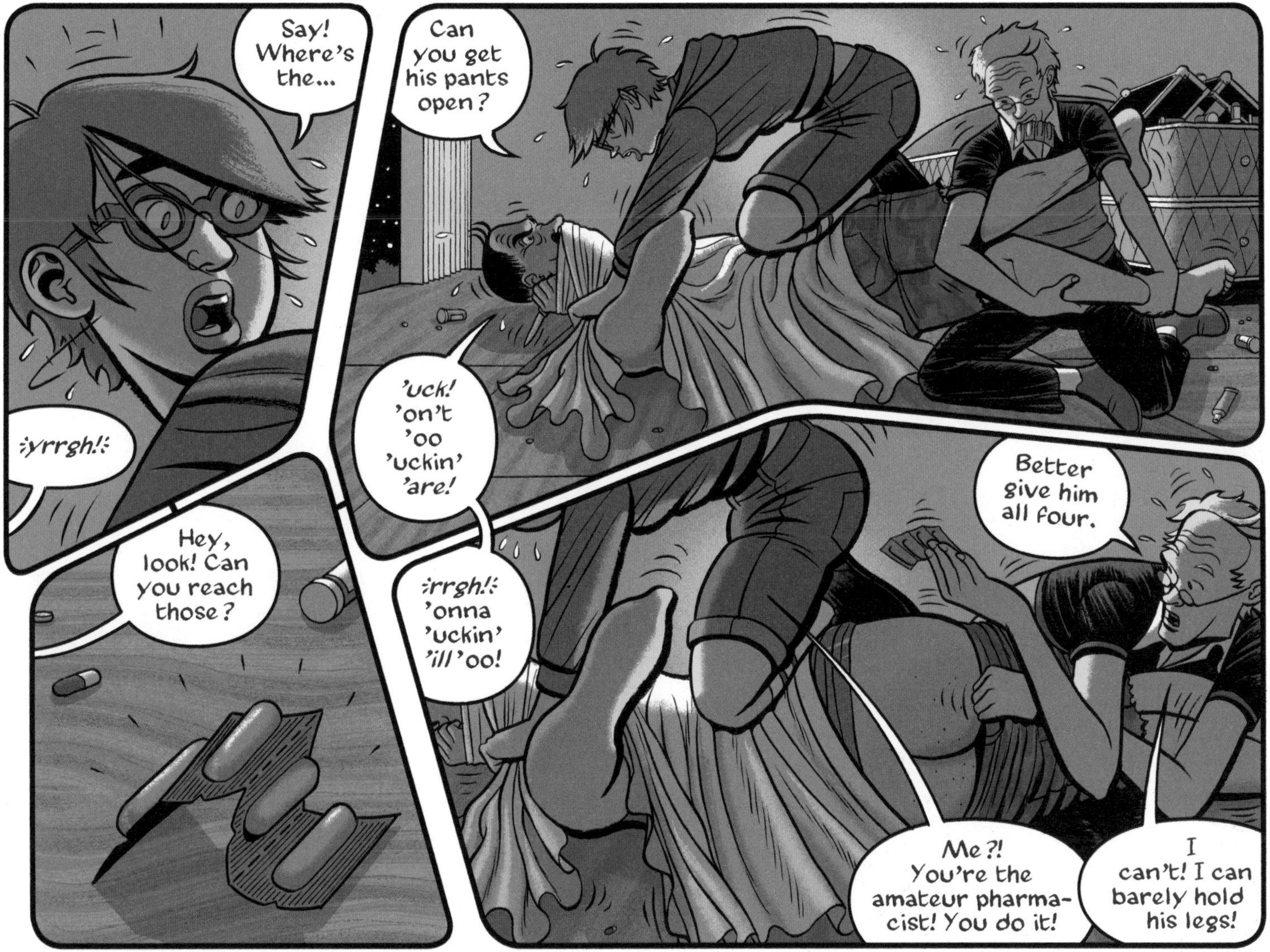
Say! Where's the...
:yrrgh!:
Can you get his pants open?
'uck! 'on't 'oo 'uckin' 'are!
Hey, look! Can you reach those?
:rrgh!: 'onna 'uckin' 'ill 'oo!
Better give him all four.
Me?! You're the amateur pharma-cist! You do it!
I can't! I can barely hold his legs!

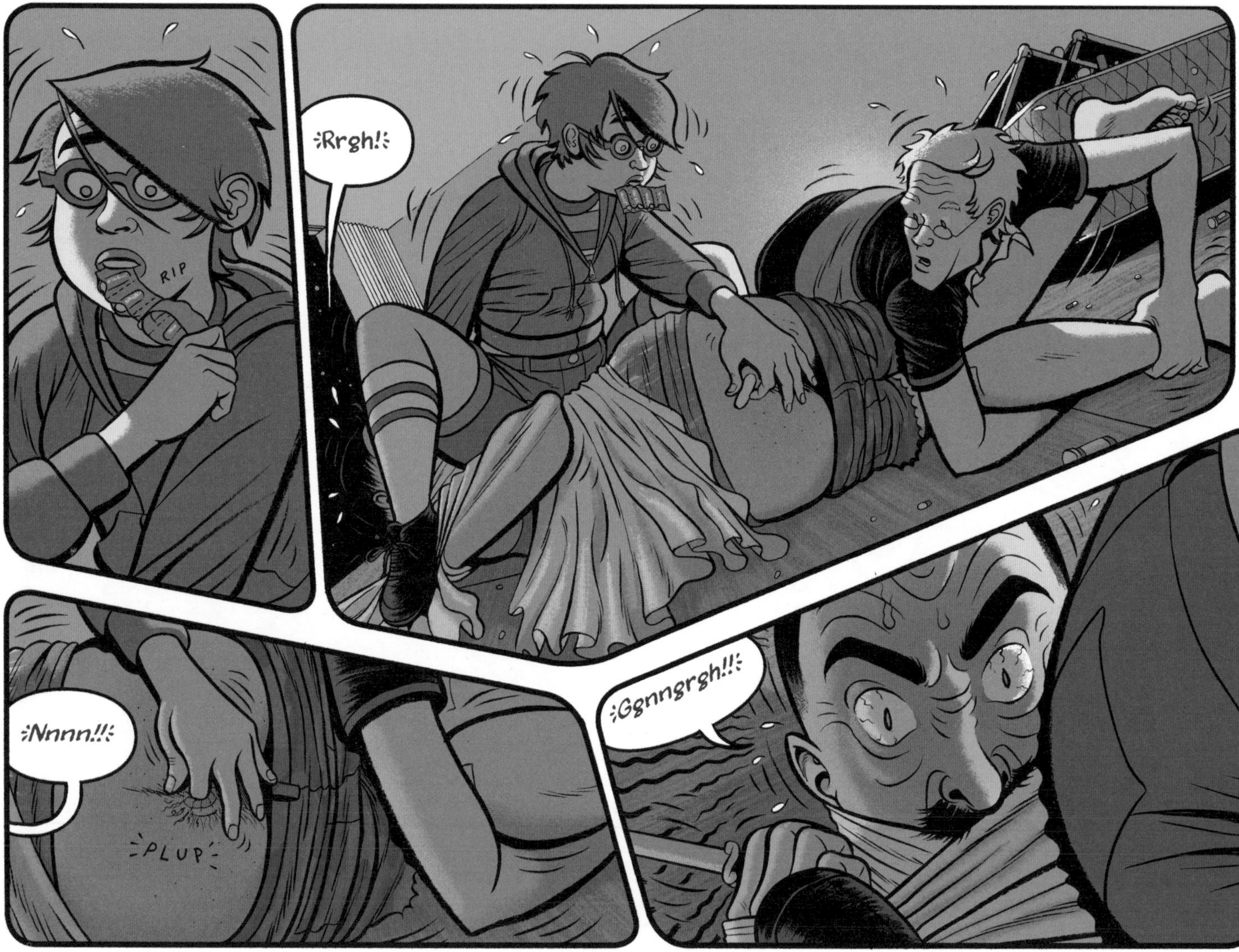
RIP
Rrgh!
Nnnn!!
PLUP
Ggnngrgh!!

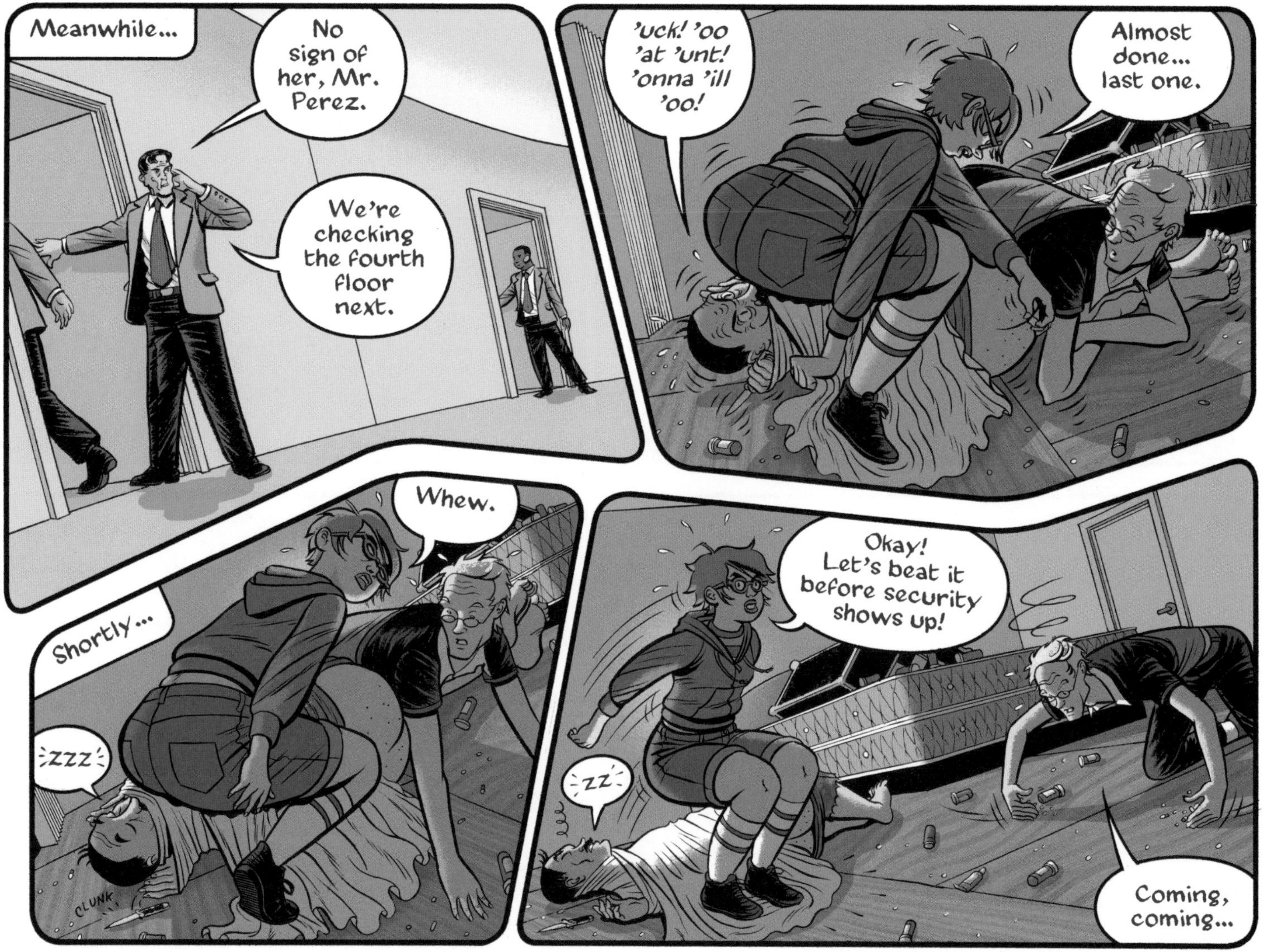
Meanwhile...
No sign of her, Mr. Perez.
We're checking the fourth floor next.
'uck! 'oo 'at 'unt! 'onna 'ill 'oo!
Almost done... last one.
Shortly...
Whew.
ZZZ
CLUNK
Okay! Let's beat it before security shows up!
ZZ
Coming, coming...

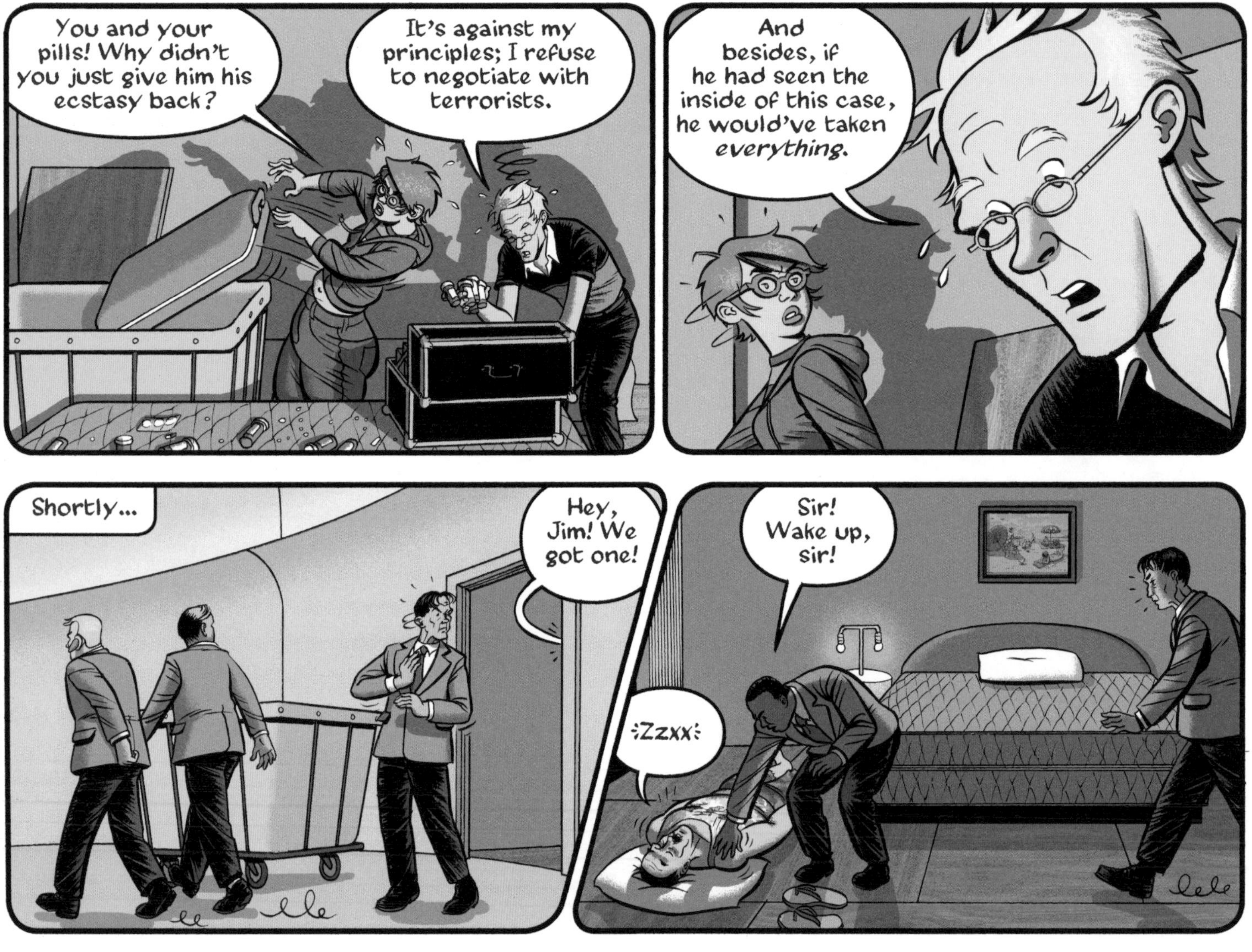

You and your pills! Why didn't you just give him his ecstasy back?
It's against my principles; I refuse to negotiate with terrorists.
And besides, if he had seen the inside of this case, he would've taken *everything*.
Shortly...
Hey, Jim! We got one!
Sir! Wake up, sir!
Zzxx

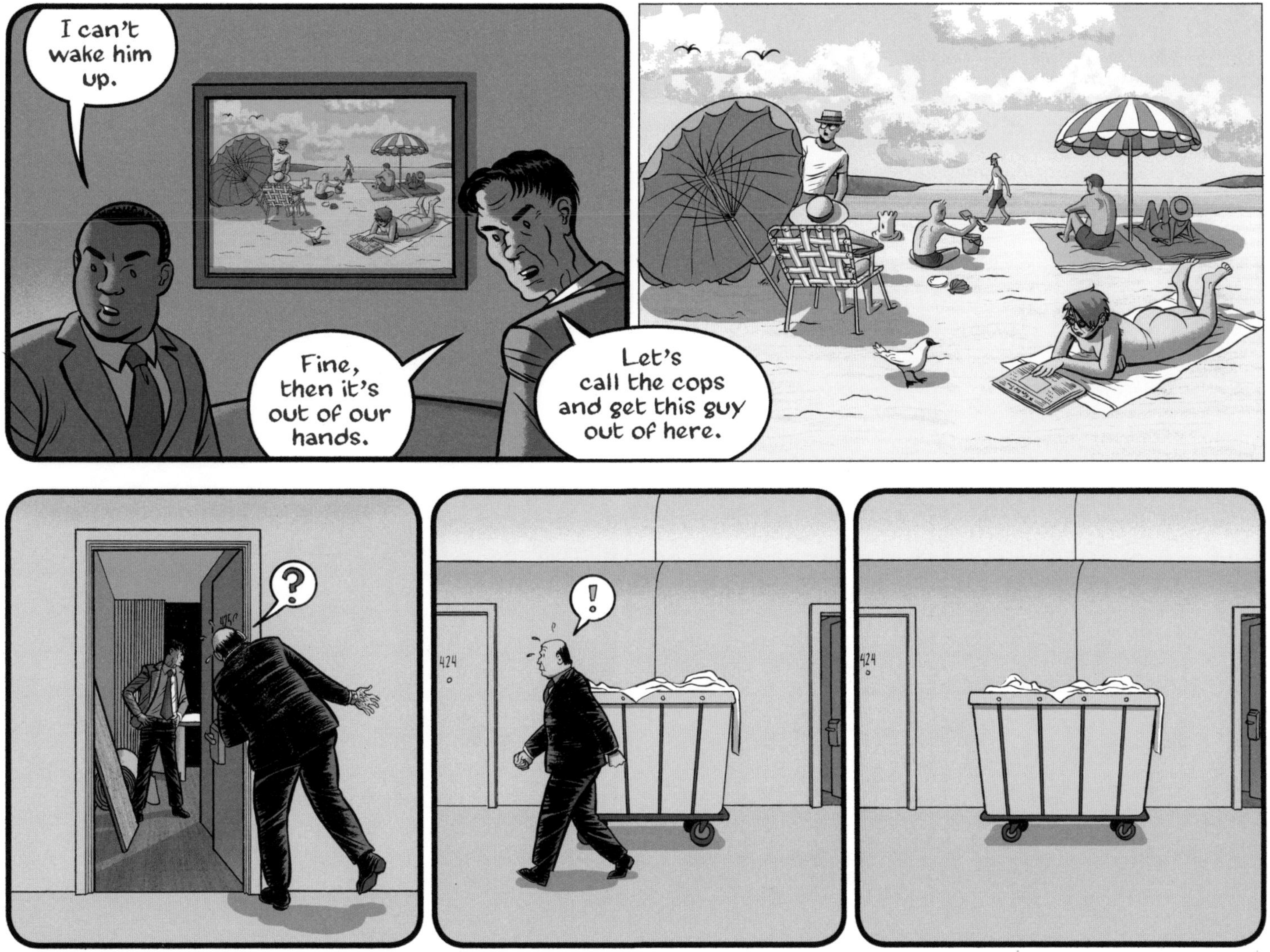
I can't wake him up.
Fine, then it's out of our hands.
Let's call the cops and get this guy out of here.
?
!
424
424

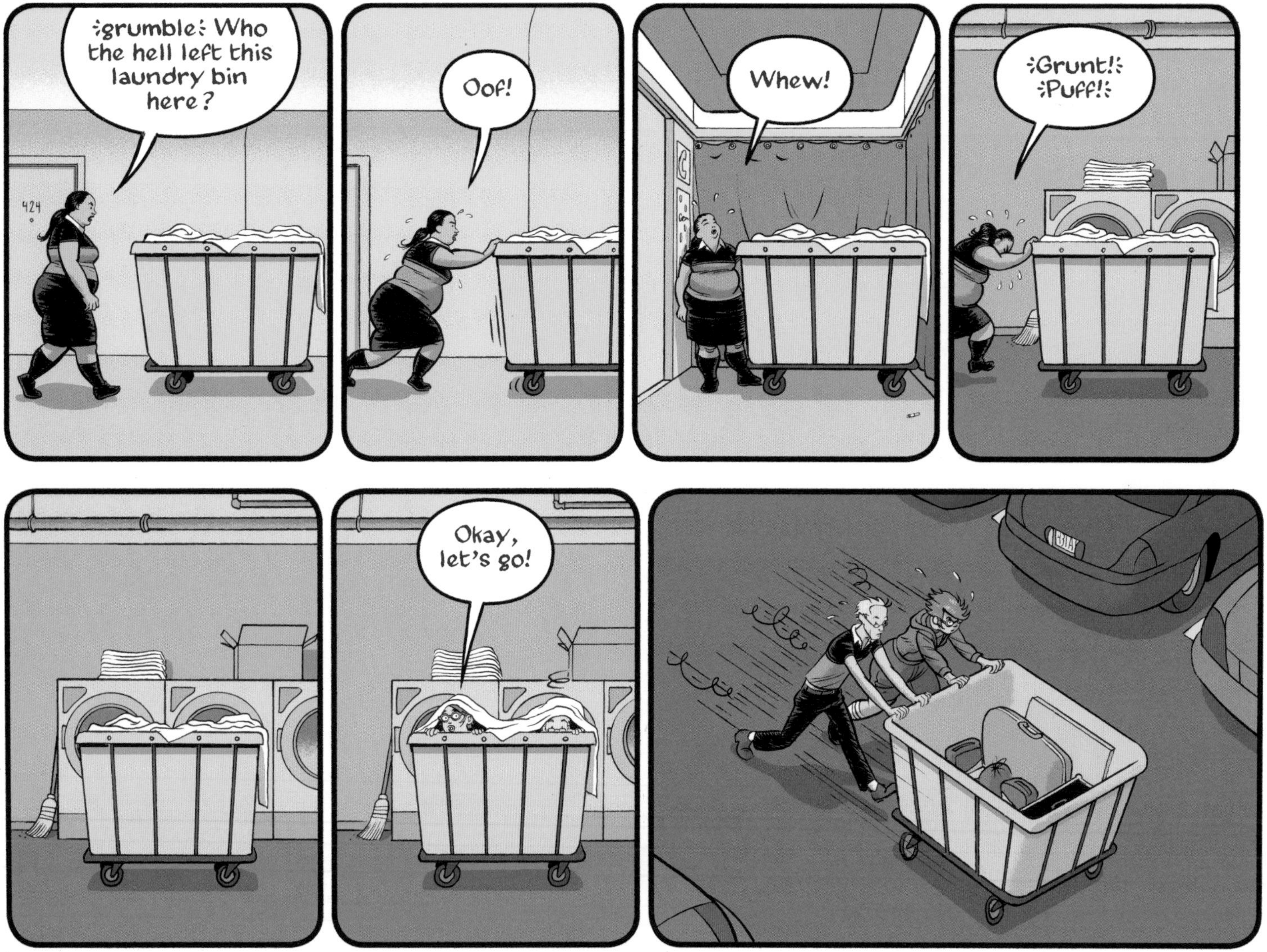
:grumble: Who the hell left this laundry bin here?
424
Oof!
Whew!
:Grunt!:
:Puff!:
Okay, let's go!

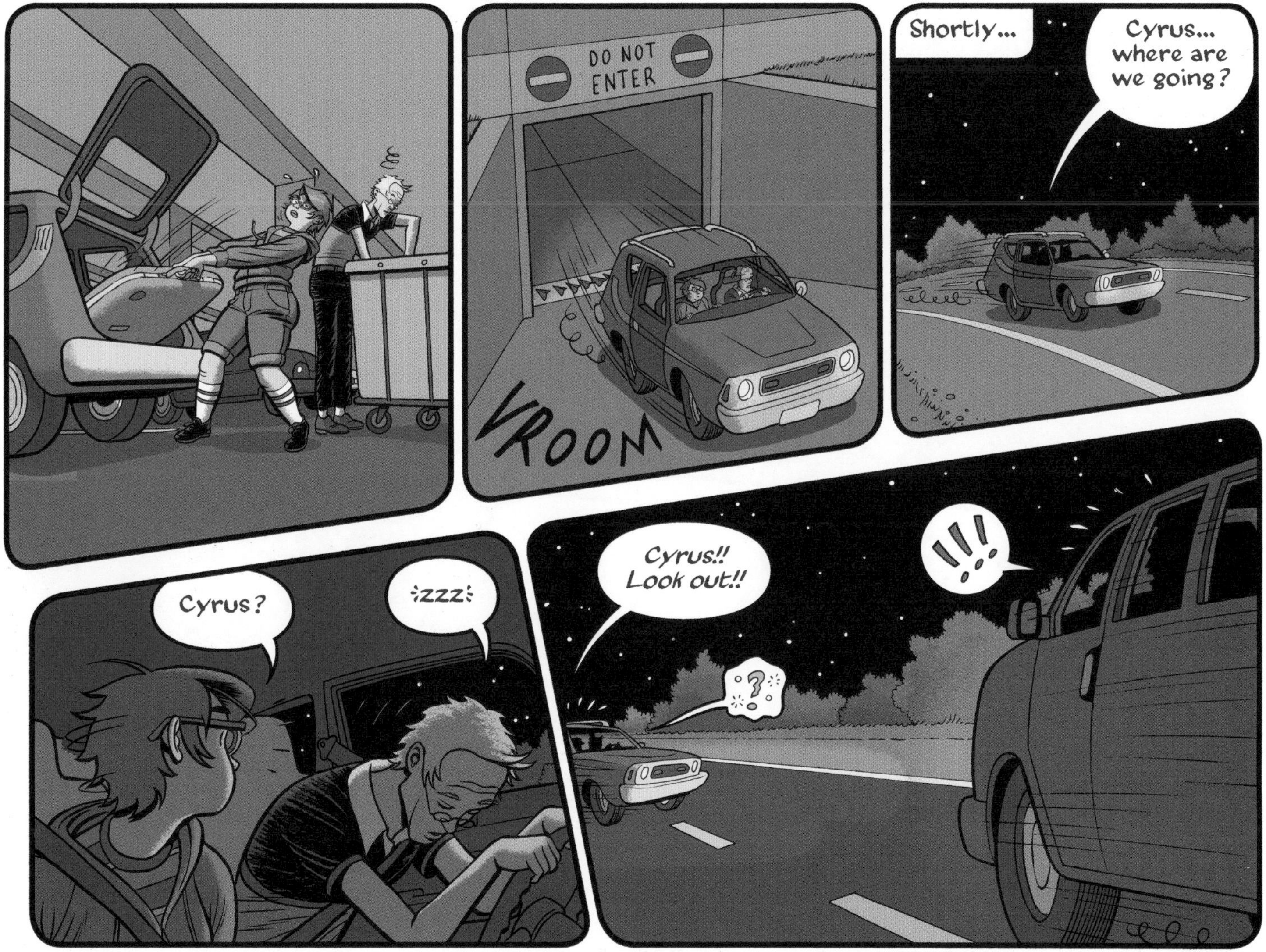
DO NOT ENTER
VROOM
Shortly...
Cyrus... where are we going?
Cyrus?
zzz
Cyrus!! Look out!!
?
!!!

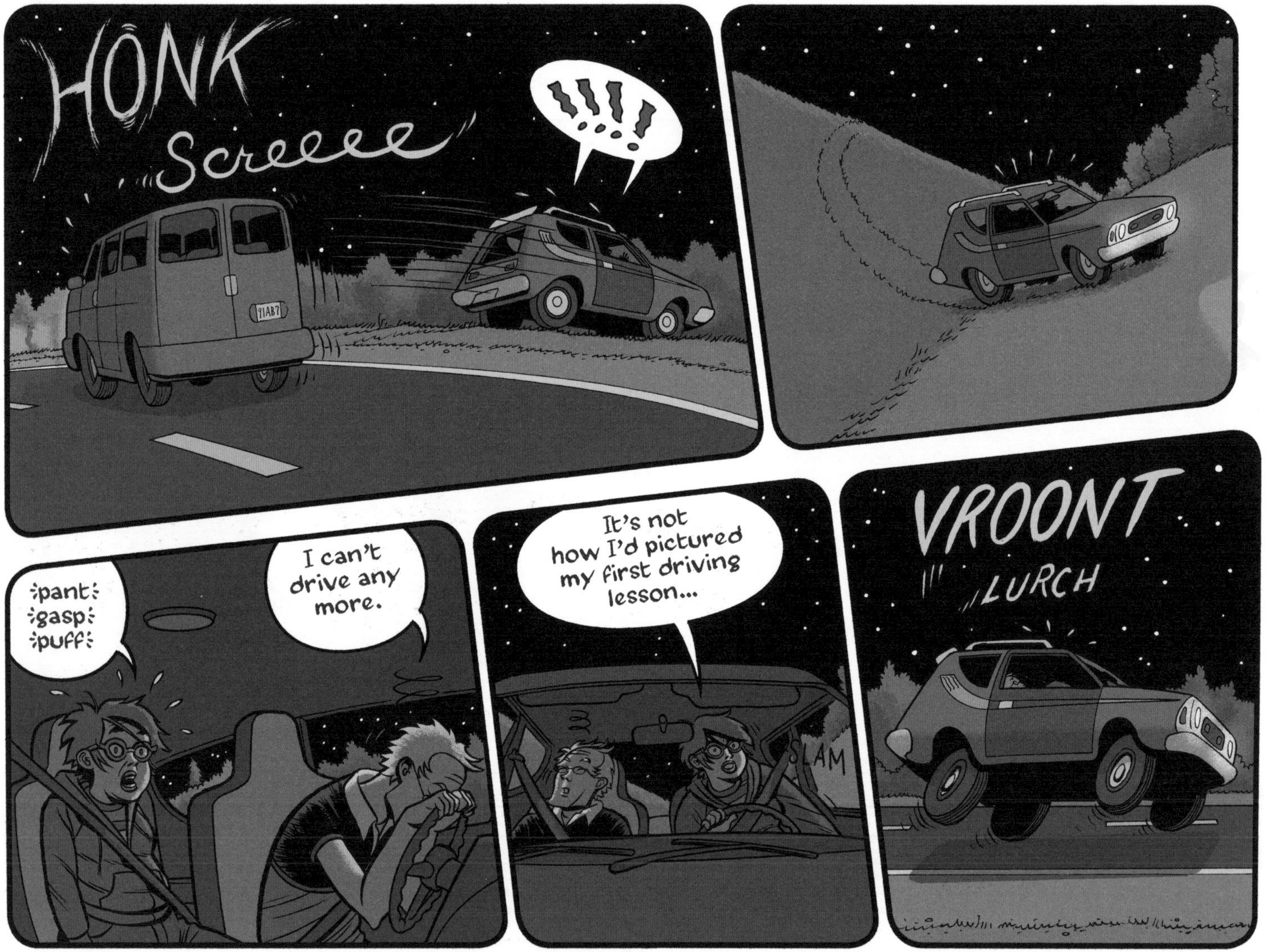
HONK
Screeee
I can't drive any more.
pant
gasp
puff
It's not how I'd pictured my first driving lesson...
SLAM
VROONT
LURCH

:ZZZ:

Meanwhile...

95
New York
City
↓

1 9
Jersey Shore
Points
EXIT ↓ ONLY

Hm.

EXIT
↗

Cyrus, wake up. We've died and gone to motel heaven.

PEA HELL MOTEL

SHURE MOTEL

VACANCY

STARFISH MOTEL

MOTEL

SURF MOTEL

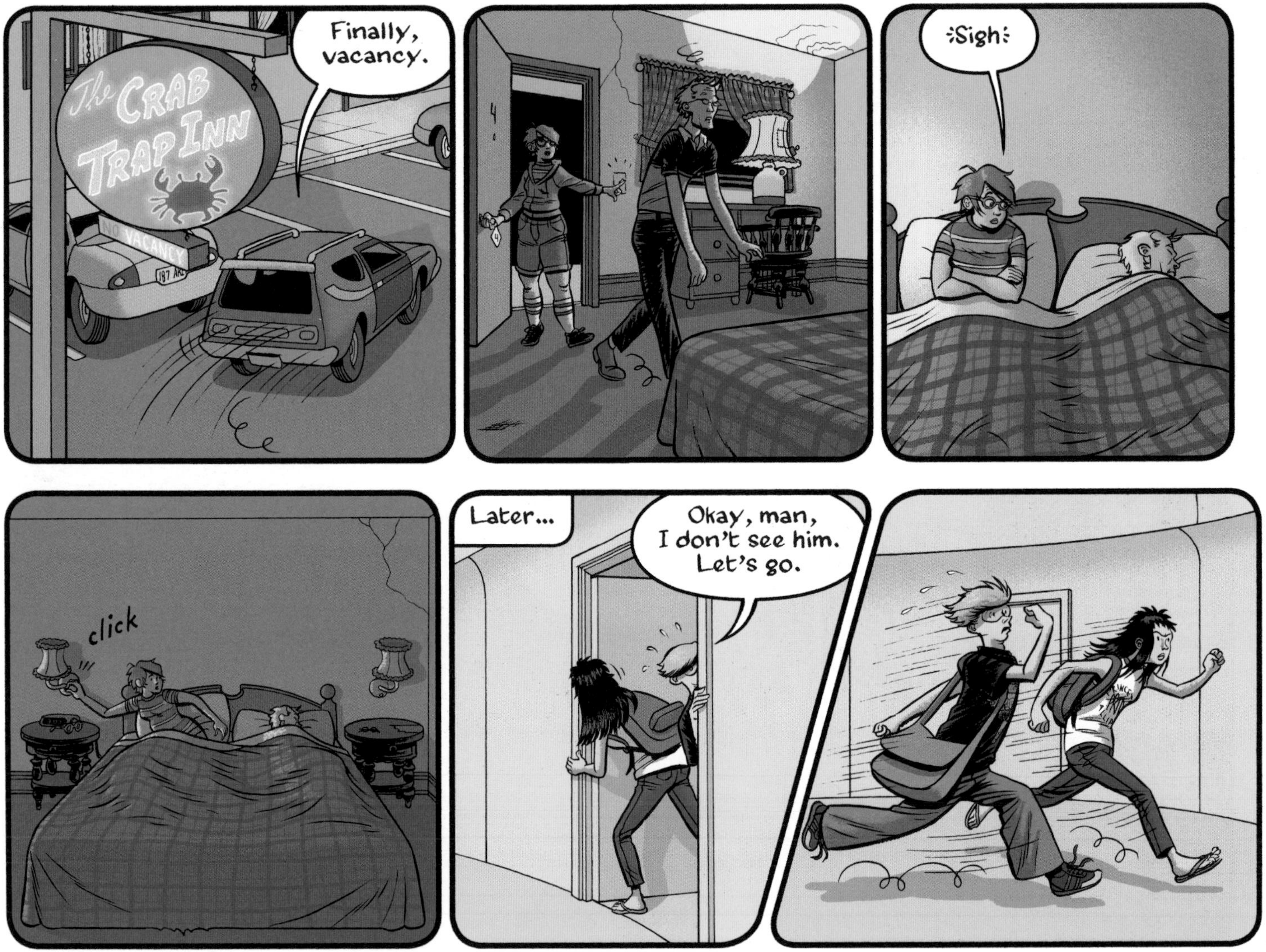
The CRAB TRAP INN
NO VACANCY
Finally, vacancy.
4
:Sigh:
click
Later...
Okay, man, I don't see him. Let's go.

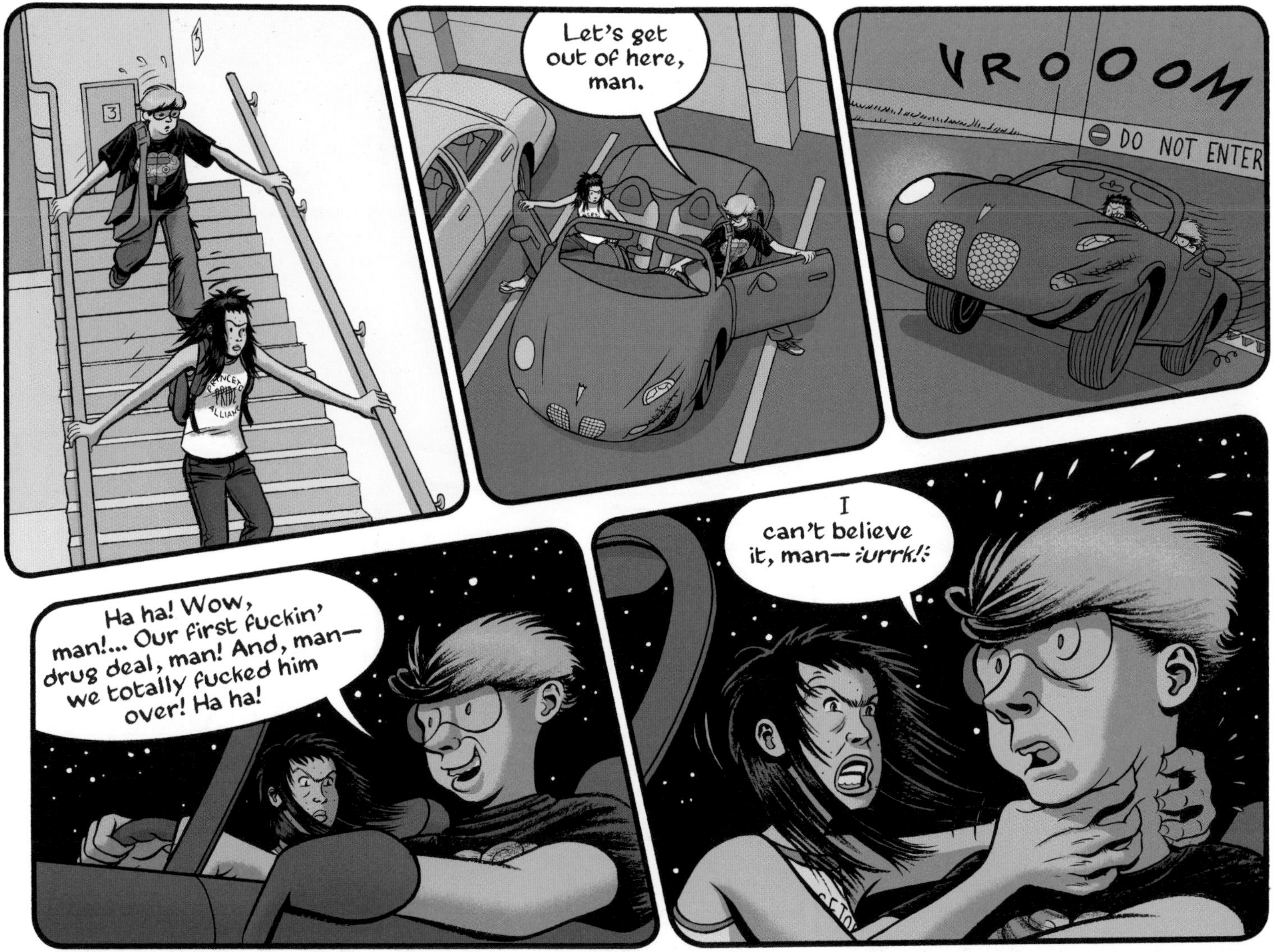

3
3
Let's get out of here, man.
VROOOM
DO NOT ENTER
Ha ha! Wow, man!... Our first fuckin' drug deal, man! And, man— we totally fucked him over! Ha ha!
I can't believe it, man— urrk!

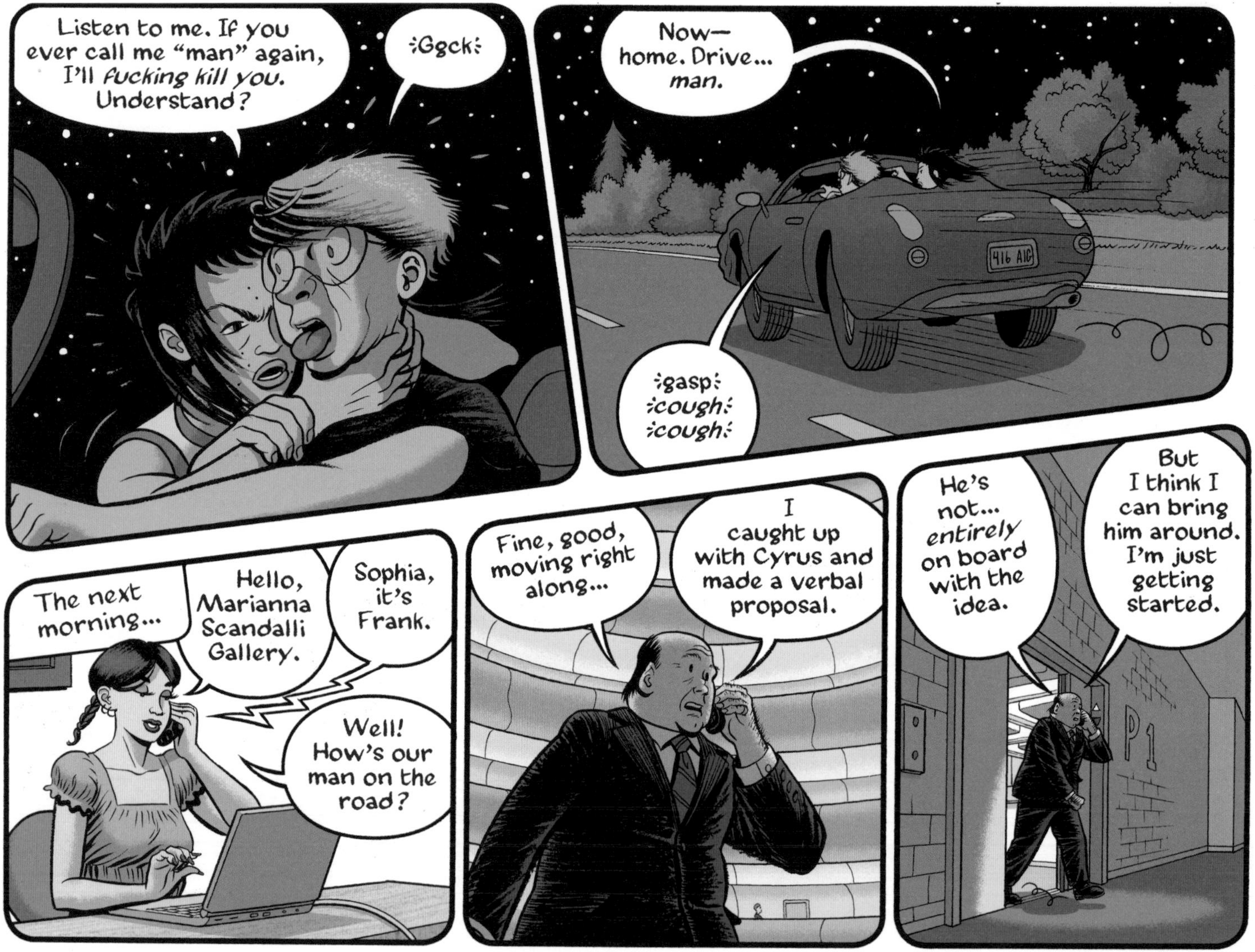
Listen to me. If you ever call me "man" again, I'll *fucking kill you.* Understand?
Ggck
Now— home. Drive... *man.*
gasp
cough
cough
416 AIC
The next morning...
Hello, Marianna Scandalli Gallery.
Sophia, it's Frank.
Well! How's our man on the road?
Fine, good, moving right along...
I caught up with Cyrus and made a verbal proposal.
He's not... *entirely* on board with the idea.
But I think I can bring him around. I'm just getting started.
P1

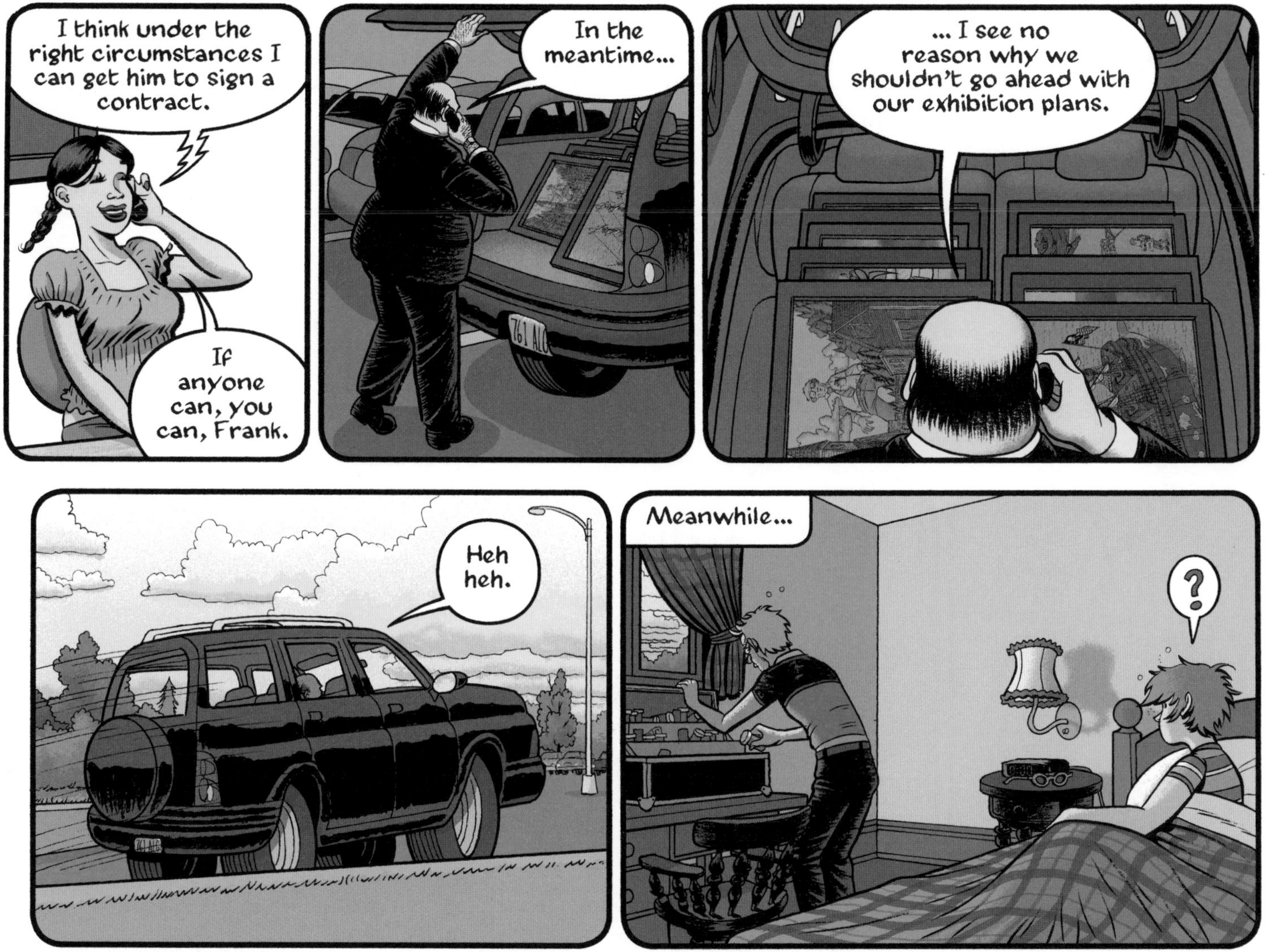
I think under the right circumstances I can get him to sign a contract.
If anyone can, you can, Frank.
In the meantime...
761 ALC
... I see no reason why we shouldn't go ahead with our exhibition plans.
Heh heh.
761 ALC
Meanwhile...
?

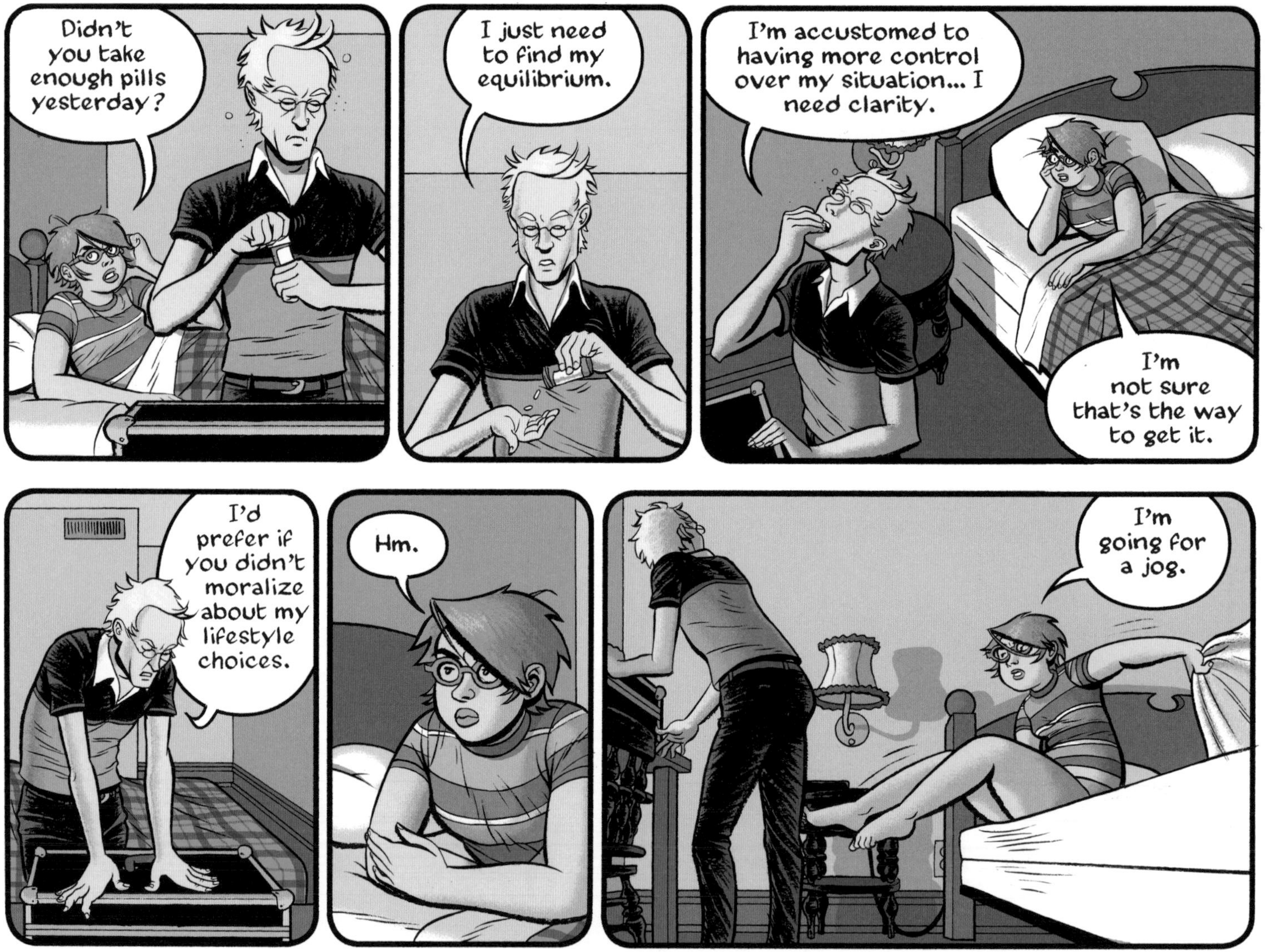
Didn't you take enough pills yesterday?
I just need to find my equilibrium.
I'm accustomed to having more control over my situation... I need clarity.
I'm not sure that's the way to get it.
I'd prefer if you didn't moralize about my lifestyle choices.
Hm.
I'm going for a jog.

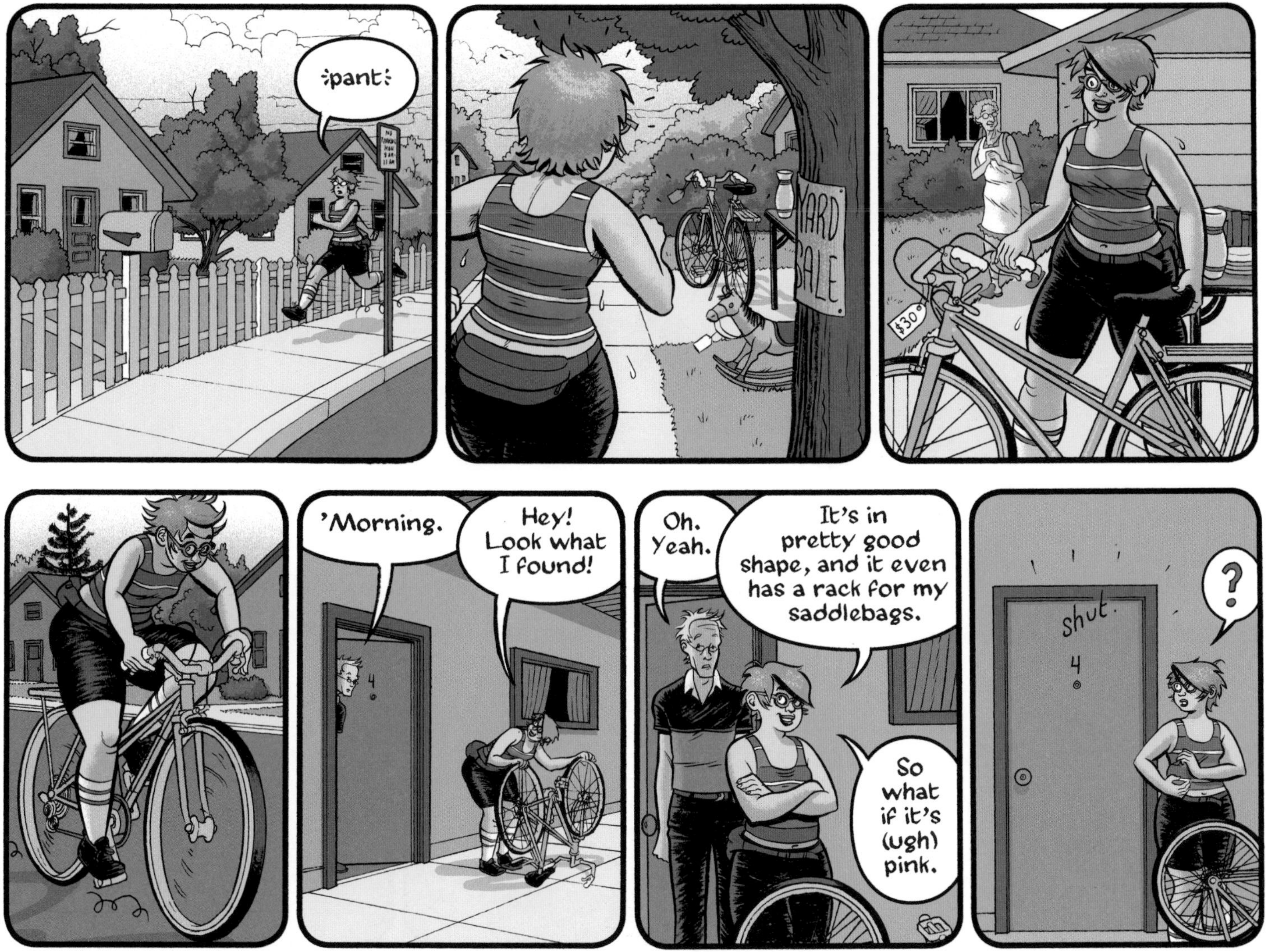
pant
YARD SALE
$30
'Morning.
Hey! Look what I found!
Oh. Yeah.
It's in pretty good shape, and it even has a rack for my saddlebags.
So what if it's (ugh) pink.
shut.
?

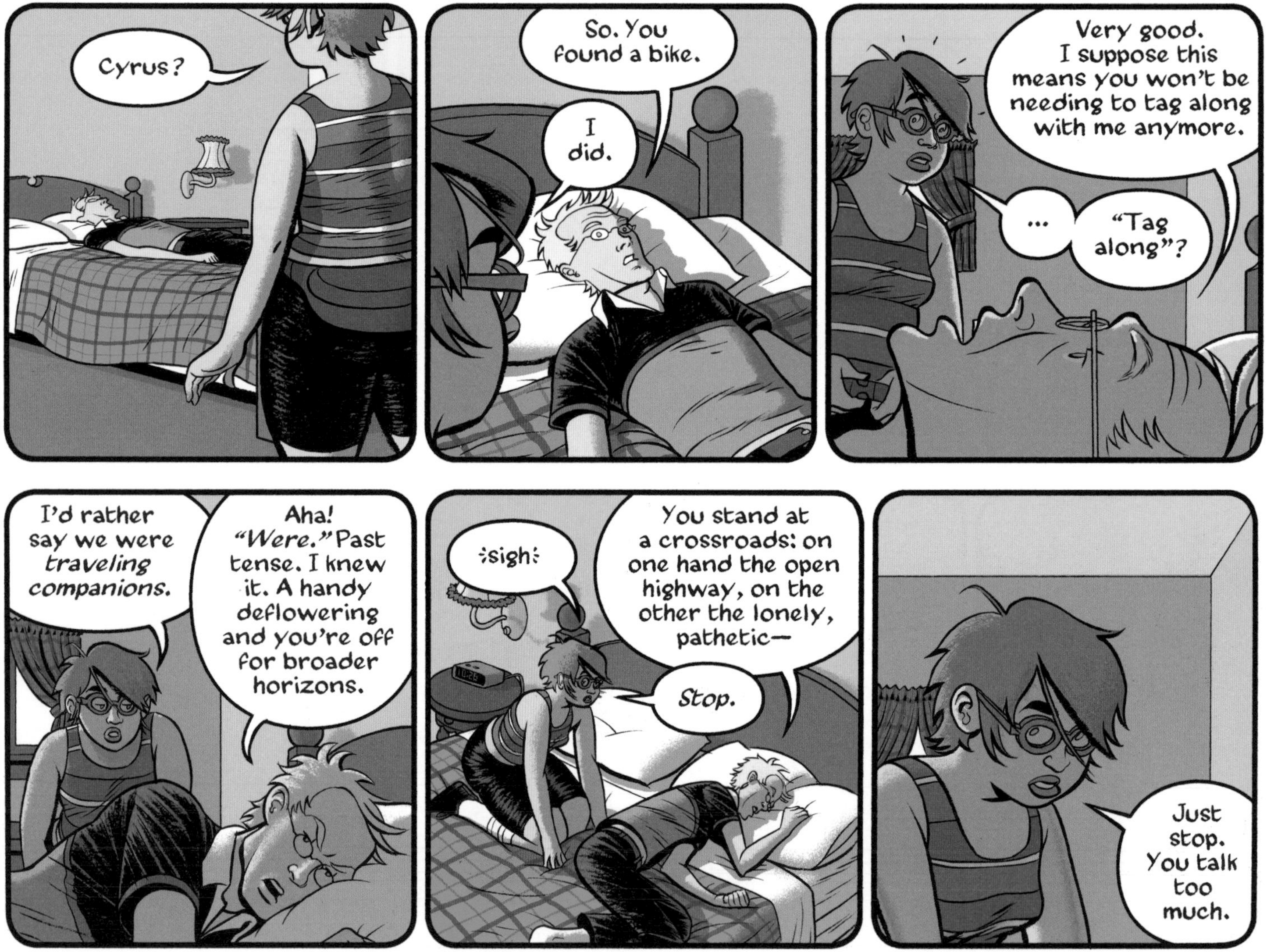

Cyrus?
So. You found a bike.
I did.
Very good. I suppose this means you won't be needing to tag along with me anymore.
...
"Tag along"?
I'd rather say we were *traveling companions.*
Aha! *"Were."* Past tense. I knew it. A handy deflowering and you're off for broader horizons.
:sigh:
You stand at a crossroads: on one hand the open highway, on the other the lonely, pathetic—
Stop.
Just stop. You talk too much.

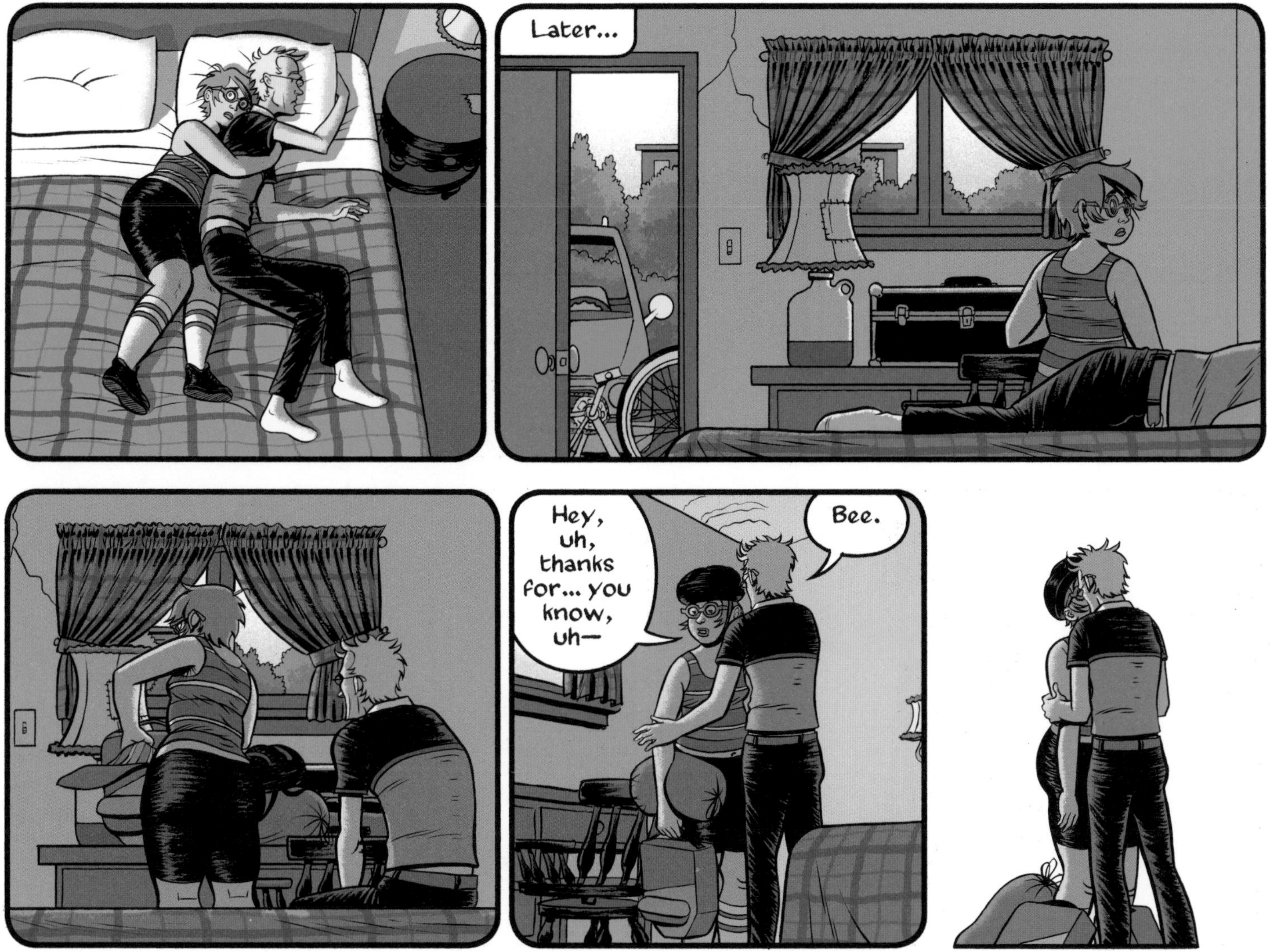
Later...
Hey, uh, thanks for... you know, uh—
Bee.

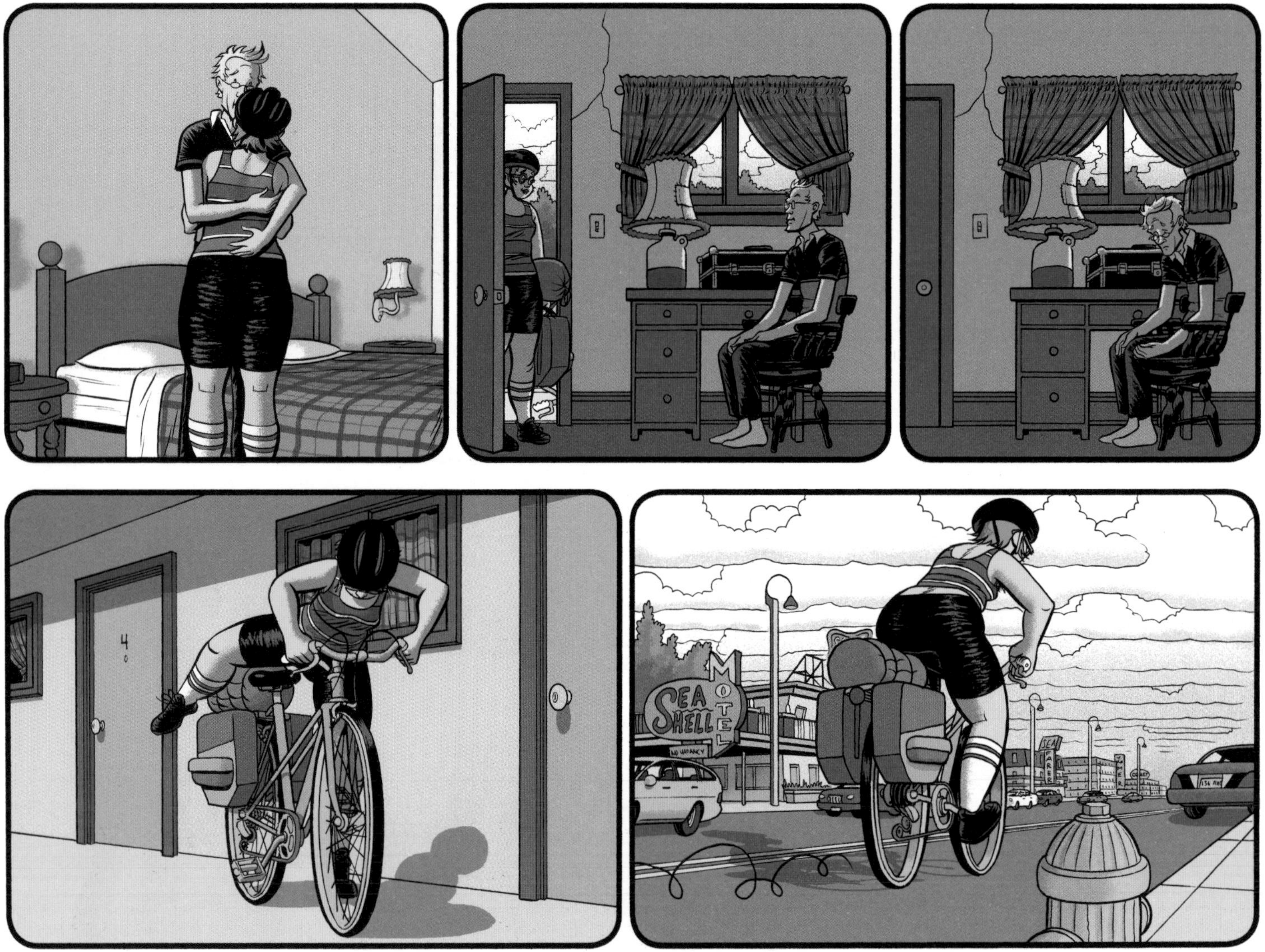
4
SEA SHELL
MOTEL
NO VACANCY

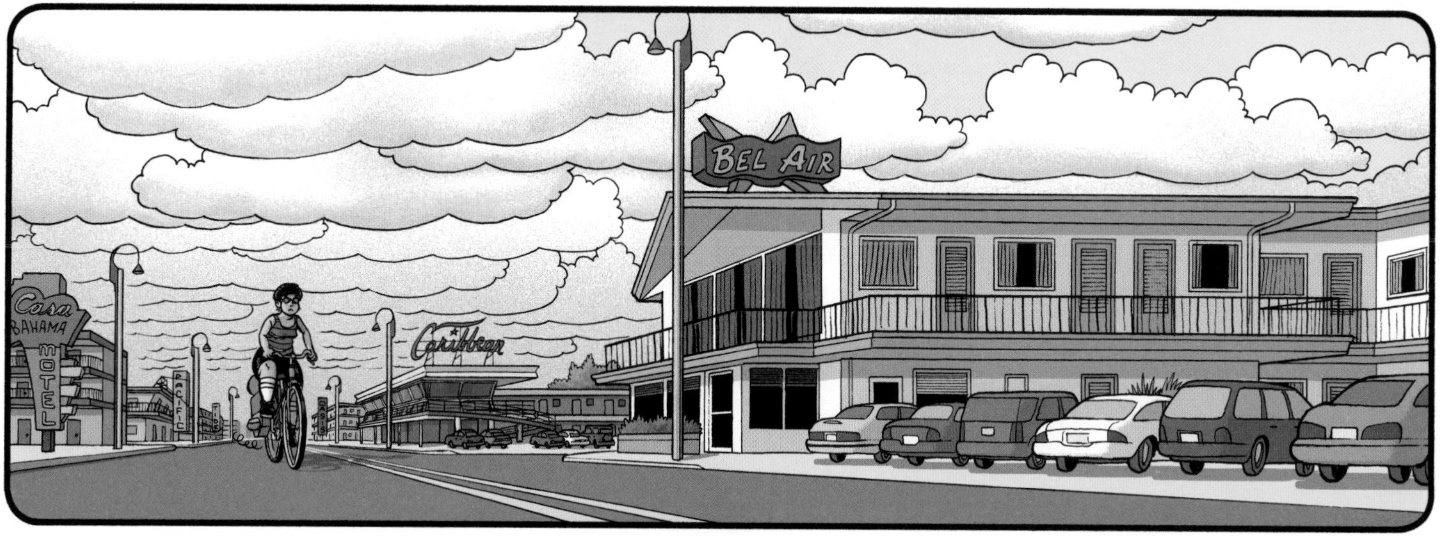
Casa
BAHAMA
MOTEL
Caribbean
BEL AIR

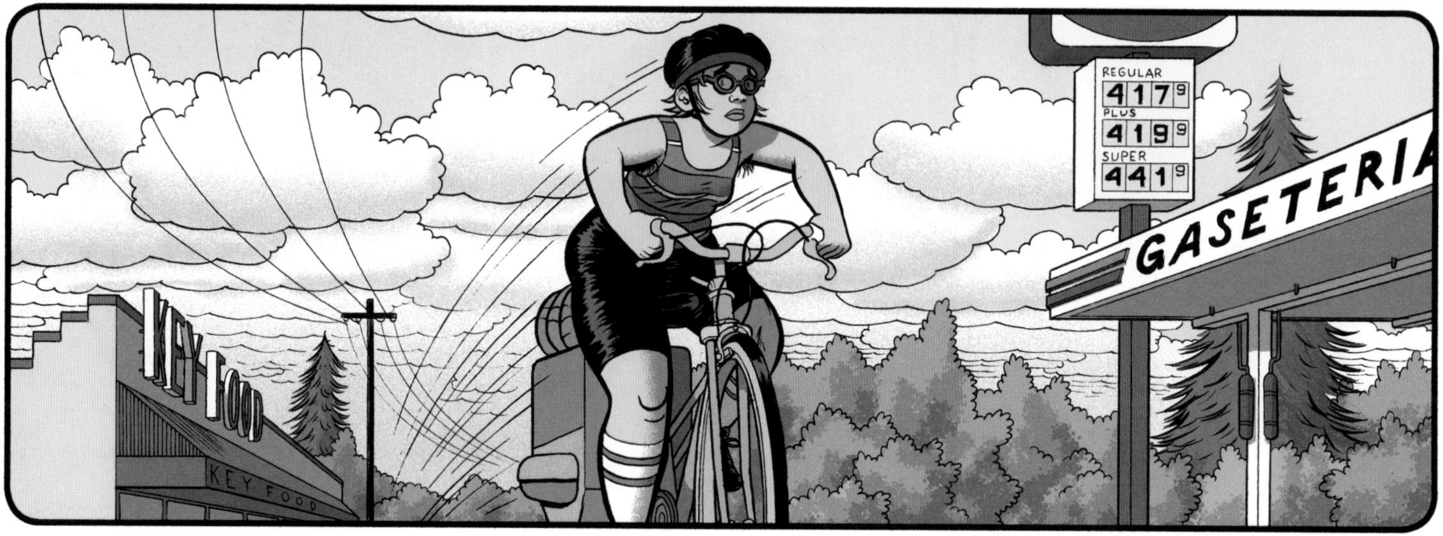
REGULAR
417 9
PLUS
419 9
SUPER
441 9
GASETERIA
KEY FOOD
KEY FOOD

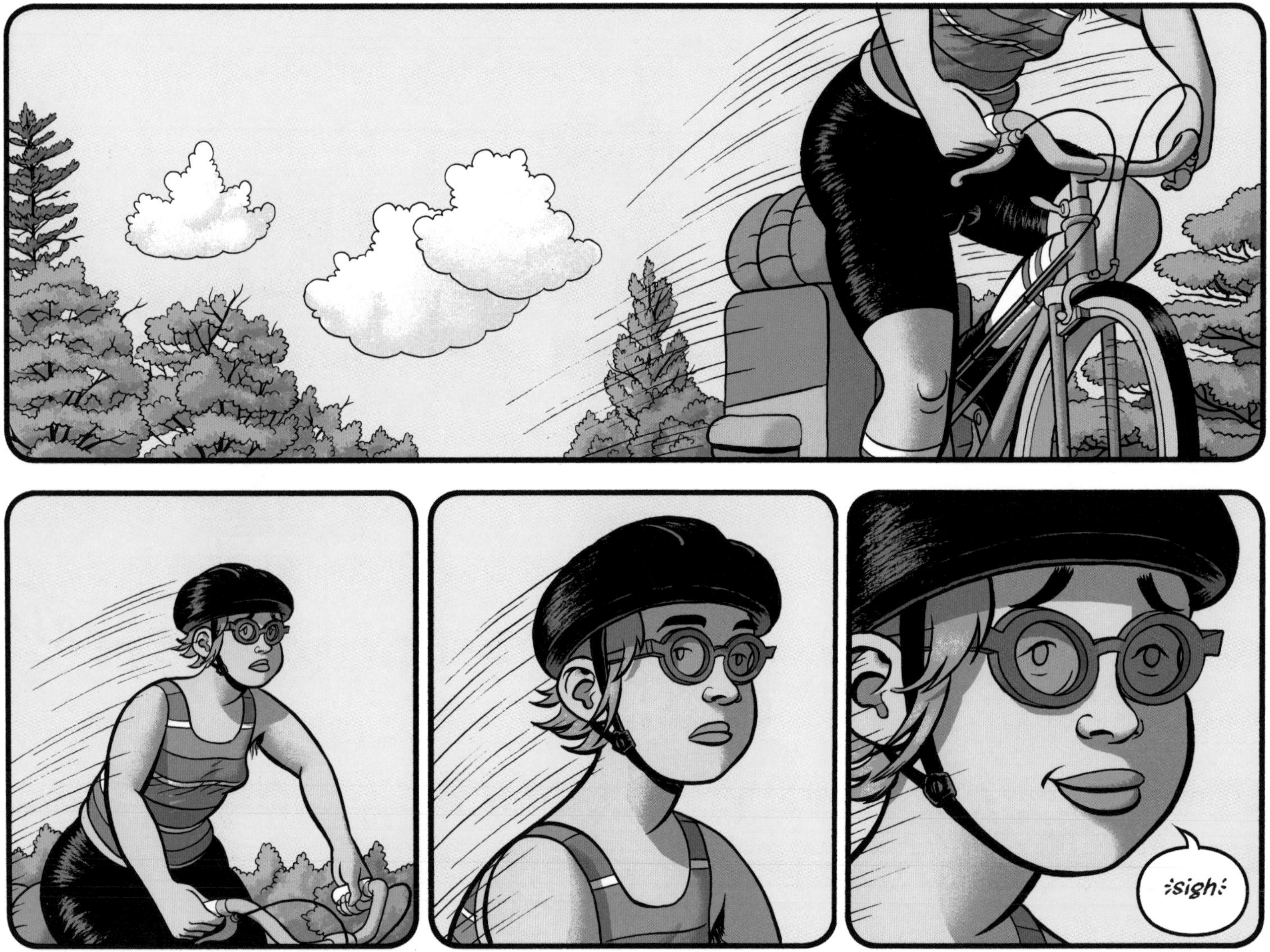
sigh

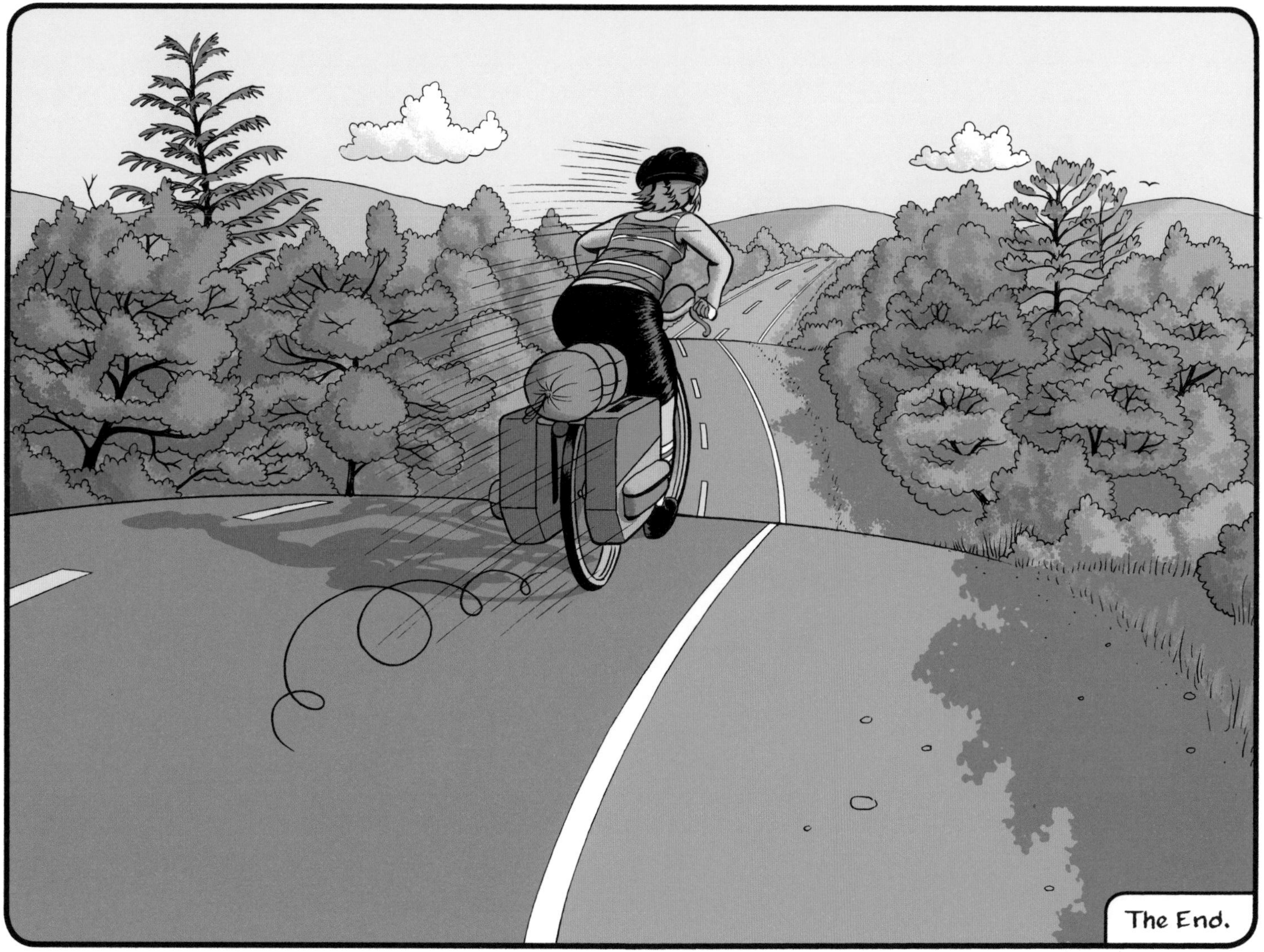
The End.

GRATITUDE

Very deeply felt thanks go to Myla for extreme patience, tolerance, and support.

Towering thanks are extended to Wendy Schmalz, Diana Schutz, Brendan Wright, Dean Haspiel, Dan Goldman, Jessica Abel, Scott McCloud, and Jennifer Hunt.

Avuncular thanks and a sandwich are extended to art assistants Raina Telgemeier, Harold Edge, Thomas Pitilli, Chisako Shioji, Brett Muller, Nicole Beguesse, Falynn Koch, Robby Barrett, Anne Baltazar, Raymon Bruwelheide, Ian Laser Higginbotham, Hilary Florido, Soo Lee, and Adrienne Little.

Profound thanks for critical reading: Nick Bertozzi, Michael Wilde, Tom Hart, Leela Corman, Daupo, Shauna Toh, Tim Kreider, Arthur Tiersky, and Oliver Broudy.

Expansive thanks to James and Sharon Harrigan for the loan of their lovely home as studio space.

Immense thanks to patient family members: M, Z, K, Mom, Dad, Diana, Chad, Mark, Ellen, Saryn, and Chris.

©2010 Myla Goldberg

Jason Little grew up haunted by the ghost of Rod Serling in Binghamton, New York. While at college in Oberlin, Ohio, he was unaware that Marge Buell was spending her last years there. Jason wrote and drew the Xeric-Grant-winning comic book *Jack's Luck Runs Out*, and Bee's previous book *Shutterbug Follies*, which earned him two Ignatz awards. Jason teaches cartooning at the School of Visual Arts in New York City, has performed cartoon slide shows with R. Sikoryak's *Carousel*, drawn storyboards at Augenblick Studios, and has curated three exhibits of comics-as-installation-art at the Flux Factory in Queens, New York. He lives in Brooklyn with author Myla Goldberg and their two daughters.

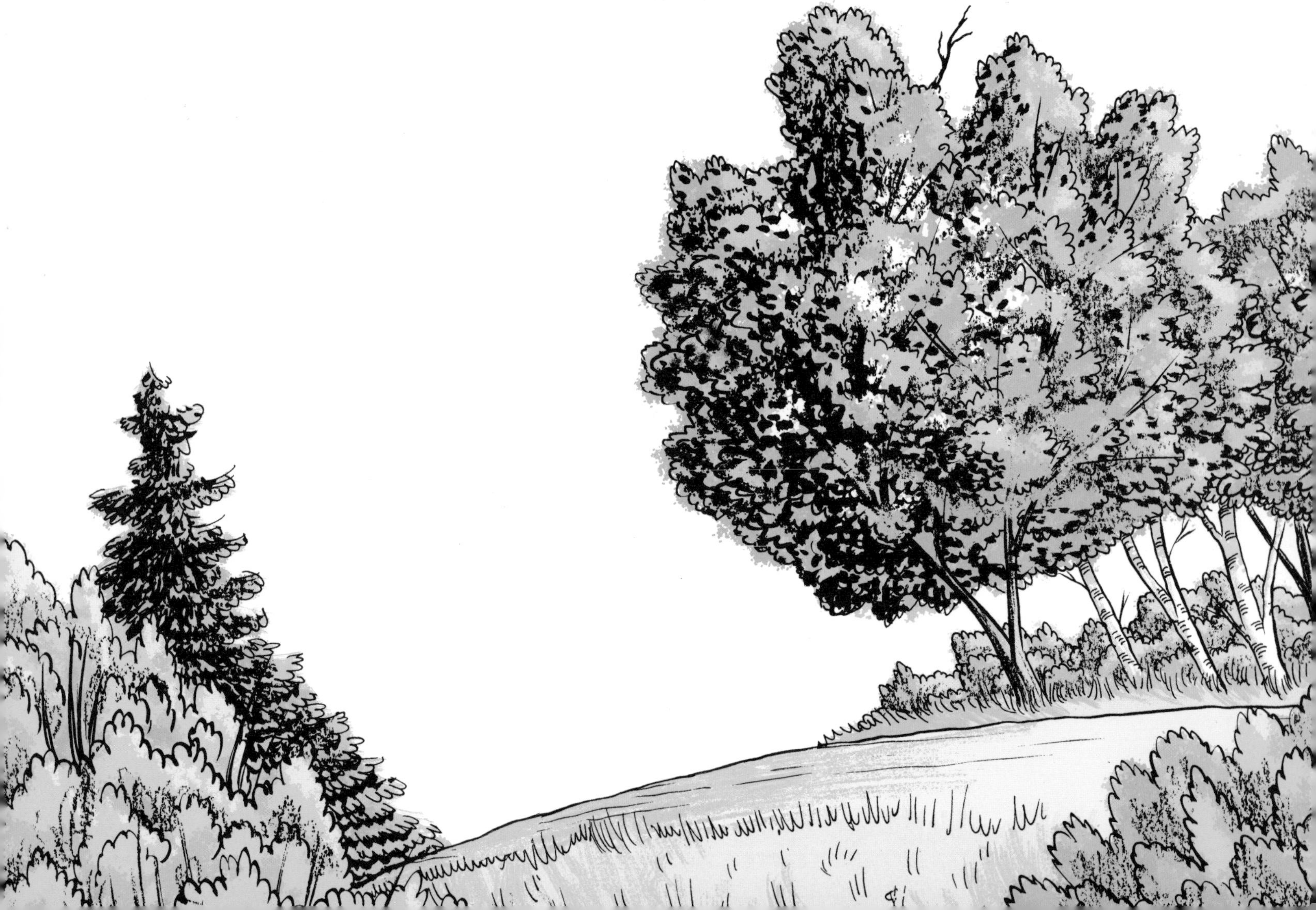